The Post-Political and Its Discontents

The Post-Political and Its Discontents

Spaces of Depoliticisation,
Spectres of Radical Politics

edited by Japhy Wilson and
Erik Swyngedouw

EDINBURGH
University Press

For Tim, in return for your Little Red Book
For Arno, Nikolaas, and Eva: the world is yours to make

Japhy Wilson acknowledges the financial support of the Hallsworth Research Fellowship. Erik Swyngedouw acknowledges the financial support of the People Programme (Maria Currie Actions) of the European Union's Seventh Framework Programme; under REAS agreeement No 289374 – 'ENTITLE'.

Edinburgh University Press Ltd
The Tun – Holyrood Road
12 (2f) Jackson's Entry
Edinburgh EH8 8PJ
www.euppublishing.com

First published in hardback by Edinburgh University Press 2014

This paperback edition 2015

Typeset in 11/13 Sabon by
Servis Filmsetting Ltd, Stockport, Cheshire,
and printed and bound in Great Britain by
CPI Group (UK) Ltd, Croydon CR0 4YY

A CIP record for this book is available from the British Library

ISBN 978 0 7486 8297 3 (hardback)
ISBN 978 1 4744 0306 1 (paperback)
ISBN 978 1 7486 8300 0 (ePub)
ISBN 978 0 7486 8298 0 (webready PDF)

Published with the support of the Edinburgh University Scholarly Publishing Initiatives Fund.

Contents

List of Contributors   vii

Seeds of Dystopia: Post-Politics and the Return of the
Political   1
Japhy Wilson and Erik Swyngedouw

Part I   Spaces of Depoliticisation

1. The Post-Politics of Sustainability Planning: Privatisation
   and the Demise of Democratic Government   25
   Mike Raco

2. The Post-Political and the End of Nature: The
   Genetically Modified Organism   48
   Larry Reynolds and Bronislaw Szerszynski

3. The New Development Architecture and the Post-
   Political in the Global South   67
   Sangeeta Kamat

4. Opening Up the Post-Political Condition:
   Multiculturalism and the Matrix of Depoliticisation   86
   Nicolas Van Puymbroeck and Stijn Oosterlynck

5. The *Jouissance* of Philanthrocapitalism: Enjoyment as a
   Post-Political Factor   109
   Japhy Wilson

6. Religious Antinomies of Post-Politics   126
   Bülent Diken

7. Post-Ecologist Governmentality: Post-Democracy, Post-
   Politics and the Politics of Unsustainability   146
   Ingolfur Blühdorn

Part II   Spectres of Radical Politics

8. Insurgent Architects, Radical Cities and the Promise of
    the Political   169
    Erik Swyngedouw

9. The Limits of Post-Politics: Rethinking Radical Social
    Enterprise   189
    Wendy Larner

10. Neither Cosmopolitanism nor Multipolarity: The
    Political Beyond Global Governmentality   208
    Hans-Martin Jaeger

11. Against a Speculative Leftism   229
    Alex Loftus

12. Spatialising Politics: Antagonistic Imaginaries of
    Indignant Squares   244
    Maria Kaika and Lazaros Karaliotas

13. After Post-Politics: Occupation and the Return of
    Communism   261
    Jodi Dean

14. The Enigma of Revolt: Militant Politics in a 'Post-
    Political' Age   279
    Andy Merrifield

    There Is No Alternative   299
    Erik Swyngedouw and Japhy Wilson

Index   313

Contributors

Ingolfur Blühdorn is Reader in Politics/Political Sociology at the University of Bath. Located at the crossroads of eco-political, democratic and social theory, his work focuses on contemporary ecological and emancipatory politics. It has informed academic and public debates in Europe, the USA and Australia.

Jodi Dean is the Donald R. Harter '39 Professor of Humanities and Social Sciences at Hobart and William Smith Colleges. She is co-editor of the international journal of contemporary theory, *Theory & Event*. Her books include *Democracy and Other Neoliberal Fantasies* (2009) and *The Communist Horizon* (2012).

Bülent Diken is Reader in Sociology at Lancaster University. His research topics are social and political philosophy, urbanism, cinema, terror and religion. His books include *The Culture of Exception* (2005, with C. B. Laustsen); *Sociology Through the Projector* (2007, with C. B. Laustsen); *Nihilism* (2009); and *Revolt, Revolution, Critique – The Paradox of Society* (2012).

Hans-Martin Jaeger is Associate Professor in the Department of Political Science at Carleton University in Ottawa. His work on international political theory and sociology, global governance, and international organisations has been published in *International Theory, European Journal of International Relations, Review of International Studies, International Political Sociology*, and other journals.

Maria Kaika is Professor of Human Geography at the University of Manchester, and Editor of the International Journal of Urban and Regional Research. Her research focuses on urban political ecology, land rent, land financialisation, urban imaginaries, iconic architecture, and European environmental policy. She is author of *City of Flows* (2005).

Sangeeta Kamat is Associate Professor in the College of Education at the University of Massachusetts at Amherst. Her areas of interest are the sociology and anthropology of development and neoliberalism. Her research is on NGOs and development in a neoliberal context, and more recently in critical geography studies in education.

Lazaros Karaliotas is Research Associate in Urban Studies at the School of Geographical and Earth Sciences, University of Glasgow. He holds a PhD in Human Geography and an MA in Development Studies from the University of Manchester. His research addresses urban restructuring, processes of post-politicization and post-democratization, radical politics, urban social movements and environmental politics.

Wendy Larner is Professor of Human Geography and Sociology at the University of Bristol. She has published widely on topics of globalisation, neoliberalism, governance and gender. Her most recent book is *Fashioning Globalisation: New Zealand Design, Working Women and the Cultural Economy* (2013, with Maureen Molloy).

Alex Loftus in Senior Lecturer in Geography at King's College London. He is the author of *Everyday Environmentalism: Creating an Urban Political Ecology* (2012), and co-editor of *Gramsci: Space, Nature, Politics* (2013).

Andy Merrifield is a writer, social theorist and urban geographer. He is the author of numerous books, including most recently, *Magical Marxism* (2011), *John Berger* (2012), *The Politics of the Encounter* (2013), and *The New Urban Question* (2014).

Stijn Oosterlynck is Assistant Professor in Urban Sociology at the University of Antwerp, Belgium. He is the director of the Center for Inequality, Poverty, Social Exclusion and the City (OASeS). His research focuses on the politics of urban development and community development, social innovation and welfare state restructuring and solidarity in diversity.

Mike Raco is Professor of Urban Governance and Development in the Bartlett School of Planning, University College London. He has published widely on urban governance, sustainability, and the politics of urban and regional development. His latest book is *State-led Privatisation and the Demise of the Democratic State: Welfare Reform and Localism in an Era of Regulatory Capitalism* (2013).

Larry Reynolds is Einstein Postdoctoral Fellow at the Freie Universität Berlin. His work develops insights from the historical materialist tradition to explore the problematic of socio-technical transition to a post-fossil fuel society. His PhD addressed the socio-technical battle around GM Crops, He has co-authored a series of articles, papers and book chapters on these questions with Bronislaw Szerszynski.

Erik Swyngedouw is Professor of Geography at Manchester University. His research interests include political ecology, urban governance, democracy and political power, and the politics of globalisation. He was previously Professor of Geography at Oxford University, and held the Vincent Wright Visiting Professorship in Political Science at Science Po, Paris, in 2014.

Bronislaw Szerszynski is Senior Lecturer in Sociology at Lancaster University. He is author of *Nature, Technology and the Sacred* (2005), and co-editor of *Risk, Environment and Modernity* (1996), *Re-Ordering Nature* (2003), *Nature Performed* (2003) and a special double issue of *Theory Culture and Society* on 'Changing Climates' (2010).

Nicolas Van Puymbroeck is a PhD candidate in Sociology at the University of Antwerp. His PhD research, which is funded by the Flanders Research Foundation, draws on theoretical insights derived from post-foundational political thought to explore the dynamics of urban immigrant integration policies.

Japhy Wilson is Research Coordinator at the National Strategic Centre for the Right to Territory (CENEDET) in Quito, Ecuador. His research explores the relationship between space, power and ideology in the politics of development. He is the author of *Jeffrey Sachs: the Strange Case of Dr Shock and Mr Aid* (2014).

Seeds of Dystopia: Post-Politics and the Return of the Political

Japhy Wilson and Erik Swyngedouw

Western democracies are only the political facade of economic power. A facade with colours, banners, and endless debates about sacrosanct democracy. We live in an era where we can discuss everything. With one exception: Democracy. She is there, an acquired dogma. Don't touch, like a museum display. Elections have become an absurd comedy, shameful, in which the participation of the citizen is very weak, and governments represent the political commissionaires of economic power. There isn't democracy, only the appearance of democracy. We live in a simulation. If we want real democracy, we will have to create it ourselves.

José Saramago (2006)

In *Seeing*, the final installment of his magisterial urban trilogy, José Saramago offers an incisive dissection of our current political predicament. A few years after a strange episode of collective blindness, city administrators are preparing for a general election. The great day for the democratic festival is a miserably rainy Sunday, and once all the ballots are counted, it turns out that a large percentage of people have spoiled their votes. The city elites of the Party of the Left, the Party of the Middle, and the Party of the Right are disquieted, if not alarmed. Something must have gone wrong, these surmise, probably the bad weather . . . A week later, the elections are repeated. This time the weather is better, but the electoral outcome is even worse: 83 per cent of the citizens vote blank. What Saramago calls 'the simple right not to follow any consensually established opinion' deeply troubles the city government. One minister refers to it as a conspiracy against the democratic system itself. In its desperate attempt to understand what is going on, and to root out what must be an organised subversion against the sacrosanct democratic principle, the government declares 'a state of emergency', unleashing all manner of repressive tactics to uncover the masterminding source of the anti-democratic plot. But none can be found. In a final desperate attempt to make the city and its citizens come to their senses, the government decides to decamp to another place, leaving the residents to their own devices and anticipating a descent into anarchic catastrophe. However, nothing of the sort happens. Everyone goes about his or her daily life, and the city continues as normal.

In this allegory, first published in 2004, Saramago ruthlessly satirises the disaffection of a growing number of people with the instituted rituals of representative democracy. Thousands of passive rebels refuse to do what is expected of them. They reject the ballot box, and just go on with life as if nothing has happened. With chilling precision, Saramago diagnoses the deadlock of contemporary 'democratic' governance. We live in times both haunted and paradoxical. Instituted representational democracy is more widespread than ever; identitarian concerns and all manner of issues and problems are made visible and politicised; 'participatory' and 'inclusive' forms of governance are nurtured and fostered on a range of geographical scales; and lifestyle preferences, the unsustainable re-engineering of our climate, the sexual escapades of the former IMF chairman, the heroic resistances of indigenous peoples, fracking, the repression of gay people in Russia, the garbage left on the sidewalk, the plight of the whale, the governments' austerity agendas to get the economy out of the doldrums – all these issues and an infinity of others are politicised in certain ways. That is, they are discussed, dissected, evaluated, raised as issues of public concern and debated at length in a variety of public and political arenas. Everything, so it seems, can be aired, made visible, discussed, and rendered contentious.

In short, democracy as the theatre of and for the pluralistic and disputed consideration of matters of public concern would appear to be triumphant. Political elites, irrespective of their particular party allegiance, do not tire of pointing out the great strides that democratic civic life has made. We are told that the great battle of the twentieth century between totalitarianism and democracy has been finally and decisively concluded in favour of the latter. The history of humanity, marked by heroic-tragic ideological battles between opposing visions of what constitutes a 'good' society, has supposedly come to an end. Democracy is now firmly and consensually established as the uncontested and rarely examined ideal of institutionalised political life. There are of course still ongoing rearguard archaic ideological battles on the geographical and political margins of the civilised world, waged by those who have not yet understood the lie of the land and the new horizon of history. When the need arises, they are corralled by any means necessary into consensual participation in the new global democratic order (although not always effectively, as the Afghanistan and Iraq disasters testify). In contrast, we – the West and its allies – will now forever live happily in the complacent knowledge that democracy has been finetuned to assure the efficient management of a liberal and pluralist society under the uncontested aegis of a naturalised market-based configuration of the production and distribution of a cornucopia of goods and services. Any remaining problems and issues will be dealt with in the appropriate manner, through consensual forms of techno-managerial negotiation.

This is supposed to be the final realisation of the liberal idyll. An untroubled, undivided, cohesive and common-sense society in which everyone knows his or her place and performs his or her duties in their own (and hence in everyone else's) interests, organised through a diversity of institutionalised forms of representative government, aided and supported by participatory governance arrangements for all sorts of recognised problems, issues and matters of public concern. Yet political apathy for mainstream parties and politics, and for the ritualised choreographies of representative electoral procedures, is at an all-time high. Indeed, as soon as the practices of government were reduced to the bio-political management of the 'happiness' of the population and the neoliberal organisation of the transformation of nature and the appropriation and distribution of its associated wealth, new spectres of the political appeared on the horizon. Insurrectional and incipiently democratising movements and mobilisations exploded in 2011, and continue to smoulder and flare: Syntagma Square, Puerta del Sol, Zuccotti Park, Paternoster Square, Taksim Square, Tahrir Square, Sao Paulo, Oakland, Montreal . . . These are just a few of the more evocative names that have become associated with emergent new forms of politicisation. Assembled under the generic banner 'Real Democracy Now!' the gathered insurgents have expressed an extraordinary antagonism to the instituted – and often formally democratic – forms of governing, and have staged, performed and choreographed new configurations of the democratic. While often articulated around an emblematic quilting point (a threatened park, devastating austerity measures, the public bailout of irresponsible financial institutions, rising tuition fees, a price hike in public transport, and the like), these movements quickly universalised their claims to embrace a desire for a fully-fledged transformation of the political structuring of life, against the exclusive, oligarchic, and consensual governance of an alliance of professional economic, political and technocratic elites determined to defend the neoliberal order by any means necessary.

It is precisely this parallax gap that sets the contours and contents of this book.

From one vantage point – usually nurtured by those who seek to maintain things as they are – democracy is alive and kicking. From the other perspective, the democratic functioning of the political terrain has been eroded to such an extent that a radical re-ordering and re-configuration of the practices of 'governing by the people for the people' is urgently required. The latter position demands a dramatic transformation of the depoliticising practices that have marked the past few decades, and that have survived the global economic crisis in the perverted form of a 'zombie neoliberalism' (Peck 2010), which staggers blindly forward in the absence of its once-inspiring master discourses. Its continuity is ensured by a range of political elites from both Right and Left, and is legitimised by their continuous election to power – a power that has become more and more enfeebled as they delegate social and political choices to those demanded, staged, figured and 'imposed' by the socially disembodied 'hidden hand of the market'.

Consider, for example, the radical austerity measures pursued by those who have no choice (like the Greek, Portuguese, Irish or Spanish governments) and by those who do (like the British, American, Dutch and Danish regimes). These measures are wholly inoperative in macro-economic terms, but are brutally effective in terms of redrawing class configurations. 'Austerity' is a class war fought by experts, consultants, economists and other elite bureaucrats and policy-makers, in close consultation with business elites and allegedly abstract and disembodied 'financial markets'. This consensualised framing of the natural order of the social stands in stark contrast to the politicising mobilisations of the past few years. The growing unrest of a large part of 'the people' has rattled the elites assembled in Davos and elsewhere, and the uprisings against austerity were labelled 'seeds of dystopia' by the World Economic Forum in its 2012 World Risk Report:

> Two dominant issues of concern emerged from the Arab Spring, the 'Occupy' movements worldwide and recent similar incidents of civil discontent: the growing frustration among citizens with the political and economic establishment, and the rapid public mobilization enabled by greater technological connectivity. A macro and longer-term interpretation of these events highlights the need to improve the management of global economic and demographic transformations that stand to increasingly define global social trends in the decade to come . . . A society that continues to sow the seeds of dystopia – by failing to manage ageing populations, youth unemployment, rising inequalities and fiscal imbalances – can expect greater social unrest and instability in the years to come. (World Economic Forum 2012: 16)

What is the relationship between these seeds of dystopia and the political desert in which they stubbornly take root? Already in the early 1990s, Philippe Lacoue-Labarthe and Jean-Luc Nancy (1997) provided an exquisitely dialectical exploration of what they labelled 'the retreat of the political', understood as both the disappearance and the re-treating of the political in theoretical musings as well as modes of appearance. A proliferating body of thought has since begun to decipher, both theoretically and empirically, the dynamics of depoliticisation, and the contours and characteristics of the alleged 'disappearance of the political'. According to this literature, contemporary forms of depoliticisation are characterised by the erosion of democracy and the weakening of the public sphere, as a consensual mode of governance has colonised, if not sutured, political space. In the process, agnostic political disagreement has been replaced by an ultra-politics of ethnicised and violent disavowal on the one hand, and the exclusion and containment of those who pursue a different political-economic model on the other. These extremes are placed outside the post-democratic inclusion of different opinions on anything imaginable in stakeholder arrangements of impotent participation and 'good governance', which ensure that the framework of debate and decision-making does not question or disrupt the existing state of the neoliberal political-economic configuration. This process is generally referred to as one of post-politicisation, institutionally configured through modes of post-democratic governance.

This book explores the contours of post-politicisation, and proposes a series of theoretical approaches to excavating the dynamics through which post-political modes of governing come into being. In addition, the book identifies a range of new forms of politicisation, which mark the present geopolitical landscape in ways that potentially open up an incipient 'return of the political'. In the remainder of this introductory chapter, we provide some conceptual clarifications regarding the nature of post-politics. We then explore the philosophical, terminological and political differences between some of the key thinkers of post-politics, focusing on the theorists whose work most consistently informs the contributions to this book: Chantal Mouffe, Jacques Rancière, and Slavoj Žižek. We conclude with an overview of the book as a whole.

The meaning of post-politics

During times of decline and reaction in which an actual transformation of the prevailing political order seems ever more unlikely, language often comes to the rescue so as to allow one to revitalize, think anew, or at the very least re-delimit the concepts of 'politics' or 'the political' with the simple yet thought-provoking addition of a prefix. (Bosteels 2011: 76)

In recent years, an emergent literature across the social sciences has conceptualised contemporary processes of depoliticisation in terms of 'post-politics', 'post-democracy', and 'the post-political' (see for example Allmendinger and Haughton 2011; Catney and Doyle 2011; Clarke and Cochrane 2013; Crouch 2004; Diken 2009; Fuller 2012; Garsten and Jacobsson 2007; Goeminne 2012; Hilding-Rydevik, Hakansson and Isaksson 2011; Kythreotis 2012; Mouffe 2005; Oosterlynk and Swyngedouw 2010; Pares 2011; Raco and Lin 2012; Rancière 1999; Rorty 2004; Schlembach, Lear and Bowman 2012; Swyngedouw 2007, 2009, 2010, 2011; Vergopoulos 2001; Williams and Booth 2013; Wilson 2013; Žižek 1999). The precise meaning of these terms is highly contested. Broadly speaking, however, they all refer to a situation in which the political – understood as a space of contestation and agonistic engagement – is increasingly colonised by politics – understood as technocratic mechanisms and consensual procedures that operate within an unquestioned framework of representative democracy, free market economics, and cosmopolitan liberalism. In post-politics, political contradictions are reduced to policy problems to be managed by experts and legitimated through participatory processes in which the scope of possible outcomes is narrowly defined in advance. 'The people' – as a potentially disruptive political collective – is replaced by the population – the aggregated object of opinion polls, surveillance, and bio-political optimisation. Citizens become consumers, and elections are framed as just another 'choice', in which individuals privately select their preferred managers of the conditions of economic necessity. Under these circumstances, as Rancière observes,

> the disenchanted opinion spreads that there isn't much to deliberate and that decisions make themselves, the work proper to politics simply involving an opportune adaptability in terms of the demands of the world marketplace and the equitable distribution of the profits and costs of this adaptability. (Rancière 1999: viii)

The contributions to this volume seek to make sense of this situation, exploring the specific mechanisms through which the post-political is constituted, and searching for the political possibilities that continue to haunt the present. They engage directly with the political theory underpinning the literature on post-politics, seeking variously to affirm, challenge, and extend the parameters of this theoretical approach, through the detailed empirical analysis of contemporary processes of post-politicisation. In the literature on post-politics, there is a great deal of confusion and divergence over the precise meaning of the term. Here we provide a theoretical introduction to post-politics, post-democracy, and the post-political, in preparation for the much more involved debates that form the substance of this book.

The post-political can be thought of as what Jacques Lacan would call a Borromean knot – a set of densely intertwined registers that constitute what we call 'reality'. Lacan named these registers the Real, the Symbolic, and the Imaginary. In Lacanian terms, the post-political can be understood as a Borromean knot comprised of the Imaginary – the ideology of the 'end of history' according to which the great ideological battles of the past have all been settled; the Symbolic – the set of institutional mechanisms and practices through which politics is reduced to the consensual management of economic necessity; and the Real – the ontological displacement or erasure of 'the political difference' between the established institutional arrangements of a given social order, and the establishment of that social order on an always absent ground.

In ideological (or Imaginary) terms, the post-political era began with Francis Fukayama's notorious proclamation of 'the end of history', according to which the fall of the Berlin Wall marked the conclusion of the long historical struggle between competing ideologies. Liberal democracy and the market economy had proved themselves to be the best possible basis for social organisation, and all that remained was for the backward parts of the world to catch up with the West (Fukayama 1992). The end of history was also declared to be 'the end of ideology' and even 'the end of politics', 'whereby both senses of "end", as a telos fulfilling itself and as an eliminating gesture, come to coincide exactly' (Rancière 1999: 75). Utopia, in short, was a thing of the past:

If we are to believe the discourse of the wise, our *fin de siècle* is the finally conquered age of realism. We have buried Marxism and swept aside all utopias. We have even buried the thing that made them possible: the belief that time carried a meaning and a promise . . . The 'end of history' is the end of an era in which we believed in 'history', in time marching towards a goal, towards the manifestation of a truth or the accomplishment of an emancipation . . . The thinkers who have made it their speciality to remind us without respite of the [twentieth] century's horrors also explain to us relentlessly that they all stem from one fundamental crime. The crime is to have believed that history had a meaning and that it fell to the world's peoples to realize it. (Rancière 2010a: 8)

Of course, the end of utopia is itself utopian, and the end of ideology is itself ideological. Yet while it is easy to deride the end of history thesis as the most transparent of ideological contrivances, it contains an important truth. In Fredric Jameson's words, the political horizon of our times is defined by the fact that 'It is easier to imagine the end of the world than to imagine the end of capitalism' (Jameson 2003: 73). The defeat of actually existing communism signified a crisis of the political imaginary of the Left, from which it has yet to recover. As Žižek has observed, 'today's predominant form of ideological "closure" takes the precise form of a mental block which prevents us from imagining a fundamental social change, in the interests of a "realistic" and "mature" attitude' (Žižek 2000: 324). In recent years, this mental block has manifested itself in the inability of the Left to mount a meaningful and sustained challenge to neoliberalism in the context of the greatest crisis of global capitalism since the Great Depression (Hall, Massey and Rustin 2013). Meanwhile, politicians, business leaders, and liberal intellectuals have persisted in their insistence that, faced with the unprecedented breakdown of the 'free market' system, there is *still* no alternative. As banks are bailed out with public money and the welfare state is dismantled in the name of austerity, electorates are told that 'We're all in this together', and are called upon to unite in support of the expert managers of the global economy. An editorial in *The Economist* explains the situation as follows:

> In the short term, defending capitalism means, paradoxically, state intervention. There is a justifiable sense of outrage amongst voters ... that $2.5 trillion of taxpayers' money now has to be spent on a highly rewarded industry. But *the global bail-out is pragmatic, not ideological.* When Francois Mitterand nationalised France's banks in 1981 he did so because he thought the state would run them better. This time governments are buying banks (or shares in them) because they believe, rightly, that public capital is needed to keep credit flowing. (*The Economist* 2008, emphasis added)

The 'pragmatic' combination of socialism for the rich and austerity for the poor has been accompanied by the continuing evisceration of political contestation from the institutional (or Symbolic) mechanisms of the global economy. In institutional terms, post-politics is defined by the reduction of the political to the economic – the creation of a 'welcoming business environment', which inspires 'investor confidence', and provides the economic guarantees deemed necessary for 'strong and stable markets'. This subordination is not purely ideological, but is embodied in concrete institutional forms, including the privatisation of central banks; the imposition of austerity on the instruction of the International Monetary Fund; the subordination of national legislation to the juridical regimes of the World Trade Organization and other multilateral organisations; the translation of corporate agendas into public policy through close formal and informal cooperation with business networks; and the delegation of numerous decision-making powers to non-state and quasi-state institutional forms (Crouch 2004; Brand 2005; Swyngedouw 2005). The economy is therefore increasingly insulated from even the most limited forms of democratic accountability, even as the state increasingly legitimises itself in terms of its capacity for 'pragmatic' and 'responsible' economic management:

> The legitimacy of state power is thereby reinforced by the very affirmation of its own impotence, of its lack of choice faced with the world-wide necessity it is dominated by. The theme of the common will is replaced by that of the lack of personal will, of capacity for autonomous action that is anything more than just management of necessity. From an allegedly defunct Marxism, the supposedly reigning liberalism borrows the theme of objective necessity, identified with the constraints and caprices of the world market. Marx's once scandalous thesis that governments are simple business agents for international capital is today the obvious fact on which 'liberals' and 'socialists' agree. The absolute identification of politics with the management of capital is no longer the shameful secret hidden behind the 'forms' of democracy; it is the openly declared truth by which our governments acquire legitimacy. (Rancière 1999: 113)

The elision of democracy with the dictates of capital has only been further consolidated by the ongoing fallout from the global economic crisis. Elected leaders slavishly follow the orders of banks, bond markets, and multilateral institutions. In the cases of Greece and Italy, they have even been deposed on the instruction of these institutions, and replaced by 'non-ideological' technocrats (Rachman 2011). The political novelty of this scenario has been noted in the pages of the *Financial Times*:

> European democracy has a new organising assumption. Citizens may still change their leaders from time to time, but only on the clear understanding that elections do not herald a change of direction. Left or right, inside or outside the euro, ruling elites are worshipping at the altar of austerity. Governments are permitted a tilt here, or a shading there. None dares challenge the catechism of fiscal rectitude. (Stephens 2012)

The situation is little different elsewhere. Around the world, notwithstanding the protests that have flared up around Occupy, the

Indignados, and the so-called Arab Spring, the global economic crisis has been mobilised not to re-politicise the economy, but to further advance its depoliticisation. We now live in a permanent state of economic, environmental and social emergency, in which

> our societies must no longer be concerned with the fight for freedom and equality . . . but with the struggle for survival, which is prey to the slightest blunder. The smallest wage rise, the smallest [fluctuation] in interest rates, the slightest unforeseen market reaction is, in fact, enough to disrupt the acrobatic balance on which our societies rest and plunge the entire planet into chaos. (Rancière 2010a: 18)

This image of a society poised above the abyss invokes the ontological (or Real) dimension of the post-political. The key thinkers of the post-political share a post-foundational ontology, according to which there is no essential ground to any social order. In contrast to political philosophies that ground society in a state of nature, a primordial hierarchy, or an economic base, post-foundational theorists begin from the position that all social orders are profoundly contingent, and structured to conceal their own absent ground. Just as Heidegger distinguished between the ontic and the ontological, and Lacan delineated reality from the Real, so these theorists distinguish between politics and the political (Bosteels 2011: 45–9). 'The political difference' (Marchart 2007) is not between politics and other social spheres, such as civil society or the economy, but between *politics* as the contingent and incomplete attempt to ground a particular set of power relations on an ultimately absent foundation, and *the political* as the ineradicable presence of this absence itself, which continually undermines the social orders constructed upon it, and which holds open the possibility of radical change. In Marchart's phrase, 'Not "everything is political", but the absent ground/abyss of everything is *the political*' (Marchart 2007: 169).

This ontological dimension is crucial to the meaning of post-politics. Indeed, we would suggest that many of the criticisms and limitations of the literature on post-politics result from a failure to adequately grasp the significance of this dimension. Orthodox Marxists, for example, accuse the theorists of post-politics of fetishising the political as a separate sphere independent of economic processes (see for example Walker 2012). But the distinction that is being drawn is not between politics and the economy, but between politics-as-social order and the political as the ontological void beneath that order – an order that includes the entirety of the 'political economy' with which orthodox Marxists concern themselves.

The post-political literature is also accused of conspiring in the

processes of post-politicisation that it claims to critique, by paint-
ing a picture of a closed world in which transformative action has
become impossible (see for example Darling 2013). This is indeed
the case for some of the secondary literature, but only to the extent
that it strips the theory of its ontological dimension, on the assumption that 'Worrying too much about the ontological status of politics
may risk causing us to overlook its everydayness' (Gill, Johnstone
and Williams 2012). It is precisely the Real dimension of the political
which ensures the impossibility of the closure of politics, and which
implies an understanding of the post-political, not as a realised totality, but as an anxiety-ridden and necessarily impossible attempt to
erase 'the ontological instance of antagonism' (Marchart 2007: 161).
If real politics and real democracy can only exist in the gap between
the post-political and the void that it denies, then 'it is the lack of
understanding of "the political" in its ontological dimension which
is at the origin of our current incapacity to think in a political way'
(Mouffe 2005: 9).

Theoretical mediators: Mouffe, Rancière, Žižek

The key thinkers of post-politics share a post-foundational ontology,
a concern with the evacuation of the political, and a commitment
to radical democratisation and egalitarian emancipation. However,
their conceptualisations of post-politics, democracy, and the political differ in significant respects, and a basic grasp of these differences
is essential for an understanding of the debates played out in this
volume. Here we will limit ourselves to a schematic presentation of
their positions. We will begin by summarising their understandings
of post-politics and the political difference, before briefly considering
their positions on the nature and possibility of radical politics today.

For Chantal Mouffe, the political is 'the dimension of antagonism
... constitutive of human societies', while politics is 'the set of practices through which an order is created' (Mouffe 2005: 9). Mouffe
equates 'politics' with the contingent construction of hegemony, and
'the political' with a we/they antagonism that she claims is the necessary condition of all political identities (Mouffe 2005: 16–17). The
political subverts any hegemonic formation, 'destroying its ambition to constitute a full presence ... as an objective reality' (Laclau
and Mouffe 1985: 127). Democracy, for Mouffe, is an institutional
arrangement in which the antagonistic confrontation between
enemies is sublimated into the agonistic engagement of adversaries
(Mouffe 2009: 551). The post-political names a hegemonic order
in which the antagonistic dimension of the political has not been

sublimated, but repressed (Mouffe 2005: 18). The demise of social democracy, the rise of the Third Way 'beyond Left and Right', and the 'unchallenged hegemony of neoliberalism' are all symptomatic of a state of affairs in which there is no longer any room for agonistic dispute (Mouffe 2005: 35–63). But because antagonism is inherent to society, the post-political results not in the end of history, but in a return of the repressed, in the form of right-wing nationalisms and religious fundamentalisms, which give expression to the antagonism that has been eviscerated from the domain of democratic contestation (Mouffe 2005: 64–72). According to Mouffe (2009: 552), 'it is the lack of political channels for challenging the hegemony of the neoliberal model of globalisation which is at the origin of the proliferation of discourses and practices of radical negation of the established order'.

Rancière agrees with Mouffe concerning the structure of the political difference, but conceptualises it in terms of a tripartite division between the political (*le politique*), politics (*la politique*), and the police (*la police*). For Rancière, the relationship between 'the political' and 'the police' is symmetrical to Mouffe's distinction between the political and politics. That is to say, society's absent ground is defined as 'the political', and the institutions that reproduce a given social hierarchy are identified as 'the police'. In contrast to Mouffe, however, Rancière uses the word 'politics' to denote 'the meeting ground' between the political and the police. Furthermore, for Rancière the absent ground of the social is defined not by antagonism, but by equality – the unconditional equality of each and every one of us as speaking (and hence political) beings (Rancière 1999: 16). The governmental order of the police determines the 'distribution of the sensible' – the systematic organisation and naturalisation of inequality as common sense. It is structured against the equality that it conceals, and operates through the exclusion of a part *of* society that is given no part *in* society (Rancière 1999: 21–42; 2001: Thesis 7).

Democracy, which for Rancière is another word for politics, is staged whenever a part of those who have no part asserts its presence, as the embodiment of the universal principle of equality (Rancière 1999: 99–101). Equality is to be understood as neither a utopian longing nor a sociologically verifiable condition, but is an ontological given, which is affirmed and given content precisely through its performative staging and enacting. Politics (or democracy) is the staging of equality that exposes a wrong, and through this, attempts to inaugurate a new partition of the sensible. Politics therefore always works on the police. It is the confrontation of the inegalitarian and oligarchic logic of the police with the logic of equality.

Rancière uses the concept of 'post-democracy' to refer to what Mouffe calls 'the post-political'. In contrast to Mouffe's approach, Rancière sees post-democracy as operating not through repression, but through disavowal. In psychoanalytic terms, disavowal denotes a defence mechanism based not on repressing pathological symptoms, but on accounting for them in such a way that their traumatic dimension is diminished. For Rancière, post-democracy involves a specific configuration of three forms of the disavowal of politics, through which the police order seeks to neutralise the political agency of the part of those who have no part. These are: archi-politics – the representation of the community as an organic whole with nothing left over (for example anti-immigrant nationalism); para-politics – the institutionalised competition for places within an established hierarchy (for example representative democracy); and meta-politics – the subordination of politics to a deeper 'essence' (for example 'the market economy') (Rancière 1999: 61–93). Post-democracy is a specific distribution of the sensible, which synthesises these forms of disavowal under the banner of 'consensus'. The outcome is the eradication of democracy in the name of democracy itself:

> Every politics is democratic in this precise sense: not in the sense of a set of institutions, but in the sense of forms of expression that confront the logic of equality with the logic of police order. It is on this basis that we use the notion of post-democracy ... to denote the paradox that, in the name of democracy, emphasises the consensual practice of effacing the forms of democratic action ... It is the disappearance of the mechanisms of appearance, of the dispute opened up by the name 'people' and the vacuum of their freedom. It is, in a word, the disappearance of politics. (Rancière 1999: 101–2)

Like Mouffe, Rancière is clear that post-democracy results not in the smooth order of rational consensus, but in the resurgence of identity politics and violent fundamentalisms (Rancière 1999: 124–5). For Rancière, however, this is not an expression of an ineradicable friend/enemy antagonism, but is a fragmented, inarticulate eruption of the demand for equality, which cannot be articulated in universal terms within the post-democratic order (Rancière 1999: 118–19).

Žižek follows Rancière in framing the political difference in terms of politics and the police. Drawing on Lacan, however, Žižek claims that Rancière 'fetishizes the order of police', by failing to take into account the violence on which it is founded, and the obscene enjoyment of power, which is the underside of its meticulous distributions of the sensible (Žižek 1999: 187, 282). Žižek also differs from Mouffe, to the extent that he identifies a historically specific form of

class struggle, rather than a transhistorical antagonism, as the void
that prevents the totalisation of society. For Žižek, class is to be
understood not in sociological terms, but as a rupture in the fabric
of capitalist society that perpetually undermines any attempt at unity
or coherence (Žižek 1991: 100). It is this rupture that is sutured by
contemporary modalities of depoliticisation.

In his account of depoliticisation, Žižek adopts Rancière's three
forms of disavowal, but adds a fourth, which he calls 'ultra-politics'
(Žižek 1999: 220–35). Ultra-politics, as embodied in the so-called
'War on Terror', establishes an absolute distinction between 'us'
and 'them', denying any shared symbolic space in which to engage
on terms other than violence. Žižek augments these four forms of
disavowal with his concept of 'post-politics'. Whereas for Mouffe
the post-political is defined by repression, and for Rancière post-
democracy is a specific form of disavowal, Žižek distinguishes post-
politics from other forms of depoliticisation on the basis that it
operates not through repression or disavowal but through *foreclosure*
– the total erasure of the political from the Symbolic. The outcome of
foreclosure is not 'a truncated symbolic order', but a seemingly complete symbolic order, which 'lacks the inscription of its lack' (Žižek
2008: xii). Foreclosure, it should be noted, is the form of denegation
peculiar to psychosis. It is this shift from disavowal to foreclosure –
from a neurotic to a psychotic ideological structure – which defines
post-politics as a modality of depoliticisation, and which explains the
violence that erupts within it:

> Today, however, we are dealing with another form of the denegation of
> the political, postmodern *post-politics*, which no longer merely represses
> the political, trying to contain and pacify the 'returns of the repressed',
> but much more effectively 'forecloses' it . . . Post-politics emphasises the
> need to leave old ideological divisions behind and confront new issues,
> armed with the necessary expert knowledge and free deliberation that
> takes people's concrete needs and demands into account . . . [However,]
> the political (the space of litigation in which the excluded can protest the
> wrong/injustice done to them) foreclosed from the Symbolic returns in
> the Real . . . in thoroughly 'irrational' excessive outbursts of violence . . .
> These violent *passages à l'acte* bear witness to some underlying antago-
> nism that can no longer be formulated in properly political terms. (Žižek
> 1999: 236–7, 243)

To summarise the respective positions of Mouffe, Rancière, and
Žižek, we can say that Mouffe is concerned with *the post-political as
the repression of antagonism*, Rancière with *post-democracy as the
disavowal of equality*, and Žižek with *post-politics as the foreclosure*

of class struggle. These divergent understandings of the nature of post-politics imply very different political projects. For Mouffe, the post-political evisceration of agonistic dispute from the public sphere threatens an escalation of violent antagonisms, and must be challenged by a reanimation of social democracy, a repoliticisation of the division between Left and Right, and a radical democracy of agonistic pluralism (Mouffe 2005: 21–3, 119). She is opposed to 'the traditional conception of revolutionary politics', and is focused not on the overthrow of liberal democracy, but on ensuring that liberal democracy realises its unfulfilled potential (Mouffe 2005: 51–3).

Žižek is highly critical of this form of 'radical democracy', arguing that it participates in the foreclosure of class struggle by limiting itself to 'palliative damage-control measures within the global capitalist framework' (Žižek 2000: 321). In her call for a modification of the police order designed to prevent the emergence of antagonism, Mouffe also differs from Rancière, who is committed to the antagonistic disruption of the police order by the staging of equality by those excluded from it. For Žižek and Rancière, as we have seen, the ontological dimension of the political difference is not structured by antagonism in the abstract, but by class struggle and equality respectively. They affirm the political potential of this dimension, and therefore ground their politics in the antagonistic moment that Mouffe seeks to avoid. Rancière defines this as the moment of 'dissensus: the putting of two worlds in one and the same world', in which a part of those who have no part presents itself as a singular embodiment of universality (Rancière 2010b: 69). For Žižek, the political moment is defined by an 'Act'. Against the post-political reduction of possibility to reality, an Act realises the impossible, by changing 'the very parameters of what is considered possible in the existing constellation' (Žižek 1999: 237).

According to Rancière, the political moment 'consists above all in the act of revoking the law of birth and wealth; in affirming the pure contingency whereby individuals come to find themselves in this or that place; in the attempt to build a common world on the basis of that sole contingency' (Rancière 2010a: 6). Žižek would endorse the egalitarian spirit of this statement, but has criticised Rancière for his singular commitment to the spontaneous uprisings of the oppressed, which he sees as politically ineffective (Žižek 1999: 281). For Žižek, 'because the depoliticized economy is the "fundamental fantasy" of postmodern politics, a properly political act would necessarily entail the repoliticization of the economy' (Žižek 1999: 432). In collaboration with Alain Badiou, Žižek has sought to rehabilitate 'the idea of communism' (Badiou 2010; Douzinas and Žižek 2010; Žižek 2013), insisting that '[t]he only true question today is ... does today's global capitalism contain antagonisms powerful enough to prevent its indefinite reproduction?' (Žižek 2010: 212).

Rancière, however, is strictly opposed to any return to the meta-politics of orthodox Marxism, which he accuses of subordinating politics to economic and historical laws, and of constructing new forms of inequality on the basis of claims to exclusive knowledge of these laws (Rancière 1999: 81–91). Such laws do not exist for Rancière, and while an anti-capitalist politics is necessary in his opinion, it cannot be derived from the internal dynamics of the capitalist system, but 'must be radically heterogeneous to the logic of capitalism and the materiality of the capitalist world' (Rancière 2010b: 82–3). For Rancière, communism is just another name for democracy, and 'Being ... communists means being thinkers and actors of the unconditional equality of anybody and everybody' (Rancière 2010b: 82). We return to the meaning of communism in the Conclusion of this book, in which we also engage with the work of Alain Badiou, as a fourth important thinker of the political.

The post-political and its discontents

The contributions to this book build on the theoretical approaches sketched here, through the exploration of specific sites of post-politicisation. The aim throughout is threefold. First, to critically engage with the theoretical literature on the post-political, mobilis-ing it as a tool of critique, and developing it in relation to the com-plexities of actually existing processes of depoliticisation. Second, to identify the discourses and practices through which the post-political is constructed in diverse spheres of reality, in order to reveal the contingency, fragility, and incompleteness of post-politics, as well as exposing its imaginaries, its strategies, and its effects. Third, to search for the spectres of radical politics that continue to haunt the post-political world, exploring their emancipatory potentialities, and confronting their political limitations.

There is no consensus among the contributions here. Indeed, the book can be read as an irruption of *dissensus*, not only against the post-political police order, but also against any attempt to police the conceptual terrain of its critique. Many of our contributors are convinced of the critical value of the theoretical literature on post-politics, and seek to put it to use, identifying its tensions and weak-nesses, while modifying and extending it in relation to a complex and ever-changing reality. But some are highly critical of this literature, drawing on specific cases of depoliticisation and repoliticisation to argue that the conceptual apparatus of post-politics is inadequate to the critical analysis of our political predicament. This is as it should be. After all, what could be more absurd than a critique of post-politics in which everyone agreed?

The book is divided into two parts. Part I explores contemporary spaces of depoliticisation, while Part II focuses on the return of the political. Part I begins with a triptych of cases of the post-political in the fields of planning, ecology, and development. Mike Raco provides a fine-grained analysis of planning reform and public-private partnerships in the UK, as an example of broader processes of post-politicisation, which operate through 'isolating and contractualising key dimensions of decision-making and removing them from the terrain of formal politics'. Larry Reynolds and Bronislaw Szersynski then discuss the post-politics of agricultural biotechnology. They trace a dialectic of depoliticisation and repoliticisation through which technology and science have been mobilised in the contested regulation of genetically modified organisms (GMOs) in the European Union. In her chapter, Sangeeta Kamat argues that post-politics is not restricted to 'the West', but is the dominant political modality of contemporary international development. Kamat critiques the ways in which seemingly democratising discourses of empowerment, inclusion and participation are mobilised within the new development architecture. Drawing on research in Andhra Pradesh, India, she shows how the formally democratic practices of women's self-help groups have failed to challenge entrenched relations of domination.

The next four chapters engage more critically with the post-political approach, questioning its political limitations and expanding its theoretical parameters. Nicolas Van Puymbroeck and Stijn Oosterlynck criticise the literature on post-politics for applying 'the notion of the "post-political condition" as a one-size-fits-all label to describe (rather than explain) currently dominant political forms associated with global capitalism and the neoliberal order'. Drawing on the work of Rancière, Puymbroeck and Oosterlynck develop a more nuanced conceptual approach, which they put to work in an exploration of the relationship between liberal multiculturalism and racist ultra-politics. Japhy Wilson then assesses the emergent development paradigm of 'philanthrocapitalism'. Building on Žižek's work on *jouissance*, Wilson uses the case of philanthrocapitalism to argue that the post-political operates not only through discursive and institutional mechanisms, but also through the mobilisation of disavowed forms of enjoyment. In his chapter, Bülent Diken draws on Žižek, Agamben, Badiou, and Marx, in an exploration of the relationship between post-politics, religion, and violence. Diken conceptualises post-politics as a form of 'economic theology', and argues that 'despite seeking to expel violence from its system of values at a surface level, post-politics itself produces a paradoxical, ecstatic violence'. The section concludes with Ingolfur Blühdorn's stark assessment of the depoliticisation of contemporary environmental governance, which he conceptualises as a 'technocratic politics of unsustainability'. Blühdorn is highly critical of the literature on post-politics, arguing that it indulges in a romantic attachment to radical political transformation, which prevents the Left from confronting the true gravity of the ecological crisis.

Part II begins with Erik Swyngedouw's account of the proliferation of insurgencies across the world's major cities since 2011. Swyngedouw argues that the spectres of the political immanent in these rebellions pose a series of theoretical and practical questions that require urgent attention. His contribution considers what to think and do *now*. Is there further thought and practice possible after the squares have been cleared, the tents have been broken up, the energies have been dissipated, and everyday life has resumed its routine practices? Where and how can fidelity to the emancipatory Idea immanent in these insurrectional events be nurtured and sustained? In her chapter, Wendy Larner takes issue with Swyngedouw, and with the post-political approach in general. Larner argues that this approach is politically disempowering, to the extent that it denies the political status of less explosive forms of contestation. Drawing on her work with a 'radical social enterprise' in the city of Bristol in the UK, Larner claims that 'it is out of such incomplete, paradoxical, and compromised experiments . . . that new political formations will emerge'. Shifting from the micro-politics of grassroots urban renewal to the geopolitical domain of global governance, Hans-Martin Jaeger makes a similar argument for the political status of a seemingly limited project. Through a critical engagement with the work of Mouffe, Rancière, and Foucault, Jaeger contrasts two visions of world order – the 'cosmopolitan' project of the EU and the 'multipolarity' of the 'BRICS' (Brazil, Russia, India, China, and South Africa). He argues that despite being integral to the global police order, the BRICS are opening a space of dissensus within it, by calling international inequalities into question.

The final four chapters return to the wave of protests and uprisings that swept across the world in 2011. In his contribution, Alex Loftus asks what the literature on post-politics can contribute to our understanding of these events. Building on Bosteels' critique of the 'speculative leftism' of post-foundational theory, Loftus challenges Laclau and Mouffe's appropriation of Gramsci's concept of hegemony, arguing that Gramsci's original Marxist project offers a more fruitful basis for radical critique. Maria Kaika and Lazaros

Karaliotas then seek to demonstrate the critical utility of the post-politics literature, though an ethnographic analysis of anti-austerity protests in Syntagma Square in Athens. Drawing primarily on Rancière, they show how the protests became divided, the 'upper square' degenerating into nationalist populism, while the 'collective self-management of the "lower square" conveyed valuable new elements for democratic politics'. In her analysis of anti-austerity protests around the world, Jodi Dean notes the tendency of protesters to frame their struggles in post-political terms, suggesting that post-politics is primarily a condition, not of the Right, but of the Left, and that 'the real political problem today is that the left accepts capitalism.' In a detailed critique of the Occupy Wall Street protests in New York's Zucotti Park, Dean claims that their concern with direct democracy prevented the realisation of their communist potential. In the final chapter, Andy Merrifield provides a freewheeling overview of the possibilities for militant politics in our time. Comparing the post-political condition to Kafka's *The Castle*, Merrifield argues that attempts to either storm or escape the castle are equally futile, and that radical politics must retain a fidelity to the conviction that 'underneath everything we see, everything we know, even beyond what we can currently imagine, there lies another reality, one uniting all hitherto ununited aspects of reality, all hitherto ununited social movements.' In the Conclusion, we reflect on the lessons to be drawn concerning the nature of our political predicament, in which radical change has never seemed less possible, yet has never been more necessary.

References

Allmendinger, P., and G. Haughton (2011), 'Post-political spatial planning in England: a crisis of consensus?', *Transactions of the Institute of British Geographers*, 37, pp. 89–103.

Badiou, A. (2010), *Communist Hypothesis*, London: Verso.

Bosteels, B. (2011), *The Actuality of Communism*, London: Verso.

Brand, U. (2005), 'Order and regulation: Global governance as a hegemonic discourse of international politics?' *Review of International Political Economy* 12: 1, pp. 155–76.

Catney, P., and T. Doyle (2011), 'The welfare of now and the green (post) politics of the future', *Critical Social Policy* 31: 2, pp. 174–93.

Clarke, N., and A. Cochrane (2013), 'Geographies and politics of localism: The localism of the United Kingdom's coalition government', *Political Geography* 34, pp. 10–23.

Crouch, C. (2004), *Post-Democracy*, Cambridge: Polity.

Darling, J. (2013), 'Asylum and the post-political: Domopolitics, depoliticization, and acts of citizenship', *Antipode*, Online First 05/07/2013 DOI: 10.1111/anti.12026.

Diken, B. (2009) 'Radical critique as the paradox of post-political society', *Third Text*, 23: 5, pp. 579–86.

Douzinas, C., and S. Žižek (2010), *The Idea of Communism*, London: Verso.

Fukayama, F. (1992), *The End of History and the Last Man*, New York: Free Press.

Fuller, C. (2012), 'Urban politics and the social practices of critique and justification: Conceptual insights from French pragmatism', *Progress in Human Geography*, Online First 21/12/2012, DOI: 10.1177/03091 32512469763.

Garsten, C., and K. Jacobsson (2007), 'Corporate globalisation, civil society and post-political regulation – whither democracy?', *Development Dialogue*, 49, pp. 143–55.

Gill, N., P. Johnstone and A. Williams (2012), 'Towards a geography of tolerance: Post-politics and political forms of contestation', *Political Geography*, 31, pp. 509–18.

Goeminne, G. (2012), 'Lost in translation: Climate denial and the return of the political' *Global Environmental Politics*, 12: 2, pp. 1–8.

Hall, S., D. Massey and M. Rustin (2013), 'After neoliberalism: Analysing the present', available at: *http://www.lwbooks.co.uk/journals/soundings/pdfs/s53hallmasseyrustin.pdf* (accessed 4 September 2013).

Hilding-Rydevik, T., M. Hakansson and K. Isaksson (2011), 'The Swedish discourse on sustainable regional development: Consolidating the post-political condition', *International Planning Studies*, 14: 2, pp. 167–87.

Jameson, F. (2003), 'Future City', *New Left Review*, 21, pp. 65–79.

Kythreotis, Andrew Paul (2012), 'Progress in global climate change politics? Reasserting national state territoriality in a "post-political" world', *Progress in Human Geography* 36: 4, pp. 457–74.

Laclau, E. and C. Mouffe (1985), *Hegemony and Socialist Strategy: Towards a Radical Democratic Politics*, London: Verso.

Lacoue-Labarthe, P. and J.-L. Nancy (1997), *Retreating the Political*, London: Routledge.

Marchart, O. (2007), *Post-Foundational Political Thought: Political Difference in Nancy, Lefort, Badiou and Laclau*, Edinburgh: Edinburgh University Press.

Mouffe, C. (2005), *On the Political*, London: Routledge.

Mouffe, C. (2009), 'Democracy in a multipolar world', *Millennium: Journal of International Studies*, 37: 3, pp. 549–61.

Oosterlynk, S., and E. Swyngedouw (2010), 'Noise reduction: The post-political quandary of night flights in Brussels airport, *Environment and Planning A*, 42, pp. 1577–94.

Pares, M. (2011), 'River basin management planning with participation in Europe: From contested hydro-politics to governance-beyond-the-state', *European Planning Studies*, 19: 3, pp. 457–78.

Peck, J. (2010), 'Zombie neoliberalism and the ambidextrous state', *Theoretical Criminology*, 14, pp. 104–10.

Rachman, G. (2011), 'Look behind you, Lucas and Mario', *Financial Times*, 15 November 2011.

Raco, M., and W. I. Lin (2012), 'Urban sustainability, conflict management, and the geographies of post-politicism: A case study of Taipei', *Environment and Planning C: Government and Policy*, 30, pp. 191–208.

Rancière, J. (1999), *Disagreement: Politics and Philosophy*, Minneapolis: University of Minnesota Press.

Rancière, J. (2001), 'Ten theses on politics', *Theory and Event*, 5: 3, pp. 1–21.

Rancière, J. (2010a), *Chronicles of Consensual Times*, London: Continuum.

Rancière, J. (2010b), *Dissensus: On Politics and Aesthetics*, London: Continuum.

Rorty, R. (2004), 'Post-Democracy', *London Review of Books*, available at *http://www.lrb.co.uk/v26/n07/richard-rorty/post-democracy* (accessed 5 October 2013).

Saramago, J. (2006), *Seeing*, New York: Harcourt.

Saramago, J., and D. Jacob (2006), 'La Démocratie est un Mensonge', interview with José Saramago by D. Jacob, *Le Nouvel Observateur*, 2190, pp. 144–5.

Schlembach, R., B. Lear and A. Bowman (2012), 'Science and ethics in the post-political era: Strategies within the Camp for Climate Action', *Environmental Politics*, 21: 5, pp. 811–28.

Stephens, P. (2012) 'Stop fretting about a French revolution', *Financial Times*, 4 May 2012.

Swyngedouw, E. (2005), 'Governance innovation and the citizen: The Janus face of governance-beyond-the-state', *Urban Studies*, 42: 11, pp. 191–206.

Swyngedouw, E. (2007), 'Impossible sustainability and the post-political condition', in R. Krueger and D. Gibbs (eds), *The Sustainable Development Paradox: Urban Political Economy in the US and Europe,* New York: Guilford Press, pp. 13–40.

Swyngedouw, E. (2009), 'The antinomies of the post-political city: In search of a democratic politics of environmental production', *International Journal of Urban and Regional Research*, 33: 3, pp. 601–20.

Swyngedouw, E. (2010), 'Apocalypse forever?: Postpolitical populism and the spectre of climate change', *Theory Culture Society*, 27, pp. 213–32.

Swyngedouw, E. (2011), 'Interrogating post-democratisation: Reclaiming egalitarian political spaces', *Political Geography*, 30: 7, pp. 370–80.

The Economist (2008), 'Capitalism at bay', 16 October 2008.

Vergopoulos, K. (2001), 'Globalization and post-democracy', in T. Pelagidis, L. T. Katseliand J. Milios (eds), *Welfare State and Democracy in Crisis – Reforming the European Model*, Farnham: Ashgate, pp. 37–49.

Walker, G. (2012), 'On Marxism's field of operation: Badiou and the critique of political economy', *Historical Materialism*, 20: 2, pp. 39–74.

Williams, S. and K. Booth (2013), 'Time and the spatial post-politics of climate change: Insights from Australia', *Political Geography*, 36, pp. 21–30.

Wilson, J. (2013), 'The urbanization of the countryside: depoliticization and the production of space in Chiapas', *Latin American Perspectives*, 40: 5, pp. 218–36.

World Economic Forum (2012), *Global Risks 2012 – Seventh Edition*, Geneva: Risk Response Network.

Žižek, S. (1991), *For They Know Not What They Do: Enjoyment as a Political Factor*, London: Verso.

Žižek, S. (1999), *The Ticklish Subject: The Absent Centre of Political Ontology*, London: Verso.

Žižek, S. (2000), 'Holding the place', in J. Butler, E. Laclau and S. Žižek (eds), *Contingency, Hegemony, Universality: Contemporary Dialogues on the Left*, London: Verso, pp. 308–29.

Žižek, S. (2008) 'Preface to the new edition: why Lacan is not a Heideggerian', in S. Žižek, *The Ticklish Subject: The Absent Centre of Political Ontology*, London: Verso (2nd edn), pp. vii–xxii.

Žižek, S. (2010), 'How to begin from the beginning', in C. Douzinas and S. Žižek (eds), *The Idea of Communism*, London: Verso, pp. 209–26.

Žižek, S. (ed.) (2013), *The Idea of Communism 2: The New York Conference*, London: Verso.

Part I
Spaces of Depoliticisation

1 The Post-Politics of Sustainability Planning: Privatisation and the Demise of Democratic Government

Mike Raco

In March 2012 the UK government introduced a new *National Planning Policy Framework* with the intention of modernising and reforming the English planning system. The core contents of the framework represent the latest manifestation of the output-centred post-political rhetoric that has dominated discourses of development since the late 1970s. Its opening words state that 'the purpose of planning is to help achieve sustainable development', and as with many contemporary planning statements it claims to reflect and help to reproduce international understandings of so-called Good Governance, while helping to 'balance' the competing needs of economic development, social inclusion, and environmental protection. As many authors have noted, the term 'sustainable development' has become something of a cliché that is used to justify a range of programmes that carry differing, and sometimes competing and contradictory, objectives. Over recent decades it has become increasingly flexible with critics of global capitalism drawing on sustainability discourses to argue that there should be 'prosperity without growth' (Jackson 2011), whilst others on the Right simultaneously use it to legitimate discourses of neoliberal capitalism and commodity-based expansion. For Swyngedouw (2009) it has therefore come to represent an impossible, post-political construction that is driven by 'non-ideological', pragmatic win-win interventions to tackle 'wicked problems', in which there are no losers and only winners.

This chapter draws on some of the key principles associated with the literature on post-politics to make sense of contemporary discourses of sustainability planning. It focuses on the relationships between contemporary uses of the discourse of sustainable development in the modernisation of the English planning system and wider changes in the political economy of capitalism. It argues that we are witnessing the establishment of a specific form of post-politics, underpinned by a contradictory *anti-utopian utopian project*. This contains many of the elements of post-political structures outlined by Rancière, Swyngedouw and others. It is focused on output-centred forms of legitimacy built around the empowerment of managerial elites; it is embedded in a discourse that undermines the value of egalitarian-based modes of democratic participation; and it purposefully removes the institutional links between decision-making, accountability, and state practices.

Moreover, as will be discussed in relation to privatisation, state 'modernisation' is increasingly used to justify and legitimate the conversion of the complex political demands associated with sustainability into a technocratic exercise to be managed and controlled by experts and those who 'know best' how to achieve tangible project outcomes. Social and economic processes are converted into discernible objects or 'things' that can be broken down, managed, accounted for, and contractualised. These contracts can then be farmed out to those with the 'expertise' to implement new modes of policy. This, in turn, has helped to create new elite networks of private actors who are then able to deliver and manage a sustainability agenda on behalf of states under contract. As Allyson Pollock (2006) and Richard Murphy (2011) note, the world's biggest business opportunities now arguably lie in capturing state welfare contracts under the guise of post-political efficiency management. Terms such as sustainability, therefore, provide an ideal cover for the rolling-out of these technocratic privatisation agendas and the fundamental transformation of relationships between states, markets, and civil society. They constitute a part of the new technical-managerial politics of good governance that has come to dominate policy-making processes and practices in democratic societies (see Dean 2009; Swyngedouw 2011). Indeed for Crouch (2011) these conceptual distinctions have become increasingly irrelevant as corporations colonise an ever-expanding range of social, political, and environmental practices that used to be seen as the everyday responsibility of government and state bureaucracies.

The chapter argues that too much of the academic and policy rhetoric around sustainability and planning is still underpinned by the core presumption that 'the state' consists of autonomous bureaucratic institutions that act under the guidance of elected politicians to provide services for citizens and communities. It is a way of thinking that underestimates the impact of modernising reforms on the structure and *modus operandi* of modern states and the new post-political economy of welfare reform that is being established in countries across the world. These reforms comprise a new mode of thinking that equates sustainability with private-led state 'efficiency' and managerialism. Paradoxically, under the rhetoric of sustainability planning, communities and citizens are told that they are 'being empowered' at a time when their capacities to influence welfare programmes are being undermined in the drive to get things done. This has become particularly significant in countries such as the UK as, under the Blair and Brown administrations, and now the Coalition government, private corporations have not only taken over an expanded range of contracted-out services but are also building and leasing out a growing proportion of the physical infrastructure of the welfare state on which citizens depend, particularly in urban areas where public sector resources have been most stretched. It is also a discourse that is fuelling so-called 'austerity agendas' across the EU and beyond in which the selling-off of welfare assets and services is seen as a prerequisite for the 'stabilisation' of indebted economies. Moreover, in the emerging markets of the Global South these new modes of state-led privatisation are being used to fund massive infrastructure investments as welfare budgets gradually expand. Post-political agendas are being used to establish new modes of inequality as the political subjectivity of modern citizens is (re)defined through the lens of consumerism. The chapter argues that they are shaping emerging programmes of sustainability planning.

The first part explores some of the wider writing on sustainability and its conversion into a post-political managerial framework. This is followed by a discussion of the changing nature of the UK state and the transfer of powers and responsibilities from democratically elected governments to new hybrids of state actors, regulators, and private corporations. The discussion uses the example of the Private Finance Initiative in the UK to highlight the form and character of contemporary change. This is followed by a section that explores the re-emergence of sustainable development discourses in the post-credit crunch English planning system. It looks at the likely impacts of the new approaches and the ways in which the post-political rhetoric of sustainability planning diverts attention away from the highly political, structural changes that are taking place in state structures and practices. It highlights the growing dissonance between democratic demands, accountability, and policy outcomes. If democratic politics is understood to consist of an equality of access to decision-making frameworks, then current shifts are indeed anti-democratic and post-political in nature.

Reducing government but expanding the state: the new progressivism

The political economy of global capitalism has changed significantly in recent decades. It is a period that is often characterised as one of 'neoliberalisation' in which the notion of a public interest, with welfare rights guaranteed by the state, has been under attack. In many ways, however, a more complex series of processes have been underway in which the regulatory power and size of state institutions and their budgets have consistently *expanded*, despite a supposed shift to a deregulated neo-liberalism. Despite recent drives to austerity, most Western states now spend more money that at any time before the so-called neoliberal era and regulate ever-greater fields of public life. The Blair and Brown governments in the UK, for example, passed over 300 new laws and regulations per year between 1997 and 2008 (*The Independent* 2008). The UK state in 2011–12 still spent approximately £680 billion or 45 per cent of GDP (*The Guardian* 2012) and this reflects a wider trend in which many states in the Global North and South are spending ever-greater sums on both welfare programmes and the regulation of public and private welfare providers. In most countries in the Global North (apart from the United States) spending has not been diverted into military or policing budgets in order to 'defend neoliberalism', but has been used to fund welfare programmes, regulatory systems, and infrastructure projects.

This expansion of the state, however, has run alongside a *systematic reduction in the size and power of government*. Under the banner of modernisation the 1990s and 2000s witnessed a remarkable degree of privatisation and the rise of what Allison Yeatman (2002) terms a 'new contractual state' in which governing has become elided with the management and organisation of contracts. This replacement of traditional forms of government reflects a wider set of political projects and the rise of so-called Third Way governance in the 1990s, or what some left-leaning authors presumptuously labelled the 'new progressivism' (see for example Pearce and Margo 2007). In Giddens's (2002: 78) terms, it was an agenda that 'aims to address the aspirations and needs of a wider constituency of the population ... and stands firmly in the traditions of social democracy – it is social democracy, brought up to date and made relevant to a rapidly changing world'. Concerns with old-fashioned democratic accountability through representational politics, it was argued, had become obsolete and theoretical in a context where populations are less concerned with ideologies and want governments to adopt a pragmatic, 'what-matters-is-what-works' approach to governance. It was a historicist vision that viewed collective politics as a relic of the past that had been replaced by processes of individualism and class fragmentation (see Beck and Sznaider 2006; Paddison 2010).

The core objective of this new progressive thinking was to reconfigure dominant understandings of political legitimacy. For Scharpf (1999), all political systems are underpinned by two distinct forms of legitimacy; *output* legitimacy and *input* legitimacy. The former is founded on tangible outputs and outcomes with governments and states being seen as legitimate if they are able to deliver high-quality and visible public services and infrastructure (see Boedeltje and Cornips 2004). The latter relates to the legitimacy of the democratic processes through which different demands are articulated and are able to influence policy-making processes. For proponents of the new progressivism, welfare-based modes of state organisation had undermined the overall legitimacy of democratic governments as they were seen as inefficient and unable to *deliver* quality outputs. As authors such as Offe note, this challenge represented a root-and-branch critique in which the 'means by which policy has been traditionally implemented, namely bureaucratic and professional intervention, seem to have lost much of their acceptance and are increasingly seen in the corrosive light of a distributional and exploitative game' (Offe 2009: 130). Rather than being seen as working towards a public interest, welfare systems were portrayed as a 'highly effective strategy of a self-serving "new class" to cement their positions of power and privilege' (Offe 2009: 130).

This is certainly a vision that advocates of the 'new' politics promoted and exaggerated in order to legitimate their policy reforms. As Tony Blair, for example, recalls in his memoires,

> The problem for all progressive parties was that by the 1960s . . . citizens on the ladder of opportunity didn't want more state help; they wanted choice, freedom to earn more money and spend it . . . They wanted a different relationship with the state: as partners or citizens, not as beneficiaries or clients. (Blair 2010: 90)

This partnering role would enable the state to support modern citizens for whom being 'well off' is about 'aspiration, ambition, getting on and going-up, making some money, keeping their family in good style, having their children do better than them' (Blair 2010: 43; see also Raco 2009). There would be an end to what Giddens (2007: 8) termed the 'phoney universalism' of old-fashioned beliefs that a welfare state system could be used to level out inequalities. The emphasis of policy should be on the achievement of clear outputs with a belief that it does not matter who delivers services or takes responsibility for state-funded programmes, as long as they are seen to be 'working' and 'efficient'.

The legitimacy conferred by these visible outputs, it was argued, strengthens the hand of governments as state institutions come to be seen as 'effective', business-like, and in control. New hospitals, roads, schools and other forms of public infrastructure provide concrete manifestations of state power and delivery, even if they are delivered and state-funded through non-democratic processes of organisation. In Tony Blair's famous term 'what matters is what works', even if that means that democratic checks and balances on the activities of policy experts need to be curtailed in order to allow them to get on with the task of delivery. The implication is that 'advancing the cause of public services and public institutions often means that government must confront the state, and seek to regulate and reform it' (Giddens 2002: 35). It is a policy utopia that sees the input of democratic engagement as a brake on modernisation and reform. Democratic governance has to be curtailed in order to save it from its own limitations (see Rancière 2006).

It is in this context that the mantras of what the United Nations and World Bank call 'Good Governance' and 'sustainability' become particularly significant. If politics becomes focused on outputs, then the logical implication is that government is replaced by the state and other 'partners' who are best able to turn policy agendas into delivery-based practice. State actors and bureaucracies become managers, who are responsible for the smooth running of (often costly) tendering, contract management, and regulatory processes. This usually requires the imposition of new contractual spaces that seek to obliterate place differences and use management techniques and practices to bring about expert-driven sustainable development. An 'effective state' becomes elided with smart rule-making, the routinisation of audit trails, the formalisation of codes, and the re-shaping of citizen expectations and understandings of risks and rewards. It is a model of governance that, for new progressives, solves 'the inherent tension between the demands of the capitalist order and democracy' (Jordana and Levi-Faur 2004: 12).

As will be discussed below, the imposition of this utopian view of governance has enormous implications for how public policy is constructed, and for the relationships between states and markets. As Crouch (2011: 72) notes, there is an obvious danger of 'regulatory capture' by private corporations as 'often the only expertise that exists about a field of activity is held within the firms concerned, so government is dependent on them for advice about how to exercise its regulation, which tends to weaken it'. This leads to the creation of new public-private hybridities made up of powerful corporations, elites, and state agencies. These become what Braithwaite (2008) terms 'communities of shared fate' that crystallise around consensus-based, technical frameworks such as those associated with sustainability indicators and planning. And these hybridities come with significant costs for governments and populations. In most cases, private companies wish to be *insulated* from the democratic demands of social groups, and look to contracts and techniques of risk management to limit the effects of policy changes on their profitability (see Riles 2008). Within contracts there are often, therefore, judicially sanctioned clauses to ensure that this separation and insulation becomes institutionalised and legally enforced.

Nothing could be more post-political in form than this contract-based, delivery-focused mode of governance. It reconstructs the political process from top to bottom so that instead of democratic politics being concerned with changing and adapting the operation of government policy and state activities, it becomes a field of contract negotiations in which state actors and citizens are required to negotiate with private delivery companies over the types of demands that they are prepared to meet. Democratic politics becomes limited to the possibilities 'outlined' by the experts who draw up management contracts, and contracts tend to become more attractive to private investors as this, it is hoped, will encourage their participation. Governments often seek to reduce 'risk' by tendering out longer-term, high-return, and state-backed contracts that insulate private investors from the threat that democratically elected governments might change their policies at a later date in response to the changing demands of citizens. This not only generates increased financial costs for the state but also imposes enormous 'liberty costs' (Levi-Faur 2011) in terms of a loss of openness and accountability. There is an erosion of the fundamental principle that governments should be able to *respond* to changing demands as and when they arise. The traditional roles and skills of state bureaucrats become increasingly obsolete with policy discussions framed through a new lexicon of management-speak that includes terms such as 'capital costs', 'competitive dialogue procurement processes', 'contractual compliance', 'revenue support' and 'risk profiles' (see Raco 2013).

The wider implication is that state managers, as well as politicians and community and voluntary groups, now have to develop new ways of thinking and acting in relation to policy-making processes. There is a greater need to employ the costly expertise of accountants, lawyers, contract-writers, and other experts. Two important outcomes have emerged from this process. First, new private elites that specialise in 'contract advice' have been enriched and have become advocates of contract-based privatisation. Companies such as PriceWaterhouseCoopers have made anything between £200 and £400 million out of advising on public private partnership contracts in the UK alone (Public Accounts Committee of the House of Commons 2011). Others also benefit enormously from the business opportunities opened up by privatisation and the ease with which welfare spending can be siphoned off and placed into tax-avoidance schemes and tax havens (for a devastating discussion of how these processes operate, see Shaxson 2011). And second, this utopian view of output-centred legitimacy underplays the very real differences in negotiating capacities that exist between multinational firms, communities, and their political representatives. Private-sector specialists are often able to extract concessions from public bodies, and their activities can have a significant impact on the rolling-out of sustainability agendas. It is a process that can create a new level of dissonance between political representatives and the publics that they serve, as politicians find their room for manoeuvre circumscribed by their contractual obligations and the need to maintain a good 'investment climate' for private firms. If new hybrids are emerging in which private actors regulate on behalf of states, and in turn are regulated by those same states, then notions of democratic accountability through representation lose their salience. In Levi-Faur's (2011: 13) terms,

> We could now be experiencing a transformation from representative democracy to indirect representative democracy. Democratic governance is no longer about the delegation of authority to elected representatives but a form of second-level indirect representative democracy – citizens elect representatives who control and supervise experts who formulate and administer policies in an autonomous fashion from their regulatory bastions.

Moreover, these changes are being reflected and reproduced in the creation of new private-sector elites. This has precipitated a new politics of the private sector. There is less and less need for formal business associations and organisations to engage in open political discourse. In their place new forms of elite 'privatism' are emerging, which aim to change the structure and capacities of the state, whilst marginalising the influence of government. This goes beyond the 'grant coalitions' (Cochrane et al. 1996) that emerged in cities in the 1990s to attract government-funded projects, and the 'growth machines' (Cox and Mair 1989) and 'structured coherences' (Harvey 1989) of the 1980s. Although strong public-private partnerships had become key pillars of policy-making by this stage, there was still an assumption that governments had not signed away many of their rights and powers for the long term and that in most cases they still had possession of key state assets and infrastructure. There was an assumption that business wanted more *market-led* interventions, whereas in the new politics of welfare many big corporations want governments to spend *more money* that they can capture and profit from. It is a form of monopoly politics, rather than market politics.

The privatisation of the state and the rolling-out of output-centred governance

All of the above makes the process of sustainability planning an extremely difficult and complex task. For at the same time as a modernising approach to governance appears to offer a progressive and inclusive way forward, based on high-quality delivery, these wider changes in the organisation of state power and global capitalism are mitigating against local control and the implementation of more radical forms of intervention. In many cases, the discourse of sustainability has been used to justify structural reforms to the state and the rolling-out of privatisation agendas, managerialism, and contractualism. The democratic promise of sustainability-inspired forms of devolution, localism, consensus, and partnership are so powerful that governments continue to reassemble sustainability programmes even where they bring about these contradictory outcomes. The problem is still characterised as one of too much govern*ment* and not enough govern*ance*.

The same is also true in relation to the ownership structures of the contemporary welfare state and the systematic removal of direct government and citizen control that has been taking place under the banner of modernisation and the desire to enhance the sustainability and legitimacy of welfare systems. The best example of this is the rolling-out of the Private Finance Initiative (PFI) in the UK, which since the late 1990s has led to the privatisation of over £300 billion worth of state assets and services (HM Treasury 2012). Under the PFI, companies finance, build, manage, and operate state infrastructure, which is then rented back to public sector authorities under contracts that normally last for twenty-five to thirty years, in some cases longer. Smyth and Edkins (2007: 233) describe them as contracts that give private investors 'responsibility for providing and servicing schools, hospitals, prisons, and other infrastructure typically for 25–40 year concessions. In return the investors receive a series of payments, a "rental", so government is paying for the services out of revenue rather than capital or debt'.

Projects include the construction of new hospitals; the management and construction of motorways and trunk roads; new schools; university buildings; community centres; training centres; prisons; and even in some cases fire engines and police stations. When the contracts expire, the infrastructure returns to the public sector, often at 'market rates' that are yet to be negotiated, but in the meantime they are not owned by the state or by electorates and any changes to the infrastructure *and/or* the services they provide require often complex contractual changes, costs, delays, and the mobilisation of expert knowledge. Contracts typically possess clauses that make their early termination prohibitively expensive, with risks transferred from the private to the public sector (see Parker and Hartley 2002; Public Accounts Committee 2011; Spackman 2002). All risks, liabilities, and uses of the sites are defined by contracts and can be commodified, repackaged, and sold on to investors such as hedge funds and investment banks under so-called 're-financing' deals.

The implications of PFI go well beyond the UK. It is a model of public-private partnership that is expanding internationally under the Good Governance rhetoric of sustainability, with significant implications for policy communities and long-term democratic governance (see Hellowell and Pollock 2009). Between 2001 and 2007, 193 PFI schemes were signed off by governments across the EU (excluding the UK) with a total capital value of €32 billion. Contracts were procured worth a further €68 billion. As investors look to expand their activities to new markets, public assets across the world are more likely than ever to become PFI targets. As Inderst (2009: 5) notes in a World Bank working paper, 'many in the infrastructure industry see the USA as the next gold rush', and there are also enormous opportunities to be found in emerging markets across the Global South and Australasia.

But it is the UK that has acted as the driving force behind the PFI. Under the consensual politics of the Blair and post-Blair eras gigantic investment and profiteering opportunities have opened up and helped to bring into being a corporate sector that specialises in lucrative public-private partnerships. The UK is seen a trailblazer that sets the standard for others which, in Deloitte's (2006) words, are 'latecomer[s] to the PPP party'. Figures 1 and 2 give a breakdown by sector of PFI expenditure up to 2011 and the total number of projects. They indicate that the key areas of private investment have been in the most lucrative welfare sectors; namely health and education.

The implications of this enormous programme of privatisation for sustainability planning are profound. PFIs represent a utopian faith in the ability of contractual governance to imagine and provide for future levels of service and repayment. The paradox of the new

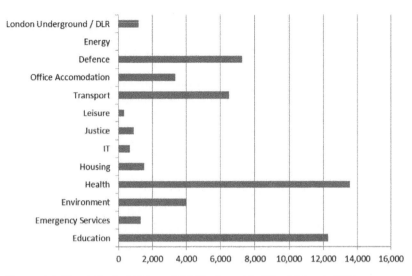

Figure 1.1 Total Capital Value of PFI Projects (£million) March 2011

Source: HM Treasury (2011)

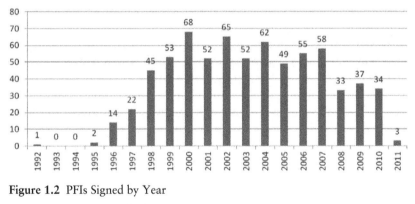

Figure 1.2 PFIs Signed by Year

Source: HM Treasury (2011)

arrangements is that welfare services are now carrying long-term financial and legally binding contractual burdens on a scale that makes it difficult to plan for future needs in an effective and sustainable way. There is a post-political rigidity to the new arrangements that seeks to 'lock out' political protest and 'take the politics out of welfare' in order to enhance the delivery of welfare. It is an extreme example of the output-centred transformation of governance now being undertaken under the label of non-political sustainability planning, a logic that is founded on the 'principle of competence [which] holds that only those actors should be involved who may make a significant contribution to the policy process' (Boedeltje and Cornips 2004: 11).

The key point about this privatisation is that it represents the logical consequence of a sustainability-driven discourse that is fiercely anti-state and pro-privatisation. Private companies have been handed the ownership of assets and resources with long-term contracts of up to forty years, and this circumscribes the possibilities for policy change for the adult lifetimes of most citizens. There has been little democratic discussion of the impacts of this PFI provision on strategic planning. The effects will be increasingly felt in a rapidly changing economic context in which the level of expected spending on welfare services is far from guaranteed. Indeed, given the financial crisis it seems likely to fall well behind the rate of inflation; a measure that is built into most PFI contract payments to insulate providers from inflationary risks. In some cases hospitals, for example, have already gone bankrupt in trying to pay off their PFI debts. In places such as south London this has effectively meant that decisions over health-care priorities and facilities have been taken away from patients, healthcare planners, and even politicians, and are now being organised by official appointed receivers, accountants, and auditors (see Raco 2012). In the absence of effective democratic inputs and checks and balances, the output becomes flawed.

The post-political nature of debates over welfare modernisation, planning, and reform have meant that these fundamental changes in governance have gone relatively unnoticed by many commentators, academics, planners, and civil society groups. The wider shift towards a sustainability consensus around which all interests can agree has been used to legitimate such reforms. The next section now looks at the latest round of modernisation and highlights the restraints that a focus on sustainability puts on the wider politicisation of planning processes. The new agendas are post-political in terms of both what they claim sustainability should be about and what they fail to acknowledge in terms of wider processes that are producing new modes of privatisation and growing inequalities.

The limits to sustainability planning and the changing nature of contemporary states

In June 2010 a coalition government was elected in the UK, led by the Conservative party. It promised a radical approach to planning in which the role of the state would be transformed to become a facilitator, rather than a driver, of economic development. It seems, ostensibly, to have promoted a new discourse that differs from that of the new progressives and Third Way thinkers of the 1990s and early 2000s. In place of target-setting, the rationale of policy is to shrink the role of the state in order to allow citizens and 'natural communities' to govern themselves. However, the differences are only to a degree. The Good Governance rhetoric of devolution is still very much in evidence, as is the focus on seeing localities and welfare systems as spaces for private accumulation and contractual acquisition at the expense of democratic accountability. This section discusses the Coalition's post-political sustainability and localism reforms and highlights their core features and potential implications.

The agendas are certainly bold in rhetorical terms. The Coalition now claims that sustainable development should represent a 'golden thread' that weaves its way through all planning policies, at all scales. There have been two key interventions – the National Planning Policy Framework (NPPF) and the Localism Act (LA) (Department for Communities and Local Government (DCLG) 2012; 2011). The former is a legally binding set of guidelines that have to be followed by planners across England. The latter is a legal Act of Parliament that sets out a series of broader reforms to the structures of government. The LA defines sustainability in procedural terms with local authorities (and their planners) required to draw up *Local Development Plans* that are supposed to take account of the needs of local communities and actors and establish local definitions of sustainability and what it includes. This, it is argued, reflects a 'traditional' English approach to planning and one that rejects the Napoleonic rational planning systems adopted in much of Continental Europe. It defines localism as an emergent property that evolves organically from the perspectives and collective discussions of local actors. It cannot be 'created' by government bureaucracies, experts, and planners. As the NPPF states, the drawing-up of local planning priorities should 'provide a framework within which local people and their accountable councils can produce their own distinctive local and neighbourhood plans, which reflect the needs and priorities of their communities' (DCLG 2011: 1).

But it is also an agenda that goes beyond this and represents a wider attack on the legitimacy of governments. For example, there are to be forced asset transfers from the public sector into the hands of communities, voluntary groups, and private actors. Local authorities and other state bodies will have to justify why they should continue to hold onto assets, as their wider legitimacy to use them in the public interest is being increasingly questioned. Government is seen as the 'problem'. Privatisation and/or community transfers are seen, by default, as preferable replacements and more in touch with the post-political rhetoric of sustainability and output-centred delivery. The proposed reforms therefore represent a fundamental critique of the legitimate existence of state planning and the apparent failures of earlier approaches that were underpinned by

> the mistaken belief that planning could both determine where growth should happen and stimulate that growth. This approach failed as it went against the grain of markets. Regional and other strategies stifled natural and healthy competition between places and inhibited growth as a consequence. (Department of Business, Innovation, and Skills (BIS) 2010: 7)

Markets and competition are equated with a natural order, whereas government is seen as an 'artificial' and 'abstract' imposition on everyday life that empowers self-selecting bureaucrats and experts at the direct expense of individual citizens living in locally oriented communities. There is thus a rhetorical attempt to reinforce the power of place and the authority of citizens and their representatives.

Within such visions, formal regions represent a particular *bête noire*, and are presented as dangerous artificial fantasies that possess little or no connection with the imaginations of 'ordinary' people or businesses. The abolition of Regional Development Agencies in England was therefore announced almost as soon as the Coalition government came to power in 2010. These bodies were based on the UK's formal EU regions and were designed to promote economic development through spatial planning. Their removal would create the conditions in which 'national and local government policies should work with and promote the market, not seek to create artificial and unsustainable growth' (BIS 2010: 7).

Under the Coalition's reforms sustainability is presented as the fundamental 'organising principle' of the planning system. However, in contrast to the 'localist' emphasis of much of the rhetoric highlighted above, its meanings and priorities are still to be centrally defined. The NPPF sets out two definitions:

> *Sustainable* means ensuring that better lives for ourselves don't mean worse lives for future generations. *Development* means growth. We must accommodate the new ways by which we will earn our living in a competitive world. We must house a rising population, which is living longer and wants to make new choices. We must respond to the changes that new technologies offer us. Our lives, and the places in which we live them, can be better, but they will certainly be worse if things stagnate. (DCLG 2012)

In order to fulfil these requirements local plans will have to adopt a *presumption* of growth, meaning that it will be up to planners, communities, and others to justify why growth should *not* take place, rather than the postwar emphasis of English planning on developers having to explain why their plans should be approved. Despite being locally derived, the NPPF makes it clear that plans *must* 'positively seek opportunities to meet the development needs of their area' (DCLG 2012: 4). So whilst on the one hand this seems to promote local autonomy, it is clear that on the other hand local plans will be determined and shaped by the NPPF's insistence that development should go ahead.

The justification for this growth-led approach is clear. Sustainability is defined as the sustainability of economic growth. It is seen as essential that the planning system 'adapts' to facilitate more growth. As the NPPF states, 'in order to fulfil its purpose of helping achieve sustainable development, planning must not simply be about scrutiny. Planning must be a creative exercise in finding ways to enhance and improve the places in which we live our lives' (DCLG 2012: 34). It is a vision that sees the existing planning system as a bureaucratic brake on development and something to be removed and converted into a dynamic, managerial structure. In line with the principles of political economic reform, the state's role is to establish partnerships with private experts, with the implication that in the longer term the system should be privatised completely, with planning conducted and regulated by 'specialist' contracted-out firms, such as PriceWaterhouseCoopers, McKinsey's, and KPMG. Such firms, in Shaxson's terms constitute a 'private police force of capitalism' as 'their audits are the main tools through which societies know about and regulate the world's biggest corporations' and states (Shaxson 2011: 176).

What such discourses amount to is a root-and-branch critique of government power in which public-sector bureaucracies are not only seen as burdensome and costly in their own right but are also to blame for the lack of competitiveness in the private sector and the erosion of active citizenship. It is a *politics of liberation* in which every effort should be made to reduce the reliance of communities and citizens on state resources and the dangerous expectations raised by decades of unsustainable welfare expansion. Thus a key part of the reforms is to establish programmes of action and governance that 'will help areas which depend too heavily on the public sector for jobs, helping create more sustainable private sector employment'. (Clegg 2010: 3). The promotion of market mechanisms becomes something of a shibboleth, a false idol that requires the structural reform of state structures to facilitate its expansion. More sophisticated understandings of the role that state power plays in facilitating market activities, which writers such as Polyani (1944), Keynes (2008) and others recognised long ago, are put to one side. In their place simple dichotomies are erected between states and markets that only serve to confuse the governance process and detach those who possess the means of governance from those who pay for and seek to influence it. It amounts to a rejection of the idea that welfare systems have been put in place to protect vulnerable communities and places from the ravages that market dynamics can bring. The welfare state has not only stifled business activity, as discussed above, but also generated dependency within poorer populations who have come to 'expect' state support. Its existence has dampened down and deflated the aspirations of individuals and whole communities.

In many ways this politics of localism is also, of course, a politics of geography. The localist agenda is particularly critical of people living in low aspirational spaces who are 'dependent' on state expenditure. It challenges some of the founding principles of Keynesianism that saw spatial equality as a core public policy objective (see Pike et al. 2006). This priority has been eroded systematically since the 1970s in countries such as the UK, where forms of what Jones (1997) terms 'spatial selectivity' have been practised that have systematically focused policy attention on the needs of 'successful' regions, whose continued success is seen as paramount to national competitiveness in an increasingly global economy. Under the Coalition's localism agenda there is a systematic attempt to institutionalise and reinforce existing inequalities and reduce the extent to which wealthier areas directly support the less wealthy through financial transfers. There has been a shift in spending towards 'growth funds' that are designed ostensibly to encourage new forms of entrepreneurialism that will 're-balance' the UK economy in the longer run.

The net effect of the changes is that citizens are being asked to take greater responsibility for their own problems, in the same way that community empowerment and sustainability agendas since the 1980s have sought to promote responsible citizenship. Localities are seen, simultaneously, as the subjects and objects of policy interventions,

> best placed to understand the drivers and barriers to local growth and prosperity, and as such localities should lead their own development to release their economic potential. Local authorities, working with local businesses and others can help create the right conditions for investment and innovation ... [aiming to] promote efficient and dynamic markets and increasing confidence to invest ... with focused investment.

It is this logic that underpins initiatives to establish networks of Local Enterprise Partnerships across localities where 'natural economies'

and 'communities' are thought to exist. In Secretary of State Eric
Pickles's (2011: 1) terms,

> We want every community to be open for business and rewarded for
> economic growth, but at the moment there is no motivation for councils
> to support local firms or create new jobs. One of the best ways we can
> change that is to free councils from their enslavement to government
> grants and put them in control of their own destiny.

This characterisation of centrally organised taxation and spending as
a form of enslavement is in itself revealing of a wider way of thinking. The philosophy is to encourage new forms of competition to
reward localities, businesses, and citizens for being successful and
this, it is imagined, will drive up standards of governance in more
deprived areas in which actors will develop their own partnerships
and ways of working.

The rolling-out of the sustainability and localism agenda has been
underpinned by post-political terminology and reform processes.
In order to incorporate consensual and inclusive language, many
aspects of the *status quo* remain conspicuously absent from discussions over reform and modernisation. The most obvious example is
that of unequal land ownership. As Cowley's (2010) research shows,
a relatively small group of just 6,000 aristocratic families in the
UK, known as the 'cousinhood' (and including the Royal family),
own large swathes of rural and urban land, almost all of which is
inherited and unearned. Approximately 69 per cent of the land area
of England is owned by just 0.6 per cent of the population. Or, in
other terms, 158,000 families own 41 million acres of land, while
24 million families live on just 4 million acres (see also Cahill 2011).
This not only concentrates wealth in a tiny number of hands, but also
precludes the implementation of sustainability planning programmes
by restricting the ownership and strategic use of assets. So whilst
local authorities and other government bodies are required to hand
their assets over to communities or investors in the name of sustainability planning, patterns of class-infused private ownership remain
unquestioned and unchallenged. They are seen as part of the 'natural
order' of British society.

Moreover, the rolling-out of the 'delivery' model of sustainability
planning under the Coalition promotes a win-win politics and fails to
engage with more contentious issues such as the growing structural
inequalities in the UK, and how localism will help to reinforce these
differences. Recent official statistics show that the richest 10 per
cent of households hold 40 per cent of the wealth and are 850 times
wealthier than those in the bottom 10 per cent (Office for National

Statistics 2012). The social and spatial geographies of the UK are becoming ever more divided, and yet the discourse of sustainability fails to give any space for the articulation of political demands for redistribution or greater social justice beyond vague commitments to future generations. In a post-political way inequalities are blamed on the failures of dysfunctional states and their inability to manage socio-economic systems and practices. What appears to be a return to input-focused forms of legitimacy, through local control, equates to a strong centralised state and privatised regulation. In the absence of strong govern*ment*, it is difficult to see how wider social and political objectives can be incorporated into meaningful local agendas. Places are instead to be left to the vagaries of private control and PFI contracts.

Conclusions

This chapter has argued that the latest phase of sustainability-inspired planning reform in England reflects and reproduces a wider set of post-political agendas that are embedded in shifting modes of capitalism. Its promises of enhanced devolution appear to offer citizens new vehicles of empowerment that will oversee the transfer of powers from old-fashioned government bureaucracies to communities and local actors. However, in practice the power of govern*ment* has been reduced. It has been replaced by new hybrids of state regulators and private corporations, working through powerful policy frameworks such the Private Finance Initiative. This process of replacement is a logical consequence of an output-centred form of post-politics that claims that the existence of strong democratic processes of engagement leads to 'confusion' and increases project costs and inefficiencies by creating new 'risks'. These, in turn, reduce the attractiveness of investment opportunities to private companies, who clamour to be insulated from the outcomes of democratic deliberation. It is a post-political logic that is reflected in mainstream discourses. UK Prime Minister David Cameron, for example, recently dismissed the planning system as a form of 'dithering' that interferes with the speedy and successful delivery of state services and assets by experts and financiers who know how to 'get things done'. Democracy represents a break on utopian models of efficiency.

The discussion has shown that this conceptualisation represents a post-political fantasy that promises an *anti-utopian managerial utopia*. It is a post-politics that disavows the utopian imaginaries of postwar Keynesianism and replaces them with an anti-utopian rhetoric of output-centred governance and management. The state becomes nothing but a contract-manager that uses managerial knowledge (that may itself be taken from the private sector through forms of consultancy) to shape the conduct of private actors and other experts to deliver policy outcomes. This, it is claimed, will make state actors and government legislators more 'legitimate' to imagined publics. As Rancière (2005: 11) points out, such approaches reproduce a wider paradox as the 'time which is no longer susceptible to realise any utopia has itself become the last utopia. Because the realism which pretends to liberate us from utopia is itself a utopia'. In Žižek's terms, the pursuit of the new politics represents the outcome of a global liberal order that

> clearly presents itself as the best of all possible worlds; its modest rejection of utopias ends with the imposition of its own market-liberal utopia which will supposedly become reality when we subject ourselves fully to the mechanisms of the market and universal human rights. (Žižek 2011: 38)

A curious parallel reality has thus emerged in which localism and sustainability are confidently elided with community responsibilisation and local control, but with no recognition of the wider structural changes that have taken place in the governance of welfare and the real limits that these place on local action and autonomy. This illusion of an output-centred shift in legitimacy and practice creates a post-political context in which political representatives are increasingly left with greater responsibilities to deliver services to citizens, but with little power to affect change. In Offe's terms it constitutes a form of 'limited statehood' in which,

> The co-option of non-state actors for the achievement of public policy goals might either increase the efficiency and effectiveness of the policy in question through the co-ordination of responsibilities, or it might lead to the systematic creation of dependency of public authorities on private actors (state capture) and outright corrupt practices. (Offe 2009: 553)

Common-sense understandings of democracy and decision-making processes are thus being eroded piece by piece by a false managerial utopianism that is creating new modes of dependency on experts. It is a surreptitious mode of change and reflects John Gray's wider concern that 'utopianism is at its most dangerous when it is least recognised' (Gray 2008: 118).

And of all this raises direct questions over political projects and demands. As a new form of politics it seeks to foreclose the potential for opposition, in part by making the state seem more 'effective' and giving publics less to react to, and also in part by isolating and contractualising some of the key dynamics of decision-making and removing them from the terrains of formal politics. However, as Swyngedouw notes, and as this chapter has shown, it is in reality an agenda that 'mobilises the commons in the interests of the elite' through a binary of utopian messages of delivery and the cultivation of a series of fears that can 'only be managed through technocratic-expert knowledge and elite governance arrangements' (Swyngedouw 2011: 378). To traverse these, Swyngedouw argues, requires 'the intellectual and political courage to imagine the collective production of space' (2011: 378). However, in more practical terms the mobilisation of post-political forms of sustainability requires publics and citizens to re-imagine political processes and to recognise the shifting modalities of (institutionalised) power in which they are now operating. It may be, for example, that there is a growing requirement for communities (and researchers) to understand and unpick the contractual relationships that now frame sustainability planning as the basis for the foundation of new imaginations. Through an enhanced understanding of the specifics of managerial utopias there may be new grounds to establish a more egalitarian politics in which the principle of 'affected interests' (Goodin 2007) plays a stronger role in shaping political agendas.

References

Beck, U., and N. Sznaider (2006), 'Unpacking cosmopolitanism for the social sciences: A research agenda', *The British Journal of Sociology*, 57, pp. 1–23.

Boedeltje, M., and J. Cornips (2004), 'Input and output legitimacy', *Research Paper*, at: *http://repub.eur.nl/res/pub/1750/* (accessed 13 August 2012).

Blair, T. (2010), *A Journey*, London: Hutchinson.

Braithwaite, J. (2008), *Regulatory Capitalism – How it Works, Ideas for Making it Work Better*, Cheltenham: Edward Elgar.

Cahill, K. (2011), 'Who owns the world?', *The New Statesman*, 17 March 2011.

Clegg, N. (2010), 'Foreword', in Department for Business, Innovation, and Skills, *Local Growth: Realising Every Place's Potential*, London: HMSO, p. 3.

Cochrane, Allan, Jamie Peck and Adam Tickell (1996), 'Manchester plays games: Exploring the local politics of globalisation', *Urban Studies*, 33: 8, pp. 1319–36.

Cowley, J. (2010), 'The coming battle over land and property', *The New Statesman*, 19 October 2010.

Cox, K. R., and A. J. Mair (1989), 'Urban growth machines and the politics of local economic development', *International Journal of Urban and Regional Research* 13, pp. 137–46.

Crouch, C. (2011), *The Strange Non-death of Neo-liberalism*, Cambridge: Polity Press.

Dean, J. (2009), *Democracy and Other Neoliberal Fantasies: Communicative Capitalism and Left Politics*, Durham: Duke University Press.

Deloitte (2006), *Closing the Infrastructure Gap*, London: Deloitte.

Department of Business, Innovation, and Skills (BIS) (2010), *Local Growth: Realising Every Place's Potential*, London: HMSO.

Department of Communities and Local Government (DCLG) (2011), *The Localism Act*, London: HMSO.

Department of Communities and Local Government (DCLG) (2012), *The National Planning Policy Framework*, London: HMSO.

Giddens, A. (2002), *The Third Way and Its Critics*, Cambridge: Polity.

Giddens, A. (2007), *Over to You, Mr Brown*, Cambridge: Polity.

Goodin, R. (2007), 'Enfranchising all affected interests, and its alternatives', *Philosophy & Public Affairs*, 35, pp. 40–68.

Gray, John (2008), *Black Mass: Apocalyptic Religion and the Death of Utopia*, London: Penguin.

Guardian, The (2012), 'Autumn statement: George Osborne slashes welfare and extends austerity', available at: *http://www.guardian.co.uk/uk/2012/dec/05/george-osborne-welfare-autumn-statement*, (accessed 7 December 2012).

Harvey, D. (1985), *The Urbanization of Capital*, Baltimore, MD: The Johns Hopkins University Press.

Hellowell, M., and A. Pollock (2009), 'The private financing of NHS hospitals: Politics, policy, practice', *Institute of Economic Affairs*, March 2009, pp. 13–19.

HM Treasury (2012), *PFI Data Summary – March 2012*, London: HMSO.

Independent, The (2008), 'More than 3,600 new offences under Labour', available at: *http://www.independent.co.uk/news/uk/home-news/more-than–3600-new-offences-under-labour–918053.html* (accessed 7 December 2012).

Inderst, G. (2009), 'Pension fund investment in infrastructure', *OECD Working Papers on Insurance and Private Pensions No. 32*, Paris: OECD.

Jackson, T. (2011), *Prosperity Without Growth*, London: Earthscan.

Jones, M. (1997), 'Spatial selectivity of the state? The regulationist enigma and local struggles over economic governance', *Environment and Planning A*, 29, pp. 831–64.

Jordana, J., and D. Levi-Faur (2005), 'The diffusion of regulatory capitalism in Latin America: Sectoral and national channels in the making of new order', *Annals of the American Academy of Political and Social Science*, 598, pp. 102–24.

Keynes, J. M. (2008), *The General Theory of Employment, Interest, and Money*, London: BN Publishing.

Levi-Faur, D. (2011), 'Regulation and regulatory governance', in

D. Levi-Faur (ed.), *Handbook on the Politics of Regulation*, Cheltenham: Edward Elgar, pp. 1–25.

Murphy, R. (2011), *The Courageous State – Rethinking Economics, Society, and the Role of Government*, London: Searching Finance.

Offe, C. (2009), 'Governance: An empty signifier?', *Constellations*, 16, pp. 550–61.

Office for National Statistics (2012), 'South East has biggest share of the wealthiest households', available at: *http://www.ons.gov.uk/ons/dcp171776_289407.pdf*, (accessed 3 December 2012).

Paddison, R. (2010), 'Protest in the park: Preliminary thoughts on the silencing of democratic protest in the Neoliberal age', *Variant*, 39/40, pp. 20–5.

Parker, D., and K. Hartley (2002), 'Transaction costs, relational contracting and public private partnerships: A case study of UK defence', *Journal of Purchasing and Supply Management*, 9, pp. 97–108.

Pearce, N., and J. Margo (eds) (2007), *Politics for a New Generation – the Progressive Movement*, London: Palgrave.

Pickles, E. (2011), 'Review could end council dependence on Whitehall grant', available at: *http://www.communities.gov.uk/news/newsroom/1866559,* (accessed 13 August 2012).

Pike, A., A. Rodriguez-Pose and J. Tomaney (2006) *Local and Regional Development*, Routledge, London.

Pollock, A. (2006), *NHS Plc – The Privatisation of Our Health Care*, London: Verso.

Polyani, K. (1944), *The Great Transformation*, Blackwell, Oxford.

Power, M. (1999) *The Audit Society*, Cambridge University Press, Cambridge.

Public Accounts Committee of the House of Commons (2011), *Lessons from PFI and Other Projects*, London: HMSO.

Raco, M. (2009), 'From expectations to aspirations: State modernisation, urban policy, and the existential politics of welfare in the UK', *Political Geography*, 28, pp. 436–44.

Raco, M. (2013), *State-led Privatisation and the Demise of the Democratic State: Welfare Reform and Localism in an Era of Regulatory Capitalism*, Hampshire: Ashgate.

Rancière, J. (2005), *Chronicles of Consensual Times*, New York: Continuum.

Rancière, J. (2006), *Hatred of Democracy*, London: Verso.

Riles, A. (2008), 'The anti-network: Private global governance, legal knowledge, and the legitimacy of the state', *Journal of Comparative Law*, 56, pp. 605–30.

Scharpf, F. (1999), *Governing Europe: Effective and Democratic?* Oxford: Oxford University Press.

Shaxson, N. (2011), *Treasure Islands: Tax Havens and the Men Who Stole the World*, London: The Bodley Head.

Smyth, H., and A. Edkins (2007), 'Relationship management in the management of PFI/PPP projects in the UK', *International Journal of Project Management*, 25, pp. 232–40.

Spackman, M. (2002), 'Public-private partnerships: Lessons from the British approach', *Economic Systems*, 26, pp. 283–301.

Swyngedouw, E. (2009), 'The zero-ground of politics: Musings on the post-political city', *New Geographies*, 1, pp. 52–61.

Swyngedouw, E. (2011), 'Interrogating post-democratisation: Reclaiming egalitarian political spaces', *Political Geography*, 30: 7, pp. 370–80.

Yeatman, A. (2002), 'The new contractualism and individualized person-hood', *Journal of Sociology*, 38, pp. 69–73.

Žižek, S. (1999), *The Ticklish Subject: The Absent Centre of Political Ontology*, London: Verso.

Žižek, S (2011), *Living in the End Times*, London: Verso.

2 The Post-Political and the End of Nature: The Genetically Modified Organism

Larry Reynolds and Bronislaw Szerszynski

The close of 'the short twentieth century' in 1991 (Hobsbawm 1994) was followed by a deluge of proclaimed endings – of history, of nature, of politics – and even, some argued, of endings themselves. Later on in the same decade Bruno Latour (1999) caught the spirit of the moment when he proclaimed that society had moved beyond the age of revolutions, and that modes of succession have become replaced by modes of coexistence. In this chapter we take one emblematic technology of that period – the genetically modified organism (GMO) as deployed in agricultural biotechnology – and use it to explore this complex moment at the end of the twentieth century. The emergence of a neoliberal global order in the 1990s had substituted technological progress for the agonistic struggles of history. However, in the story of GM crops and the 'biotech revolution', we find that this neutralised technological agenda became challenged and obstructed. In this situation, those attempting to govern the GM controversy in the European Union of the early twenty-first century resorted to rhetorics and regimes of 'coexistence' between parallel agro-food socio-technical systems. Here, instead of the triumphant succession of one technological and social system over another, it was suggested that three separate agro-food systems – GM agriculture, 'conventional' industrial agriculture, and organic alternatives – could and should 'coexist' in the same time-space. Tropes of progress in *time* became eclipsed by ones of coexistence in *space*, as capitalism tried to establish a new spatio-temporal fix (Jessop 2006). For the public controversy around GM food, the enabling of consumer choice through labelling represented the dissolution of political antagonisms over 'the environment' into apparently mutually compatible and individualised market choices. At the same time, a new machinery of public participation attempted to incorporate opposition within consensual regimes, through government-sponsored events like 'GM Nation?' (Reynolds and Szerszynski 2007). In the architecture of this 'deliberative' process the opinions of 'engaged publics' who attended events were 'balanced' by neutralised samplings of a 'general public' constructed as dispassionate and uncommitted – and therefore somehow more legitimate (Reynolds 2013). Regimes of choice, consensus and coexistence were thus deployed to defuse the strange and complex political charge that was building up around GM crops and foods.

The history of the EU GM controversy therefore provides a prime site to explore current debates around the post-political condition. Yet this is no simple story of the eclipse of the political by neutralised tropes of the technical. Whilst Carl Schmitt in 1929 may have observed the rise of a new ground of depoliticisation and neutralisation in the technical (Schmitt 1993), the closing decades of the twentieth century provide the scene for the proliferation of struggle around technology, science and the environment, as these grounds themselves became politicised. Indeed, these decades can be understood to mark the end of the period when the technical was seen as the neutral foil to the political. This occurred amidst a wider destabilisation of perhaps the most fundamental ground of neutralisation and depoliticisation of the entire modern epoch – that of 'the natural' itself (McKibben 1990; Smith 1984). Thus the figure of the GMO, entering the stage of political contestation in this millennial period of endings and destabilisations, would come to represent the collapse of long established categories of 'life' and 'technology', and of 'nature' and 'politics', into each other.

In this chapter we first lay the grounds for this story by setting out the theoretical resources we will draw upon, including the recent political philosophy of the post-political, debates in science and technology studies (STS) about the democratisation of science, and Schmitt's theory of neutralisation and depoliticisation. We then consider the political-economic and cultural context which shaped the emergence of biotechnology in general and GM crops in particular, a context hidden behind narratives of neutral, autonomous and inevitable technological progress. This is followed by the story of the 'release' of the GMO onto the public stage in three acts: those of regulation, of resistance, and of the attempted neutralisation of that resistance. We conclude by considering the wider implications of the story of the GMO for the relationship between technology and politics in the twenty-first century.

The post-political and the age of neutralisations

Our reading of the GMO is informed by an encounter between two areas of debate – those around the notion of the 'post-political', and those in STS around the 'politics of nature' and the 'democratisation of science'. From a Latourian perspective, debates around the 'post-political' connect to the question of what counts as due process in the constitution of our common world (Latour 2004a), and the way in which managerial, technical or consumerist discourses and practices might illegitimately short-circuit the agonistic play of political visions and interests. Yet concerns about the erosion of the conditions of possibility of political subjectivity, discourse and action had been raised long before this question of 'how to bring the sciences into democracy'. For Hannah Arendt (1958), the political required concerted human action in the public sphere, animated by a metapolitical attention to the goals and character of the political itself. Arendt suggested that in the modern period the rise to dominance of an understanding of politics as administration, of life as continuous production and consumption, and of culture as conformity had blurred the classical distinction between the private (the realm of necessity and the meeting of needs) and the public (the shared realm of meaningful action and self-realisation – the polis) and given rise to 'the social' – a post-political realm preoccupied not with public meanings but with private needs (Arendt 1958: 46). For Habermas (1971), the problem was the 'scientisation of politics', which approaches the social world in the same way that we treat the natural world, and thus reduces political questions to questions of technique and efficiency. For Latour (2004a), the political is erased by the very 'modern constitution' that separates the 'houses of Nature and Society' in the first place. Both of these are 'illicit assemblies': the first, convened by Science without recourse to 'due process', is a world constituted by prematurely foreclosing the question of what beings and properties exist; the second, convened by Politics but lacking the reality of things, shatters into a profusion of ultimately incommensurate and ineffectual points of view.

But it is the period since around 1991, the dusk of Hobsbawm's 'short twentieth century' and the seeming final victory of the 'free' market over state 'communism', that has been singled out as the time of 'the post-political'. For both Rancière (1999) and Mouffe (2005), the core characteristic of the political is the dissensus and agonism which is constitutive of human living together, and which crucially involves the challenging of existing power relations. By contrast, the post-democratic or post-political order was one instead based around consensus, thus stilling the dialectic through which the tensions within society drive history forward. As proclaimed by Francis Fukuyama, after the collapse of soviet communism, history as succession seemed to be over, and we were to be left with just the endless incremental development of liberal Western society, led by technological innovation (Fukuyama 1992).

The literature on the post-political that emerged at that time enumerated many mechanisms that seemed to be preventing the arising of a sort of agonism that could produce genuine social change: management, administration and bureaucracy; science and technical reasoning; a consensual socio-economic order in which questions of *eudaimonia* – of the nature of human flourishing – seem to have been settled once and for all; the elevation of consumption and market choice as the vehicle of human fulfilment and the distribution of goods; the canvassing of public opinion; and mechanisms of conflict resolution and mediation (Swyngedouw 2011: 371–2).

Despite emerging at the time of this apparent erasure of the political, GMOs became the focus of intense political debate and struggle. The promoters of this controversial new technology were keen to frame the new agricultural biotechnologies as a neutral, technological solution to problems they also defined primarily in technological terms, ignoring their socio-ecological complexities and entanglements. The regulatory frameworks and discourses legislating for this new techno-social domain were also expressed in an exclusively biophysicalist register – in terms of a trade-off between agronomic efficiency and possible biophysical harm to environments or human populations. Even the debates in parliaments, media and wider society were initially dominated by this technicist discourse. However, as the controversy intensified, complex new forms of contestation and meaning emerged, often speaking in hybrid forms that mixed scientific, political and ethical discourses. The attempt to frame the GMO as a technical solution to a technical problem failed, and the technology came to be read as a form of 'politics by other means' (Latour 1987). This can therefore be taken as another symptom of the twilight, not just of 'the political', but also of the carefully constructed neutral and legitimising other of liberal politics: 'the technical' (Ezrahi 1990).

We develop this diagnosis here by drawing on the work of Carl Schmitt. In his 'Age of neutralizations and depoliticizations', Schmitt posited that the dominant belief was now that 'the absolute and ultimate neutral ground has been found in technology, since apparently there can be nothing more neutral' (Schmitt 1993). In Schmitt's schema, the turn to technology as a principle outside politics and conflict was just the latest in a historic series of 'wanderings' in search of a neutral sphere that could constitute an imaginary ground for the rest of society:

In an age of economic or technical thinking, it is self-evident that progress is economic or technical progress. To the extent that anyone is still interested in humanitarian-moral progress, it appears as a byproduct of economic progress. If a sphere of thought becomes central, then the problems of other spheres are solved in terms of the central sphere – they are considered secondary problems, whose solution follows as a matter of course only if the problems of the central sphere are solved. (Schmitt 1993: 135)

And yet, Schmitt argued, each such wandering would inevitably be frustrated when the newly found neutral ground was itself politicised: 'Europeans have always wandered from a conflictual to a neutral sphere, and always the newly won neutral sphere has become immediately another arena of struggle' (1993: 138). As political contestations become translated into the vocabulary of a new neutral territory, this vocabulary becomes increasingly contested and loses its ability to function as a neutral 'other' to politics, leading to the search for a new neutral ground. Tracing this dynamic through a series of ill-fated depoliticisations since the sixteenth century – first theology, then science, then humanitarianism, then economics – Schmitt suggested that it was only with the turn to technology in the twentieth century that it was finally felt that 'universal peace begins here'. However, he argued, although technology as a means to an end is neutral, its particular kind of neutrality would prevent it from inspiring a concept of cultural progress or a form of society, resulting in an irruption of political contestation around technology itself (1993: 139).

If we follow Schmitt's broad schema, we would expect to see the grounds on which the post-political is founded – science and technology, bureaucracy and administration, market individualism and the sovereign consumer, and representations of the popular will – to progressively lose their capacity to be seen as neutral others to the agonism of politics, and to become politicised themselves. In the case of the GMO we can indeed detect the failure of technology to remain as an imagined neutral ground beyond politics. For most of the twentieth century, societal problems were understood in technological, physical terms, so that the solutions were also seen to lie in the realm of technology. But in the last quarter of the century this neutralisation began to lose its force in a series of conflicts over the introduction of new technologies: technology became political and politics became technological, and the GMO emerged at this crisis point. Beyond the break-up of the technical neutral ground, even deeper tectonic shifts were underway. Indeed, the technological can be understood as the latest variant of a more fundamental ideological neutralisation, that of 'the natural' (Williams 1980). 'Nature', cast as separate from and beyond its social co-producer and legible only to science, has been the increasingly necessary foil to 'politics' since the capitalist mode of production took hold at the end of the fifteenth century and the age of modernity began to be proclaimed. As the late twentieth century recognition of ecological crisis began to be read as 'the end of nature', the very concept of 'the natural' was being subverted.

GMO as metonym

The GMO stands as a metonym of this period – as a particular technology that embodies the general constellation of technology, politics and economics that characterised the time: the establishment of a neoliberal global regime, the attempt to govern life through markets, a 'risk society' fixated on potential threats to the environment and human health, and the endeavour to govern these new concerns through 'participatory' and 'consensual' mechanisms. As heralds of a promised 'biotech century', GM crops had emerged from the laboratories of the North American and European university-industrial complex into the post-cold war globalising order of the World Trade Organization (WTO), the International Monetary Fund (IMF) and the multinational corporation (Reynolds 2010). Since its inception in the 1970s, biotechnology had been an ostensibly technological project. Nevertheless, the project had been imbued with social and political significance, symbolising economic growth, competitiveness and the possibility of a new 'green' set of bio-based productive forces. Such innovations, it was hoped, would transcend the crisis of petro-industrial modernity, a crisis symbolised by the 1973 'oil shock' and the end of the long economic boom of the mid-twentieth century.

Biotechnology started in the 1970s as a state-funded and directed political project, in response to that crisis. But it was shaped by two trends that had already been gestating in the decaying Fordism of the 1960s: neoliberalism and environmentalism. The GMO appeared as an emblematic technology for the neoliberal age: a technology that was also a patented, informational commodity and that facilitated the further penetration of agro-food systems by corporate power and market forces. Yet both the production and the reception of agricultural biotechnology were shaped by environmentalism: the GMO was presented as an inherently green technology, but also entered a world in which environmental movements were contesting and politicising technology and nature to an unprecedented extent. The GMO thus emerged in a time of epistemic and ontological crisis at the proclaimed 'end of history', where apparently stable binary categories such as the nation and the globe, the scientific and the political, the natural and the social, the human and the non-human were starting to collapse.

From their inception, the life sciences had carried a portentous symbolic charge, epitomised by Crick and Watson's 1953 boast in a Cambridge public house that they had found 'the secret of life' (Watson 2003). Amidst the crisis of the early 1970s, the advent of recombinant DNA (rDNA) appeared as both a promise and a threat. The metaphor of DNA as a 'genetic code' that could at first be 'read' and now (with the advent of rDNA) 'reprogrammed' promised huge instrumental power, suggesting that biological species could soon be optimised to suit corporate trajectories and accumulation strategies. But at the same time, rDNA technology seemed to mark the implosion of the fundamental modernist categories of 'life' and 'technology' – an implosion signalled by the portmanteau term of 'biotechnology' itself. As an ontopolitical object, the definitions and boundaries of the GMO were contested and uncertain. How should this new object be received? As a technology? A commodity? A form of life? A form of pollution?

This blurring of categories meant that GM crops were vulnerable to being understood within different conceptual and legal framings. While some saw the new technology as a further sign of humanity's Promethean prowess, for others it was 'playing god' and subversive of the natural order. While, for some, the way that 'biotechnology' collapsed the categories of 'life' and 'technology' seemed to promise new levels of control over biological processes, for others it suggested that the products of human ingenuity had become wild or alien things, beyond our control. New apprehensions emerged of the technology creating a form of self-replicating 'living pollution' that might be qualitatively more risky than familiar forms of chemical pollution. The hype and the soaring hopes of investors and 'bio-entrepreneurs' were thus matched by fears in other quarters. Biotechnology was seen as either promising cornucopia or threatening catastrophe – but rarely as a merely mundane development.

From its inception, the project of biotechnology and rDNA engineering had been an object of techno-economic promise and a target of funding for the state-political sphere. However, a new phase opened in the late 1980s, as the first potentially commercialisable products in the form of GM crops took shape, and their creators sought their dissemination as experimental and marketable objects. The question of how the state would regulate these new objects thus became one of the first iterations of the (post-)politics of the GMO. Given all the possible interpretations and apprehensions of these new beings, within which register of onto-political concern might the state seek to regulate their release into the world?

Regulating release

As the post-cold war order took shape, the first GM crops were ready to make their way out of the laboratories and into the fields, ecosystems, supermarkets and digestive systems of the world – a process regulators would call 'deliberate release'. Organisations such as the WTO and the European Union were keen to create homogeneous regulatory spaces that could both stabilise and allow the circulation of entities such as the GMO (Reynolds and Szerszynski 2011). In 1986 various regulatory discussions and processes began simultaneously in the US, the EU and its member states, and also at the international level through bodies concerned about global regulatory harmonisation, such as the Organisation for Economic Co-operation and Development (OECD). Reflecting the trend towards de-regulation and 'regulatory relief' amidst concerns about national economic competitiveness, the US developed a minimalist regulatory style, based on the assertion of the OECD that there was 'no scientific basis for specific legislation for the implementation of rDNA technology and applications' (Office of Science and Technology Policy (OSTP) 1986: 19) The US therefore chose to treat GM objects as 'substantially equivalent' to their conventional counterparts, denying the need for any special legislative framework or regulatory category – a regulatory style extended globally through WTO dispute settlement procedures.

The European Union took a different route to the regulation of GMOs. The EU's main regulatory tool – the 1990 Deliberate Release Directive (DRD) – constituted GMOs as a separate regulatory class of objects, a move that marked a divergence from the approach favoured by the USA (Council of the European Communities 1990). This was a precautionary move by the EU with respect to the GMO, in an acknowledgement of scientific uncertainties and controversies surrounding the new technology. At first sight, the EU's approach therefore appeared to be more in keeping with Latour's call for 'due process' in composing the common world, opening up debate as to what is considered to exist (Latour 2004a). However, the EU's Directive shared the USA's narrowly positivistic understanding of what the issues around the new technology might be, confining them to physical risk to human health and the environment, and thus amenable to a technocratic risk management paradigm. In this sense, the EU followed the USA in treating the GMO within the realm of what

Latour calls 'matters of fact', as opposed to 'matters of concern' (Latour 2004b).

This framing of the GMO treated it in purely physical terms. Potential problems with or objections to the new technology were posed in the reductionist register of physical threats to health or the environment. This narrow, depoliticised framing neglected a range of socio-political concerns raised by critics of the technology, such as how the monopoly granted by patents and other intellectual property rights might dispossess farmers and increase monopoly control of the food chain, or how GM crops might accelerate an intensification of industrial agriculture and globalisation and thereby undercut other agricultures. Furthermore, the particular and concrete forms taken by the technology – crops engineered to be resistant to proprietary herbicides and/or to carry their own insecticide – seemed to presuppose an industrial agricultural model (Reynolds and Szerszynski 2011). Such political questions around future agro-social forms and alternatives could not be addressed within the discourses or committees of the regulatory system found in the UK and the rest of the EU. These frameworks simultaneously constituted the GMO as a regulatory object, and constructed the regulatory spaces required for its smooth circulation within institutions such as the EU and the WTO. The nation state, as a series of borders which might restrict or regulate the flow of objects like GMOs and subject them to a territorially bounded polity, was apparently displaced in favour of a global, borderless regime where rules are formulated by panels of technocrats and framed in neutralised terms of standards setting and harmonisation.

Resisting release

Yet this attempt to govern the GMO in a purely technocratic register would not succeed. The controversy that erupted around the first attempts at commercial cultivation of GM crops in the latter half of the 1990s overwhelmed and paralysed the EU's regulatory system. The first commercially grown GM crops – a crop of Monsanto's Roundup Ready soyabeans – were ready for harvest in October 1996, in the USA's agricultural heartlands of Iowa. In one manifestation of the unease and hostility the new bio-technological creations would provoke, Greenpeace activists symbolically marked one of these fields with a gigantic 100ft 'X' and the word 'biohazard'. The 'X' symbol, echoing the then-popular TV series *The X-Files*, emphasised the alien and alienating resonances of a dystopian sci-fi present. This symbolic labelling, creating an iconic media image, would then follow the crop as it crossed the Atlantic, as activists staged demonstrations and blockades at major European ports as the ships carrying the GM soya arrived.

GM soya first arrived in Europe mixed in with conventional soya shipments (it was 2 per cent of the 1996 shipments, growing to 15 per cent in 1997). This led to demands for the segregation and labelling of GM products in the food chain. In July 1996 EuroCommerce, representing a large section of the European retail, wholesale and international trade sectors, started to call for labelling on GM products (Friends of the Earth Europe 1996). In September of the same year, EuroCommerce held a press conference with the Greens in the European Parliament calling for a boycott of products made from the GM soybeans until these were adequately labelled. At the same time, environmental NGOs including Greenpeace began to mobilise public protest campaigns, and several large European supermarket chains and wholesale organisations declared that they would not stock products containing the GM soya unless they were separated and labelled.

The first shipments of GM crops added urgency to a range of concerns articulated by an array of forces including European legislators, the news media, consumer groups, food retailers, dissident scientists, churches, trades unions, women's groups and environmental NGOs. Concerns were voiced in various registers, from the 'naturalness' and 'safety' of the technology, to questions of social justice, environmental sustainability, and the ethics of 'playing god'. However, in a move that echoed Schmitt's argument that the 'central spheres' of society provide the language not only for power but also for resistance, the narrow physicalist and technicist framings set out in the governmental and regulatory regimes also shaped oppositional discourses. Critics of the technology often had the greatest impact when raising questions around possible harm, understood in terms of biophysical impacts on health or the environment.

By 1997 the EU's harmonised regulatory space was fracturing, as a series of member states began implementing their own national bans on the new GM crop varieties. Under the 1990 Deliberate Release Directive, once one member state's competent scientific authority had given consent to a GM variety, the principle of the internal market meant that the GMO in question must be accepted by every other member state. However, the 1990 directive had an 'opt-out' clause under its Article 16. This clause allowed a member state to impose its own provisional prohibition on the sale or use of a GM variety within its territory if it had justifiable reasons to consider that product 'a risk to human health or the environment' (Council of the European Communities 1990). Thus a range of possible negative effects on human health or the environment of the GM crop tech-nology became the currency of public and political contestation in different parts of the EU. These included the possibility of negative health effects from the modified DNA; the concern that antibiotic resistance might spread following the use of antibiotic markers in the creation of the GM crops; the safety of the herbicides connected to the herbicide resistant GM crops; and the effects of the associated herbicide management regime on agricultural biodiversity.

In the UK, the question of biodiversity became an important focus of the controversy. By 1996 environmental NGOs such as Greenpeace and Friends of the Earth were aligned with the 'wildlife establishment', including the government's statutory body English Nature and the Royal Society for the Protection of Birds, in calling for a moratorium on the commercial cultivation of herbicide-resistant GM crops. In response, the UK government improvised a substantial programme of 'Farm Scale Evaluations' on the impacts on agricul-tural biodiversity. These FSEs enlisted both the agrobiotech industry and the wildlife establishment in their implementation, and helped to head off calls for a commercial moratorium, while also visibly pro-ceeding with the GM project. All this could now be done under the supposedly neutral cover of a scientific experiment.

However, the FSEs provoked a new set of political critiques and interventions in a number of registers: of *science* – that the inevitably reductionist nature of the FSEs would not produce valid knowledge about the GM socio-ecological complex; of *democracy* – that the FSEs were being foisted on local populations without their consent; and of *risk* – that the FSEs were themselves a form of pollution. A pattern of public participation began to emerge around the FSEs, ranging from village meetings, picnics and trespasses on the sites, to 'crop-trashings' (Szerszynski 2005). The trials thus became the cause and focus of yet more anti-GM activism and popular/civic unrest; rather than closing down and narrowing the debate into purely 'tech-nical' issues, they produced a more complex and turbulent situation.

In these contests around the FSEs and their associated GM crops, key areas of debate arose about how GM crops might spread to and 'contaminate' other crop varieties as a form of 'living pollution'. The extent of adequate separation distances between GM crops and other forms of land use, along with the movements of pollen and the behav-iour of bees, suddenly became a new currency of social contestation and forms of activism. The unstable terrain of the technical-neutral ground was crumbling, and new and mutating forms of contestation and agonism were sprouting through the cracks. Arenas previously understood as zones of scientific neutrality, such as the UK national 'Seed List Hearings' in 2000 and 2002, became populated with forms of public contestation and criticality (Gray 2002; Friends of the Earth 2004).

Thus the seemingly neutral foundations of technical questions and positive risk began to break up beneath the European GM regulatory system. This should come as no surprise. Following Schmitt, we would indeed expect the next flowering of the political to break out precisely on the previously neutralised ground of the technical. Yet because politics erupts within the technical, it is expressed within that same language or speaks in hybrid mixtures. Bees, birds, butterflies and bacteria became 'politicised' nodes of public association and debate, around which a range of groups from beekeepers to ornithologists were drawn into the controversy. There is no retreat from the political into the technical in this mutual crisis of political and scientific authority and the subversion of the binarisms that draw the borders between them.

Regulating resistance

Faced with such destabilisation, governments across Europe staged a temporary retreat to past stabilisations of 'the political'. These found a moment of resurrection in the mobilisation of territorial tropes around the nation state, especially in the national bans invoked under Article 16 of the Deliberate Release Directive, which mobilised powerful discourses of national sovereignty and the defence of borders from alien pollutants, followed by a de facto EU-wide moratorium. As a condition for lifting the de facto moratorium and national bans, EU member states called for a new regulatory framework around labelling, traceability and the segregation of GM and non-GM food products. At the same time, the combined actions of retailers and social movements had already helped to create a segregated market, with premiums for conventional non-GM as well as organic and other 'quality' agrofood products. The logic of segregation then began to pervade seed production and distribution, crop cultivation and the agricultural landscape itself. As an attempt to unblock the EU GMO moratorium and lift the national bans, this 'regime of coexistence' represented a bid to re-institute a single harmonised European regulatory space for the GMO, but one in which borders have not been eradicated but subtly reterritorialised. The regulatory membrane now moved away from national borders and bans, and started to follow new contours that flowed within and through nation states, between labelled products in grain silos and on supermarket shelves, and between GM and non-GM crops in fields and the wider landscape.

We have seen how attempts had been made to control the hybrid forms of politicised collective contestation that had been 'contaminating' the previously pristine spaces of technicist neutrality. But with the mutual crisis of political and scientific authority blocking any simple retreat from the political to the technical terrain, new forms of neutralisation and depoliticisation began to be experimented with, ones involving tropes of 'choice' and 'consensus'. This involved the dispersal of collective antagonists and their arenas of contestation through two modes of subjectivisation.

The first of these was the framing of GM as a question of personal consumer choice and market mechanisms. Mandatory labelling of GM would enable individual consumers to exercise choice, making political conflict over agro-food futures unnecessary. In 2003 new updated EU food regulations came into force, requiring the labelling of GM-derived products, their traceability along the food chain, and their segregation from 'conventional' products. These led to proposals for the remaking of agricultural landscapes, and their partition into zones for the different kinds of agricultural production. In July 2003 the European Commission published its Guidelines for the Development of National Strategies and Best Practices to Ensure the Co-Existence of Genetically Modified Crops with Conventional and Organic Farming (Council of the European Communities 2003). The preamble to these guidelines outlined ten general principles, which partially abandoned the previously dominant vision of progress towards a singular technological future of intensive, productivist, high-tech agriculture. Instead, the preamble embraced a plurality of agricultures. The first principle declared that: 'No form of agriculture, be it conventional, organic, or agriculture using GMOs, should be excluded in the European Union', and the second insisted that 'the ability to maintain different agricultural production systems is a prerequisite for providing a high degree of consumer choice'. In the coexistence guidelines, as in the updated food regulations, the emphasis was on the autonomy and authority of the individual – not as a citizen who might work with others towards realising a shared public vision of the future of agriculture, but as a consumer exercising private values and preferences.

Subjectivisation was also carried out in a second register – that of public participation and deliberation. Publics were convened to debate whether GM crops should be commercially grown, for example in the 2003 'GM Nation?' consultation in the UK, in which over 30,000 members of the public participated through activities such as attending meetings or completing questionnaires. However, despite this apparent loosening of technocracy, the public debate would be an exercise yielding purely sociological information about the public and its 'values' to the government; 'facts' would be left safely within the domain of expert discourses, unmolested by any uncontrolled exposure to public participation. Participants were interpellated not as knowledgeable, materially entangled beings but as detached individuals with only values and attitudes (Reynolds 2013; see also Latour 2004c).

This attempt to control the unruly nature of the politics of GM through the subjectification of the public was reinforced by a reassertion of technocracy at the European level. A new European Food Safety Authority (EFSA) was used to declare products approved under the Deliberate Release Directive as safe, thus rendering the questions of contamination and coexistence as purely about economic damage to a producer's GM-free marketing value. By insisting that questions of risk could be settled by a single 'centre of calculation' (Latour 1987), the EU's bio-regulatory coexistence architecture assumed that the question of harm to health or the environment had been already settled by the initial approval process for each variety. Therefore the risk of contamination of non-GM by GM was relegated to a threat to the GM-free 'sign value' accrued by conventional or organic growers, and to the right of consumers to buy commodities which were consistent with their own personal beliefs.

The European Commission now attempted to manage the GM controversy via an institutionalised bifurcation, constructing two purified realms; the 'purely scientific' realm of powerful bodies like the new European Food Safety Authority (EFSA) and the 'purely economic' realm of coexistence and labelling. This bifurcated regime represented an attempt to simultaneously incorporate and transform the participatory subject: henceforth, the publics of GM were called upon, not to be publics collectively deliberating on 'the facts' and their contexts, but as individualised consumers expressing subjective values and tastes through the market. This move to defuse the threat of any genuinely reflexive modernisation through an individualised and marketised regime guaranteed by science performed a division between a 'House of Nature' in which questions had all been answered, and a 'House of Society' in which questions did not matter (Latour 2004a).

Yet this new regime remains unsettled. For example, the rise of the GM-free regions movement saw the GMO struggle respatialised and manifested as a battle over the scale at which coexistence between GM and non-GM agriculture should be institutionalised: that of the largest possible territorial blocs proposed by GM opponents, or that of the farm-scale molecular management favoured by the European Commission. More significantly, the GM-free regions movement contested the very logic of the regime of coexistence. One of its founding conferences in Berlin in 2005 issued a manifesto which challenged the rhetoric of choice central to the European Commission's emerging GM governance strategy, arguing that 'Choices about the use of reproductive material in a common environment cannot be made individually, as they affect all people sharing these commons' (European Conference on GM-Free Regions 2005). In the manifesto, individual choice is thus trumped by the collective responsibilities imposed by sharing a 'common environment', and the living nature of agricultural biotechnology is presented as requiring collective and regional democratic governance.

Conclusion

After the fall of communism and the apparent triumph of neoliberal capitalism in the 1990s, history, in the sense of the clash of ostensibly alternative systems and the possibility of radical change, did indeed seem to have come to an end. But although 'history' appeared to have been slain, it was at once resurrected, stripped of all politics, antagonisms and contradictions, as 'progress'. And smuggled in beneath the fanfare of the end of ideology was a particular ideology, one in which technological innovation became the only marker that we were no longer in the past. Although we were a very long way from the height of centralised planning and the classical modernist state of the middle of the twentieth century (Scott 1998), we still seemed to be firmly in the grip of Schmitt's 'technological neutral'.

And yet, as the GMO moved from the laboratories of corporations to the fields and supermarkets of Europe, the technological – and indeed the natural – failed to function as a neutral, depoliticised ground. The very constitution of biotechnology as a chimera of the biological and the technological had already evidenced the unsettling of the modernist division between the natural and the artificial, between nature and culture. But the GMO also entered a post–1960s world in which social movements had turned technology and science into fundamentally contested domains. The wider unsettling of the technological neutral of which these were all manifestations derailed any simple succession from 'conventional' to 'GM' agriculture.

So why did the GMO, once the herald of the brave new world of the 'coming biotech century' (Rifkin 1998; Oliver 2000), suddenly find itself merely meekly asking to 'coexist'? As Latour intuited in 1999, coexistence as a general condition seems to be thrust upon us all in the current historical conjuncture – and nowhere more than in the case of technology. As the 1990s and our post-historic times began to unfold, technological innovation seemed to take a new course – neither incremental improvements of existing forces of production nor their replacement with new ones, but simply a piling up of new technologies which are fated to exist side by side. We seem to be inhabiting a technological plateau, a moment of 'great stagnation' (Cowen 2011), closely linked to the breaking of the long wave of mid-twentieth-century capitalist development. It is rather as if the owl of Minerva got suspended in mid-flight, and has been fluttering like a moth around the light-emitting diode, at the moment of neither dusk nor dawn, where Y2K bugs failed to bite, and where both technological utopias and millennial apocalypses are forever present but forever postponed (Reynolds and Szerszynski 2012).

But the demise of the technological neutral does not necessarily mean any straightforward restoration of the political. In the case of GM, we have seen a manifestation of the more general use of marketised regimes for the governance of environmental and health issues through labelling schemes and appeals to consumer choice. The rise of apparently plural food and agro-social worlds is linked to the fragmentation and segmentation of mass markets, where saturated or mature sectors require the generation of new accumulation strategies based upon identity, taste and social distinction. Thus we are usually presented in the supermarkets with a choice between organic, or Fairtrade, or other ethical and eco-labels: a systemic alternative is not available for purchase, only the marketised fragments of one. In such a context, alternative agro-food systems seem destined to remain alternatives *within* the system, rather than systematic alternatives *to* the system. Thus while GM has not 'succeeded', neither do alternative agricultures seem to be able to make the succession; all are forced to coexist, caught in the bottleneck of history.

However, despite the apparent plurality of different consumer worlds, environmental activists insist that there is somehow 'one world' which is inextricably entangled. Thus the Berlin Manifesto declared that 'in most cases and for most species there is no realistic chance for coexistence between GM and non-GM farming, just as there is none between silence and noise in a room' (European Conference on GM-Free Regions 2005). Such voices of opposition still believe in the systemic clash of alternatives and the possibility of succession, in the spirit of the early twenty-first century alterglobalisation slogan that 'another world is possible'. However, if a coherent politics of social change is to occur under contemporary conditions, it will have to involve a recognition of the profound implications for politics of the end of the technological neutral.

References

Arendt, H. (1958), *The Human Condition*, Chicago: University of Chicago Press.

Council of the European Communities (1990), 'Council Directive 90/220/ EEC of 23 April 1990 on the deliberate release into the environment of genetically modified organisms', *Official Journal of the European Communities*, L 117, 08/05/1990 P. 0015 – 0027, available at *http:// eur-lex.europa.eu/LexUriServ/LexUriServ.do?uri=CELEX:31990L0220: EN:HTML*.

Council of the European Communities (2003), *Commission Recommendation of 23 July 2003 on Guidelines for the Development of National Strategies and Best Practices to Ensure the Co-Existence of Genetically Modified Crops with Conventional and Organic Farming*, Brussels: CEC, available at: *http://ec.europa.eu/agriculture/publi/reports/coexistence2/guide_ en.pdf*.

Cowen, T. (2011), *The Great Stagnation: How America Ate All The Low-Hanging Fruit of Modern History, Got Sick, and Will (Eventually) Feel Better*, Harmondsworth: Penguin.

European Conference on GM-Free Regions (2005), *Berlin Manifesto for GMO-free Regions and Biodiversity in Europe: Our Earth, Our Future, Our Europe*, unpublished declaration from the European Conference on GM-Free Regions, Biodiversity and Rural Development, Berlin, 22–3 January, available at: *http://www.gmo-free-regions.org/past-conferences/ gmo-free-conference–2005/berlin-manifesto.html*.

Ezrahi, Y. (1990), *The Descent of Icarus: Science and the Transformation of Contemporary Democracy*, Cambridge, MA: Harvard University Press.

Friends of the Earth Europe (1996), *Friends of the Earth Europe Biotechnology Programme Mailout*, 2(6), 15 September.

Friends of the Earth (2004), 'Legal challenge warning on GM maize', press release, 21 February, available at *http://www.foe.co.uk/resource/press_ releases/legal_challenge_warning_on_20022004.html*.

Fukuyama, F. (1992), *The End of History and the Last Man*, New York: Free Press.

Gray, A. (2002), Professor Alan Gray on *Farming Today*, BBC Radio 4 (27 April).

Habermas, J. (1971), *Toward a Rational Society*, London: Heinemann.

Hobsbawm, E. (1994), *The Age of Extremes: The Short Twentieth Century, 1914–1991*, London: Michael Joseph.

Jessop, B. (2006), 'Spatial fixes, temporal fixes and spatio-temporal fixes', in N. Castree and D. Gregory (eds), *David Harvey: A Critical Reader*, Oxford: Blackwell, pp. 142–66.

Latour, B. (1987), *Science in Action: How to Follow Scientists and Engineers Through Society*, Cambridge, MA: Harvard University Press.

Latour, B. (1999), 'Ein ding ist ein thing: a (philosophical) platform for a Left (European) party', *Soundings*, 12, pp. 12–25.

Latour, B. (2004a), *Politics of Nature: How to Bring the Sciences into Democracy*, Cambridge, MA: Harvard University Press.

Latour, B. (2004b), 'Why has critique run out of steam? From matters of fact to matters of concern,' *Critical Inquiry*, 30, pp. 225–48.

Latour, B. (2004c), 'Whose cosmos, which cosmopolitics? Comments on the peace terms of Ulrich Beck', *Common Knowledge*, 10, pp. 450–62.

McKibben, B. (1990), *The End of Nature*, London: Penguin.

Mouffe, C. (2005), *On the Political*, London: Routledge.

Oliver, R. W. (2000), *The Coming Biotech Age: The Business of Bio-Materials*, New York: McGraw Hill.

Office of Science and Technology Policy (OSTP) (1986), *Coordinated Framework for the Regulation of Biotechnology*, Washington, DC: White House Office of Science and Technology Policy.

Rancière, J. (1999), *Disagreement: Politics and Philosophy*, Minneapolis: University of Minnesota Press.

Reynolds, L. (2010), *The Production, Governance and Contestation of Genetically Modified Food and Crops*, unpublished PhD thesis, Colchester: University of Essex.

Reynolds, L. (2013), 'The contested publics of the UK GM controversy: A tale of entanglement and purification', *Science as Culture*, 22: 4, pp. 452–75.

Reynolds, L. and B. Szerszynski (with Maria Kousis and Yannis Volakakis (2007), *Workpackage 6: GM Food – The Role of Participation in a Techno-Scientific Controversy*, report for European Commission Sixth Framework project PAGANINI (Participatory Governance and Institutional Innovation) (available at *http://www.univie.ac.at/LSG/paganini/*).

Reynolds, L. and B. Szerszynski (2011), 'Contested agro-technological futures: The GMO and the construction of European space', in Peter Robbins and Farah Huzair (eds), *Exploring Central and Eastern Europe's Biotechnological Landscape*, Berlin: Springer.

Reynolds, L. and B. Szerszynski (2012), 'Neoliberalism and technology: Permanent innovation or permanent crisis?', in L. Pellizzoni and M. Ylönen (eds), *Neoliberalism and Technoscience: Critical Assessments*, Farnham: Ashgate, pp. 27–46.

Rifkin, J. (1998), *The Biotech Century: Harnessing the Gene and Remaking the World*, New York: Jeremy P. Tarcher/Putnam.

Schmitt, C. (1993), 'The age of neutralizations and depoliticizations', *Telos*, 96, pp. 130–42.

Scott, J. C. (1998), *Seeing Like a State: How Certain Schemes to Improve the Human Condition Have Failed*, New Haven, CT: Yale University Press.

Smith, N. (1984) *Uneven Development: Nature, Capital and the Production of Space*, New York: Blackwell.

Swyngedouw, E. (2011), 'Interrogating post-democratization: reclaiming egalitarian political spaces', *Political Geography*, 30: 7, pp. 370–80.

Szerszynski, B. (2005), 'Beating the unbound: Political theatre in the laboratory without walls', in G. Giannachi and N. Stewart (eds), *Performing Nature: Explorations in Ecology and the Arts*, New York: Peter Lang, pp. 181–97.

Watson, J. D. (2003), *DNA: The Secret of Life*, London: Heinemann.

Williams, R. (1980), *Problems in Materialism and Culture*, London: New Left Bookclub.

3 The New Development Architecture and the Post-Political in the Global South

Sangeeta Kamat

Neoliberalism has fundamentally transformed development policy and practice in the Third World. This calls for new conceptual tools that move beyond earlier analyses of depoliticisation, anti-politics, alternative development and post-development. As many commentators have pointed out, neoliberalism is more than a set of economic policies aimed at eliminating trade barriers, promoting foreign investment and hollowing out the nation state. Rather, neoliberalism 'reaches from the soul of the citizen-subject' and 'involves *extending and disseminating market values to all institutions and social action*' (Brown 2003, emphasis in original). Drawing on Foucault's work on governmentality, Wendy Brown (2003) has argued that the distinctiveness of neoliberalism lies in the way democratic principles of freedom, rights and equality are merged so thoroughly with market rationality that an emancipatory politics appears hopeless and unjustified. She claims that neoliberalism cloaks itself in a liberal democratic discourse, while simultaneously dismantling democratic institutions and values. Brown concludes that this use and abuse of democracy confronts the Left with a fundamental paradox in developing an antidote to neoliberalism. While I am in broad agreement with Brown's analysis, this chapter argues that the analytics of neoliberal governmentality must be supplemented with a critique of the post-political in order to effectively engage with this paradox.

The chapter draws on empirical work in India to think through the ways in which post-politics is constitutive of the new development architecture in the 'Global South'. The post-political conjuncture signals a new political formation in which democratic norms and practices have become central to sustaining the ideological complex of neoliberalism. This emphasis on the centrality of 'democracy' to neoliberal ideology sets post-political analysis apart from the literature on governmentality, according to which discourses of freedom, rights and choice are only a legitimating gesture of pro-market regimes (Brown 2003: 27). The authoritarian capitalist state is assumed to be the 'real' face of neoliberalism, and insistence on democratic principles is seen as a mere rhetorical 'shell' that is disingenuous and 'void of substance' (Brown 2003: 11–15). Most critiques of development similarly argue that 'democracy promotion' by Western aid agencies is merely an illusion, a smokescreen for predatory capital in its global expansionary phase. World Bank programmes are understood as distorting the true content of democracy to promote a 'market rationality' of free enterprise and the flexible worker (Rankin 2004; Elyachar 2005). As I illustrate in this chapter, this analysis underestimates the ideological consequences of the democratic surplus and minimises the political fallout of neoliberalism. I argue that democratic discourses of empowerment, inclusion and participatory development are not false gestures but institute a political culture that is indispensable to the neoliberal growth strategy.

The chapter examines the democratic discourse in the context of neoliberal development in India. My claim is that the legacy of state-led development, citizen entitlements, and the persistence of the commons in the postcolony has embedded neoliberal rationality and market moralism in a welfare-developmentalist discourse, in contrast to the discrediting and dismantling of welfare programmes in the West. In the postcolony, neoliberal rationality not only promotes market values of competitive individualism, but fuses these with democratic norms of participation, community empowerment and inclusion. However, the idealisation of these democratic principles is at the same time profoundly undemocratic in its disavowal of the *politics* of poverty and inequality. This duality of embodying the democratic ethos while simultaneously repudiating conflict and contradiction is the essence of post-politics. As readers of this volume are already well aware, post-politics refers to a new mode of governance in which antinomies are effectively vanquished and liberals and conservatives speak a common language of public-private partnership, civic participation and the promotion of democracy as the path to economic growth and sustainable development. The post-political formation is one in which dissent is not suppressed but made irrelevant, where all concerned parties have a voice and difference is acknowledged, while conflict and oppositional politics are considered redundant (Mouffe 2005; Swyngedouw 2009). Post-political society is therefore also post-democratic, in the sense that democratic norms and the demos are passionately defended while agreement on fundamentals is assumed and consensual politics is expected to prevail (Rancière 2000; Dean 2005; Žižek 2004).

In advanced capitalist states in which liberal democracy is hegemonic, the rise of 'Third Way politics' and 'the new progressivism' are the hallmarks of post-political society. However, while much of the literature on post-politics relates to advanced capitalist democracies, I argue that the imperatives of global capitalism produce similar tendencies in the 'Global South'. In the field of international development, the post-political operates in multiple registers, from global policy formulation to local community interventions, through which the established divisions between public and private, state and market, individual and community are dissolved to form a post-ideological global compact on growth and democracy. The contestations that defined development in the postwar postcolonial period are replaced by a politics of consensus that unites governments and NGOs, communities and corporations in a shared vision of development and governance, which operates with impunity in the face of staggering levels of poverty, inequality and dispossession. Established modes of representative government that allow for contentious politics have been replaced by a new 'art of government' that relies upon collaboration, coordination and integration, in which competing interests are harmonised to propose a 'win-win' situation for all (Lemke 2007; Cruikshank 1993; Swyngedouw 2009). In this distinctively post-political framework, interests are seen only in particularistic terms, and are denied their universal content (Žižek 1999).

The first part of the chapter presents an overview of the new development architecture at the global scale, reflected in policy propositions that inaugurate the post-political formation. The second part considers the mainstream appropriation of the 'alternative development' discourse of 'participation' and 'empowerment', which nullifies its political content. The final section reviews a micro-credit and 'self-help' programme in the Indian state of Andhra Pradesh, which embodies the post-political approach. This flagship programme provides a classic instance of the mechanisms through which India's 'political society' (Chatterjee 2011) is made to conform to a post-political governance framework. I conclude that the ideological implications of neoliberal development are best understood through the analytical lens of post-politics.

Development in the neoliberal conjuncture

In a speech in New Delhi in 2012 on 'The future of international development', the Permanent Secretary for the UK's Department for International Development (DFiD) declared 'We live in a new global order, an order which no longer follows the tired old rules of the

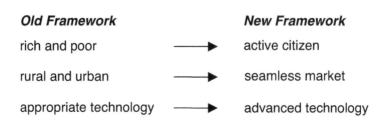

Figure 3.1 The New Development Architecture

rich and the poor; the donor and the recipient; the first world and the third' (Lowcock 2012). Such easy rhetoric is commonplace in an era in which historic antagonisms are said to have been replaced by 'open societies and open economies' (Lowcock 2012). References to the 'new architecture of aid and assistance' circulate in global policy rhetoric, and are retrofitted as the new enlightened approach to development in the Third World. During my recent research on the NGO sector in Andhra Pradesh, I stumbled upon a particularly compelling instance of the 'new architecture' at a workshop organised by the Centre for Good Governance for district-level government and NGO staff. The highlight of the workshop was a slide reproduced in Figure 3.1.[1]

The 'old framework' referred to the perspective that supposedly informed state planning in the welfare developmentalist period, and workshop participants were encouraged to consider the new charter as one more conducive to India's new growth strategy of market liberalisation. The theme song of the 'new framework' is that binaries are redundant, oppositions constrain progress and a fresh new conceptual approach is needed that rejects boundaries, hierarchies and difference in favour of a new equivalence in social class and geography. In contrast to the authoritarianism and exclusion that characterised the top-down development planning of the past, the new architecture deploys a progressive and democratic orientation by flattening out hierarchies and inequalities and adopting an equalising approach – the poor must be provided with the same opportunities to become 'active citizens' as the rich, and markets must thrive in rural as well as urban areas.

This new paradigm is reflected in 'good governance' arrangements that project a unity of interests between multilateral development agencies, First World and Third World governments, multinational corporations, and a diverse NGO sector, all of which are represented as equal stakeholders in the development enterprise (see Raco, Chapter 1 of this volume). More recently, philanthropic foundations such as the Gates Foundation have emerged as influential agenda-setters and key interlocutors of the development mission on a global scale (see Wilson, Chapter 5 of this volume). The institutional apparatus is complex and multi-scalar, with a wide range of tasks and responsibilities shared among a disparate set of actors rather than a straightforward transfer of power from state to market or to civil-society organisations. The World Bank and the IMF lead the financing and overall coordination of development policies along with multinational corporations and their associated foundations, while numerous NGOs, independent consultants and government departments are enlisted as subcontractors to carry out the 'deliverables' in a given policy arena. From the 1990s onwards, the extensive 'NGOisation' of the development sector led to the depoliticisation of development, through which political-economic responses to poverty and inequality have been discredited in favour of a techno-managerial approach (Feldman 2003; Kamat 2002; Jad 2007; Miraftab 2004a). NGOisation also implies a 'project' approach whereby economic and social problems are managed through externally funded initiatives that are required to demonstrate measurable outcomes in the short term, and has been accused of systematically undermining social movements and mass organisations of workers, peasants and the disenfranchised (Kamat 2004; Khalidi and Samour 2011; Miraftab 2004b).

The postcolonial state is repositioned in the new architecture. No longer a victim at the mercy of Western donor institutions – a representation that was at any rate only partially accurate in the postcolonial phase of development – the balance of power between Third World countries and the United States and Europe has now shifted in ways that challenge earlier narratives of development as imperialism (see Jaeger, Chapter 10 of this volume). Postcolonial and post-communist countries now enthusiastically endorse neoliberalism as an economic regime in their own best interests. Similarly, the subject of development is reconditioned in the current context. The neoliberal subject is encouraged to be entrepreneurial, flexible, risk-taking and adaptable to precarious life conditions, in contrast to the postwar development discourse, in which the Third World subject was construed as an abject figure and a beneficiary of aid and state patronage (Dean 1991).

The new development architecture emphasises 'stakeholder participation', in which 'the poor are to be consulted to ask what it is they want' (Lowcock 2012). The Third World subject is imbued with the 'will to improve' (Li 2007), and public-private governance is the order of the day. In this context, critiques of development as depoliticised and disempowering are seemingly obsolete. Locally generated development solutions can no longer be easily distinguished from externally imposed interventions, and binaries between sovereign national ('good') development and Western Eurocentric ('bad') development are becoming increasingly difficult to uphold. Critiques that frame development as an imperialist enterprise appear untenable, as the chief architects of imperialist development such as the World Bank and the IMF are now vocal advocates of locally led, small-scale projects, and are the largest funders of the very principles of capacity building, people's participation, civic empowerment, and self-governing communities that once defined the oppositional framework of 'alternative development'.

New institutional economics and post-politics

The transformations in development discourse in the neoliberal context have been identified by a number of scholars (Cooke and Kothari 2001; Harris 2001; Ferguson 2006; Li 2007; Hout and Robison 2008; Miraftab 2004b). However, the logics that drive these transformations and their implications for Left politics have not been adequately theorised. A popular though naive view is that democratic norms of inclusive development and empowerment are deployed as a ruse to deflect criticism or to appease opponents, a sentiment expressed in the post-development scholarship:

> When taking into consideration the radical nature of the participatory proposal for social transformation and the neo-liberal structural-adjustment context in which it has been co-opted, the *incompatibility between the two might seem far too deep-seated to permit such a co-optation to take place*. But if we factor in the growing social discontent, popular mobilisations, and anti-SAP riots that were taking place across the Third World, we begin to understand how the development industry could not simply ignore the increasing critiques and challenges to its reigning paradigm ... The challenge that participation posed to development orthodoxy was 'too serious to be brushed away or frontally imposed' (Leal 2007: 541, emphasis added).

An empirical history of development economics complicates this simplistic thesis and suggests that the democratic project of participatory governance is deeply implicated in neoliberal development. My claim is that the 'radical democratic' proposal of people's participation and empowerment is not a threat to the development industry, but has played a crucial role in post-politicisation, as evidenced by the meteoric rise of the New Institutional Economics (NIE). The NIE endorses the 'alternative development' principles of 'participation', 'localisation', 'empowerment' and 'inclusion', but aims to identify the ways in which these practices can be structured for the success of market-friendly reforms in the Third World. Initially derided by neoclassical economists as 'intuitive', 'extraneous', 'political' and 'culturalist', the NIE has emerged as the 'new frontier' of development economics, and now shapes development policy and practice throughout the Third World (Meier and Stiglitz 2001).

The primary thesis of the NIE is that institutions, ideologies and values matter for markets to function efficiently. NIE scholars reject the neoclassical proposition of the 'invisible hand' that regulates markets by 'getting prices right', and argue that 'getting institutions right' is the precondition for a productive economy and a stable society. They argue that the fundamentals of neoclassical economics – resources, technology and rational choice – are insufficient for capitalism to succeed, and that it is equally necessary to harmonise institutions, cultures and individual behaviour with the imperatives of capitalism. In other words, capitalism must become as much part of the 'deep structure' of developing societies as it is in the First World. Through 'disciplined analysis', the NIE aims to devise the precise interventions required to achieve this objective (Meier and Stiglitz 2001; North 1994).

NIE economists generate theoretical models and data through experimental research to identify the 'ecology' (social, cultural, institutional context) in which private enterprise, the utility-maximising individual, and market relations are mutually optimised. According to the NIE, an 'ecology' suitable for capitalism is largely absent in the Third World. The NIE acknowledges that each society has its own history (in NIE language, 'path dependence'), and emphasises that institutions and values that are supportive of capitalism must be tailored to each particular 'ecology'. For this reason, capitalism cannot be externally imposed, but must grow in capillary form to become the internal rationality of a given society.

NIE theorists are strong advocates of the stakeholder model of governance, according to which rules to manage 'common pool' assets such as water are only effective when the interests of different asset users (that may include a poor farmer and a rich industrialist) are taken into consideration. In the NIE perspective, elected bodies are not always the ideal representatives in such situations, and just as firms may specialise in the production of a given commodity, variegated governance arrangements can be organised to accomplish different development outcomes. Local decision-making and direct democracy are positive elements as long as these function efficiently, meeting defined objectives and minimising costs. The broad thrust of the NIE is to develop mechanisms that link people to markets and manage economic and social goods more efficiently, while expanding the global pool of private assets. Social forestry, community-based forestry, village education committees, village health committees, self-help groups, micro-enterprises and micro-credit groups are all examples of the NIE approach in the development sector.

From the 1990s onwards, the NIE has gained credibility as a multi-disciplinary approach that extends neoclassical economics in ways that are appropriate to Third World societies (Herrera 2006). Each macro-economic crisis since the East Asian financial crisis of 1997 has been used to validate the micro-economic approach of the NIE as a scientifically tested set of interventions that will ensure the durability of capitalism in a dysfunctional Third World. NIE proponents such as Joseph Stiglitz and Paul Krugman are heralded as critics of the one-size-fits-all policies of the World Bank and the IMF, (such as the notorious Structural Adjustment Programmes). Their endorsement of the NIE is seen as progressive and pro-Third World, on the grounds that people and context, institutions and power are finally being taken seriously by economists. Much of the new language in development studies that has now gained currency among World Bank economists – such as 'social capital', 'participatory development', 'inclusive growth', 'capacity building', 'the commons', 'collective action', 'decentralization' and 'good governance' – is inspired by the NIE literature.

With the help of the NIE, the development fraternity has been able to abandon the much criticised Washington Consensus and endorse a Post-Washington Consensus that emphasises state, people, institutions and norms as necessary ingredients for market-led growth. Many consider the abandonment of market fundamentalism a victory for the Left. However, this change in stance is anything but an admission of the failure of capitalism. On the contrary, it typifies the dialectical process through which capitalism innovates to overcome its own limits and to become more robust. The rise of the NIE in the development sector suggests that the World Bank's promotion of participation and inclusive governance is not a democratic fig leaf to defend itself against its critics, but is essential to the viability of capitalism in the Global South. As the remainder of this chapter demonstrates, the NIE provides a fresh approach to engineering neoliberal rationality in the Third World *in and through democratic processes*, which is best understood though the analytical lens of post-politics.

The 'self-help movement' in Andhra Pradesh – a case of post-politics

Self-help groups are among the most recent inventions of the new development architecture, in which development is delivered through 'self-managed organisations' of 'disadvantaged communities'. Self-help programmes are promoted as examples of inclusive development and empowerment, in which those excluded from development take charge of their own social and economic needs rather than relying on the state or the NGO sector. In this new formulation, state agencies and NGOs are classified as 'self-help promoting institutions' (SHPIs) that facilitate 'capacity building' and 'skills training' for self-help groups (SHGs). The primary function of SHGs is to generate capital by members pooling their savings and obtaining small loans ('micro-credit') from government bodies, NGOs or private-sector banks. The capital that a group generates is loaned out to group members or other local residents and the group as a whole is required to ensure timely repayment of loans. Members receive loans only if the group has a proven record of regular repayment rates (that is, a good credit rating). Women's groups are particularly encouraged, and 'women borrowers [have become] the target of an aggressive "self-help" approach to development' (Rankin 2001: 18; see also Kabeer et al. 2012). The repayment rates of women's groups in Bangladesh made international headlines in the mid–1990s, and SHGs are now widely promoted as the primary strategy for empowering the poor in the Third World. Estimated to be a \$20 billion industry globally, micro-credit is the fastest growing segment of international aid and investment, with India representing the largest micro-lending market (Thakur 2008). The southern Indian state of Andhra Pradesh has the highest concentration of SHGs in the world, and accounts for 50 per cent of SHGs in the country. According to current estimates, of a total rural population of nearly 25 million women in Andhra Pradesh, 11 million have been mobilised into as many as 2 million SHGs. On average there are seven to eight SHGs per village, each comprising an average of ten to fifteen members, and the initiative has been expanded to towns and urban areas. Also known as the 'micro-credit plus' approach, the success of the Andhra Pradesh government in enlisting virtually every poor rural household into the 'self-help movement' has drawn the attention of venture capitalists and donor agencies as a model programme to be exported to other regions and countries around the world (Ramesh 2007).

Economic studies confirm that micro-credit does not alleviate poverty, and suggest that its utility is limited to 'consumption smoothening' (Bateman and Chang 2009). Studies also show that class structures and inequalities are reproduced as poor and vulnerable individuals become increasingly dependent on loans, while the well-off use their savings and loans to lend to poor families at high interest rates, reproducing the role of the usurious village money-lender (Fernando 1997). Ethnographic research argues that micro-credit functions to constitute the 'rational economic woman' who is disciplined, self-reliant, ambitious yet fiscally prudent (Rankin 2001). Research conducted in various countries similarly illustrates that self-help groups facilitate market relations and competitive individualism among the rural poor and serve as strategic mechanisms for embedding neoliberal rationality in the global South (Fernando 2005; Elyachar 2005; Rankin and Shakya 2007).

This research demonstrates the extent to which the alternative development discourse of empowerment and inclusion has been assimilated into a project of neoliberal governmentality. However, these critiques are not sufficiently attentive to the post-democratic dimension of self-help programmes, which I argue is critical to their success. The 'self-help movement' in Andhra Pradesh embodies the post-democratic formation in several ways. In the first place, it is not limited to the minimalistic promotion of economic entrepreneurship, but claims to instill a sense of entitlement and ownership of the 'commons'. The state's flagship self-help programme, known as DWCRA (Development of Women and Children in Rural Areas), encourages collective action and women's leadership in tackling serious social issues of domestic and sexual violence, child marriage, child labour and the harassment of women related to dowry or other patriarchal 'evils'. Discriminatory treatment of *dalits* (scheduled castes) and *adivasis* (scheduled tribes) is similarly sanctioned as an area of intervention for DWCRA (colloquially pronounced 'dwacra') women's groups. The efficacy of DWCRA groups in responding to these issues varies greatly depending on the group's leadership, support from political parties such as the women's wing of communist parties, and the general history of women's activism and political militancy in their region. DWCRA is promoted by NGOs and the state as a governance framework that encourages direct collective action among women who are often economically vulnerable and illiterate, on issues that impact them in their homes and workplaces, such as domestic violence, alcoholism and child marriage. If this is not democracy and empowerment, what is?

The SHP in Andhra Pradesh also facilitates a sense of citizen rights and public entitlements that echoes the pre-neoliberal developmentalist state. Self-help groups receive a host of public services and subsidies such as free health and dental check-ups, subsidised rice and cooking fuel (Deepam scheme), subsidised housing (Rural Permanent

Housing Programme), student scholarships, adult literacy classes and leadership training. In appropriate cases, self-help groups are expected to facilitate access to benefits and subsidies that are specifically for poor women and their families. Moreover, the state enlists women and men to form 'common interest groups' (CIGs) such as mothers' committees, health committees, school education committees, forest protection committees, water conservation committees and village development committees to identify problems impacting them in these specific areas, and to understand, analyse and develop solutions that they consider appropriate. Members may solicit advice and support from NGOs, local state officials and party leaders, but the group is responsible for its actions.

The 'self-help movement' is coordinated through federations of SHGs at the village level, cluster level, mandal level, district level and state level, which form a multi-scalar nested arrangement with members at each level electing representatives to the next level. SHG federations constitute 'soft spaces' of governance that are neither formal nor informal and exist parallel to official administrative arrangements and representative institutions of government. Such 'soft spaces' of governance are increasingly common as part of neo-liberal experimentation in diverse countries representing 'collaborative consensus-seeking stakeholder arrangements' that are flexible, diverse and provisional (Haughton et al. 2012).

Democracy as consensual politics and the partition of the sensible

Micro-credit and self-help programmes are criticised for promoting a singular rationality of market-led development. However, the strategy in Andhra Pradesh involves the pluralisation and differentiation of self-help groups that are at the same time strategically linked and co-ordinated. There are self-help groups for every conceivable development objective. The mandate of DWCRA groups is to encourage women's participation and therefore empowerment, especially in the areas of social development that affect them the most. Each of the 'common interest groups' is entrusted with a specialised role such as community oversight to ensure the proper functioning of the local school, mobilising community participation for reforestation and kitchen gardens, ensuring judicious water use, constructing good roads as part of model village programmes, and so forth. Membership may overlap among these groups and among DWCRA and savings and credit groups, but each self-help group has a specialised and distinctive function and identity that connects to a broad rural development agenda. The critique of development as depoliticisation does not apply to the 'self-help movement' in Andhra Pradesh. On the contrary, in this self-help programme '*everything is politicised*, can be discussed, but only in a non-committal way and as a non-conflict. Absolute and irreversible choices are kept away; politics becomes something one can do without making decisions that divide and separate' (Diken and Lausten in Swyngedouw 2009: 609, emphasis added). An ode entitled 'Hail the SHG woman', written by a district-level project director, describes the ideal self-help group meeting in which 'Intellectual and political deliberations conclude without differences/ Cultural meetings sum up without protests/ The congregation is punctual and resolve to abide by their decisions'. These, the poem concludes, are the 'unsung champions', 'the SHG members in their periodical (*sic*) meetings'.[2]

Consensual decision making is promoted as the norm for self-help groups, and group leaders and members are exhorted to maintain unity and harmony within the group, regardless of the social problem being addressed, and whether there may be differences among members. Caste and class hostilities that structure the rural economy and are palpable in the spatial organisation of the village are bracketed in this context. An early attempt by the state to facilitate mixed-caste groups failed, and groups are fairly homogenous in their class and caste composition. The DWCRA women see themselves as 'doing politics' in other ways: confronting government officials for being slow in sanctioning funds that the village is supposed to receive for a development activity; negotiating with political leaders to lend support on an issue; pressuring a school teacher to show up and teach their kids; and even pooling savings to nominate members from their network to contest elections (*Times of India* 2012). Self-help groups regard themselves not 'at a distance' from politics, but as deeply enmeshed in politics and as political actors in a direct-democracy-kind-of-way. The state and the NGO sector acknowledge that self-help groups have emerged as new 'power centres', which advocate for themselves and build alliances on issues that they perceive to be in their common interest (Ramesh 2007). The concern in this case is not that politics is being subverted by technocratic rationality and the 'rule of experts' (Ferguson 1994). Instead, the question is how to theorise the 'properly political' (Swyngedouw 2009: 603–4).

Each self-help group or cluster of SHGs is read as an 'interest group' with its specific caste, class, gender and occupational identity and aspirations. As stakeholders, the interests of the bureaucracy, the aid industry, NGOs, banks and the business sector are also represented in this 'silent revolution'. To meet project goals that may range from an awareness and treatment campaign for HIV/AIDS

to increasing primary school enrolment or ensuring 'total financial inclusion' of the very poor, stakeholders negotiate contractual
arrangements with self-help groups, such that each party is seen to
pursue its specific interest in a cooperative manner. This is governance by absolute consensus that 'insists on the "democratic" inclusion of all, thereby suturing the totality of the social' (Swyngedouw
2009: 609). It is a totalitarian form of democracy that is essentially
post-democratic, in the sense that dissensus or antagonism between
the state and 'the people' is foreclosed, and governance is 'reducible to the sole interplay of state mechanisms and combinations of
social energies and interests . . . It is the practice and theory of what
is appropriate with no gap left between the forms of the State and
the state of social relations' (Rancière, quoted in Swygnedouw 2009:
610). Rancière identifies this as a post-democratic policy arrangement, in which interests of all types have a place, but 'politics proper'
– that is, any kind of challenge to the existing order – has no space:

> Consensus is thus not another manner of exercising democracy . . . [It]
> is the negation of the democratic basis for politics: it desires to have
> well-identifiable groups with specific interests, aspirations, values and
> 'culture' . . . Consensualist centrism flourishes with the multiplication of
> differences and identities. It nourishes itself with the complexification of
> the elements that need to be accounted for in a community, with the per-
> manent process of autorepresentation, with all the elements and all their
> differences: the larger the number of groups and identities that need to
> be taken into account in society, the greater the need for arbitration. The
> 'one' of consensus nourishes itself with the multiple. (Rancière 2000: 125)

The paradox of post-political, post-democratic society is that on the
one hand there is a heightened pluralism of identities and differentiation of roles and responsibilities, and on the other there is a normative
consensus in the way problems are enumerated, desires articulated
and issues catalogued. This normative consensus is achieved by a
specific 'partition of the sensible', in which 'a particular activity is
visible and another is not,' and where a certain 'speech is understood
as discourse and another as noise' (Rancière, quoted in Swyngedouw
2009: 606). Rancière's thesis captures the 'self-help movement's
lack of engagement with the agrarian crisis that has gripped Andhra
Pradesh and led to farmer suicides of epidemic proportions. More
than a decade of neoliberal reforms have eliminated farm subsidies
and agricultural price regulations, while subsidising private investment in the 'hi-tech' city regions. These reforms have promoted
hybrid and genetically modified crops that are risky and expensive,
leading to high levels of rural indebtedness, which are exacerbated by

increased water and energy costs resulting from privatisation. All this has caused severe economic distress among small and marginal cultivators who comprise the majority of the rural economy. In Andhra Pradesh, the official tally for debt-related farmer suicides between 1997 and 2005 is 16,770 – three times the general suicide rate of the state (Sainath 2007). Astonishingly, the self-help movement has not mobilised against the agrarian distress that directly impacts its own members. Women and children are severely affected by a debt-induced suicide in their household, and in certain cases DWCRA group members have mobilised to secure compensation or debt redressal for households routinely excluded from the official suicide tally (Sainath 2009). Yet despite their neo-communitarian organisation and intimate knowledge and experience of rural distress, SHGs and their federations have not protested against the economic policies that have resulted in 'farmer suicides'.

The SHG 'partition of the sensible' ensures that members are occupied with generating savings; ensuring high repayment rates; achieving 'total financial inclusion' through the 'SHG-Bank linkage movement'; skills training; generating income from contracts on government projects such as the school midday meal scheme; and advocacy on 'women's issues' such as domestic violence. SHG members' concerns relate to rates of savings and borrowing; accounting and book-keeping; and disbursing capital in a prudent manner so the group remains viable. There is constant talk about which SHG is doing well, comparisons of group leaders and politicking on whom to recruit to the group. Common-interest groups and DWCRA groups are expected to maintain records of numbers of children enrolled in primary school; midday meals supplied; trees planted; kitchen gardens grown; trainings received; health camps organised; BPL (below poverty line) households verified; welfare benefits distributed; atrocity cases filed.

The vast network of self-help groups is mobilised 'to reduce the overall demand (complaint) of a particular group to just this demand, with its particular content' (Žižek, quoted in Swyngedouw 2009: 609). There is an absence of

> debate on the sensible givens of a situation, a debate on that which you see and feel, on how it can be told and discussed, who is able to name it and argue about it . . . about the very configuration of the visible and the relation of the visible to what can be said about it. (Rancière, quoted in Swyngedouw 2009: 610)

The particular of each is 'elevated to the status of the political. Rather than politicising, such social colonisation of the political, in fact, erodes and outflanks the proper political dimension of egalibertarian universalization' (Swyngedouw 2009: 615). The universal demand for a dignified life is suppressed in the particular. The demand for a 'fidelity that, although always particular, aspires to become public, to universalize' is rendered invisible in a post-democratic, post-political formation in which the enunciation of particular, multiple, disjointed demands is permissible only in certain ways (Swyngedouw 2009: 614).

Conclusion: development, democracy and neoliberal governance

This chapter has demonstrated the theoretical purchase of post-politics in making sense of the apparent contradictions of contemporary development theory and practice. The critique of post-politics adds an important dimension to critiques of neoliberalism and shows how democratic discourse is far more deeply implicated in securing capitalist hegemony than is generally acknowledged. There are three main insights that require emphasis. First, the case of the SHG supports an understanding of post-politics as a radical form of depoliticisation, in which consensual democracy becomes the organising principle of politics, despite being essentially anti-democratic (Žižek 2004: 307). To interpret the 'democratic turn' as the electoral expediency of political parties is to misrecognise its critical function in diffusing antagonism and struggle (Reddy 2002). As Perry Anderson (2000) concludes, 'What is strong is not democratic aspiration from below, but the asphyxiation of public debate and political difference by capital above. The force of this order lies not in repression, but in dilution and neutralization'.

A second related observation is that not all identities and interests are neutralised; rather, some are given primacy over others. While the main thrust of the new development architecture is economic empowerment, class identities and relations of production are sealed off from this ostensibly democratising agenda, and self-help groups are organised primarily on the basis of gender, caste and tribal identities. Here I find Žižek's argument persuasive contra Laclau and Mouffe – post-politics is the sublimation of class contradictions into other forms of difference and conflict that is necessary for the reproduction of capitalism (see Wilson, Chapter 5 of this volume). Identities and interests are not repressed and may even be encouraged, so far as these do not threaten the neoliberal capitalist order.

Third, I have argued that post-politics is institutionalised in the Third World through the New Institutional Economics, which represents a new 'science' of economic development. As the self-help model indicates, the NIE facilitates the development of institutions 'of the poor for the poor by the poor'. In this context, the agenda of Wendy Brown (2003) and others of 'enhancing the capacity of citizens to share power' and developing 'practices and institutions of shared popular power' is greatly compromised as an effective counter to neoliberalism.

The ingenuity of post-politics is that it allows the accumulationist project to remain firmly anchored in a populist discourse of 'one world, one people' that privileges liberal democracy as the 'ultimate horizon of our politics' (Dean 2005). In this respect, critical scholars of development would do well to pay heed to Žižek's caution:

> Anti-capitalism without problematizing capitalism's political form . . . is not sufficient, no matter how radical it is. Perhaps the lure today is the belief that one can undermine capitalism without effectively problematizing the liberal-democratic legacy, a legacy that – as some leftists claim – although engendered by capitalism, acquired autonomy and can serve to criticize capitalism. (Žižek 2006: 567)

My argument here is not to oppose democracy. Rather, it is to be attentive to the ways in which democratic aspirations are being mobilised towards capitalist ends, which imply that political democracy cannot be the litmus test of anti-capitalist politics and struggles.

Notes

1. Thanks to Anant Maringanti of the Hyderabad Urban Lab for first bringing this to my attention.
2. Author meeting with Mr A. Ramesh Kumar, project assistant director, Rangareddy district, Andhra Pradesh, November 2011.

References

Anderson, P. (2000), 'Editorial: Renewal', *New Left Review*, 1 pp. 1–9.

Bateman, M., and H.-J. Chang (2009), 'Microfinance and the illusion of development: From hubris to nemesis in thirty years', *World Economic Review*, available online *http://wer.worldeconomicsassociation.org/article/view/372012*.

Brown, W. (2003), 'Neoliberalism and the end of liberal democracy', *Theory and Event*, 7:1, available at *http://muse.jhu.edu/journals/theory_and_event/v007/7.1brown.html*.

Chatterjee, P. (2011), *Lineages of Political Society*, Delhi: Permanent Black.

Cooke, W., and U. Kothari (eds) (2001), *Participation: The New Tyranny?* London: Zed Books.

Cruikshank, B. (1993), 'Revolutions within: Self-governance and self-esteem', *Economy and Society*, 22: 3, pp. 327–44.

Dean, J. (2005), 'Žižek against democracy', *Law, Culture and the Humanities*, 2, pp. 154–77.

Dean, M. (1991), *The Constitution of Poverty: Toward a Genealogy of Liberal Governance*, London: Routledge.

Elyachar, J. (2005), *Markets of Dispossession: NGOs, Economic Development, and the State in Cairo*, Durham: Duke University Press.

Feldman, S. (2003), 'Paradoxes of institutionalisation: The depoliticisation of Bangladeshi NGOs', *Development in Practice*, 13: 1, pp. 5–26.

Ferguson, J. (1994), *The Anti-Politics Machine: Development, Depoliticization and Bureaucratic Power in Lesotho*, Minneapolis: University of Minnesota Press.

Ferguson, J. (2006), *Global Shadows: Africa in the Neoliberal World Order*, Durham: Duke University Press.

Fernando, J. (1997), 'Nongovernmental organizations, micro-credit, and empowerment of women', *The Annals of the American Academy of Political and Social Science*, 554: 1, pp. 150–77.

Fernando, J. (ed.) (2005), *Perils and Prospects of Micro-credit: Neoliberalism and Cultural Politics of Empowerment*, London: Routledge.

Harris, J. (2001), *Depoliticizing Development: The World Bank and Social Capital*, New Delhi: LeftWord

Haughton, G., A. Allmendinger and S. Oosterlynck (2012), 'Spaces of neo-liberal experimentation: soft spaces, post-politics, and neoliberal govern-mentality', *Environment and Planning A*, 45, pp. 217–34.

Herrera, R. (2006), 'The neoliberal "Rebirth" of development economics', *Monthly Review*, 58: 1, available at *http://monthlyreview.org/2006/05/01/the-neoliberal-rebirth-of-development-economics*.

Hout, W., and R. Robison (2008), *Governance and the Depoliticisation of Development*, New York: Taylor & Francis.

Kabeer, N., S. Mahmud and J. Castro (2012), 'NGOs and the political empowerment of poor people in rural Bangladesh: Cultivating the habits of democracy?', *World Development*, 40: 10, pp. 2044–62.

Kamat, S. (2002), *Development Hegemony: NGOs and the State in India*, New Delhi: Oxford University Press.

Kamat, S. (2004), 'The privatization of public interest: NGOs in the neolib-eral era', *Review of International Political Economy*, 11: 1, pp. 155–76.

Khalidi, R., and S. Samour (2011), 'Neoliberalism as liberation: The Statehood program and the remaking of the Palestinian National Movement', *Journal of Palestine Studies*, 15: 2, pp. 6–25.

Jad, I. (2007), 'NGOs: Between buzzwords and social movements', *Development in Practice*, 17: 4–5, pp. 622–9.

Leal, P. A. (2007), 'Participation: The ascendancy of a buzzword in the neo-liberal context', *Development in Practice*, 17: 4–5, pp. 539–48.

Lemke, T. (2007), 'An indigestible meal? Foucault, governmentality and state theory', *Distinktion: Scandinavian Journal of Social Theory*, 8: 2, pp. 43–64.

Li, T. M. (2007), *The Will to Improve: Governmentality, Development, and the Practice of Politics*, Durham: Duke University Press.

Lowcock, M. (2012), 'The future of international development', DfID Permanent Secretary speech in New Delhi, 16 October 2012, *https://www.gov.uk/government/speeches/mark-lowcock-the-future-of-international-development*.

Meier, G. and J. Stiglitz (eds) (2001), *Frontiers of Development Economics: The Future in Perspective*, Washington, DC: World Bank Publications.

Miraftab, F. (2004a), 'Making neo-liberal governance: The disempowering work of empowerment', *International Planning Studies*, 9: 4, pp. 239–59.

Miraftab, F. (2004b), 'Public-private partnerships: The Trojan horse of neoliberal development?', *Journal of Planning Education and Research*, 24, pp. 89–101.

Mouffe, C. (2005), *On the Political*, New York: Routledge.

North, D. (1994), 'Economic performance through time', *American Economic Review*, 84: 3, pp. 359–68.

Priyadarshee, A., and A. K. Ghalib (2011), 'Andhra Pradesh micro-finance crisis in India: Manifestation, causal analysis, and regulatory response', Brooks World Poverty Institute Working Paper, available at: *http://www.bwpi.manchester.ac.uk/resources/Working-Papers/working-papers–2011.html*.

Ramesh, J. (2007), 'Self help groups revolution: What next?', *Economic and Political Weekly*, 8 September.

Rancière, J. (2000), 'Dissenting words: A conversation with Jacques Rancière', *Diacritics*, 30: 2, pp. 113–24.

Rankin, K. N. (2001), 'Governing development: neoliberalism, microcredit and the rational economic woman', *Economy and Society*, 30: 1, pp. 18–37.

Rankin, K. N. (2004), *The Cultural Politics of Markets: Economic Liberalisation and Social Change in Nepal*, London: Pluto Press.

Rankin, K. N., and Y. B. Shakya (2007), 'Neoliberalizing the grassroots? Microfinance and the politics of development in Nepal', in K. England and K. Ward (eds), *Neoliberalization: States, Networks, Peoples*, Oxford: Springer, pp. 48–76.

Reddy, G. K. (2002), 'New populism and liberalisation regime shift under Chandrababu Naidu in AP', *Economic and Political Weekly*, 2 March.

Sainath, P. (2007), 'One farmer's suicide every 30 minutes', *The Hindu*, 15 November.

Sainath, P. (2009), 'Neo-liberal terrorism in India: The largest wave of suicides in history', *Counterpunch*, 12 February, available at: *http://www.counterpunch.org/2009/02/12/the-largest-wave-of-suicides-in-history/*.

Shylendra, H. S. (2006), 'Microfinance institutions in Andhra Pradesh: Crisis and diagnosis', *Economic and Political Weekly*, 20 May 2006.

Swyngedouw, E. (2009), 'The antinomies of the post-political city: In search of a democratic politics of environmental production', *International Journal of Urban and Regional Research*, 33: 3, pp. 601–20.

Thakur, R. (2008), 'Macro potential of the microfinance industry', India Brand Equity Foundation, available at: *http://www.ibef.org/down load/finance_260908.pdf*.

Times of India (2012), 'SHGs hold sway over panchayat elections', 8 February, available at *http://articles.timesofindia.indiatimes.com/2012–02–08/bhubaneswar/31037043_1_shg-members-gram-panchayat-sar-panch*.

Žižek, S. (2004), 'The ongoing "Soft Revolution"', *Critical Inquiry*, 30: 2, pp. 292–323.

Žižek, S. (2006), 'Against the populist temptation', *Critical Inquiry*, 32: 3, pp. 551–74.

4 Opening Up the Post-Political Condition: Multiculturalism and the Matrix of Depoliticisation

Nicolas Van Puymbroeck and Stijn Oosterlynck

In recent years a broad scholarly consensus has acknowledged far-reaching alterations in Western political systems (Crouch 2004). From the advent of stakeholder democracy, consensus building and good governance to the rise of populism at both the Left and Right ends of the political spectrum, all of these developments are said to announce a rupture in the workings of national liberal-democratic regimes. While eminent sociologist Ulrich Beck (1997) identified the changes as a 'reinvention of politics' in a (necessary) process of 'reflexive modernization', a heterogeneous collection of scholars has recently developed a more critical account. Instead of tackling the democratic deficits associated with representative government or politically accommodating a plurality of lifestyles, the institutional and discursive innovations of 'governance-beyond-the-state' (Swyngedouw 2005) are now increasingly portrayed as symptoms of the strengthening of disciplinary control over the life of citizens and even of deepening authoritarianism.

These critical reflections on the proliferation of new political forms have been increasingly addressed from the perspective of the distinction between politics and the political (Dikeç 2005; Swyngedouw 2011). Politics refers to the practices that institute society and create social order. For social order to arise, politics necessarily implies the instauration of social differentiation, which establishes societal hierarchies between class, race, gender or any other imaginable classification. However, a crucial insight of post-foundational political thought, as this critical approach is sometimes called (Marchart 2007), is the impossibility of any social order to sustain itself in the same form indefinitely. Since there is no ultimate ground for society and the hierarchical differences on which it rests, any social order is open to disruption by those who happen to be excluded and marginalised by it. According to Marchart (2007), it is in this moment of disruption that the 'political difference' between the society-as-instituted on the one hand and its absent ultimate ground on the other comes to the fore as the inevitable political condition of society.

By putting this political difference centre-stage in their analysis, scholars aim to criticise much celebrated new political forms and practices such as 'good governance', 'consensus building' and 'stakeholder democracy'. Erik Swyngedouw (2007; 2008; 2009) has labelled these 'post-political' to indicate that they paper over the inequalities which run through society, disavowing the rifts in society, and foreclosing potential struggles for alternative political futures. These governmental innovations deny the absent ground of society and proclaim the end of meaningful dispute about society as the 'end of politics'.

This chapter subscribes to the need to place the political difference at the centre of any critical analysis of new political forms and practices, and to devote more explicit attention to the political significance of current governance innovations. However, despite its justified critique of the fixation of much political analysis on just one side of the political difference (i.e. the side of politics), in this chapter we will argue that this critical approach runs the risk of being less productive than it could be in empirical terms, by failing to develop an analytical framework that can capture the full complexity and manifold ways in which the political difference can play out in actually existing social formations. This is, as we aim to show, due to an across-the-board application of the notion of the 'post-political condition' as a one-size-fits-all label to describe (rather than explain) the currently dominant political forms and practices associated with global capitalism and the neoliberal order. The concomitant call for 'the return of the political' as a momentous disruption of the currently hegemonic political forms and practices that institute hierarchical social formations is equally misleading in that it raises the promise of a genuine political society, instead of acknowledging the inevitable tension between each particular societal ordering and its absent ultimate ground.

If post-foundational political thought really wants to capture the analytical imagination of social scientists, it needs to open up the multiple tactics of disavowing society's absent ground, which are now being congealed under the conceptual short-hand of the post-political condition. Instead of a relentless search for 'genuine' politics (or 'politics proper'), we need to focus our analysis on the specific moments and places where politics and the political meet and the different political effects they (can) produce. The notion of the post-political condition lacks the analytical leverage to identify the multiplicity of possible relations that characterise the political difference.

In order to boost this analytical leverage, we draw on Rancière's work to construct a matrix of different figures of depoliticisation that disavow the political.[1] For the purpose of clarification, we illustrate the matrix of depoliticisation by applying it to the relation between cultural diversity and the state.

Rethinking 'the political'

> Politics is always at work on the gap that makes equality consist solely in the figure of the wrong. It works at the meeting point of police logic and the logic of equality. But the whole problem is knowing how to interpret this gap. (Rancière 1999: 62–3)

For Erik Swyngedouw, one of the most prolific writers on the 'post-political condition' in the social sciences, the importance of this concept derives from the limited acknowledgement of the political salience of contemporary governmental innovations (Swyngedouw 2006; 2008). The frequent use of Foucault's notion of governmentality to describe these governmental innovations (see for example Raco 2003; 2009; Jessop 2007; Uitermark 2005) is exemplary here. By cutting off the King's head in political theory, Foucault (2004) not only revealed the locus and scope of power inequalities beyond the state, he also problematised power's relation to politics. While Foucault scrutinised the capillary nature of power, however, Jaeger (Chapter 10 of this volume) points out that he did not probe for its political surplus. In this regard, Rancière (1999: 32) remarks that

> while it is important to show, as Michel Foucault has done magnificently, that the police order extends well beyond its specialised institutions and techniques, it is equally important to say that *nothing is political in itself merely because power relations are at work in it*. (Emphasis added)

Initially Swyngedouw explored the role of the political in a Marxist analysis of contemporary societal transformation through the notion of 'democratic deficit'. A democratic deficit comes about when citizens lose the capacity to establish, change and contest their relationship to society through the state (Merrifield and Swyngedouw 1996). Across different socio-spatial scales of government, democratic deficits were said to be expanding (Swyngedouw 2000; Swyngedouw, Moulaert and Rodriguez 2002), despite the widespread celebration of the newly emerging networked governmental arrangements as 'empowering, democracy enhancing and more effective forms of governance compared with the sclerotic, hierarchical and bureaucratic static forms'

(Swyngedouw 2005: 1992). This acknowledgment of the Janus-faced nature of governmental innovations inspired Swyngedouw to replace the descriptive notion of democratic deficit with a full-blown theoretical argument on the nature of democratic politics. He became increasingly aware that contemporary institutional innovations (like the stakeholder-based arrangement of multi-level governance) and populist discursive regimes (like the apocalyptic imaginary surrounding climate change) are not sources for the revitalisation of the political sphere, but are its very negation. As such, they are said to constitute 'the performative expression of a post-political condition' (Swyngedouw 2010: 227).

The term 'post-politics' is borrowed from Slavoj Žižek, who adds it to Rancière's different types of disavowing the political, which will be discussed in the second part of this chapter (Žižek 1999b). For Žižek, post-politics is a specifically postmodern form not just of repressing, but also of foreclosing political disagreement. Post-politics would reduce politics to serving the needs of global capitalism and multicultural humanitarianism, by mobilising expert knowledge and techniques of deliberation. In post-politics old ideological divisions are left behind, but critique and debate have become an endogenous and institutionalised part of society, projecting a dynamic and apparently democratic public sphere (Diken 2009). At the same time, the basic organising principles of our societies are institutionally and discursively pacified and pushed beyond the boundaries of critique and debate. Global capitalism is naturalised to the extent that debate and criticism is restricted to the management and distribution of its consequences. Put differently, the post-political condition is an exaggerated denial of 'the absent ground' of the particular twenty-first-century institutionalisation of society (Marchart 2007).

Through his account of the post-political condition, Swyngedouw has revived the political difference between the contemporary society-as-instituted and its always absent ultimate ground, significantly moving beyond, for example, Foucauldian accounts of neo-liberal governmentality. Although Foucauldians obviously do not herald a foundationalist account of society, according to which society unfolds from a pregiven essence, the political saliency of governmental innovations escapes from their view. Foucauldians lay bare how the analytics of power works, not why. Swyngedouw, on the other hand, shows that the machinations of power work towards a particular goal, namely papering over the fundamental divides in society and thus disavowing the possibility of an alternative.

In his attempts to transcend post-politicisation, we would argue that Swyngedouw oscillates between the call for a 'communist' revolution on the one hand and the call to revive an agonistic political sphere on the other (Swyngedouw 2009). Each of these stances derives from a particular interpretation of the articulation between the two sides of the political difference. Contemporary thinkers of the political difference have developed competing views on the articulation between the political and politics. As we will show below, this articulation is often dealt with in a non-relational way, either by labeling current politics as 'post-political', which should be overcome by an entirely new society (the so-called purification approach) or by calling for a distinct institutionalised space of 'genuine politics' intended to mediate the lack of societal grounding (the so-called three-term approach) (Chambers 2011a).

Searching for the genuinely political: from pure to mediated politics

The 'purification approach' wants to supplant political difference with a genuine form of politics. It advances the hypothesis that a radically different society beyond antagonism is a real possibility. Swyngedouw sometimes gravitates towards a purification approach, most notably in his exploration of the 'communist hypothesis'. Building on insights from Badiou, he claims that the idea of communism is about equality and democracy and the belief that these can be *realised* through sustained political struggle (Swyngedouw 2009: 299). It entails 'the faithful belief and relentless call for and struggle over the staging of equality and freedom, sustained by the conviction that this is immediately realizable and immanently practical' (Swyngedouw 2009: 311). Swyngedouw claims that communism 'involves the self-organisation and self-management of people, and, therefore, will eliminate the coercive state as the principal organizer of political life' (Swyngedouw 2009: 300). He calls for a politics around the notion of the commons, which aims for the 'the shared ownership of each and everyone under common stewardship' and 'the production of collective institutions for the democratic management of the commons' (Swyngedouw 2009: 304).

The influence of Badiou and Žižek is palpable here. To call the communist hypothesis utopian is 'foolish', says Badiou (2008: 35), because this would neglect its immanent and practical origins. Indeed, it is the immanent contradiction of the present society, and not some floating image of heaven, which supposedly calls for a leap into a so-far unimaginable future. In his recent book *Living in the End Times*, Žižek (2011: x) defends the premise that 'the global capitalist system is approaching an apocalyptic zero-point' which calls for a specifically adapted mode of realising the communist invariant today (Badiou 2008). Žižek and Badiou thus call for a radical rupture with society as we know it and the embrace of a new act of political foundation. They do not solely call for re-establishing a tension between society as an instituted social order on the one hand, and the always disruptive pulse of democracy and equality properly understood on the other, but move beyond that by asking for a moment of 'divine violence', 'the terrifying point of direct intervention of the noumenal into the phenomenal', which should lead to the realisation of the idea of communism as a new political foundation (Žižek 2011: 392).

Admittedly, Swyngedouw repeatedly ventures backwards and forwards between this purified account of the genuinely political and the more mediated form described below, thus doubting how real the possibility of communism is. On some occasions, he describes the 'communist hypothesis' as a 'historical invariant' that 'stands for the eternal return of the heroic-tragic historical-geographies of emancipatory struggles sustained by the eternally returning, albeit in different historical forms, desire/struggle for emancipation, freedom, and equality' (Swyngedouw 2009: 304). On others, he insists that 'realizing the communist hypothesis entails a voluntaristic (subjective) moment to revive this communist invariant, that is the will of the individual to join up in common with others to realize politically the idea of communism' (Swyngedouw 2009: 304).

Ultimately, however, Swyngedouw seems to side with Badiou in his belief that the spark of politics can catalyse a 'proper democratic political sequence' that remains true to its original egalitarian inspiration (Swyngedouw 2009: 302). For Badiou (2008: 41), keeping the act alive is a real practical possibility: politics 'is not simply a matter of a momentary encounter with the impossible: that would be heroism'. Politics is about courage, endurance and 'a fidelity to a political truth procedure' (Swyngedouw 2011: 8). What Swyngedouw and Badiou call for is the purification of the political difference in favour of a society of politics. Paradoxically however, in their post-antagonist society, politics will become redundant and lose its meaning, leading to the post-political society par excellence.

While the purification approach to the political difference aims to transcend the tension between the two terms, another approach, termed the 'three-term approach' by Samuel Chambers, preserves the tension but makes it politically productive by mediating it spatially and institutionally. Mouffe's argument on the transformation of antagonism into agonism is illustrative of this strategy. The three-term approach implies that the political disagreements generated by attempts to ground society can be mediated in a space of encounter where opposing societal views can enter into a civilised battle. Laclau and Mouffe frame this argument with the notion of the 'radicalization of democracy' or 'de-MORE-cracy' (Boucher 2010). This refers to a second stage of the democratic revolution, a realisation of what is already potentially present in our so-called democratic societies. Laclau and Mouffe (2001: xv) stress that 'it is important to understand that liberal democracy is not the enemy to be destroyed in order to create, through revolution, a completely new society.' Instead, Mouffe (1993: 6) argues that the fragile balance of the liberal-democratic paradox between the ethico-political values of freedom and equality is the condition of possibility for what she calls a 'healthy democratic process'. The latter arises from a true understanding of the political, which she defines as 'the dimension of antagonism . . . constitutive of human societies' (Mouffe 2005: 9). For Mouffe, human societies are constituted internally and externally through establishing relational differences, which are reflected in specific interpretations of equality and liberty, and this is what makes societies political. This approach may be seen to run counter to the purification approach, because Mouffe's attempt to revive an agonistic public sphere is aimed at making room for staging discussion and encounter and hence does not necessarily tackle the inequalities in which every social order is grounded.

Yet political antagonism always implies the lurking threat of violence, of a paradoxical annihilation of the difference constitutive of its own identity. If societies want to avoid the real truth of the political and be 'healthy', then they will need to acknowledge the existence of the political and transform antagonism into pluralist agonism. This sublimation should come about by the acknowledgement of warring enemies that they 'belong to the same common symbolic space' (Mouffe 2005: 20). Thereby 'the category of the "enemy" does not disappear but is displaced' (Mouffe 1993: 4). Mouffe is therefore particularly concerned with the basic political institutions through which antagonism is transformed to agonism, with the institutional space where the political difference is articulated. Illustrations of this three-term approach are to be found, for example, in the call of Oosterlynck and Swyngedouw (2011: 1591) for 'a space in which demands for different socioenvironments from those currently in place can be voiced, articulated, and discussed, whereby antagonistic positions are translated into agonistic encounter,' or in Swyngedouw's reference to 'democracy as the instituted space of agonistic encounter' (Swyngedouw 2011: 372).

Rancière's relational approach to the political difference

The purification approach and the three-term approach are both problematic. As Boucher (2010) has convincingly shown, the revolutionary vanguardism of Žižek and Badiou is nothing other than an inversion of Laclau and Mouffe's radical democracy. They each respectively lean to a different side of the political difference. The purification approach leans over to the political in its ambition to radically disrupt the currently existing social order. In its attempt to undo the inequalities underlying the existing societal order without taking distance from the idea of society as such, it proposes a new society devoid of power, inequality and politics. It wants to overcome the current post-political condition by replacing it with a genuine political society, thus undoing the political difference. The three-term approach is equally problematic because its attempt to devise a proper space for the political already domesticates it. It leans over to the side of societal order in trying to channel and institutionalise the ultimate absent ground. Its support for a legitimate space of plural agonistic encounter already channels what should be political and what should not.

If we want to hang on to the post-foundational insight that society can never ultimately be grounded and the tension between politics and the political should be kept open, we should opt instead for a 'relational' approach which tries to think through the opening between society and its always absent ground. This relational approach to the tension of grounding what cannot be grounded in principle was developed by Rancière. Rather than promising a new and genuine political society, it enables us to see and explain the manifold ways in which this political tension is addressed, thus allowing for an empirical account of what is produced in terms of political effects by the operation of the political difference.

Rancière's relational account of the political difference of what he calls 'politics' and 'the police' is situated in between the latter two approaches. Rancière borrows the notion of police from Foucault to refer to a societal 'system of distribution and legitimization . . . an order of bodies that defines the allocation of ways of doing, ways of being, ways of saying' (Rancière 1999: 28–9, emphasis added). This police order refers to a partitioning of society understood as a 'sensible' collectivity in which citizens 'partake' materially and temporally according to their ascribed 'parts' (in the sense of roles in a play). So Rancière admits that 'The idea of the partition of the sensible is no doubt my own way of translating and appropriating for my own account the genealogical thought of Foucault – his way of systematizing how things can be visible, utterable, and capable of being thought' (Rancière et al. 2000: 13).

Nevertheless, as Rancière confides to his readers in *The Difficult Legacy of Michel Foucault*, Foucault's work remains haunted by the possibility of emancipatory struggle (Rancière 2010). Defining politics as the scrupulous interruption of the police order by pointing out its blind spots, 'the part of those who have no-part', Rancière indicates that 'it's the question of equality – which for Foucault had no *theoretical* pertinence – that makes the difference between us' (Rancière et al. 2000: 13).

Contrary to Laclau and Mouffe, for whom society *is* political because it builds on internal and external relational differences, or Žižek and Badiou, for whom society is instituted by a political moment, Rancière contends that society *'becomes'* political when its order is disrupted. The political disruption of the police order follows a specific 'rationality of disagreement' (Rancière 1999: 43). It occurs when the fundamental equality of human beings as human beings is invoked, which only happens rarely. The enactment consists of the collective becoming of a different subject, a yet unseen and unheard part whose appearance can only disrupt the existing social order, not found a new one:

> Politics is a matter of subjects or, rather, modes of subjectivation. By *subjectivation* I mean the production through a series of actions of a body and a capacity for enunciation not previously identifiable within a given field of experience, whose identification is thus part of the reconfiguration of the field of experience. (Rancière 1999: 35)

As such, there is no proper time and place for politics in the order of the police (Dikeç 2002; 2005), nor is there a privileged subject bringing societal change. Politics takes place and reconfigures it into a temporary stage for the manifestation, demonstration and verification of equality. In theatrical terms, politics is a disruptive 'performance' that creates its own stage and subject to enact the presupposition of human equality within the audience of society (Hallward 2009).

To avoid both the purification approach and the three-term approach, it is crucial to highlight the deeply paradoxical nature of Rancière's specifically relational conception of the political difference. There are no given places for politics, nor does politics ever bring about a society beyond societal hierarchies. For Rancière, politics is, on the one hand, radically opposed to the police order, yet on the other, it is deeply endebted to it because 'politics has no objects or issues of its own' (Rancière 1999: 31). Although nothing *is* political per se for Rancière, only the police order can *become* political. Therefore the political cannot simply re-turn; instead politics 'twists' the order of the police (Deranty 2003). The relationship between politics and police is thus an intimate 'entanglement of both logics. Politics acts on the police. It acts in the places and with the words that are common to both, even if it means reshaping those places and changing the status of those words' (Rancière 1999: 33). This entanglement is only untied at the moment when politics takes place: 'political activity is none other than the activity that parcels them out' (Rancière 1999: 28). And even then 'the distinction between politics and police takes effect in a reality that always retains a part of indistinction. It is a way of thinking through the mixture. There is no world of pure politics that exists apart from a world of mixture' (Rancière 2010: 207).

To put it differently, Rancière's relational approach to the political difference does not lean towards one of its two sides, but instead tries to hold open and think through their tension:

> What is proper to politics is thus lost at the outset if politics is thought of as a specific way of living. Politics cannot be defined on the basis of any pre-existing subject. The political 'difference' that makes it possible to think its subject must be sought in the form of its relation. (Rancière 2001: no. 4)

This relational approach is more suitable for an empirical investigation of the articulation of the two terms of the political difference, paying particular attention to the different tactics of depoliticisation arising in the police order in order to obscure the absence of an ultimate ground of any societal order.

Operationalising the relational approach: multiple figures of depoliticisation

> Depoliticization is the oldest task of politics, the one which achieves its fulfillment at the brink of its end, its perfection on the brink of the abyss. (Rancière 1995: 19)

Drawing on the first two approaches to the political difference, 'Post-politics refers to a politics in which ideological or dissensual contestation are replaced by techno-managerial planning, expert management and administration', whereby '"doing politics" is reduced to a form of institutionalized social management' (Swyngedouw 2010: 225). In this second part of the paper, we argue that this perspective on contemporary society lacks sufficient analytical leverage to identify the multiplicity of forms through which society's absent ultimate ground is disavowed today.

From our perspective, post-politics constitutes a conceptual shorthand to identify the current interplay of different generic tactics of disavowing the political. Conceptually, post-politics is therefore insufficient to disentangle the multifarious forms of depoliticisation that are at work in the political field. As will be explained below, Rancière's (1999; 2001) conception of archi-, meta-, and para-politics, and Žižek's (1999) addition of ultra-politics provide us with the conceptual tools to crack open the black box of the post-political condition and develop a truly relational approach to the political difference. Today's society is not characterised by a new form of post-political depoliticisation. For Rancière (2004), using the notion of 'post-democracy' instead of 'post-politics', the current order is one of 'advanced plutocratic consensus' in which the different generic figures of disavowal he identified interlock in an ever more effective way.

To be sure, Swyngedouw (2011) has already referred to these tactics of disavowal in the margins of his writings, for example to identify contemporary insurgent outbursts of violence as ultra-politics, or to label the rise of eco-villages as a fundamentalist regression to archi-politics. Nevertheless, he sees them as the mere reactionary counterpart of this new post-political condition: 'It is nothing but the flipside of the disavowal of the violence of consensual governance. They are the Manichean counterpunch to rituals of resistance' (Swyngedouw 2011: 8). Such tactics of disavowal are therefore treated as derivative of the prevalence of a post-political condition, and do not have their own rationale of existence. They are nothing but signals of 'the possibility for a return, a retreating, of "the political"' (Swyngedouw 2011: 4). Building on Rancière's relational interpretation of the political difference, according to which the political cannot return but can only twist the reigning order of the police, we suggest that these tactics of disavowal should be afforded a much more central role in the analysis of contemporary political dynamics and treat them as components of a typology of figures of depoliticisation.

In his magnum opus *Disagreement: Politics and Philosophy* (1999), Rancière discusses different ways in which the absent ground of society can be disavowed. Rancière's goal is not only, as Bosteels (2010: 80) has argued, 'to come to an understanding of politics without prefixes, of the real of politics set free from the typical efforts of philosophers to appropriate, displace, cover up and/or unmask its essential scandal'. It is also to understand the various forms of depoliticisation that stand in between the political difference of politics and the police. Archi-, meta- and para-politics are described by Rancière as particular logics of policing that aim to put off the possibility of a different society. These figures of depoliticisation represent a systematisation of his earlier accounts of political philosophy, described at length in *The Philosopher and his Poor* (Rancière 2004). While the latter discussed the polymorphic disavowal of politics in three particular political philosophies (Platonism-Marxism-Bourdieusianism), *Disagreement* discussed them as instances of societal tactics of disavowal.

Each of these figures of depoliticisation combines a 'diagnosis' (Rancière 1999: 62) with a 'reply', which is also a 'replica' (Bosteels 2010: 83). The diagnosis concerns the 'unfounded state of politics' (Rancière 1999: 62), which reveals the contingency of any social order. Figures of depoliticisation are thus ways to acknowledge the existence of the political difference. Yet, they simultaneously try to advance a societal order that would transcend the difference between politics and the police, thus attempting to close what cannot be closed in principle. In reply to the diagnosis that recognises the contingency of any societal order, figures of depoliticisation aim to install a certain partition of the sensible (or police order) that would overcome hierarchical societal differentiation. This reply is a replica, in the sense of being a false mirror-image, of what politics aims for. While politics momentarily shows the scandal of each societal order by uncovering particular forms of injustice, figures of depoliticisation believe they can overcome inequality all together, thus simultaneously obscuring and repressing the existence of the political difference. Figures of depoliticisation are therefore 'reflective operations to suppress a scandal in thinking proper to the exercise of politics' (Rancière 1999: xii).

Put differently, figures of depoliticisation are aimed at grounding the police's partition of the sensible so the existing inequalities become invisible or harmless. They want to twist the 'naturalness of policing' (Rancière 1999: 64), and are devoted to the order of the police: they aim to achieve and eliminate politics at the same time. This is 'the primordial tension . . . the coincidence between the wish "truly" to do political things . . . and the wish to put an end to politics, to hear nothing more about it' (Rancière 1995: 12). Figures of depoliticisation saturate the police order to eliminate the possibility of disruptive politics. As such, they are what stand in between the political difference of politics and the police.

The matrix of depoliticisation

Now that we have defined what figures of depoliticisation are, this section will describe the generic forms they can take. Put simply and crudely, *archi-politics* is a tactic of disavowal which grounds a police order in the idea of a harmonious community. The populist politics of nationalism or neo-communitarian projects such as 'the Big Society' offer a particularly apposite contemporary example of archi-politics, as they consider the real possibility of an undivided and harmonious society. *Para-politics* is a tactic of depoliticisation which does accept that society is not harmonious and homogeneous, but differentiated along multiple axes. Para-politics nevertheless rids existing hierarchical societal differentiations of their disruptive qualities by channelling and reducing them to a superficial competition between different opinions and parties (Rancière 1999; Marchart 2007; Žižek 2004). In doing so it erects rules or institutions for where and when this competition can and must take place, as in the case of deliberative dialogue procedures and the increasingly popular stakeholder consultation boards. *Meta-politics* denounces these channelling devices as the false appearances of underlying social structures. It denounces the absent ground of society instead by deducing all societal inequalities from one primordial source of inequality. We can see this at work in certain forms of Marxism according to which parliamentary institutions are considered as no more than a distraction from the fundamental contradictions and inequalities in the economic sphere.[2] Neoliberal ideologies that trace all existing inequalities to a statist interference in the personal freedom of natural subjects also follow a meta-political rationale. Lastly, *ultra-politics*, which Žižek (1999a; 1999b; 2004) has added to Rancière's triptych, is a figure of depoliticisation which undermines the possibility of challenging the existing societal order by constructing a radically different enemy, with which there can be no 'common ground for symbolic conflict' (Žižek 1998: 70).[3] Terrorism and the extreme Right are contemporary illustrations of ultra-politics, as they legitimate 'the attempt to depoliticize the conflict by bringing it to its extreme via the direct militarisation of politics – by reformulating it as the *war* between "Us" and "Them", our Enemy' (Žižek 1998: 70).

One could argue then that post-politics is a particular historical combination of: (1) para-politics in the form of governance-mediated searches for consensus around specific issues amongst a plethora of different stakeholders; (2) a meta-political reduction of the social order to the mere product of atomising market-based relations of competition; and (3) an ultra-political projection of any ideological alternative to a capitalist free market society beyond the boundaries of the present into a failed past, often backed up by (4) an archipolitical appeal to a harmonious and undivided national, regional or local community of supposedly equals.

Žižek's extension of Rancière's triptych with a fourth figure of depoliticisation has led him to organise them in a two-by-two matrix. The goal of classifying figures of depoliticisation into a matrix is to show that they are related to each other, and so can also mutate from the one into the other, depending on the strategic circumstances. At the same time, it allows us to think through what Diken (Chapter

6 of this volume) calls the 'antinomies' of post-politics. Understood as a particular historical combination of tactics of disavowal, post-politics intricately unites fundamentally conflicting strategies of depoliticisation. In Figure 4.1 below, we have adapted Žižek's matrix (1999a), now projecting the respective figures of disavowal onto a distinction between the two structural aspects of any figure of depoliticisation described above: a figure of depoliticisation always consists of a diagnosis and a reply.

In response to the disruptive potential of politics, the different figures of disavowal develop two different diagnoses to avoid the political claim for equality. *On the one hand*, archi- and ultra-politics work from the assumption that society is not internally split. They do so by grounding the harmonious community in shared values, beliefs and destiny (archi-politics) or by projecting social divisions beyond the boundaries of the community (ultra-politics). *On the other hand*, meta- and para-politics accept that society is internally split. Nevertheless, claims for equality are diverted by considering societal differences as a matter of individual preference open for negotiation (para-politics) or by reducing them to a pregiven primordial structure of inequality (meta-politics).

Now, from the diagnosis to the reply is not a one-to-one correlation. *On the one hand*, the reply of para- and ultra-politics consists of splitting up and institutionalising a distinction between a social and a political part. Taking the example of a stakeholder consultation board as a para-political reply, the board meetings are said to be the political place and time where disputes of opinions can compete. Outside these institutional arenas is the social part of society, where voices that call for equality are out-of-place. The example of the extreme Right's discriminatory treatment of 'foreigners' illustrates how this reply plays out in ultra-politics. Extreme-right tactics do not deny that foreigners partake in the police order, for example when they are hired in secondary wage labour sectors. However, politically speaking they are said to belong to a different and subordinate group, which denies them an equal voice as fellow members of the community. Therefore it is legitimate to discriminate against foreigners' rights on the grounds of their belonging to a different political group. *On the other hand,* the symmetrical reply between archi-politics and meta-politics stems from their attempt to eliminate any distinction between prescribed social or political parts of society. Instead of policing by division, their reply rests on uniting. Archi-politics, which strives for 'the total elimination of politics as a specific activity' (Rancière 1999: 70), promises an all-inclusive society to which everyone can join in principle. This avowed openness resonates for example in populist versions of cosmopolitan humanitarianism. In

		DIAGNOSIS	
		Society is not internally split	Society is internally split
REPLY	Policing through a Specifically Political Sphere	ULTRA-politics	PARA-politics
	Policing through the Denial of any Specifically Political Sphere	ARCHI-politics	META-politics

Figure 4.1 The matrix of depoliticisation: four figures that disavow the possibility of politics by combining a diagnosis and a reply

meta-political tactics of disavowal, there equally is no need for a specifically political response to the necessarily unequal nature of any social order. The reply, however, takes a different form: the claim for equality is accommodated by reducing different types of inequality to one fundamental source of equality, which has to be undone in its own right. For example, claims to equal recognition for sexual preference or cultural belonging are said to reflect underlying unequal distributions of economic resources or the unequal effects of statist violence on the personal sphere.

An empirical puzzle of disavowal: cultural diversity and the state

In contrast to the one-dimensional notion of the 'post-political condition', the matrix of depoliticisation enables a more nuanced empirical understanding of the polymorphic relation between society-as-instituted and its always absent ultimate ground. Multiple figures of depoliticisation aim at the foreclosure of disruptive politics by intervening in the police order. For the purpose of clarification, we now illustrate the matrix by applying it to an empirical puzzle regarding cultural diversity and the state (see Figure 4.2). Ever since Žižek's (1996; 1998; 1999b) early writings on the topic of 'liberal multiculturalism', this puzzle has appeared front-stage in the debate on the post-political condition, especially after the recent backlash against multiculturalism in Europe (Ahmed 2008; Bond 2012; van Baar 2011; Žižek 2008; 2009; 2011). From the perspective of the political difference, any institutionalised articulation between

		DIAGNOSIS	
		Society is not internally split	Society is internally split
REPLY	Policing through a Specifically Political Sphere	ULTRA-politics = New Racism	PARA-politics = Liberal Multiculturalism
	Policing through the Denial of any Specifically Political Sphere	ARCHI-politics = Civic Republicanism	META-politics = Ethnostratified Class-Struggle

Figure 4.2 The matrix of depoliticisation illustrated: disavowing alternative relations between the state and cultural diversity

cultural diversity and the state is doomed to produce exclusion and inequality. We aim to show that the across-the-board generalisation of the relation between cultural diversity and the state as post-political multicultural humanitarianism obfuscates the multifarious strategies that have been developed to foreclose claims for equality.

Before the recent backlash, liberal multiculturalism constituted the hegemonic figure of disavowal. According to the matrix, it follows a para-political rationale. The diagnosis reads that although the existence of different cultures in one state can lead to societal hierarchies, the threat of antagonism can be contained by institutionally capturing these cultures. The tolerant multiculturalist regime calls for an institutional neutralisation of cultures. The aim is 'to absorb them as a specific "way of life"' (Žižek 1998: 225) dependent on the life choices of free individuals: 'This leads us to today's tolerant liberal multiculturalism as an experience of the Other deprived of its Otherness – the decaffeinated Other' (Žižek 2010). Accordingly, the liberal multiculturalist reply institutes a separate sphere in society where the political antagonisms arising from cultural differences are policed in para-political fashion. This separate sphere is shaped by the 'diversity paradigm' and encompasses the multicultural policies pursued by public authorities, the diversity management of companies, civil society associations and public organisations, and the promotion of intercultural competencies of individual citizens (Faist 2009; 2010). The diversity paradigm polices cultural differences by incorporating them in the social order as 'competencies' to be developed by individual citizens, 'human capital' to be managed by organisations and 'assets' that enrich society. The move away from concerns with discrimination and the structural disadvantage of ethnic minorities and towards organisational efficiency effectively forecloses the invocation of the equality of humans as cultural beings. Put differently, it designates 'how multicultural policies have become a form of "planned pluralism" that makes difference tolerable to the majority order' (Bond 2012: 219).

As public condemnations by the German Chancellor Angela Merkel and former French president Nicolas Sarkozy indicate, liberal multiculturalism has recently been under siege. Ahmed (2008) argues that 'the best description of today's hegemony is "liberal monoculturalism" in which common values are read as under threat by the support for the other's difference'. Although the growing ascendency of extreme-right populism in Europe surely influenced the backlash against multiculturalism, the matrix shows that it would be wrong to argue that the civic republicanism of liberal monoculturalism equals the extreme Right's new racism. Both the ultra-political new racism and the archi-political civic republicanism advance the productive lie of a society that is not internally split, yet they defend different replies.

For Žižek, new racist ultra-politics stand for the 'restoration' of historically defined and naturalised monocultural states which are internally beyond antagonism because they exclude foreign cultures. Its reply projects antagonism beyond its territorial borders, making the other an absolute Other external to the political body. By contrast, the neo-communitarian project of civic republicanism (Schinkel and Van Houdt 2010) papers over internal cultural differences and forecloses the antagonisms that they generate. Instead, it advances a common public culture which all can join in principle. This supposedly colour-blind monoculture should emphasise what unites us, thus restoring a form of national pride and belonging. In contrast to multiculturalist para-politics that channels antagonisms generated by cultural differences into a competition between different subcultures from which citizens can freely choose, archi-political republicanism imagines a broadly shared set of values and norms that are embodied by the state and reproduced through public institutions like the education system.

Lastly, defenders of an ethnostratified class struggle would agree with the archi-politics of civic republicanism that any separate political sphere to stage cultural antagonism must be abolished. Nevertheless, the meta-political diagnosis reads completely differently from the archi-political one, because it does not believe that a society beyond societal hierarchy is possible. For meta-politics, cultural differences are nothing but a smokescreen that obscures the shared objective interests of the working class, and that serves to legitimate the unequal distribution of material resources across cultural groupings, which is the 'real' source of societal antagonism. Therefore meta-politics calls for the lifting of the veil of identity politics and the joining of social forces against class-based relations of domination and exploitation.

Conclusion: the whereabouts of post-democracy

The 'post-political condition' has recently emerged as a welcome theoretical innovation to account for the Janus-faced nature of contemporary governmental changes. Its introduction has made scholars aware of the political difference between the contemporary society-as-instituted and its always absent ground, leading them to reveal the fundamentally political mechanisms that continuously work to veil the possibility of a radically different society. Today's discursive and institutional governance innovations are not innocent improvements to tackle deficits associated with national liberal-democratic regimes. Instead they represent ever more effective forms of disavowing the contingency of contemporary societies, and they silently paper over the multiple hierarchical differences that structure them.

This chapter has attempted to derive a set of operational concepts from post-foundationalist political thought in order to unravel in precise empirical terms just how the possibility of a radically different society is postponed. Our central claim is that the post-political condition has so far been used as a one-size-fits-all label and a conceptual short-hand to group currently hegemonic political forms. Instead, we call for the need to crack open the black box of the post-political condition to see the multifarious generic policing tactics that combine to depoliticise society.

We think this is necessary, first, to be able to further explore and assess the empirical role of each of the generic figures of depoliticisation. It will enable us to develop a better understanding of how the importance of different tactics of disavowal changes over time and how their articulation works to improve or reduce the effectiveness of depoliticisation. Secondly, adopting a relational account of the political difference, and thus keeping open the tension-ridden relationship between politics and the police, implies a cautionary warning for self-proclaimed promises of a 'return of the genuinely political'. In their revolutionary spirit and longing for pure equality, these run the risk of concealing very real political inequalities which inevitably continue to exist in radically transformed societies. Thirdly, and relatedly, a relational account of the political difference helps to see how the always present possibility to disagree fundamentally with particular existing inequalities is the source of new transformative political subjects, as harbingers of repoliticisation through temporal disturbances and interruptions of the status quo.

Notes

1. Rancière's use of 'politics' differs from other theorists of the political difference. See Wilson and Swyngedouw's introduction to this volume for a discussion of these important terminological differences.
2. Given the commitment of Marxism to an egalitarian society, it may appear strange to refer to Marxism as the paradigmatic case of meta-politics. It therefore needs to be clarified that Marxism is meta-political in the sense that it is predicated on the impossibility of equality *within* the existing capitalist order and on the reduction of the internal split in society to one primordial source of inequality (economic inequality). Contrary to post-foundationalist political thought, Marx believed it was both possible and desirable to overcome the political difference (and hence move past the political).
3. While Rancière did not elaborate in detail the idea behind ultra-politics in *Disagreement*, we argue that his later work on 'the ethical turn' of politics essentially covers this fourth figure of disavowal. In Rancière's words: 'the political community thus tends to be transformed into an ethical community, the community of only one single people in which everyone is supposed to be counted ... The excluded, therefore, has no status in the structuration of the community ... he or she becomes *the radical other*, the one who is separated from the community for the simple fact that he or she is alien to it, that he or she doesn't share the identity that binds each to all, and that he or she threatens the community in each of us' (2006: 6–7, emphasis added). For the sake of consistency, we retain 'ultra-politics' instead of 'the ethical turn of politics'.

References

Ahmed, S. (2008), 'Liberal multiculturalism is the hegemony – it's an empirical fact – a response to Slavoj Zizek', *Darkmatter*, 19 February 2008.
Badiou, A. (2008), 'The communist hypothesis', *New Left Review*, 49.
Barnett, C. (2004), 'Deconstructing radical democracy: Articulation, representation, and being-with-others', *Political Geography*, 23, pp. 503–28.
Beck, U. (1997), *The Reinvention of Politics: Rethinking Modernity in the Global Social Order*, Cambridge: Polity.
Bond, S. (2012), 'The multicultural paradox: The role of critique, the post-political and a radical democracy', *Dialogues in Human Geography*, 2: 2, pp. 218–20.

Bosteels, B. (2010), 'Archipolitics, parapolitics, metapolitics', in J. P. Deranty (ed.), *Jacques Rancière: Key Concepts*. Durham: Acumen, pp. 80–92.

Boucher, G. (2010), 'An inversion of radical democracy: The republic of virtue in Zizek's revolutionary politics', *International Journal of Zizek Studies*, 4: 2, pp. 1–25.

Chambers, S. A. (2011a), 'Jacques Rancière and the problem of pure politics', *European Journal of Political Theory*, 10: 3, pp. 303–26.

Chambers, S. A. (2011b), 'The politics of the police: From neoliberalism to anarchism, and back to democracy', in P. Bowman and R. Stamp, *Reading Rancière*, London: Continuum, pp. 9–43.

Crouch, C. (2004), *Post-Democracy*, Cambridge: Polity.

Davis, O. (2010), *Jacques Rancière*, Cambridge: Polity.

Dean, J. (2009), 'Politics without politics' *Parallax*, 15: 3, pp. 20–36.

Deranty, J.-P. (2003), 'Rancière and contemporary political ontology', *Theory & Event*, 6:4.

Dikeç, M. (2002), 'Police, politics, and the right to the city', *GeoJournal*, 58, pp. 91–8.

Dikeç, M. (2005), 'Space, politics, and the political', *Environment and Planning D: Society and Space*, 23: 2, pp. 171–88.

Diken, B. (2009), 'Radical critique as the paradox of post-political society', *Third Text*, 23 (5), pp. 579–86.

Faist, T. (2009), 'Diversity – a new mode of incorporation?', *Ethnic and Racial Studies*, 32:1, pp. 171–90.

Faist, T. (2010), 'Cultural diversity and social inequalities', *Social Research*, 77:1, pp. 297–325.

Foucault, M. (1978), *The History of Sexuality. Volume I: An Introduction*, New York: Pantheon.

Foucault, M. (2004), *Society Must Be Defended*, London: Penguin.

Guénoun, S et al. (2000), 'Jacques Rancière: Literature, politics, aesthetics: approaches to democratic disagreement', *SubStance* 29: 2, pp. 3–24.

Hallward, P. (2009), 'Staging equality: Rancières theatrocracy and the limits of anarchic equality', in G. Rockhill and P. Watts (eds), *History, Politics, Aesthetics: Jacques Rancière*, Durham: Duke University Press.

Jessop, B. (2007), 'From micro-powers to governmentality: Foucault's work on statehood, state formation, statecraft and state power', *Political Geography*, 26, pp. 34–40.

Laclau, E. and C. Mouffe (2001), 'Preface to the Second Edition', in E. Laclau and C. Mouffe, *Hegemony and Socialist Strategy: Towards a Radical Democratic Politics*, London: Verso, pp. vii–xix.

May, T. (2008), *The Political Thought of Jacques Rancière: Creating Equality*, Edinburgh: Edinburgh University Press.

May, T. (2010), *Contemporary Political Movements and the Thought of Jacques Rancière*, Edinburgh: Edinburgh University Press.

May, T. et al. (2008), 'Democracy, anarchism and radical politics today: An interview with Jacques Rancière', *Anarchist Studies*, 16: 2, pp. 173–85.

Marchart, O. (2007), *Post-Foundational Thought: Political Difference in*

Nancy, Lefort, Badiou and Laclau, Edinburgh: Edinburgh University Press.

Marchart, O. (2011), 'The second return of the political: Democracy and the syllogism of equality', in P. Bowman and R. Stamp, *Reading Rancière*, London: Continuum, pp. 129–47.

Merrifield, A., and E. Swyngedouw (1996), 'Social justice and the urban experience: An introduction', in A. Merrifield and E. Swyngedouw, *The Urbanization of Injustice*, London: ; Lawrence and Wishart, pp. 1–17.

Mouffe, C. (1993), *The Return of The Political*, London: Verso.

Mouffe, C. (2005), *On the Political*, London: Routledge.

Nash, K. (1996), 'Post-democracy, politics and philosophy: An interview with Jacques Rancière', *Angelaki*, 1: 3, pp. 171–8.

Oosterlynck, S. and E. Swyngedouw (2010), 'Noise reduction: The post-political quandary of night flights at Brussels Airport', *Environment and Planning A*, 42: 7, pp. 1577–94.

Raco, M. (2003), 'Governmentality, subject-building, and the discourses and practices of devolution in the UK', *Transactions of the Institute of British Geographers*, 28: 1, pp. 75–95.

Raco, M. (2009), 'From expectations to aspirations: State modernisation, urban policy, and the existential politics of welfare in the UK', *Political Geography*, 28, pp. 436–44.

Raco, M. and R. Imrie (2000), 'Governmentality and rights and responsibilities in urban policy', *Environment and Planning A*, 32: 12, pp. 187–204.

Rancière, J. (1989), *The Nights of Labor. The Workers' Dream in Nineteenth-Century France*, Philadelphia: Temple University Press.

Rancière, J. (1992), 'Politics, identification, and subjectivation', *October*, 61, pp. 58–64.

Rancière, J. (1995), *On The Shores of Politics*, London: Verso.

Rancière, J. (1999), *Disagreement: Politics and Philosophy*, Minneapolis: University of Minnesota Press.

Rancière, J. (2004a), 'On war as the ultimate form of advanced plutocratic consensus', *Contemporary French and Francophone Studies*, 8: 3, pp. 253–8.

Rancière, J. (2004b), *The Philosopher and His Poor*, Durham: Duke University Press.

Rancière, J. (2004c), 'Who is the subject of the Rights of Man?', *The South Atlantic Quarterly*, 103: 2/3, pp. 297–310.

Rancière, J. (2006), 'The ethical turn of aesthetics and politics', *Critical Horizons*, 7: 1, pp. 1–20.

Rancière, J. (2009), 'A few remarks on the method of Jacques Rancière', *Parallax*, 15: 3, pp. 114–23.

Rancière, J. (2010), *Chronicles of Consensual Times*, London: Continuum.

Schaap, A. (2011), 'Enacting the right to have rights: Jacques Rancière's critique of Hannah Arendt', *European Journal of Political Theory*, 10: 1, pp. 22–45.

Sharpe, M. and G. Boucher (2010), *Žižek and Politics: A Critical Introduction*, Edinburgh: Edinburgh University Press.

Schinkel, W. and F. Van Houdt (2010), 'The double helix of cultural assimilationism and neo-liberalism: Citizenship in contemporary governmentality', *The British Journal of Sociology*, 61: 4, pp. 696–715.

Swyngedouw, E. (2000), 'Authoritarian governance, power, and the politics of rescaling', *Environment and Planning D: Society and Space*, 18, pp. 63–76.

Swyngedouw, E. (2005), 'Governance innovation and the citizen: The Janus face of governance-beyond-the-state', *Urban Studies*, 42: 11, pp. 1991–2006.

Swyngedouw, E. (2006), 'Impossible sustainability and the post-political condition', in D. Gibbs and R. Kreuger (eds), *The Sustainable Development Paradox: Urban Political Economy in the United States and Europe*, pp. 13–40.

Swyngedouw, E. (2007), 'The state of the situation: post-political cities', in S. Gatz, S. Van Rouveroij and C. Leysen (eds), *The State of the City/ The City is the State*, Brussels, VUBPRESS.

Swyngedouw, E. (2008), 'Where is the political?', paper delivered at the Annual Conference of the Association of American Geographers, Boston.

Swyngedouw, E. (2009), 'The communist hypothesis and revolutionary capitalisms: Exploring the idea of communist geographies for the twenty-first century', *Antipode*, 41: 1, pp. 298–319.

Swyngedouw, E. (2011), 'Interrogating post-democratization: Reclaiming egalitarian political spaces', *Political Geography*, 30: 7, pp. 370–80.

Swyngedouw, E., F. Moulaert and A. Rodriguez (2002), 'Neoliberal urbanization in Europe: Large-scale urban development projects and the new urban policy', *Antipode*, 34: 3, pp. 542–77.

Uitermark, J. (2005), 'The genesis and evolution of urban policy: A confrontation of regulationist and governmentality approaches', *Political Geography*, 24: 2, pp. 137–63.

van Baar, H. (2011), 'Commentary: Europe's Romaphobia: problematization, securitization, nomadization', *Environment and Planning D: Society and Space*, 29: 2, pp. 203–12.

Žižek, S. (1996), 'Multiculturalism, or, the cultural logic of multinational capitalism', *New Left Review*, 225, pp. 28–51.

Žižek, S. (1998), 'A leftist plea for "Eurocentrism"', *Critical Inquiry*, 24: 4, pp. 988–1009.

Žižek, S. (1999a), 'Carl Schmitt in the Age of Post-Politics', in C. Mouffe (ed.), *The Challenge of Carl Schmitt*, London: Verso, pp. 18–37.

Žižek, S. (1999b), *The Ticklish Subject: The Absent Centre of Political Ontology*, London: Verso.

Žižek, S. (1998), 'For a leftist appropriation of the European legacy', *Journal of Political Ideologies*, 3: 1 pp. 63–78.

Žižek, S. (2004), 'The lesson of Rancière', in J. Rancière, *The Politics of Aesthetics*, London / New York: Continuum, pp. 69–79.

Žižek, S. (2008), 'Tolerance as an ideological category', *Critical Inquiry*, 34: 4, pp. 660–82.

Žižek, S. (2009), 'Appendix: Multiculturalism, the reality of an illusion', available at *http://www.lacan.com/essays/?page_id=454*.

Žižek S. (2010), 'Liberal multiculturalism masks an old barbarism with a human face', *The Guardian*, 3 October.

Žižek, S. (2011), *Living in the End Times*, London: Verso.

5 The *Jouissance* of Philanthrocapitalism: Enjoyment as a Post-Political Factor

Japhy Wilson

What is needed is a new 'social contract' between the rich and everyone else . . . For the rich, there should be a clear set of rules, so that they know what they must do in order to win society's acceptance. Call this the 'Good Billionaire Guide'. For everyone else, there should be a clear under-standing of how society will behave towards the rich if they abide by these rules . . . A truly fair social contract might actually allow the rich who give generously more grace than their peers to indulge themselves free from criticism in their yachts, space flights, and Rod Stewart-serenaded birthday parties. Philanthrocapitalism need not go hand in hand with Puritanism. (Bishop and Green 2008: 258)

In ideology, all is not ideology (that is, ideological meaning), but it is this very surplus which is the last support of ideology . . . The criticism of ideology [must aim] at extracting the kernel of *enjoyment*, at articulating the ways in which – beyond the field of meaning but still internal to it – an ideology implies, manipulates, produces a pre-ideological enjoyment structured in fantasy. (Žižek 1989: 125)

In *Philanthrocapitalism: How the Rich Can Save the World and Why We Should Let Them*, the US Business Editor of *The Economist*, Matthew Bishop, and his co-author Michael Green celebrate the potential for a new form of philanthropy to resolve problems of disease and extreme poverty in Africa and beyond. Unlike tradi-tional philanthropists, who were content to write cheques for good causes, 'philanthrocapitalists' such as Bill Gates and George Soros closely monitor their projects, transforming development aid by infusing it with the business principles of innovation, efficiency, and entrepreneurship. Bishop and Green argue that philanthrocapitalism provides the potential basis for a new social contract in Western soci-eties, in which increasing inequality is to be accepted in exchange for 'the rich regarding their surplus wealth as the property of the many, and themselves as trustees whose duty it is to administer it for the common good' (Bishop and Green 2008: 15). The book has received widespread acclaim in the international business press and amongst the luminaries of global liberalism. Its website includes enthusiastic reviews in publications such as *Forbes* and the *Financial Times*, and leads with an endorsement from Bill Clinton, who asserts that, 'We have to transform the world into one of shared responsibilities, shared opportunities, and a shared sense of community. Bishop and Green show us how to do it'.[1]

This chapter develops an analysis of philanthrocapitalism, based on the psychoanalytic social theory of Slavoj Žižek. In his popular writings, Žižek has characterised Bill Gates and George Soros as 'liberal communists', who believe that 'market and social responsibility can be reunited for mutual benefit' (Žižek 2008: 15). Philanthropy, he suggests, shares an ideological structure with chocolate laxatives. In both cases, the poison – chocolate that constipates, capital that exploits – is presented as the cure to its own pathological symptoms (Žižek 2008: 18). Though suggestive, these analogies are not further developed by Žižek, and bear little relation to the theory of ideology that he has developed in his philosophical work. As such, they are typical of Žižek's failure to adequately apply his own theoretical approach to the analysis of global capitalism, despite his increasingly strident calls for a return to the critique of political economy (Sharpe 2004: 196–1). This chapter argues that Žižek's approach contains the potential for a critique of philanthrocapitalism as an ideological formation, which extends beyond both his own writings on philanthropy and the broader critical literature on the topic, and which can contribute to our understanding of the post-political tendencies of contemporary global governance.

The majority of the critical literature on philanthrocapitalism challenges it on the basis of its depoliticisation of development and its erosion of representative democracy. This literature points out that development assistance in philanthrocapitalism is not channelled through democratically elected governments, but is delivered by unelected, unaccountable foundations, whose preference is for technocratic, top-down forms of intervention. Market solutions are prioritised, and projects are conceptualised in isolation from the broader political-economic dynamics in which they are located (Bosworth 2011; Desai and Kharas 2008; Edwards 2009, 2011; Jenkins 2011; Ramdas 2011; Rogers 2011). In these respects, philanthrocapitalism is typical of the post-political modality of contemporary depoliticisation, which is characterised by the evisceration of the properly political moment of 'agonistic engagement' or 'dissensus' from the sphere of politics, and its replacement with forms of consensual governance and expert administration operating within the confines of neoliberal orthodoxy (Mouffe 2005; Rancière 2010).

This understanding of philanthrocapitalism as post-politics is accurate up to a point, but misses certain dimensions of its ideological operation. As we saw in the Introduction to this volume, Žižek criticises the literature on post-politics for its neglect of class struggle and its failure to adequately account for the ideological operation of *jouissance* – or 'enjoyment' (Žižek 2000a; 1999: 282–3). Here I develop Žižek's ideas in this regard, through a critique of philanthrocapitalism as a form of post-politics rooted in class struggle, which operates through the mobilisation and regulation of *jouissance*. I do so with reference to Bishop and Green's book – as the key ideological text of philanthrocapitalism – and to Millennium Promise, a philanthropic organisation established in 2005 by the celebrity development economist Jeffrey Sachs and the billionaire venture capitalist Ray Chambers, which Bishop and Green discuss as an example of philanthrocapitalism in practice (Bishop and Green 2008: 206–7). Funded by George Soros, among others, and including Bono and Angelina Jolie among its celebrity supporters, Millennium Promise finances and promotes the Millennium Villages Project in sub-Saharan Africa (Wilson 2014).

In this chapter, I argue that philanthrocapitalism operates as a post-political strategy by mobilising distinct but interrelated forms of *jouissance*. In the first place, philanthrocapitalism encourages 'us' (the populations of 'Western' nations) to identify with the philanthropists through the vicarious experience of the warm glow of their charitable giving. Secondly, we are offered a colonial fantasy of 'Africa' as the location of a primitive and inaccessible *jouissance* against which our shared identity with the philanthrocapitalist is further constituted. Thirdly, in the structure of its development projects, philanthrocapitalism provides a narcissistic mirror-image in which we are invited to enjoy an imaginary reflection of our own society as an organic whole.

Philanthrocapitalism as an ideological formation

Much of the literature on post-politics is avowedly 'post-Marxist' in its rejection of the political and conceptual privileging of class struggle. Chantal Mouffe's understanding of the post-political has been particularly influential in this regard (Mouffe 2005; 2009; and see Jaeger and Loftus, Chapters 10 and 11, respectively, in this volume). Mouffe's approach is rooted in her 'radical democracy' project with

Ernesto Laclau, according to which there is no natural order or essential ground to society, and class is just one (increasingly insignificant) political identity amongst the postmodern profusion of differences (Laclau and Mouffe 1985). Žižek endorses this post-foundationalist ontology, and his early work was explicitly identified with the radical democracy project (Žižek 1989). His subsequent embrace of Marxism, however, has led Žižek to criticise Laclau and Mouffe's approach for rejecting the enduring significance of class struggle, and thus naturalising global capitalism as the horizon of our political possibilities (Žižek 2000a; Daly 2009). Rather than asserting an essentialist understanding of class as the foundation of social order, however, Žižek conceptualises class as the constitutive antagonism that perpetually undermines any such order (Žižek 2000b: 316–26). Class is not just another identity in the pluralistic play of differences, but is the void around which society perpetually strives to organise itself. From this perspective, the primary function of post-politics is the suturing of class antagonism, through a variety of ideological mechanisms that prevent or displace its political articulation.

In response to Laclau and Mouffe's denial of the relevance of class struggle in the post-political era, Žižek argues that, 'The very absence of struggle and resistance – the fact that both sides involved in [capitalist social] relations accept them without resistance – *is already the index of the victory of one side in the struggle*' (Žižek 2000b: 320, emphasis in original). Philanthrocapitalism can be understood as a form of class struggle in this sense, to the extent that it operates to foreclose the political articulation of the struggle itself. In *Philanthrocapitalism*, Bishop and Green explicitly frame the project in these terms, as a strategy to legitimate the intensification of inequality that has accompanied globalisation, in order to prevent a return to the redistributive policies of the welfare state. They warn that if 'the rich' are not seen to be sufficiently generous, 'they risk provoking the public into a political backlash against the economic system that allowed them to become so wealthy' (Bishop and Green 2008: 11). This danger is well understood by '[t]he leading beneficiaries of the winner-takes-all society, [who] worry increasingly about the political risks of growing inequality and are concluding that philanthropy may be one of the best ways to manage those risks' (2008: 20). Discussing the previous 'golden ages' of philanthropy, in Victorian Britain and the pre-New Deal USA, Bishop and Green note that 'Each past boom in giving was associated with massive wealth creation . . . accompanied by political unrest that seemed to threaten capitalism, adding urgency to the need for a philanthropic response' (2008: 21). They accept that the welfare state was a political necessity during the period of actually existing communism, as this was 'the only way of buying off the working class to defeat the revolutionary appeal of the growing socialist movement' (2008: 26). The contemporary moment, however, is celebrated as a 'new golden age of capitalism', in which state retrenchment 'has made space for the philanthrocapitalists' to engage in charitable acts that replace the social functions of the state (2008: 27).

Bishop and Green set out the political agenda of philanthrocapitalism in unambiguous terms. No critical tools are required to demonstrate that it *is* a class strategy. However, the question of *how* it functions as such is rather more complex. There is, I suggest, something obscene in the ideological formation of philanthrocapitalism, in which the spectacle of global inequality is not so much discursively concealed as viscerally *enjoyed*. This indicates that philanthrocapitalism operates ideologically through a specific mobilisation of what Žižek calls *jouissance*. Žižek's conceptualisation of *jouissance* is drawn from Lacanian psychoanalysis, and cannot be reduced to our commonsense understanding of 'enjoyment'. *Jouissance* is better understood as the raw libidinal energy of the bodily drives, which is only experienced as enjoyment when structured by specific fantasies that underpin our sense of reality. Our constitution as subjects in early childhood occurs through abandoning the realm of unmediated *jouissance* at the unsymbolised level of the Real, and entering the Symbolic order of language, from within which *jouissance* can only ever be experienced in mediated form, via fantasies located in the Imaginary register, which structure our enjoyment in specific ways.[2] From beyond the realm of the Symbolic, however, *jouissance* continues to exert a powerful hold over the subject, as an obscure source of enjoyment that is both compelling and potentially horrifying in its alien material persistence (Žižek 1997: 55–106; Braunstein 2003; Declercq 2004). Žižek's most original contribution to the critique of ideology has been to demonstrate how, beneath the articulation of discourses, the organisation of institutions, and the arrangement of social relations, *jouissance* is mobilised and regulated through disavowed social fantasies that structure relations of domination in ways that displace or foreclose their constitutive antagonism.

It is from this perspective that philanthrocapitalism can be grasped as an ideological formation, which projects a profoundly conservative semblance of natural order and shared purpose onto the increasingly diffuse and unequal societies of contemporary capitalism, through post-political discourses and institutional structures underpinned by a specific economy of *jouissance*. The following sections discuss the organisation of *jouissance* around a spectacle of philanthrocapitalist largesse, in which the populations of Western nations are invited to identify with the philanthrocapitalist against the unbearable *jouissance* of the African Other, and to enjoy an Imaginary reflection of the wholeness and unity of Western capitalist societies.

The warm glow of canned giving

The most overt form in which *jouissance* is mobilised in philanthrocapitalism is in the 'warm glow' that is said to accompany acts of charity. In *Philanthrocapitalism*, Bishop and Green emphasise the significance of this experience, claiming that philanthropy produces 'the dopamine-mediated euphoria often associated with sex, money, food, and drugs' (Bishop and Green 2008: 39). Their descriptions of philanthrocapitalist activity are saturated with language suggestive of (distinctly gendered) enjoyment. The philanthrocapitalist 'pours billions of dollars of his spectacular earnings . . .', 'grows an even bigger pile to give away . . .', and 'gets the maximum bang from every one of the billions of bucks at his disposal . . .' (2008: 41, 52). Reporting on Shakira's performance at a philanthrocapitalist 'debate-cum-party, screened live on MTV', Bishop and Green tell us that 'Shakira's hips don't lie – and Bill Clinton can't take his eyes off them. Nor, to be fair, can most of the audience' (2008: 8). Their description of Bill Gates 'rocking back and forth in his chair as he gets excited about . . . ending disease and reducing poverty' (2008: 3–4) again conveys a certain enjoyment. This enjoyment is also evident in Gates's own language in an interview with *The New Yorker*:

> 'You think in philanthropy your dollars will just be marginal, because the really juicy obvious things will all have been taken. So you look at this stuff and we are, like, '*Wow!* . . .We can save many lives for hundreds of dollars each . . .' It's fun, and it's also an enormous responsibility. (Quoted in Specter 2005)

The enjoyment implicit in this description of saving human lives as 'fun' and 'juicy' is sanctioned by *The New Yorker*'s celebratory portrait of Gates, while Bishop and Green conclude their discussion of 'the warm, fuzzy feeling' by dismissing criticism of such motivations and turning to the philanthrocapitalists with a nudge and a wink: 'Oh, go on. *Just enjoy it*' (Bishop and Green 2008: 42–3, emphasis added). These invocations of the *jouissance* of the philanthrocapitalists in the popular media function ideologically by inviting the populations of Western nations to participate vicariously in their enjoyment. Žižek conceptualises such forms of experience-through-another in terms of 'interpassivity' or 'substitution', which he explains with reference to canned laughter – when we come home tired from work and watch a comedy show, the television laughs on our behalf, and at the end of the programme we feel the relief associated with laughter, despite the fact that we may not have laughed ourselves (Žižek 1997: 140–4). In a homologous way, when popular audiences are offered spectacular mediatised representations of philanthrocapitalist largesse, appealing to ideals of sacrifice and salvation, yet saturated with the language and imagery of enjoyment, they are being encouraged to vicariously experience the warm glow of charitable giving enjoyed by the philanthrocapitalists, as if the audience themselves had given. In Bishop and Green's account, as we have seen, the MTV audience are united with Bill Clinton and the attendant philanthropists in their shared fixation on Shakira's hips, while following Warren Buffet's donation of US$31 billion to the Gates Foundation, we are told that 'the two tycoons smiled and shook hands *as the crowd cheered wildly*' (Bishop and Green 2008: 1, emphasis added). Similarly, Jeffrey Sachs tells his audience 'not to blame the rich for the poverty of the poor' (Sachs 2007), encouraging us to enjoy the spectacle of their 'transformative billionaire philanthropy' (Sachs 2008: 327), while joining him in marvelling at their luxurious lifestyles and their vast accumulated wealth:

> There are now around 950 billionaires in the world, with an estimated combined wealth of $3.5 trillion. That's an amazing $900 billion in just one year. Even after all the yachts, mansions, and luxury living that money can buy have been funded many times over, these billionaires will still have nearly $3.5 trillion to change the world ... All in all, it's not a bad job for men and women who have already transcended the daily economic struggle faced by the rest of humanity! (Sachs 2008: 327–8)

Just as we are encouraged to vicariously enjoy the wealth of the philanthrocapitalists, we are equally invited to experience extreme poverty through their eyes. In a widely acclaimed MTV documentary, Jeffrey Sachs escorts Angelina Jolie on a visit to a Millennium Village in Kenya. Images of African poverty and disease are spliced with intimate studio footage of Jolie directly addressing the audience. At one point we are treated to the spectacle of the highest-paid female actor in Hollywood (Child 2011) encountering an impoverished old woman, who is digging in a field. The translator tells Jolie that the old woman 'eats only when people have sympathy with her and give her a little flour or a little maize. If she doesn't eat then she just sleeps.' The documentary then shows Sachs and Jolie laughing as they till the soil alongside her with makeshift hoes, before cutting to Jolie in the studio, smiling radiantly into the camera as if talking confidentially to a friend: 'I'm a city girl, I got some blisters. Yeah, it's embarrassing'. The old woman is not seen or heard of again. The documentary thus presents a seductive confection of human tragedy and complacent frivolity, in which the audience is invited to participate in the emotional highs and lows of the celebrity philanthropist, in contrast to the abject suffering of the African Other.[3]

The Thing called 'Africa'

Africa is the favoured site for philanthrocapitalist development initiatives, which reproduce familiar colonial tropes in their representation of the continent as an abject space in contrast to the peace and prosperity of the West (Mbembe 2001: 1–3). In his promotion of philanthropy, Jeffrey Sachs depicts Africa as 'a place of unrelieved crisis' in which people are 'hungry, thin and ill' (Sachs 2005b: 210, 227). *The New Yorker*'s portrait of Bill Gates similarly describes Africa as a land in which 'hundreds of millions of children, and almost as many adults, suffer needlessly from illnesses that most people in the West have never heard of' (Specter 2005: 56). At a purely discursive level, such representations depoliticise global capitalism by displacing its contradictions into a putatively external space, and deny the political agency of Africans by reducing them to the status of suffering victims (Ferguson 2006; Comaroff 2007). At a deeper level, however, this representation of 'Africa' also mobilises specific forms of *jouissance* that reinforce its post-political functionality. Here it is important to emphasise that *jouissance* is not reducible to 'enjoyment' in the commonsense understanding of the term, but is a much more ambiguous phenomenon, which is experienced not only as intense pleasure, but also in the form of horror and revulsion, as 'a paradoxical pleasure procured by displeasure itself' (Žižek 1989: 202). This experience is often fixated on a specific object, which Lacan called the Thing – a phantasmatic object that comes to both terrify and fascinate the subject, through its apparent embodiment of an unbearable *jouissance* (Žižek 2002: 32). In the ideological structure of philanthrocapitalism, the Imaginary representation of 'Africa' functions in this way, as a Thing 'embodying horrifying *jouissance* . . . and as such an object which simultaneously attracts and repels us' (Žižek 1989: 180).

In *The Sublime Object of Ideology*, Žižek cites a story by Franz Kafka, which includes a graphic description of worms writhing in an open wound. Žižek draws our attention to the fascination that such images hold over us, suggesting that their horrifying appeal lies in the access they seem to offer to the essence of a pre-Symbolic *jouissance*, understood as 'the life-substance in its most radical dimension of meaningless enjoyment' (Žižek 1989: 76). This same fascination is discernible in philanthrocapitalist narratives addressing malaria as a cause of poverty. Despite poverty being the issue at hand, this literature often digresses into biological descriptions of malaria that communicate a similarly horrified experience of raw, unmediated *jouissance*, such as the following passage from *The New Yorker*'s portrait of Bill Gates:

> Anopheles mosquitoes require a meal of blood in order to lay their eggs – and they always feed at night . . . Once sporozoites enter the body, they glide into the bloodstream and travel to the liver, where they divide repeatedly. . . .. They then invade red blood cells and begin to feed on them, and within two weeks they will number thirty billion. (Specter 2005: 69)

Such representations take hold of their audience at the level of affect, rather than argument, and take the place of rational debate concerning alternative political-economic explanations of the causes of poverty. As Jeffrey Sachs put it, following a similarly detailed biological account of malaria, 'Africa has it bad intrinsically. Not because . . . its public health system is whatever, but because it has anopheles gambiae mosquitoes' (Sachs 2006). Such casual naturalisations of poverty are facilitated by the mobilisation of *jouissance* in the form of emotive representations of disease. This is further demonstrated by the representation of HIV/AIDS in philanthrocapitalist discourse, which appeals not to the unmediated *jouissance* of the virus itself, but to persistent colonial representation of Africa as a place of primal sexual enjoyment, according to which it is assumed that 'the colonized enjoy access to some hidden kernel of enjoyment that always eludes the colonizer's grasp' (Lane 2002: 194). This fantasy is mobilised by Bono's Product RED organisation, which donates a percentage of the profits of its branded products to the Global Fund to combat HIV/AIDS in Africa. As Richey and Ponte have argued, 'like fashion, rock music, or celebrity, AIDS is about money, power, and sex' (Richey and Ponte 2011: 68). Bono weaves these factors together in his promotion of RED, claiming in *Vanity Fair* to be bringing 'some sex appeal to the idea of wanting to change the world' (Bono, quoted in Richey and Ponte 2011: 69). In a more sober tone, Jeffrey Sachs raises the possibility in *The End of Poverty* 'that in Africa there is more sexual activity outside of long-term stable relationships' (Sachs 2005b: 200). Though acknowledging that 'the data . . . cast doubt on this widely believed hypothesis', he nevertheless goes on to assert that 'sexual networking is different in Africa, for example there are more relationships between older men and younger women and more concurrent relationships' (Sachs

2005b: 200). As in the case of malaria, this disavowed mobilisation of an enjoyment-of-the-Other stands in for rational argument, facilitating the execution of a post-political manoeuvre in which poor health is represented as a cause of extreme poverty rather than as its consequence (Sachs 2005b: 201).

The voyeurism implicit in sexualised representations of HIV/AIDS is equally evident in the philanthrocapitalist representation of extreme poverty, which indulges in the explicit images of starvation and disease criticised as 'poverty porn' (Selinger and Outterson 2009; Mooney and Hancock 2010). This term again indicates the mobilisation of *jouissance* within the ideological formation of philanthrocapitalism, suggesting that the audience of such representations does not merely empathise with the sufferer, but rather derives a certain disavowed pleasure from its proximity to the unbearable *jouissance* of the Other in its extreme and unknowable suffering. The voyeuristic power of poverty porn is mobilised in the first chapter of *The End of Poverty*, which Sachs introduces with a nightmarish description of a village in Malawi, including the following phrases:

> The presence of death . . . a lifetime of toil . . . withered crops that have died . . . a handful of semi-rotten, bug-infested millet . . . high fever . . . coma . . . horrific catastrophe . . . stunted from years of under-nutrition . . . strangers sharing a death bed . . . the room is full of moans . . . a dying chamber . . . swabbing dried lips . . . watching their loved ones die . . . (Sachs 2005b: 5–9).

As Žižek has noted in a different context, representations such as this construct 'a phantasmatic image of the Third World as Hell on Earth, as a place so utterly desolate that no political activity, only charity and compassion, can alleviate the suffering' (Žižek 1997: 24). As in the case of the biological descriptions of malaria discussed above, such representations operate at the level of affect rather than meaning, silencing critical thought with the demand to 'Act now!', which contains 'Don't think!' as an implicit injunction. They also reinforce the imagined unity of Western capitalist societies, in which billionaire philanthropists are united with the broader population in 'our' shared prosperity against the unknowable and unbearable *jouissance* of the African Other.

The mirror and the (w)hole

The enjoyment derived from such experiences of imagined wholeness and coherence constitutes a further dimension of *jouissance* within the ideological formation of philanthrocapitalism. This is reinforced by the representation of philanthrocapitalist development projects in Africa, which function as a mirror in which the social body of Western capitalism is reflected as a harmonious order cleansed of its constitutive antagonism. This corresponds to what Lacan calls the mirror-stage of childhood development, in which personal identity is first established. It is only through seeing its reflection in a mirror, or in the gaze of an Other, that a child first formulates its understanding of itself as a unified and distinct subject, and this initial experience of self-identity is replete with narcissistic *jouissance* (Bailly 2009: 28–40; Bohm and Batta 2010: 356). Similarly, in the form of its development interventions, philanthrocapitalism reflects an idealised image of capitalist society back onto itself, contributing to the formation of its own narcissistic self-image. This is evident in the philanthrocapitalist enthusiasm for development projects that construct individuals in the philanthropist's favoured self-image as a self-made entrepreneur – hence the popularity amongst philanthrocapitalists of micro-credit programmes, business training schemes, and entrepreneurship awards (Bishop and Green 2008: 127, 132, 181).

More significant in terms of the broader ideological formation of philanthrocapitalism, however, are projects such as the Millennium Villages, which operate not only to produce entrepreneurial individuals, but to engineer entire social orders based on an image of capitalist society undisturbed by the rupture of class antagonism. Model villages have held a peculiar attraction for philanthropists since the nineteenth century, when British capitalists constructed utopian settlements in which to house their workers, and colonial philanthropists established model communities in Africa (Bishop and Green 2008: 177, 191). The consistent objective of such projects has been to produce a model society in which the contradictions of capitalism are to be resolved without the transformation of capitalist social relations. The Millennium Villages Project continues this tradition, aiming to create an idealised model of capitalist society in eighty villages with a combined population of approximately 500,000 inhabitants, organised in fourteen clusters across ten countries in sub-Saharan Africa (Millennium Villages Project 2011). The objective of the Project is to demonstrate the viability of Jeffrey Sachs's strategy for achieving the Millennium Development Goals, as set out in his bestselling manifesto, *The End of Poverty*. The Project includes an integrated set of development interventions that aims to raise the villagers' levels of human, social, natural, physical and financial capital to the point at which self-sustained growth can be achieved (Sanchez et al. 2007). This strategy is premised on the assumption that 'If every village has a road, access to transport, a clinic, and other essential inputs, the villagers in poor countries will show the same determination and entrepreneurial zeal of people all over the world' (Millennium Project 2005: 15). Yet rather than exacerbating the inequalities on which capitalism is premised, Sachs insists that the profits resulting from this eruption of 'entrepreneurial zeal' will be reinvested in the community, as 'The poor . . . are ready to govern themselves responsibly, ensuring that any help they receive is used for the benefit of the group rather than pocketed by powerful individuals' (Sachs 2005b: 242).

The assumption of a universal entrepreneurial spirit and the representation of poor African villages as egalitarian communities are of course profoundly problematic in themselves (Oya 2010; Mueller 2011). When confronted by such phantasmatic scenes, however, Žižek suggests that we should not immediately seek to challenge them with an alternative account of 'reality', but should first ask for whom they are being staged (Žižek 1997: 21). The obvious response in this case is that the Millennium Villages are staged for the narcissistic enjoyment of the philanthrocapitalists themselves. After all, the image of hardworking entrepreneurs ready to reinvest their profits for the good of the community is precisely the story that philanthrocapitalism likes to tell about itself. Yet I would suggest that the Millennium Villages are primarily staged as an Imaginary mirror held up before the gaze of Western capitalist societies, in which their populations are invited to enjoy a reflection of capitalist social relations in which the traumatic rupture of their own class antagonism is sutured by a fantasy of rural village harmony. As such, the Millennium Villages embody what Žižek, following Rancière, calls archi-politics, the attempt 'to define a traditional close, organically structured homogenous social space that allows for no void in which the political moment-event can emerge' (Žižek 1999: 224).

It is on the basis of such fantasies that philanthrocapitalism is able to construct its more grandiose utopian visions. Writing in *The Times* in 2005, Jeffrey Sachs imagines Africa in 2025, after the Millennium Villages Project has been implemented on a continental scale. Africa is now fully 'developed', and its modern science facilities have just saved the world from a deadly virus:

The Rwandan President . . . praised her country's scientists, declaring: 'From the heart of darkness has come light' . . . Songs of thanks . . . reverberated through the churches, mosques, temples, and city plazas of the world. The most popular of these was the classic 'One', written decades earlier by U2's Bono: 'We're one but we're not the same, We get to carry each other, carry each other . . .' Yes, the world was one interconnected whole . . . (Sachs 2005a).

Bishop and Green conclude *Philanthrocapitalism* with an alternative but entirely complementary vision of the world in 2025. The philanthrocapitalists are celebrating Bill Gates's seventieth birthday in Richard Branson's 'luxury eco-friendly space mansion':

> From above, planet Earth has never looked better, and . . . back on the ground things look pretty good too . . . Gates has helped to save millions of lives and . . . has also inspired many of the world's growing army of billionaires . . . to join him . . . to tackle some of the biggest problems facing humanity . . . Gates feels justifiably proud of what he and his philanthrocapitalist friends have achieved . . . Smiling, Gates gazes at the shining planet before him . . . (Bishop and Green 2008: 253–4)

Like the Millennium Villages, each of these visions presents an image of global capitalism stripped of its constitutive antagonism, holding up 'utopia as a mirror, reflecting back from an imaginary elsewhere the qualities that allow it to . . . be taken in by its own form' (Clarke 2011: 952). For Sachs, Africa is no longer a 'heart of darkness', while for Bishop and Green the world is a harmonious globe seen from the God-like perspective of the philanthrocapitalists in their space-mansion. What this vision disavows, of course, is the howling void of deep space that separates the philanthrocapitalists from planet Earth. In their denial of the void of class antagonism, such utopias are inherently reactionary. As Jodi Dean has pointed out, 'Rather than beginning from a universality posited from a point of exclusion, from antagonism or class struggle . . . right-wing politics attempts to restore a ruptured society to its original unity' (Dean 2006: 126). Indeed, this fantasy of a capitalist society divested of class antagonism – of 'capitalism without capitalism' (Žižek 2002: 131) – is for Žižek the defining feature of fascism, which similarly seeks to suture real social antagonisms through appeal to the collective *jouissance* of an imagined unity, 'in order to legitimize the continuation of relations of social domination' (Žižek: 1999: 217). This is not to suggest that philanthrocapitalism is in any way 'fascist'. But it does indicate the reproduction of certain ideological structures within the putatively 'post-ideological' universe of global capitalism.

Conclusion

Philanthrocapitalism contributes to broader processes of post-politicisation, through its transition of authority from elected to non-elected bodies; its reduction of development to a technocratic exercise divorced from political-economic structures; its construction of the recipients of development as sufferers rather than agents; its populist appeal to celebrity leaders; and its articulation of apocalyptic discourses that foreclose political contestation. Beyond identifying these generically post-political dimensions of philanthrocapitalism, however, my analysis endorses the analytical and political utility of a specifically Žižekian conceptualisation of post-politics. Against Laclau and Mouffe's rejection of the continued significance of class struggle, the case of philanthrocapitalism supports Žižek's conceptualisation of class as the antagonistic rupture at the heart of post-political order. Equally, the example of philanthrocapitalism indicates the significance of Žižek's theorisation of enjoyment as a post-political factor, by demonstrating the ideological mobilisation of *jouissance* as the substance that is suturing this void.

The significance of *jouissance* within the ideological formation of philanthrocapitalism raises the question of 'how we are to relate to enjoyment, how we can ... traverse the fantasies that provide it, even as we acknowledge enjoyment as an irreducible component of what it is to be human' (Dean 2006: 43). The problem, as Terry Eagleton has put it, is that 'ideological power rests finally on the libidinal rather than the conceptual, on the way we hug our chains rather than the way we entertain beliefs' (cited in Sharpe 2004: 32). Yet the solution cannot be to divest ourselves of enjoyment itself, as *jouissance* is existentially inescapable. According to psychoanalytic theory, we can only hope to understand the ways in which *jouissance* is being mobilised and regulated, and in doing so, to open the possibility of transforming our relations to it (Declerq 2004: 247). Rather than bathing in the reflected glow of philanthrocapitalist largesse, we could begin by returning to Robert Tressell's simple insight, made over a century ago in *The Ragged Trousered Philanthropists*. Tressel points out that, under capitalism, the true philanthropists are the working classes of the world, and the true beneficiaries of their charitable giving – in the form of surplus value – are the capitalists, who even appropriate the moral garb of philanthropy for themselves (Tressell 2005). The enduring validity of this insight calls for a renewed politics of radical egalitarianism, through which a reimagining and redistribution of enjoyment becomes possible. This implies the abolition of philanthropy through fidelity to its true meaning: *philos-anthropos, love of humanity*. One possible name for such a politics is 'communism':

> Future forms of the politics of emancipation must be inscribed in a resurrection, a re-affirmation, of the Communist idea, the idea of a world that isn't given over to the avarice of private property, a world of free

association and equality . . . In such a framework, it will be easier to re-invent love than if surrounded by the capitalist frenzy. (Badiou 2012: 72–3)

Notes

1. *http://www.philanthrocapitalism.net/* (accessed 10 April 2012).
2. As in the case of 'enjoyment', Lacanian 'fantasy' is radically different from the commonsense meaning of the term, as Žižek explains: 'Fantasy does not simply realize a desire in a hallucinatory way: rather . . . it provides a schema according to which certain positive objects in reality can function as objects of desire . . . to put it in somewhat simplified terms: fantasy does not mean that when I desire a strawberry cake and cannot get it in reality, I fantasise about eating it; the problem is, rather; *how do I know that I desire a strawberry cake in the first place?* This is what fantasy tells me" (Žižek 1997: 7).
3. The documentary is entitled *MTV Diary: Angelina Jolie and Dr Jeffrey Sachs in Africa.* It was first aired in 2005. It can be watched online at *http://www.youtube.com/watch?v=uUHf_kOUM74* (accessed 19 April 2012).

References

Badiou, A. (2012), *In Praise of Love*, London: Serpent's Tail.
Bailly, L. (2009), *Lacan*, Oxford: Oneworld.
Bishop, M., and M. Green (2008), *Philanthrocapitalism: How the Rich Can Save the World and Why We Should Let Them*, London: A. & C. Black.
Bohm, S., and A. Batta (2010), 'Just doing it: enjoying commodity fetishism with Lacan', *Organization*, 17, pp. 345–61.
Bosworth, D. (2011), 'The cultural contradictions of philanthrocapitalism', *Society*, 48, pp. 382–88.
Braunstein, N. (2003), 'Desire and jouissance in the teachings of Lacan', in J.-M. Rabate (ed.), *The Cambridge Companion to Lacan*, Cambridge: Cambridge University Press, pp. 102–15.
Child, B. (2011), 'Angelina Jolie and Sarah Jessica Parker ranked Hollywood's richest women', *The Guardian*, 6 July.
Clarke, D. B. (2011), 'Utopologies', *Environment and Planning D: Society and Space*, 29: 6, pp. 951–67.
Comaroff, J. (2007), 'Beyond bare life: AIDS, (Bio)politics, and the neoliberal order', *Public Culture*, 19:1.
Daly, G. (2009), 'Politics of the political: Psychoanalytic theory and the Left(s)', *Journal of Political Ideologies*, 14: 3 pp. 279–300.
Dean, J. (2006), *Žižek's Politics*, New York: Routledge.
Declercq, F. (2004), 'Lacan's concept of the real of jouissance: Clinical

illustrations and implications', *Psychoanalysis, Culture and Society*, 9, pp. 237–51.

Desai, R., and H. Kharas (2008), 'The California consensus: Can private aid end global poverty?', *Survival: Global Politics and Strategy*, 50: 4, pp. 155–68.

Edwards, M. (2009) 'Gates, Google, and the ending of global poverty: philanthrocapitalism and international development', *Brown Journal of International Affairs*, 15: 2, pp. 35–42.

Edwards, M. (2011), 'Impact, accountability, and philanthrocapitalism', *Society*, 48, pp. 389–90.

Ferguson, J. (2006), *Global Shadows: Africa in the Neoliberal World Order*, Durham: Duke University Press.

Jenkins, G. W. (2011), 'Who's afraid of philanthrocapitalism?', *Moritz College of Law Working Paper Series no. 149*.

Laclau, E., and C. Mouffe (1985), *Hegemony and Socialist Strategy*, London: Verso.

Lane, J. F. (2002), 'The stain, the impotent gaze, and the theft of jouissance: Towards a Žižekian reading of Robbe-Grillet's La Jalousie', *French Studies*, 56: 2, pp. 193–206.

Mbembe, A. (2001), *On the Postcolony*, Berkeley: University of California Press.

Millennium Project (2005), *Investing in Development: A Practical Plan to Achieve the Millennium Development Goals*, New York: United Nations Development Programme.

Millennium Villages Project (2011), *Millennium Villages Project: The Next Five Years: 2011–2015*, New York: Millennium Villages Project.

Mooney, G., and L. Hancock (2010), 'Poverty porn and the broken society', *Variant*, 39/40, pp. 14–17.

Mouffe, C. (2005), *On the Political*, New York: Routledge.

Mouffe, C. (2009), 'Democracy in a multipolar world', *Millennium*, 37, pp. 549–61.

Mueller, B. E. T. (2011), 'The agrarian question in Tanzania: Using new evidence to reconcile an old debate', *Review of African Political Economy*, 38: 127, pp. 23–42.

Oya, C. (2010), 'Rural labour markets in Africa: The unreported source of inequality and poverty', *Development Viewpoint*, 57.

Ramdas, K. (2011), 'Philanthrocapitalism: reflections on politics and policy making, *Society*, 48.

Rancière, J. (2010), *Dissensus: On Politics and Aesthetics*, London: Continuum.

Richey, L. A., and S. Ponte (2011), *Brand Aid: Shopping Well to Save the World*, Minneapolis: University of Minnesota Press.

Rogers, R. (2011), 'Why philanthro-policymaking matters', *Society*, 48, pp. 376–81.

Sachs, J. (2005a), 'How Africa lit up the world', *The Times*, 3 July.

Sachs, J. (2005b), *The End of Poverty: How We Can Make It Happen in Our Lifetime*, London: Penguin.

Sachs, J. (2006), 'The Millennium Villages Project: A new approach to ending poverty', Washington, DC: Centre for Global Development.

Sachs, J. (2007), 'The Forbes One Billion', forbes.com 10/08/2007, available at *http://www.forbes.com/forbes/2007/1008/094.html* (accessed 11 November 2011).

Sachs, J. (2008), *Common Wealth: Economics for a Crowded Planet*, London: Penguin.

Sanchez, P. et al. (2007), 'The African Millennium Villages', *Proceedings of the National Academy of Sciences*, 104: 43, pp. 16775–80.

Selinger, E., and K. Outterson (2009), 'The ethics of poverty tourism', *Boston University School of Law Working Paper no. 09–29*.

Sharpe, M. (2004), *Slavoj Žižek: A Little Piece of the Real*, Aldershot: Ashgate.

Specter, M. (2005), 'What money can buy', *The New Yorker*, 24 October, pp. 56–71.

Tressell, R. (2008), *The Ragged-Trousered Philanthropists*, Oxford: Oxford University Press.

Wilson, J. (2014), *Jeffrey Sachs: The Strange Case of Dr Shock and Mr Aid* London: Verso.

Žižek, S. (1989), *The Sublime Object of Ideology*, London: Verso.

Žižek, S. (1997), *The Plague of Fantasies*, London: Verso.

Žižek, S. (1999), *The Ticklish Subject: The Absent Centre of Political Ontology*, London: Verso.

Žižek, S. (2000a), 'Class struggle or postmodernism? Yes, please!', in J. Butler, E. Laclau, and S. Žižek, *Contingency, Hegemony, Universality*, London: Verso, pp. 90–135.

Žižek, S. (2000b), 'Holding the place', in J. Butler, E. Laclau and S. Žižek, *Contingency, Hegemony, Universality*, London: Verso, pp. 308–29.

Žižek, S. (2002), *Welcome to the Desert of the Real*, London: Verso.

Žižek, S. (2008), *Violence*, London: Profile.

6   Religious Antinomies of Post-Politics

Bülent Diken

... if it is true that God is the place where humans think through their decisive problems ... (Agamben 2011a: 4)

... the criticism of religion is the first premise of all criticism. (Marx 1957: 41)

When much is written about a phenomenon, when it appears to occupy a central position in thought, it is often a sure sign that the phenomenon is about to vanish, illuminating, like a dead star, in the very process of disappearing. One could say that, along the same lines, the concept of 'post-politics' gestures towards articulating a vision of a disappearance of 'politics' in its radical sense, as the attempt to change society. Indeed interest in 'politics' in this sense has been absent in the philosophical and social scientific discourses, except, that is, in the works of a few leftist philosophers such as Badiou, Negri, Rancière and Žižek. Did their efforts not signify the last, cramp-like movements of a dying concept?

The paradox, however, is that we live as ever in a world saturated with enormous conflicts and misery, and that there is all the more reason to criticise existing and emerging forms of oppression and injustice. After all, if we look at the contemporary world through the prism of radical politics, what we see is precisely a more or less permanent 'revolutionary situation' characterised by the co-existence of extreme poverty and extreme wealth. What needs to be explained in such a world is stability rather than destabilising tendencies; why nothing happens, or, why the counter-revolution has been so stable and so strong.

Yet that which has disappeared often returns. Hence phenomena considered to be far away, 'historical', or even dead are constantly knocking on our doors, catching us unprepared and perplexed. Were we not told, for instance, more than a few times, that modernity means increasing secularisation, that it inevitably brings with it the disappearance of religion from the political, social and cultural scene? But seen in the prism of contemporary troubles, if there is anything that has not disappeared, it is religion, to the extent that our 'civilization' today defines itself with reference to religion, accepting it as the main yardstick to differentiate itself from others.

Hence my main argument: the resurgence of religion (and religious violence) is not an exception to the post-political order. While I discuss this, I also maintain that post-politics is a problematical concept. One can neither refer to an original 'politics' nor to a past that is simply 'post'. The post-political condition *is* an ideological fiction. Exactly for this reason, however, the concept illuminates some essential paradoxes that define the contemporary political imaginary. Fiction, after all, functions as a support for the real. Therefore I start by considering some of the paradoxes that become visible in the horizon of post-political society. The pivot around which this discussion is organised is the sovereignty-governmentality-visibility nexus. In this context I am especially interested in the relationship between sovereignty and governmentality, which, I argue, takes the form of a disjunctive synthesis. Then, to articulate the religious motives that are constitutive of this paradoxical relationship, I turn to political and economic theology. To finish, I discuss capitalism as religion, linking this back to the concept of post-politics.

Post-politics as revision

If politics is politicisation, that is, the ongoing critique of what exists, post-politics designates a political way of emptying out the political. In this sense post-politics is a particular, particularly banalised form of politics in which already recognised groups compete and negotiate interests without challenging the hegemonic relations in a given political constellation. Politics as game-playing without the possibility of changing the game. Thus consensus is the essence of post-politics, provided that 'consensus' is not thought of only as the avoidance of conflict. At a deeper level, it is an agreement regarding the terms of disagreement (see Rancière 2010: 144). That is, consensus allows one to have different opinions, to disagree, criticise, but only in a given framework of sensibility, which is effectively justified each time such permitted critique takes place. This is also why the ultimate target of radical politics is this framework itself; not playing a given game, indulging in its officially recognised transgressions, but changing the game itself. Politics is a process of separation, of dis-identification, vis-à-vis a given framework of the sensible. To politicise is to open up a space for what can be said, seen and thought otherwise. Only then there transpires a new sociality that is in excess of what already exists.

Crucially, the banalisation of politics in the 'post-political' society occurs against the background of a ban. This ban, the single most important imperative of today's dominant ideology, is encapsulated by Badiou in three words: 'live without Idea' (2009: 511). But social life can become a 'problematic', that is, an object of critique and change, only on the condition that people can imagine the possibility of a different society. 'All . . . events belong to the class of possibilities, which are not present in daily reality in any other way but ideally' (Bauman 1976: 35). 'Idea', in other words, is that which enables us to contemplate our present condition in the prism of the possible, without which social life would turn into bare repetition.

Ultimately, therefore, the term post-politics designates a society that cannot imagine radical events. This is, to use a forgotten expression, its counter-revolutionary aspect. After all, the straightforward aspect of all counter-revolutionary thought is its definition of the existing world as an invariant and its direct opposition to ideas that promise another world. But in a second, more sinister and more interesting sense, counter-revolution signifies the revision, internal perversion of, rather than opposition to, ideas. It designates not merely an external force but a strategic field of formation in which the struggle revolves around appropriating, accommodating and revising ideas and principles. In this second sense, post-politics knows that 'life without idea' is an absurd idea. Counter-revolution does not necessarily mean to extinguish creativity and critique as such, but it means docile critique without consequences.

Indeed, the history of modernity is the history of how the founding concepts of modern revolutions, starting with the French Revolution, are appropriated and revised, thereby suppressed, by capitalism and the state. The way the concepts of freedom, equality and fraternity have been captured forms the problematique of post-politics, or, contemporary democracy.

Following Badiou, the main axiom of contemporary democracy is: 'there are only bodies and languages' (Badiou 2009: 1, 34). This democracy recognises only bio-political bodies as objective existence, without a virtual, metaphysical dimension to their being. Yet, this 'materialist' consensus is also 'democratic', for it recognises the plurality of languages, cultures. Concomitantly, its vision is limited to relations between 'bodies' and 'languages', without any attempt at incorporating within the narrative a political truth. As such, contemporary democracy is an 'atonic' world in which time collapses into a permanent present, a bare repetition that consists of a succession of disconnected 'episodes' (Badiou 2009: 121, 420). This post-political democracy reduces freedom to a negative rule, the rule of what exists, in the sense that one can speak of freedom only insofar as no cultural prohibition prevents individual bodies from actualising their capacities (Badiou 2009: 34). Consequently, freedom often appears as an effect of governmentality. A similar fate meets the concept of equality. Thus the demand for equality is often reduced to a demand for 'more' in a taken-for-granted system of distribution, without restructuring the social space itself. Further, as the concepts of freedom and equality are internally perverted in democratic materialism, the concept of fraternity is subsumed under the concept of community (Badiou 2008: 148). It, too, has become a governmental term through which particular communal substances (ethnic, consumptional, sexual, religious and so on) are constantly classified, mapped and re-mapped (see Rose 1999: 175–7).

What is significant here is that governmentality implies an infinite 'plurality' of what is to be governed and perceives what is to be governed as 'specific finalities' (Foucault 1991: 95). In this sense post-politics deals with 'bodies and languages' as a matter of managing the 'infinity of finite things' (Dillon 2011), of finitudes, without allowing these finitudes to universalise themselves.

Post-political governmentality reduces singularities, which refer to infinity, to finite particularities, to 'bodies and languages' only. For the same reason, it does not oppose but asks for constant critique. In a knowledge-based 'control society' one never finishes learning; on the contrary, 'continuous assessment' becomes an imperative (Deleuze 1995: 179). Thus everybody is invited, encouraged and forced to continually assess and revise their particular empirical position. Obsessed with the question of distribution of particular identities, post-political governmentality is preoccupied with 'critique'. Not with radical, emancipatory critique, but with revisionist critique – critique as continuous revision, revision as disseminated critique – which flattens transcendent idea(l)s, reducing singularity to particularity, universality to generality, and dissensus to a consensus-generating dispositif. A 'critique', which paradoxically consolidates what exists. This is why nothing really changes while everything and anything is constantly criticised in post-political society. Ours is a society in which critique (of critique of critique . . .) of the system is a component of the system itself. Moreover, this 'critique' has a pre-emptive effect regarding radical critique for it functions like the recent police tactic, 'kettling', a device to contain within barriers the mobility of a demonstration, preventing its massification. In 'continuous' critique one is continuously kettled; one's critique never reaches the dimension of a universality but remains organised, regulated and controlled in its own particularity.

Post-politics as political theology

But this is not the whole story. Despite its negation of 'the political', of antagonistic politics, post-politics is not unrelated to it. Rather, it seems as if the lack of antagonism in post-political society is countered with an excess of antagonism. So, we are witnessing in post-politics also the revival of sovereignty as a radical, ultra-political version of the disavowal of the political by depoliticising conflicts via direct militarisation of politics and sublimation of order as an absolute value in the Schmittian sense (see Žižek 1999). When politics is foreclosed, bare life becomes the main object of politics. Sovereign violence and post-politics are thus complementary ideological operations (Žižek 2008: 34). This uneasy relationship, it seems to me, is mediated around three obligatory points of passage: a domesticated, trivialised version of messianism; a paradoxical form of violence; and a new, revised rendering of Orientalism.

First a few words on post-political messianism. As is well known, the key image of thought in the war against terror, the trademark of contemporary post-politics, is 'clash', the clash of civilisations and of religions. In this prism Western power is perceived to be essentially different from and opposed to Islamic fundamentalism. The West is either understood as a secular society obsessed with consumerism (Barber 1996) or as a humanistic version of the Christian faith (Huntington 1997): it is, in both cases, a civilised, non-antagonistic and non-crusading civilisation that counters a barbaric version of Islam. Islamic fundamentalism becomes, in this context, a synonym for chiliastic apocalypticism.

Hall (2009) provides a perfect example. His main point is that although apocalypticism has historically been a strong militant tendency in all three monotheistic religions, in the West, especially through the Reformation, it is 'tamed'. The protestant ethic brought with it an emphasis on worldly vocations and a religious accommodation of 'rationalized time' (Hall 2009: 84). Thus, wasting time turned into 'the first and in principle the deadliest of sins' (Weber 2003: 157). Consequently, articulated with chronological time, the apocalypse was 'secularized' in modernity (Hall 2009: 164). Salvation became a matter of individual faith. Modern governmentality has, in other words, pacified the 'apocalyptic tradition', in which Paul, Müntzer and Robespierre are included (Hall 2009: 195). In this perspective, contemporary Islamic terrorism, too, like Leftist terror and Marxist guerilla movements in the twentieth century, is an 'apocalyptically structured' ideology that insists on the sacred in a secularised world (Hall 2009: 164, 173).

Hall's narration is an illustration of how religion and terror are brought together in the horizon of contemporary post-politics, not only by glossing over decisive differences between the apocalyptic tradition and the contemporary fundamentalist terrorism, but also by mystifying the content of the 'taming' here – its historical links to counter-revolution. To discuss this, I am tempted to contrast the contemporary katechontic take on the apocalypse, which legitimises counter-revolution in general and the war on terror specifically, with Taubes's revolutionary eschatology, which seeks a total deligitimisation of power. In this framework the 'katechon' signifies the justification of power with reference to the divine, while the 'eschaton' stands for the endorsement of the divine with a view to resisting power. Taubes is a relevant figure in this respect, for while Schmitt's political theology elevates the katechon and thus evacuates the eschaton, Taubes's work marks the beginning of a response to Schmitt, informing the basis upon which one can contest the katechontic understanding of history. The relevance of this discussion is to point out the katechontic tendency inherent in the reduction of politics to the post-political logic of (economic) administration.

For Taubes (2009), the starting point of eschatological apocalypticism is the concept of alienation. In the existing world, injustice is abundant, and both man and God are alienated. Beyond *this* world, there is *that* other world, the world to come, which promises freedom. But this difference between *this* and *that* is not a blueprint for nihilistic escapism; rather, it implies a transvaluation in the properly Nietzschean sense, questioning the value of (existing) values with a view to seizing the untimely moment of an event to come, to creating a better world. And corresponding to the two sets of values, there are two Gods: the God of creation, of the existing world, and the God of redemption. The latter will come by annihilating the existing world. This God to come, who is *'new* to the world', is also a promise of a revolution, a 'turning point': he 'will annihilate the world and then appear in his might' (Taubes 2009: 10). Since freedom from what exists is its goal, revolution necessarily looks beyond *this* world. It brackets the actual order and existing beliefs, which are the foundations of the actual world. What is significant is that, in this tradition, spanning from the Gnostic theology to the Exodus to Maccebean revolt, the Zealots and Thomas Müntzer, the dialectic between *this* (natural) and *that* (supernatural) world interlock not in the heart of the individual, as a personalised faith, but as two different but interrelated systems, two 'kingdoms'. The 'moment when "this" world touches "that" world . . . is the *kairos*' (Taubes 2009: 68).

Eschatological intervention is always an 'untimely' undertaking, which consists in 'acting in a non-present fashion, therefore against time and even on time, in favour . . . of a time to come' (Nietzsche quoted in Deleuze 1983: 107). An intervention into time to change its course, with a view to bringing forth a new future; a 'suspension of time in expectation of a future always to come' (Dillon 2008: 13). As such, as a strategic decision which aims to seize the moment, *kairos* is opposed to chronological time. But it is not external to it. Rather, it is an 'operational' time internal to chronology, transforming it from within. *Kairos* is a 'seized' *chronos*, the time in which 'man' autonomously seizes the moment, 'chooses his own freedom', in opposition to chronological time (Agamben 2005: 69; 2007: 115). As the temporal dimension of the event, it signifies the timing of actualisation, that is, the recognition, articulation and the decision to actualise an event; a moment of opportunity, which can be seized by an untimely intervention on the basis of reading the symptoms, signs, available in a given situation.

To be sure, what we have in Taubes is a transcendent/theological philosophy which operates with concepts such as eternity, the God of redemption, and so on. But what is noteworthy is its structure, its understanding of revolution as a relation to the virtual infinity and of *kairos* as 'the mystery of the universe' (Taubes 2009: 68). However, it must be emphasised that this promissory aspect of *kairos* is not necessarily messianic in a religious sense; *kairos* is not the Messiah (see Dillon 2008: 14). Messianism is not necessarily a religious experience. Within the communist and democratic tradition there is a messianism which is not reducible to religion through any deconstruction; a messianism which consists in an experience of the 'emancipatory promise' (Derrida 1994: 74). This promise, according to Derrida, is an 'absolutely undetermined messianic hope', that is, its content is not, in contrast to religion, determined. It is a promise independent of the three monotheistic religions, even when they oppose one another, for it holds to the anti-nihilist belief that 'faith without religion' is possible (Derrida 2004).

The same structure can be endorsed from the point of view of power as well. Schmitt, for instance, the 'apocalyptician of counter-revolution' (Taubes quoted in Ratmoko 2009: xvi), puts *kairos* in the service of power, seeking a theological legitimation of the political. Thus, while the apocalyptic world-view seeks redemption in the 'end' of the world, Schmitt advocates *translatio imperii*, that is, the evolution of the Roman Empire into the Holy Roman Empire and the Third Reich. However, this worldly power cannot become 'holy', according to the apocalyptic tradition, for the holy is, precisely, the 'measure' of the God to come: 'The holy is the terror that shakes the foundations of the world. The shock caused by the holy . . . bursts asunder the foundations of the world for salvation' (Taubes 2009: 194).

In this radical sense, the idea of messianic apocalypse cannot be really assimilated by sovereignty. Thus it is revised and transformed. The Reformation, or 'Copernican Christianity' as Taubes (2009: 108) calls it, is 'modern' in the sense that it takes for granted the loss of heaven, of the idea that there is a heaven above the world in which the new God lives. But 'under an empty heaven', in a world in which the virtual collapses into the actual, to act for salvation becomes irrelevant – when salvation is reduced to the work of grace, which does not necessitate actors' active participation, 'man's fulfillment of the law becomes pointless' (Taubes 2009: 108). In other words, in the apocalyptic tradition, the dialectic between the actual and the virtual, the earth and heaven, is preserved; divine justice must be found, resurrected, in *this* world. In Copernican Christianity, by contrast, rebirth (resurrection) ceases to have a power to shape the actual world. When reconciliation is distinguished from redemption, when heaven and earth are separated as two distinct points of view, it becomes possible to envisage 'a secular world in which all spirituality is subordinated to, and defenseless against, worldly power' (Taubes 2009: 109).

Seen in this perspective, a double movement is visible: while it 'sacralizes' power through political theology, modernity also 'secularizes' eschatology, excluding it by accommodating it (Bradley and Fletcher 2010: 2). This tamed, decaffeinated version of eschatological apocalypse, fit for a passive nihilist society, is also the 'blind spot' of contemporary liberal democracy or post-politics. Consider Fukuyama's neo-evangelistic 'good news' that the 'end of history' has arrived, that all regimes in the world, including dictatorships, now evolve towards liberal democracy (1992: xii-xiii, 212). On the one hand, this thesis sacralises a particular, actual expression of temporal power, the market, turning it into the telos of history (Bradley and Fletcher 2010: 2). But on the other hand, this divinised liberal democracy is distinguished from its empirical manifestations, arguing that it is a 'trans-historical', that is, an infinite, virtual idea that cannot be reduced to its actual, finite manifestations or delegitimised by use of empirical evidence (see Fukuyama 1992: 139):

> *With the one hand*, it accredits a logic of the empirical event which it needs whenever it is a question of certifying the finally final defeat of . . . everything that bars access to the Promised Land of economic and political

liberalisms; but *with the other hand*, in the name of the trans-historic . . . ideal, it discredits this same logic of the so-called empirical event . . . to avoid chalking up to the account of this ideal and its concept precisely whatever contradicts them in such a cruel fashion: in a word, all the *evil*, all that is *not going well* in the capitalist States and in liberalism . . . (Derrida 1994: 86)

As such, the eschatology-lite does not really exclude the dialectic between the actual and the transcendent. Rather, it flattens it so that the 'idea' loses its power of destroying and transvaluating what exists, becoming instead the potentiality of an already sacralised liberal democracy. In a sense, Fukuyama is doing here to the 'trans-historical' idea what Schmitt did to the concept of exception, turning its revolutionary potentiality into a counter-revolutionary justification of the given. His novelty lies in using the tools of passive nihilism as well as political theology in this endeavour. Thus, while he sacralises the liberal democratic market, he also levels the transcendent ('heaven') and the actual (the 'earth') in a way that the idea of revolution, of something other than liberal democracy, becomes redundant. His is, in other words, a chiliasm without divine violence. And herein we arrive at the central paradox of post-political society:

On the one hand, it abolishes the eschatology and infinitely prolongs the history and the government of the world; on the other, it finds that the finite character of its paradigm returns ceaselessly . . . (Agamben 2011b: 163)

And for all its condemnation of violence, this tamed, secularised eschatology is not less violent than the revolutionary eschatology. The difference is not between violence and non-violence but between two forms of violence: the eschaton and the katechon.

A recent film, *The Hurt Locker,* can illustrate this point. Described variously as 'reckless', a 'rowdy boy' and a 'real wild man' by his colleagues, the protagonist, James, is motivated by a desire to break through numbness or narcosis in search of intense experience. He takes risks, drinks, smokes, listens to heavy metal music at high volume, is uncommunicative and so disliked by the other soldiers that they briefly discuss killing him. While the passive nihilist or 'post-political' society is obsessed with security, James is addicted to danger. Whereas this society opts for a decaf reality devoid of passions, James is ready to trade off the social bond for his passionate attachment, his addiction. Hence the bomb, the ultimate symbol of terror in a society of fear, is James's only object of fascination (see Bennett and Diken 2011).

Thus, in James, courage and obsession, risk and responsibility become indistinguishable. Throughout the film his lack of self-control progressively becomes a threat to everybody around him, culminating when he unnecessarily leads his men into the alleys of Baghdad at night on a speculative hunt for some bombers. Despite this, a commentator, Richard Corliss, writes that, 'the Army needs guys like James' (Corliss 2008). In a sense, therefore, James is the new 'Marlboro man': the soldier 'smoking while Iraq burns', an 'icon of American impunity' (Klein 2004). Significantly in this context, like Kurtz in *Apocalypse Now*, James in *The Hurt Locker* incarnates an obscene enjoyment which does not subordinate itself to any symbolic law (see Žižek 2005). Thus he dares to face the abyss of the real, in the form of war, as a terrorising *jouissance*. However, while both Kurtz and James are the excesses of the system, the system eliminates Kurtz because he challenges it politically and ethically. In stark contrast, in *The Hurt Locker* the system has nothing against James. Rather, the internal excess is justified and accommodated as a war hero. Consider the case of General Stanley McChrystal, the man who stayed in charge of the US mission in Afghanistan from June 2009 to June 2010:

> McChrystal . . . fashioned himself a 'bad-ass' early on in life. At the military academy he attended, he cultivated the art of insubordination, and was rewarded for it: when he got 100 hours of demerits, his classmates applauded him as a 'century man'. In the Bush administration, his willingness to go rogue in the name of accomplishing his objectives, and his commitment to ignoring niceties like the chain of command, the truth (he was accused of involvement in the cover-up of a friendly-fire incident) or the rules of engagement (he was connected to a prisoner-abuse scandal) were likewise rewarded. He was not disciplined; he was given Afghanistan. (Doyle 2010)

What we get here is a picture in which the lack of antagonistic politics is countered with the inherent excess of the system. In this way, despite seeking to expel violence from its system of values at a surface level, post-politics itself produces a paradoxical, ecstatic violence:

> a violence cut off from its object and turning back against that object itself – against the political and the social. It's no longer anarchistic or revolutionary . . . It's not interested in the system's internal contradictions; it targets the very principal of the social and the political. (Baudrillard 1998: 66)

This violence does not mirror a (political) conflict but the level of consensus; it produces no value, no object and no ends except the reproduction of (addiction to) violence. The culture of passive nihilism which James hates, its zeal for 'over-protection', leads to the loss of immunity; like redundant 'anti-bodies' that turn against the organism in which they live, James incarnates an auto-immune pathology of the system (see Baudrillard 2002: 93).

That brings us to another crucial aspect of the post-political political theology: its Orientalism. Recall the Arab Spring. When the world woke up to the unexpected revolts, it first supported the dictators in the name of stability. Tony Blair articulated this instant in his exemplary rhetoric when he described the Egyptian dictator, Mubarak, as 'immensely courageous and a force for good', warning against the possibility that a revolt might bring the Muslim fundamentalists to power (Blair in McGreal 2011). The question, for him, was how these countries were going to 'evolve and modernise, but do so with stability' (Blair in Sparrow 2011). This is of course ironic, outrageous and hypocritical: Blair is one of the few who legitimised the Iraq war with the promise of 'bringing democracy', that is, on the basis of an assumption that a revolution cannot come from below in the Muslim Orient. And precisely at the moment it came, in 2011, the first thing Blair did was instinctively to support the dictator.

But this is half the story. Gradually, the response of the establishment shifted from reacting to revising, to mystifying the spirit of the revolts. Thus it quickly translated the reason of the revolts into its own language: people's fight for 'democracy' under 'totalitarian' regimes and so on. And in this process the event was orientalised: the totalitarian despots versus their victims.

Let us therefore dwell on the concept of despotism. In its origin, in ancient Greece, the rule of the despot, *oikonomia*, designated a specific power relation that takes place only in the household, that is, in the domestic sphere. 'Political' power, in contrast, was seen as something that pertains to the city/polis, as a relationship between free men concerning the common good. In the household, the despot governs three kinds of subjects: his children, his wife and his slaves. Aristotle draws a parallel between the power relation between the despot and his children on the one hand and that between the king and his people on the other. The defining aspect of this parallel is that both relations are to the benefit of the ruled (people/children). To his wife, the despot relates as husband; not force but equality determines the terms of this 'democratic' relation which is beneficial for both parties. To his slaves, by contrast the despot relates as a tyrant or as a master, and since slaves are not free this relation is only to the benefit of the master.

On this account, the existence of the slave, that is the process of primitive accumulation, is the main reason why *oikonomia* cannot be political. But precisely such a displacement occurs in eighteenth-century Europe, when 'despotism' starts to signify perversion or abuse of regal power (the king ruling his 'people' as if they were his 'slaves'). As such, 'despotism' figuratively connotes a political way to pervert or depoliticise politics. Significantly, in the same period, the concept of despotism becomes the cornerstone in Orientalism, which perceives in the Orient a space of perversion that sustains a forbidden eroticism: the despot as the sole owner of all enjoyment, including the multitude of harem women (Grosrichard 1998: 141–6). A space in which everything exists for the despot, whose power terrifies and terrorises all his powerless subjects who are reduced to slaves and are motivated by fear rather than courage and individual will (Grosrichard 1998: 36–40). A system in which no separation of powers exists, where everything exists for and belongs to the Sultan and thus nothing has an independent being or existence (Grosrichard 1998: 55–70).

As such, the relationship between the West and the Orient is not merely that of a difference between two elements within the same space. Rather, the Orient signifies a ground zero, that which is prior to difference. Hence, the eunuch, not the woman, is the emblem of the Orient. Similarly, despotism is not merely a political form as monarchy, tyranny and democracy, but rather an *a*political 'formlessness'; the Orient is defined by the lack of form as such (Grosrichard 1998; Boer 1996: 46). It is a discursive representation of a space that cannot be represented, a space beyond the symbolic.

Herein lies, too, the phantasmatic background of the post-political imagination. While the very consistency of the contemporary society is marked by the link between sovereignty and post-politics, sovereignty is disavowed and externalised to the Orient in the formless form of 'despotism'. But this attempt always ends up in paradoxes: on the one hand, the post-political society is marketing liberal democracy as the best rule, which is based on 'freedom', and on the other, it presents security politics (for example, the war against terror) as a sacred token of sovereignty, as if sovereignty were not a political issue, demonstrating repeatedly that 'despotism' is the apolitical kernel of politics (cf. Grosrichard 1998: 14). Thus, if you say that we live in a post-political society in which governmentality is the dominant form of politics, you are right. If you say that we live in a biopolitical society in which the sovereign decision (or micro-decisions) is the dominant form of politics, you are also right. If you say this is contradictory, you are also right for the machine at work here is a paradoxical machine, which works not in spite of but because of its antinomies. For this reason (for its theology is not reducible to political theology) we need to consider the economic theology of the post-political society together with its political theology.

Post-politics as economic theology

Just as the conception of sovereignty is grounded in (political) theology, governmentality is rooted in (economic) theology. Significantly in this respect, through Christian theology (at the end of the classical civilisation), the Greek term *oikonomia* has moved into the theological field, signifying a divine design, the 'divine plan of salvation' (Agamben 2011b: 20). As such, *oikonomia* is the theological answer to the question of what is to be done in a world ontologically created by God, which must be redeemed by the religious praxis of a separate person, the Son. This is also to say that the economy (the praxis which is to be followed to reach the goal of salvation) has no foundation in ontology (in creation). 'However, this anarchic and unfounded praxis must be reconciled with the unity of the substance' (Agamben 2011b: 65). Praxis (the Son) must be related to ontology (God). God and his government of the world must be brought together. Hence the significance of the concept of free will, which, Nietzsche insisted, was 'fabricated' by monotheistic religions to make humanity 'accountable' to a transcendent God (Nietzsche 1969: 53). Through this concept, which is 'in agreement with the theological *oikonomia*' (Agamben 2011b: 56), Christian Trinitarian monotheism seeks to overcome the Gnostic split between two Gods, and to unite God's creation and government of the world. In this sense, insofar as it sought to reconcile a transcendent God which is inoperative in relation to the existing world, and a saviour/redeemer as the ruler of the world, Christian theology is not only political but also economic-managerial from the start (Agamben 2011b: 66). The apolitical paradigm of governmentality has political consequences.

Crucially, this relation between ontology and praxis, sovereignty and governmentality does not constitute a dialectic that results in a synthesis. Rather, it constitutes 'a bipolar machine, whose unity always runs the risk of collapsing and must be acquired again at each turn' (Agamben 2011b: 62). Or, a disjunctive synthesis, in which the two poles can neither be united nor fully separated. The King/God reigns but does not administer, a task beyond his dignity. At the same time, however, his power cannot be separated from him. That is, the two poles are not completely unrelated either; they operate together, within the same 'functional system' (Agamben 2011b: 79).

Power articulates itself at two different levels: it is, at the same time, transcendent and profane, virtual and actual. In this prism 'post-politics' (the reduction of politics to governmentality) is rooted in economic theology, in *oikonomia*. Thus while political theology (sovereignty) thinks along the lines of absolutism, economic theology (post-politics) follows a democratic model in which the administration of the law parallels the divine economy (see Agamben 2011b: 142–3).

Here we also arrive at the point at which political and economic theology intersect: glory. Power needs glory. Acclamations, protocols, ceremonies, exclamations of praise, often accompanied by ritually repeated bodily gestures, are indispensible to power because they form a public opinion and express consensus (Agamben 2011b: 169–70). In its Judaic origin, glory signifies the manifestation, becoming visible of God as a consuming (thus blinding) fire. In this sense it is an 'objective' aspect of the divine. At the same time, however, it has a 'subjective' dimension: the glorification of this divine reality by God's subjects, by human praxis. In this sense 'glorification stems from the glory that, in truth, it founds' (Agamben 2011b: 199). Glory is what establishes the link between the Kingdom and *oikonomia*, between sovereignty and governmentality. Thus it does not disappear with increasing modernisation; rather, it shifts to the domain of public opinion, or consensus, as the modern way of acclamation:

> Contemporary democracy is a democracy that is entirely founded upon glory, that is, on the efficacy of acclamation, multiplied and disseminated by the media beyond all imagination. (Agamben 2011b: 256)

And insofar as post-politics designates consensus politics, it is worth recalling that what is glorified in a neoliberal world in which people can imagine the end of the world but not that of capitalism (Žižek 2009: 78) is first and foremost capitalism itself. In this regard, it might be illuminating to rethink the link between religion and capitalism. Let us start, again, from *oikonomia*.

In *Politics* Aristotle is at pains to differentiate between economy and the *chērematistikē*. That is, between the 'natural' form of acquisition, which consists in attaining 'true wealth', property or goods that are necessary for the life of the household or the state, on the one hand, and the 'unnatural' form of acquisition, which consists in selfish profit, on the other (Aristotle 1995: 23, 326). What we have in the first case is the simple circulation of commodities whereby the household manages the availability of the supply of use-values, by selling and buying commodities. As Marx articulates it, the logic here operates in the form of C-M-C: Commodity is sold for Money in order to buy another Commodity (1976: 252). In the second, 'unnatural' case, however, one is solely concerned with money. Here the main objective is no longer to accumulate necessary use-values but to accumulate wealth in the form of money-capital. Aristotle makes two essential points here: first, referring to Midas, he says that money is a 'nonentity' that is 'useless' and 'worthless' in itself (Aristotle 1995: 26). This is also why wealth accumulated only in terms of money is 'unnatural'. And second, he adds that whereas the art of household management has a natural limit, in this second logic 'there is no limit to wealth' (Aristotle 1995: 24). That is, with the invention of money, the art of acquisition which was originally focused on necessity and use-values gradually 'grew into chrematistics, into the art of making money' (Marx 1976: 253). Now money becomes both the beginning and the end of the process of exchange: M-C-M. 'The movement of capital is therefore limitless' (Marx 1976: 252).

But the problem is that, despite the differentiation, there *is* an overlap between the two forms, between 'economy' and the 'Chrematistic' principle. As noted already by Aristotle, the two modes are 'not identical yet ... not far removed' (Aristotle 1995: 24). It is as if what is 'unnatural', the accumulation of money-capital *ad infinitum*, is already at the heart of 'natural' *oikonomia*, and has a potentiality to become its ultimate aim. Aristotle detects a contradiction between the two modes, but cannot fully resolve it. As such, his discussion serves as *locus classicus* both for a generic concept of capital and for its moral-ethical critique (Albertsen 2011: 2).

In this respect, Weber's discussion of the 'spirit' of capitalism is significant. Since capitalism is a world without value, an inherently nihilistic system, it is constantly in need of moral justification, which can only come to it from outside. This external source is the protestant ethic, which originally provided capitalism with a religious basis, with a 'spirit', although the pact between capitalism and Protestantism has later weakened to the point that 'victorious capitalism ... needs its support no longer' (Weber 2003: 181–2). Secularisation is disenchantment.

However, theology persists as an active force in modern economy. Capitalism and Christianity are structurally linked together. Weber discusses the relation between Christianity and capitalism in two directions: on the one hand, the protestant ethic was a cause, a precondition for the development of capitalist economy and culture; on the other, Protestant Christianity itself was a result of capitalism. The question, however, is whether a third sphere articulates their relation (see Hamacher 2002: 86). That third sphere is debt, or guilt. Hence Benjamin insists that capitalism is a religion, a cult religion which does not expiate but produces guilt:

> An enormous feeling of guilt not itself knowing how to repent, grasps at the cult, not in order to repent for this guilt, but to make it universal,

to hammer it to consciousness and finally and above all to include God himself in this guilt, in order to finally interest him in repentance. (Benjamin 1996: 259)

Just as the religious economy presupposes a guilty god, capitalism as religion presupposes a god in debt. Through the mechanism of debt (credit) value begets surplus-value, a process that resembles 'a god's genesis out of something that *is not*', a god's self-generation out of nothing (Hamacher 2002: 92). Thus, in Marx, the law of value functions as an abstract law that governs the relations of equivalence among commodities, that is, as a transcendent moment within the immanent relations of equivalence. 'Money is therefore the god among commodities' (Marx 1993: 221).

The paradox here consists in the movement through which abstract value becomes totally value-free, or, 'valueless:' abstract capital that seeks out further capital accumulation whenever, wherever, regardless of whatever. Ultimately, therefore, the concept of value can say nothing on value, or rather, nothing other than surplus value. To be sure, in this sense, the capitalist concept of value is nihilistic: capital as an abstract entity that, instead of relating itself to an exteriority, relates itself only to itself. The world of capitalism is essentially a world without value. However, this cynicism must not be mistaken as the absence of a religious dimension in capitalism. It is coupled with cult, with 'a strange piety,' which functions like a 'spiritualized Urstaat,' enabling the illusion that all production in a capitalist society emanates from 'God-capital' (Deleuze and Guattari 1983: 225). Capitalism posits an infinite debt to capital, which is the fetish object, the 'body without organs' of the capitalist society. Just as the sovereign miracle in political theology, capital is that which performs miracles in economic theology.

This 'strange piety' also constitutes an eschatology in the sense that capital 'is always also an anticipation of an imagined future' (Goodchild 2005: 143). Capital is always something 'to come', the promise of a future-return in the form of profit. And insofar as the promise or the future is linked to credit (*credos*) one can say that capitalism not only levels desires and beliefs, but itself creates beliefs and desires. In this respect capital reveals itself as the truth of *oikonomia* rather than a deviation from it. Credit, or debt to the future, thus appears as *kairos*, that which mediates ontology and praxis.

Religion, says Feuerbach, takes over the best qualities of humans and allocates them to God, affirming in God what is negated in man (1989: 27). Hence the paradox of religious alienation: the more God is valued, the more human life is devalued. Marx repeats the same logic in the *1844 Manuscripts*, where he depicts capital as a source of economic alienation: the more wealth the workers produce in capitalism the poorer they become (Marx 2007: 119). But where does this process originate? Original accumulation, which is not the result of capitalist production but rather the starting point of all accumulation processes, was called 'previous accumulation' by Adam Smith. Marx says that 'primitive accumulation plays approximately the same role in political economy as original sin does in theology' (Marx 1976: 363). In this fictional phase (reminiscent of the 'state of nature' in political theology), we are told, while the diligent and intelligent accumulated wealth, the 'lazy rascals' were condemned to poverty, a situation in which they have 'nothing to sell except their own skins' (Marx 1976: 363). As such, the starting point of capital is divorcing the producer from the means of production, his expropriation from the soil. Just as religion captures what is profane and sacralises it through glorification, capitalism captures the commons and commodifies them through the spectacle.

Just as religion demands the infinite increase (subjective glorification as infinite guilt) of what cannot be increased (objective glory of God), capitalism demands infinite accumulation (subjective glorification of capital) of what is beyond human agency ('objective glory' of abstract capital). In both cases 'glorification is . . . what produces glory' (Agamben 2011b: 216, 227). And in both cases the paradox is a cover for the fact that the centre of the machine is empty. And in both cases what is at stake is human life, which is inoperative, that is, without purpose. Its essence is non-utilitarian 'play'. The human is 'the Sabbatical animal par excellence' (Agamben 2011b: 246). What religion does is to capture this inoperativity and inscribe it in a religious sphere by sacralising it, only to ration it, to partially return it in the form of the 'sabbath', a situation in which all 'work', all economy ceases to exist and everything falls back upon inoperativity, which eschatology awaits. What capitalism does is to capture the multitude's inoperativity, its freedom, and inscribe it in a utilitarian sphere, only to partially return it as permitted freedom, as holiday, which is the main promise of work in capitalism. A post-political promise, in which work (hell) is replaced by play (paradise).

Conclusion: ass festival

The idea of God, it is commonly held, does not seem to be compatible with the expert-scientific ideals and capitalist/utilitarian ideology of post-politics. But the enlightened rejection of religion does not amount to a consistent atheism. Indeed, post-political subjectivity merely replaces monotheistic religions with an earthly, decaf deity, a cult, with 'capitalism as religion' (Benjamin 1996).

Towards the end of *Thus Spoke Zarathustra*, we meet some of Zarathustra's guests who all think they have 'unlearned' from Zarathustra the religious sentiment, the despair that follows from feeling weak in this world and that prompts humans to imagine a transcendent heaven in which pain and antagonism no longer exist. They are therefore in a carnival mood. Yet Nietzsche makes it clear that killing God is not enough to get rid of him. A materialist, hedonist world is prone to new, this-worldly illusions, even new gods and idols. At one point in the carnival, therefore, the noise abruptly stops and, precisely when they think they have overcome it, the crowd falls back upon a religious mood. 'They have all become *pious* again, they are *praying*, they are *mad*!' (Nietzsche 1961: 321). But what they worship is a this-worldly God: an ass. They explain that the ass carries their burden, he is patient and never says 'No', indeed he never speaks, and so on. 'Better to worship God in this shape than in no shape at all' (Nietzsche 1961: 322). In *Zarathustra*, it is the 'ugliest man', the passive nihilist, who has murdered God and delivers the tribute to the ass that has 'created the world after his own image, that is, as stupid as possible' (Nietzsche 1961: 322). In the brave new post-political world, too, providence takes its cue from men: the ass is embodied in utilitarianism, and the desire for change, for transfiguration, has disappeared into the cry of the ass. Brave New World is founded on the despotism of the useful.

In this sense post-politics plays one side of the bipolar machine against the other, pushing to an extreme the administrative logic of economic theology, to a point of eliminating the transcendent God/ Kingdom. An ideology in which

> the world created by God is identified with the world without God, and where contingency and necessity, freedom and slavery all merge into one another, the glorious center of the governmental machine appears clearly. Modernity, removing God from the world, has not only failed to leave theology behind, but in some ways has done nothing other than to lead the project of the providential *oikonomia* to completion. (Agamben 2011b: 287)

References

Agamben, G. (2005), *The Time That Remains*, Stanford: Stanford University Press.
Agamben, G. (2011a), *Nudities*, Stanford: Stanford University Press.

Agamben, G. (2011b), *The Kingdom and the Glory: For a Theological Genealogy of Economy and Government*, Stanford: Stanford University Press.

Albertsen, N. (2011), 'Kapitalismens krematistiske varieté: gamle og nye numre', unpublished working paper.

Aristotle (1995), *Politics*, London: Oxford World's Classics.

Badiou, A. (2008), *Conditions*, New York: Continuum.

Badiou, A. (2009), *Logics of Worlds: Being and Event 2*, New York: Continuum.

Barber, B. R. (1996), *Jihad vs McWorld: How Globalism and Tribalism are Reshaping the World*, New York: Ballantine Books.

Baudrillard, J. (1998), *Paroxysm*, London: Verso.

Baudrillard, J. (2002), *Screened Out*, London: Verso.

Bauman, Z. (1976), *Socialism: The Active Utopia*, New York: Holmes & Meier Publishers.

Benjamin, W. (1996), 'Capitalism as religion', in M. Bullock and M. W. Jennings (eds), *Selected Writings Vol. 1, 1913–1926*, Cambridge, MA: Harvard University Press, pp. 288–91.

Bennett, B., and B. Diken (2011), 'The Hurt Locker', *Cultural Politics*, Vol. 7: 2, pp. 165–88.

Boer, I. E. (1996), 'Despotism from under the veil: Masculine and feminine readings of the despot and the harem', *Cultural Critique*, 32: 1, pp. 43–73.

Bradley, A. and P. Fletcher (2010), 'The politics to come: a history of futurity', in A. Bradley and P. Fletcher (eds), *The Politics To Come*, New York: Continuum, pp. 1–12.

Corliss, R. (2008), '*The Hurt Locker*: A Near-Perfect War Film', available at *http://www.time.com/time/arts/article/0,8599,1838615,00.html*.

Deleuze, G. (1983), *Nietzsche and Philosophy*, New York: Columbia University Press.

Deleuze, G. (1995), *Negotiations*, New York: Columbia University Press.

Deleuze, G., and F. Guattari (1983), *Anti-Oedipus: Capitalism and Schizophrenia*, Minneapolis: University of Minnesota Press.

Derrida, J. (1994), *Specters of Marx*, London: Routledge.

Derrida, J. (2004), 'For a justice to come', Lieven De Cauter's interview with Derrida, available at *http://archive.indymedia.be/news/2004/04/83123.html*.

Dillon, M. (2008), 'Lethal freedom: divine violence and the Machiavellian moment', *Theory and Event*, 11: 2, pp. 1–22; *http://muse.jhu.edu/login?uri=/journals/theory_and_event/v011/11.2.dillon.html*.

Dillon, M. (2011), 'Specters of biopolitics: finitude, eschaton and katechon', *The South Atlantic Quarterly*, 110: 1, pp. 782–94.

Doyle, S. (2010), 'Gen McChrystal and the myth of macho', *The Guardian*, 26 June.

Feuerbach, L. (1989), *The Essence of Christianity*, New York: Prometheus Books.

Foucault, M. (1991), 'Governmentality', in G. Burchell, C. Gordon and

P. Miller (eds), *The Foucault Effect*, Chicago: The University of Chicago Press, pp. 87–104.

Fukuyama, F. (1992), *The End of History and the Last Man*, New York: The Free Press.

Goodchild, P. (2005), 'Capital and Kingdom: An eschatological ontology', in C. Davis, S. Žižek and J. Milbank (eds), *Theology and the Political*, Durham: Duke University Press.

Grosrichard, A. (1998), *The Sultan's Court*, London: Verso.

Hall, J. R., (2009), *Apocalypse*, Cambridge: Polity.

Hamacher, W. (2002), 'Guilt history. Benjamin's sketch 'Capitalism as religion'', *Diacritics*, 32: 3–4, pp. 81–106.

Huntington, S. P. (1997), *The Clash of Civilizations and the Remaking of World Order*, London: Simon and Schuster.

Klein, N. (2004), 'Smoking while Iraq burns', *The Guardian*, 26 November.

Marx, K. (1957), 'Contribution to the critique of Hegel's Philosophy of Right: Introduction', in K. Marx and F. Engels, *On Religion*, Moscow: Foreign Languages Publishing House, pp. 41–58.

Marx, K. (1976), *Capital Volume I*, London: Penguin.

Marx, K. (1993), *Grundrisse*, London: Penguin.

Marx, K. (2007), *Economic and Philosophic Manuscripts of 1844*, New York: Dover.

McGreal, C. (2011), 'Tony Blair: Mubarak is "immensely courageous and a force for good"', *The Guardian*, 2 February.

Nietzsche, F. (1961), *Thus Spoke Zarathustra*, London: Penguin.

Nietzsche, F. (1969), *Twilight of Idols*, London: Penguin.

Rancière , J. (2010), *Dissensus*, New York: Continuum.

Ratmoko, D. (2009), 'Preface' to J. Taubes, *Occidental Eschatology*, Stanford: Stanford University Press.

Rose, N. (1999), *Powers of Freedom: Reframing Political Thought*, London: Cambridge.

Sparrow, A. (2011), 'Blair says leak of Palestine papers "destabilising" for peace process', *The Guardian*, 28 January.

Taubes, J. (2009), *Occidental Eschatology*, Stanford: Stanford University Press.

Weber, M. (2003), *The Protestant Ethic and the Spirit of Capitalism*. New York: Dover.

Žižek, S. (1999), 'Carl Schmitt in the age of post-politics', in C. Mouffe (ed.), *The Challenge of Carl Schmitt*, London: Verso, pp. 18–37.

Žižek, S. (2005), 'With or without passion', available at *http://www.lacan.com/zizunder.htm*.

Žižek, S. (2008), *Violence*, London: Profile Books.

Žižek, S. (2009), *First as Tragedy, Then as Farce*, London: Verso.

7 Post-Ecologist Governmentality: Post-Democracy, Post-Politics and the Politics of Unsustainability

Ingolfur Blühdorn

International climate politics and sustainability politics more generally have entered a visibly novel phase. There is now an unprecedented consensus that the established economic order, patterns of resource exploitation, wealth distribution and lifestyles in Western(ised) consumer societies are profoundly unsustainable and in urgent need of comprehensive structural change. Yet this coincides with a form of actual policy-making that more explicitly and determinedly than ever points in precisely the opposite direction. In the wake of the financial crisis, in particular, huge public investment has been injected into re-stabilising rather than radically overhauling the existing order of unsustainability. Recent policies of debt consolidation and economic recovery have further curtailed the ability of the state to politically regulate the market and steer the economy towards sustainability. They have massively aggravated social inequality, reinforced the depletion of social capital, and provided new stimuli for accelerated resource exploitation. In the policy literature, the rhetoric of structural change has by no means disappeared, yet, in eco-politics the paradigm of 'adaptation' and 'resilience' to supposedly 'inevitable' environmental and social change has become dominant, and politics more generally seems to have been reduced to a best-practice competition in the execution of non-negotiable market imperatives. Partially reflecting this, the recent eco-sociological literature displays a marked loss of confidence not only in the achievability of meaningful international climate agreements, but also in a range of other narratives which were once major sources of eco-political hope: the belief in increasingly powerful and international grassroots movements for an ecologically more benign socio-economic order; the 'ecological modernisation' promise of techno-managerial resource-efficiency revolutions (Mol and Sonnenfeld 2000); the narrative of 'political consumerism' and 'shopping for sustainability' (Micheletti

2003; Seyfang 2005); or the claim that new forms of 'ecological citizenship' (Dobson and Bell 2006) and 'alternative hedonism' (Soper 2007, 2008) are already emerging. None of these – either individually or in combination – is likely to deliver anything like the structural transformation which is required if established norms of social justice, democratic self-determination and environmental integrity are to be maintained. Modern societies therefore seem inescapably locked into a technocratic *politics of unsustainability* (Blühdorn 2007a, 2009a, 2011a).

The objective of this chapter is to explore what the growing body of thought on post-democracy and post-politics might contribute to a more detailed understanding of this politics of unsustainability. Prima facie, the history of environmental movements, the close association of environmentalism with the struggle for a more authentic democracy, and the centrality of sustainability concerns in recent mass protests such as Occupy and the *Indignados* may suggest that the thinking on post-democracy and post-politics is not a very promising tool for the purposes of eco-political analysis. Yet, as I have argued elsewhere (e.g. Blühdorn 2010, 2011b, 2013a, 2013b), the theories of post-democracy and post-politics can indeed be used to sharpen the analysis of contemporary eco-political discourse and practice. Erik Swyngedouw has also demonstrated this in a powerful way (Swyngedouw 2007, 2008, 2009, 2010a, 2010b, 2011a, 2011b). Drawing on the work of Badiou, Mouffe, Rancière, Žižek and other neo-Marxist critics of hegemonic market-liberalism, he has argued that politics and the political have been evacuated wholesale from today's institutionalised environmental policy, that the prevailing technocratic-managerial approaches, more than anything, reinforce and police the established order of liberal consumer capitalism, and that this mainstreamed policy discourse not merely illustrates the post-democratic and post-political condition, but in fact renders environmental policy one of the key arenas through which the post-political frame is forged and configured, and the hegemony of neoliberal thought entrenched.

Swyngedouw's work delivers centrally important insights. Arguably, however, it does not unlock the full analytical-explanatory potential that the post-democracy/post-politics paradigm has with regard to contemporary eco-politics. It has deficits in terms of its underlying social theory; it is potentially counter-productive from an eco-activist perspective; and its understanding of the politics of unsustainability is far too superficial. In what follows I will develop the notions of post-democracy and post-politics, and relate them to eco-political discourses, in a way that moves well beyond the work of Swyngedouw and others following the post- or neo-Marxist tradition. I begin, drawing largely on Swyngedouw's work, with an account of the neo-Marxist perspective on contemporary eco-politics as a neoliberal ploy. The second section outlines how, since the late 1980s, a profound shift in culture and social values has given rise to a new eco-political governmentality that has to be understood, not as an imposition by ideological neoliberals, but as an emancipatory achievement. The third section then reinterprets today's post-democratic and post-political politics of unsustainability as the product of this new governmentality. Throughout the chapter, I consciously refrain from directly engaging in any (eco-) political campaign. Yet, although I argue that the politics of unsustainability and its underlying post-ecologist governmentality are (at least *also*) the result of emancipatory processes, and will therefore be extremely difficult to adjust, the analysis is driven by the hope that exposing the anatomy of the politics of unsustainability may ultimately release more genuinely transformative potentials than the neo-Marxist campaign against ideological neoliberals. Indeed, I harbour an underlying concern that the neo-Marxists' simplistic rhetoric may, more than anything, contribute to the 'discourses of simulation' (Blühdorn 2004, 2006, 2007b, 2013b) that play such a crucial role in sustaining the politics of unsustainability.

The ecological crisis as a neoliberal ploy

The environmental issue first entered the political arena as a radical challenge to the order of consumer capitalism and liberal representative democracy. When trying to force their ecological concerns onto the political agenda, the new social movements of the 1970s and early 1980s had to confront significant resistance. Their diagnosis of a relatively prosperous society as socially alienating, ecologically destructive, and heading towards comprehensive catastrophe, and their vociferous demands for a transformation of the existing social order, economic model, political structure, and relationship to nature all triggered deep ideological divisions and implied radical political confrontation. In contemporary Western consumer democracies, by contrast, these conflicts have been largely pacified and environmental concerns have been fully institutionalised and integrated into the policy process. The diagnosis of significant environmental challenges is largely uncontested; there is broad political commitment to taking them seriously; scientific experts are fully devoted to assessing the problem and finding out how to address it most effectively; and a whole range of technocratic bodies are monitoring the implementation of national and international sustainability plans. As yet, none of this has really resolved the problems which the emancipatory social movements once put on the political agenda. But environmental politics has clearly metamorphosed from a highly political and politicising terrain into a largely depoliticised and post-political issue.

Critical observers in the tradition of post- or neo-Marxist critical theory have interpreted this development as part of a general shift, engineered by ideological neoliberals, towards a post-democratic and post-political condition. 'Post-democracy' is their name for a form of governance which formally retains all democratic institutions and rituals, but relocates political power and decision-making to arenas where corporate interests rule largely insulated from democratic participation and accountability (Crouch 2004; Rancière 2006). For these scholars, 'post-politics' implies the reign of supposedly objective necessities and non-negotiable imperatives (Boggs 2000; Žižek 2009). In particular, it is seen as the condition where 'a consensus has been built around the inevitability of neoliberal capitalism' (Swyngedouw 2009: 609), with 'public administration' and 'the new public management' technocratically executing 'systemic' imperatives of market efficiency, economic competitiveness, public austerity and the lean state. The consolidation of post-political arrangements, Swyngedouw suggests 'runs parallel to the rise of a neoliberal governmentality that has replaced debate, disagreement and dissensus with a series of technologies of governing that fuse around consensus, agreement, accountancy metrics and technocratic management' (Swyngedouw 2009: 604). From this perspective, the prevalent forms of contemporary eco-politics are not only a 'perfect expression' of the post-political order, but neoliberals have also turned the environmental crisis into a major catalyst for the post-political consensus (Swyngedouw 2007: 18). Eco-political debates, Swyngedouw suggests, crucially 'contribute to the making and consolidation of a post-political and post-democratic condition' (Swyngedouw 2009: 604). Consensually established concerns like climate change, he believes, 'sustain the deepening of a post-political condition' and promote its institutionalisation 'through forms of post-democratic governing' (Swyngedouw 2010a: 225). The widely echoed warnings that serious consequences are looming unless drastic action is taken immediately are for Swyngedouw, more than anything, a 'populist ploy' (Swyngedouw 2007: 25) and a neoliberal strategy to reinforce the depoliticised rule of the market. Indeed, he portrays the 'pervasive apocalyptical imaginary' as a 'perfect example' of neoliberal tactics (Swyngedouw 2009: 602, 611) and 'an integral part of the new cultural politics of capitalism' (Swyngedouw 2010a: 219).

Swyngedouw challenges this neoliberal seizure of the ecological issue, and aims to mobilise against the curious pact between a diverse range of environmentalists on one side and the market-liberal agents of post-democracy and post-politics on the other. In doing so, he reminds us that 'nature out there' as a singular extra-societal point of reference does not exist, but only a multiplicity of culturally loaded and coded visions of nature and the natural, and that, accordingly, 'there is nothing foundational in nature that needs, demands, or requires sustaining' (Swyngedouw 2007: 9). 'Sustainability', he suggests, as an empty conceptual shell that different political actors may want to fill with very diverse normative content and political objectives, is, *eo ipso*, neither 'possible' nor actually 'desirable' (Swyngedouw 2007: 9). In clear contrast to his own political intentions, Swyngedouw gets strangely close to the (mostly neoliberal) deniers of climate change and the sustainability crisis more generally (see for example Jacquesa et al. 2008; Norgaard 2011), by suggesting that 'If we were to believe that the earth is really in the dismal state we are told it is in, we would not be sitting around writing and reading arcane academic journal articles' (Swyngedouw 2010a: 219). In an ironic twist he even describes ecology as the neoliberals' 'new opium for the masses' (Swyngedouw 2010b). Discarding the ritualised 'apocalyptic warnings of catastrophe' (Swyngedouw 2010a: 217), he insists that the key issue is neither the protection of specific bio-physical conditions, nor the achievement of resource efficiency or the decarbonisation of fossil-fuel societies. Any environmental policy that focuses on these issues, he argues, 'avoids asking the politically sensitive, but vital, question as to what kind of socio-environmental arrangements do we wish to produce, how can this be achieved, and what sort of natures do we wish to inhabit' (Swyngedouw 2007: 9). Put differently, he demands that ecological communication and environmental policy are explicitly reconnected to social values and notions of subjectivity. And as any imaginable socio-environmental arrangement invariably produces winners and losers, he demands that eco-political debate and policy once again places changing 'power geometries' into the centre of attention (Swyngedouw 2007: 31).

As regards the specific modes in which contemporary eco-politics is practically executed, Swyngedouw (2008: 14) notes:

> Not only is the political arena evacuated from radical dissent, critique and fundamental conflict, but the parameters of democratic governing itself are being shifted, announcing new forms of governmentality, in which traditional disciplinary society is transfigured into a society of control through disembedded networks of governance.

He takes issue with the proliferation of new modes of devolved stakeholder governance which in environmental policy, in particular, are widely presented and perceived as enhancing the legitimacy and effectiveness of policy-making, and as a commendable approximation to the ideals of emancipatory and participatory social movements. Swyngedouw radically questions this established policy orthodoxy. He portrays these innovative policy arrangements as 'fundamentally Janus-faced' (Swyngedouw 2005: 1993) in that they claim to fully embrace the norms and objectives which the emancipatory social movements had campaigned for, whilst in fact they are 'an integral part of the consolidation of an imposed and authoritarian neoliberalism, celebrating the virtues of self-managed risk, prudence, and self-responsibility' (Swyngedouw 2005: 1998). As they (1) are rarely based on codified and transparent rules, (2) tend to be highly selective as regards which actors are accredited stakeholder status and allowed to participate, (3) are ill-defined in terms of the nature of the representation they offer and the legitimacy they generate, (4) often remain ambiguous in terms of their political objectives and priorities and (5) disperse political responsibility and obscure chains of accountability, Swyngedouw describes them as 'the Trojan Horse' that the neo-liberal enemy secretly introduces in order to 'diffuse and consolidate the market as the principal institutional form' (Swyngedouw 2005: 2003). He criticises the new networks of governance as inherently 'contradictory' and producing 'perverse effects' in that, whilst 'appearing to empower civil society', they in fact contribute to a 'substantial democratic deficit' (Swyngedouw 2005: 1999–2001). Arguing along very similar lines, Davies portrays the new 'governing networks as micro configurations of the [Gramscian] integral state' with 'considerable hegemonic efficacy' (Davies 2012: 2687–8). Rather than 'cultivating trust', he argues, these networks foster political 'hierarchy and closure' (Davies 2012: 2687). Rather than building new alliances for profound structural change and securing broad engagement in the societal transition towards sustainability, Swyngedouw adds, these new forms of governance-beyond-the-state are really designed 'to ensure that the world as we know it stays fundamentally the same' (Swyngedouw 2010b: 309).

So from the neo-Marxist perspective, these depoliticised modes of stakeholder governance are not only eco-politically ineffective but, even more importantly, they are perceived as anti-democratic, indeed, essentially authoritarian. They disempower the democratic sovereign and suspend the promise of autonomous self-determination; they present as inescapable and without alternative what is in fact just the self-serving agenda of neoliberal elites; and they close the discursive space for the formation and articulation of new subjectivities, which could potentially challenge the social, economic and political order of hegemonic market-liberalism. Accordingly, the critics of the neoliberal appropriation of eco-politics are struggling for 'the recuperation of the horizon of democracy as the terrain for the cultivation of conflict and the naming of different socio-economic futures' (Swyngedouw 2007: 33). Their 'political program is to enhance the democratic content of socio-environmental construction by means of identifying the strategies through which a more equitable distribution of social power and a democratically more genuine mode of the production of natures can be achieved' (Swyngedouw 2007: 32). They seek to recentralise the 'notions of equality and freedom', and explore 'perspectives for re-vitalising the political possibilities of a spatialized emancipatory project' (Swyngedouw 2011: 370). Indeed, beyond any engagement with eco-politics, their agenda is, ultimately, to reinstate the emancipatory project and reinstall the notion of the autonomous subject as the centre of an authentically democratic politics.

Second-order emancipation

This neo-Marxist analysis highlights a number of important points. First, as outlined above, contemporary eco-politics is indeed largely technocratic and managerial, and its depoliticisation has indeed been strategically pursued. However, this is neither a phenomenon of the recent present, nor is it adequately portrayed as an innovation and campaign by ideological neoliberals. Secondly, it is certainly correct to insist that there is no such thing as a singular 'nature out there', or a scientifically measurable 'environmental crisis' that is the common point of reference for eco-political debates and that provides an uncontested normative foundation for a prescriptive politics of sustainability. But the assumption of a singular nature and the 'phantasmagorial imaginaries' of eco-apocalypse are not neoliberal innovations, and neoliberals do not strongly, or even primarily, rely on such imaginaries to legitimise and push their anti-political agenda. On the contrary, they much more commonly downplay the seriousness of the ecological-cum-social crisis and the urgency of remedial action. Thirdly, neo-Marxists are entirely right in challenging the eco-political effectiveness of depoliticised techno-managerial policy approaches. Yet, their suggestion that a repoliticisation and re-subjectivation of eco-politics may change this in any significant way is sociologically unfounded. Fourthly, it is undoubtedly correct that in advanced modern consumer democracies an entirely new kind of governmentality has emerged. However, the neo-Marxists' account of the causes and driving factors of this shift in political culture is rather simplistic, as is their analysis of its implications for the conduct of eco-politics. Finally, it is also true that with their strong reliance on scientific experts and technocratic elites, the prevalent depoliticised modes of eco-governance have disowned and disempowered emancipatory social movements, turning the eco-issue into a means of justifying the restriction of civil liberties, the regulation of personal lifestyles and other intrusive interventions into the private sphere. Yet this is not simply a matter of neoliberal elites instrumentalising the environmental crisis for their anti-democratic and anti-political purposes. This apparently anti-emancipatory turn has much more complex causes – and politically very irritating effects – which the neo-Marxist critique conveniently leaves unaddressed.

A more nuanced understanding of the post-political shape of contemporary eco-politics requires, first of all, a recognition that practices of depoliticisation have, in fact, always been a constitutive element of eco-political communication. Even the most political and politicising strands of the environmental movement have always firmly relied on such strategies and presented their demands on the basis of non-negotiable fundamentals and categorical eco-imperatives, which supposedly do not allow for any alternatives. Secondly, a more complex understanding of contemporary post-democratic and post-political eco-politics needs to pay much closer attention to the new governmentality on which it is based. As indicated above, neo-Marxists also diagnose this new governmentality, but their explanation of its origins is reassuringly simple, and they do not adequately explore what this governmentality actually means for contemporary eco-politics.

The starting point for a detailed analysis must be the specific notion of subjectivity which underpinned the thinking of political ecology, and of the emancipatory social movements' new politics more generally. This particular ideal and its constitutive norms of autonomy, integrity and dignity, had emerged in the context of the European Enlightenment and was incrementally installed as an uncontested social and political norm through a long sequence of emancipatory movements, culminating in the 'silent revolution' (Inglehart 1977, 1997, 2007) or 'participatory revolution' (Kaase 1984; Blühdorn 2009) of the 1970s and 1980s. But in the course of this long sequence of emancipatory struggles, this specifically modernist norm did not, of course, remain static. It was continuously redefined in line with the ongoing modernisation (differentiation, acceleration, individualisation, economisation, technicisation, and so on) of modern societies. The two interrelated changes which are, arguably, most relevant in the present context are, firstly, the transformation of the ways in which modern individuals realise, articulate and experience their subjectivity and identity and, secondly, the incremental differentiation, fragmentation and flexibilisation of the modernist subject. The former had for a long time been debated by the critical Left as the permeation of the supposedly autonomous subject by the market, its colonisation by the culture and consumer industry and its manipulation by the advertising machine. Indeed, the bourgeois-modernist tradition, reinforced by the Christian contempt for anything material and emphemeral, had conceptualised subjectivity and identity-formation as explicitly distinct and independent from the market. Self-realisation was imagined as the development of innate qualities of character and *inner values* whereby the market and material values and pleasures appeared, more than anything, as obstructing and corrupting authentic freedom, self-determination and identity. More recently, however, it has been acknowledged in less normative terms that, for the purposes of their identity construction, self-expression and self-realisation, individuals in advanced post-industrial societies very strongly rely on acts of consumption and the choices provided by the market (Lodziak 2002; Bauman 2007; Featherstone 2007).

The latter – that is, the pluralisation and flexibilisation of identity – had for a long time been discussed under the headings of popular culture and postmodernisation (Kellner 1995). More recently, Zygmunt Bauman (2000) has sought to capture it within his paradigm of 'liquid modernity'. Taking up the Marxian idea of the process of modernisation 'melting all that is solid into air', Bauman suggests that individual identity, which had once been conceived of as unitary, consistent and solid, is becoming increasingly fragmented, volatile and liquid. Indeed, the bourgeois-modernist tradition had understood identity formation as a steady and lifelong process of maturation culminating in a rounded and stable personality defined by firm moral principles, consistent tastes and interests, and reliable features of character. Yet, as contemporary societies are becoming ever more differentiated and subject to accelerated change; as the life-worlds of modern individuals are becoming ever more complex, information-rich and virtualised, this traditional notion of identity is giving way to multiple, fragmented and flexible forms of identity. The qualities in demand today are versatility, mobility and openness to change. Lifelong learning and strategic image-management are imperatives of the modern labour market and professional success. Also, more flexible notions of identity, which are more open to inherent contradictions, appear to facilitate a much richer experience of life and more personal fulfilment, whereas the earlier ideals of subjectivity and identity – with their implicit demand for consistency, commitment, loyalty and rational-cum-moral self-restriction – are turning into an obstacle and liability. Accordingly, the more progressive parts of contemporary societies, in particular, are adapting their understanding of their Self and their norms of identity. Borrowing the words of Inglehart and Welzel (2005: 23), such value change may be seen as an 'evolutionary process in which those values that are best suited to cope with life under given existential conditions have a selective advantage over values that are less suited to these conditions'.

In line with the tradition of critical theory, these developments have been described in terms of alienation, the incremental decline of the individual, the colonisation of its life-world, and the expansion of the apparatus of domination and control. Yet, taking into account its emancipatory drivers and potentials, this ongoing cultural shift can also be framed in terms of liberation – as many postmodernist thinkers have done. Indeed, the emergence of liquid identity could be conceptualised as the outcome of 'second-order' or 'reflexive' emancipation. If 'traditional' or 'first-order' emancipation refers to the long-winded rise of the 'autonomous' subject of traditional modernity, culminating in the alternative culture and 'DIY politics' of the new social movements, the term second-order or reflexive emancipation could be used to refer to its replacement by more contemporary notions of subjectivity and identity. It captures the trends of depoliticisation, outsourcing and delegation to service providers that have been noticeable since the 1990s (see Raco, Chapter 1 of this volume). It entails the partial deliverance from the very responsibilities (autonomy) which the social movements had enthusiastically struggled for. In a nutshell, while first-order emancipation is the installation of the modernist autonomous subject, second-order emancipation is the liberation from specific implications of this modernist ideal, which in the contemporary context appear overly demanding and restrictive.

Eco-politically, this modernisation-induced value- and culture-shift may be conceptualised as a 'post-ecologist turn' (Blühdorn 2002, 2004). It undermines the very foundations of political ecology's radical critique and vision, and it comprehensively reconfigures the normative frame of reference of ecological communication. Political ecology and the emancipatory new social movements had been driven by the longing for, and the belief in, the 'authentic Self' beyond the individualised and predominantly materialist consumer lifestyle; 'real fulfilment' beyond the alienating treadmill of competitiveness and efficiency; pacified social and natural relations beyond social and ecological instrumentalisation, exploitation and destruction, and genuinely empowering forms of political and economic organisation beyond the only formally democratic order of liberal consumer capitalism (see for example Goldsmith 1972; Porritt 1984; Die Grünen 1980). In the wake of the post-ecologist turn, however, this profound unease with the alienation of scientific-technological-industrial modernity, and this belief in a better alternative, have largely evaporated. Ecologist ideals – small-scale, low-tech, steady-state, localised, post-consumerist, self-sufficient – retain little of their earlier appeal. Scientific-technological-industrial modernity and its consumerist lifestyles have been more firmly embraced than ever before. Ever-expanding needs in terms of, for example, mobility, individuality, technology, protein intake, travel or attractive shopping opportunities have become essentially non-negotiable (depoliticised). Prevalent notions of wellbeing and quality of life imply that ways *must* be found to meet them. Of course, contemporary eco-political communication is, as noted above, also shaped by an unprecedented awareness of the multi-dimensional unsustainability of post-industrial consumer societies, yet non-negotiable norms of subjectivity and identity imply that sustaining the established order, at least for the time being, is a categorical imperative.

As regards the struggle for democracy, which has always been at the very heart of the emancipatory project (as well as political ecology), this reflexive emancipation from the traditionally-modern norms of subjectivity and identity raises the question to what extent democratic structures and processes are actually still desirable at all. After all, democracy, rather than being an intrinsic value has, first and foremost, always been valued as a tool for the realisation of the specifically modernist notion of the subject. Yet, if in the wake of second-order or reflexive emancipation the established understandings of subjectivity and identity are being revised, it cannot simply be assumed that the established norms and forms of democracy are still an appropriate strategic tool. On the contrary, such structures might easily appear distinctly unappealing. The plethora of seductive opportunities for self-realisation, the frantic struggle against mounting uncertainties, and the management of increasingly complex personal lifestyles all reduce the time and energy available for democratic participation. Even more importantly, many of the priority tasks for personal fulfilment and social wellbeing in advanced modern societies – for example, stimulating the economy, generating and securing jobs, providing affordable consumer goods, fighting terrorism, mitigating climate change – can, it seems, be addressed much more effectively in non-democratic ways. Furthermore, at a time when the economic, ecological and social limits to growth have become more evident and uncontested than ever before, whilst the prevalent forms of self-determination and self-realisation more exclusively than ever rely on continuously expanding and accelerating consumption, the egalitarian and redistributive values of democracy are turning into a serious problem – not only for wealthy elites, but also at the grass-roots of society.

Thus, in the realm of democratic politics, too, the process of second-order emancipation comprehensively reconfigures the emancipatory-progressive project and nurtures a new governmentality. In significant respects, this value- and culture-shift moves beyond the modernist notion of identity and subjectivity. Yet it also continues the journey towards ever more freedom, self-determination and subjectivity. In fact, it radicalises the claims for emancipation and participation, and makes contemporary citizens ever more uncompromising in their demand for representation. Therefore, second-order emancipation is very unlikely to lead to the 'end', 'death', or even 'hatred' of democracy (Guéhenno 1993; Keane 2009; Rancière 2006). But it does imply a profound transformation of democracy which, by analogy to the post-ecologist turn, may be conceptualised as a 'post-democratic' turn (Blühdorn 2013a, 2013b). In contrast to the widespread polemical use of the term post-democracy as a strategic weapon in the campaign against anti-political neoliberals and for the resuscitation of 'authentic' democracy, this notion of the post-democratic turn suggests that the democratic norms which Crouch, Swyngedouw and many others aim to revive might have become historically obsolete. It takes seriously the possibility that the democratic project, as the new social movements had framed and promoted it, has meanwhile become exhausted, and cannot be revived, because it no longer corresponds to the values and needs, i.e. the ideals of subjectivity and identity, which are prevalent in contemporary consumer societies.

Reactionary ecology

This account of the post-ecologist turn and its counterpart in the participatory-democratic dimension of emancipatory politics takes us well beyond the neo-Marxist narrative of depoliticised ecology and post-political governance as a neoliberal ploy. It facilitates a much more nuanced understanding of depoliticisation, post-democracy and post-politics in advanced modern societies. It reveals, firstly, that the new governmentality which in contemporary consumer democracies underpins the techno-managerial management of societal affairs is by no means simply a product and tactic of anti-democratic and anti-political elites. Undoubtedly, neoliberals are putting substantial resources into nurturing this new governmentality, but at least as much as it is imposed from the top down, this governmentality emerges from the bottom up. It is an emancipatory achievement just as much as it is an instrument of domination. Analytical approaches which fail to recognise that prevalent norms of subjectivity play an important part in its evolution remain invariably reductionist. They ignore a distinctive characteristic of the post-ecologist, post-democratic and post-political constellation – one that actually provides the depoliticised management of societal affairs with some kind of bottom-up legitimacy.

Secondly, the analysis of second-order emancipation raises fundamental doubts about the neo-Marxist agenda of 'reclaiming political democracy'. The demand that democratic politics and the spaces for democratic engagement 'need to be taken back from the post-political oligarchic constituent police order' (Swyngedouw 2008: 5); the campaign for 'genuine democracy' and 'a return to the polis' (Swyngedouw 2008: 16); the desire to 'revitalise the emancipatory project' and reclaim the 'notions of equality and freedom' (Swyngedouw 2011: 371) all echo widely through the activist literature and popular political debate. They are comforting in that they suggest that the established ideological compass is still intact. They are reassuring – especially in times of political disorientation – in that they provide clear ideological directions couched in a familiar political language. Yet, they are deceptive and entail a false promise: they disregard that the polis (political subject) to which they wish to return no longer exists; that the political enemy is complex, intangible and most certainly not simply the neoliberal other; and that the emancipatory project, rather than being dead and waiting for resuscitation, is in fact very much alive – albeit in a reconfigured form. Furthermore, they ignore that there is no such thing as 'genuine' democracy, and that the meaning of this ideal, rather than being static, has always been in flux, continuously being reconfigured and redefined in line with evolving notions of subjectivity and identity. Therefore, the attempt to revive earlier incarnations of the democratic-emancipatory project is not only unpromising in a political-practical sense, but it is also ideologically questionable. It paternalistically prescribes an 'authentic' interpretation of democracy; and in as much as it seeks to reactivate something which the emancipatory project has successfully overcome, it may actually be regarded as reactionary.

As we have seen, the contemporary politics of unsustainability is no longer oriented towards the transformation of established social values and societal structures, but is fully focused on stabilising the already existing order. According to the neo-Marxist account, this reflects the vested interests of ideological neoliberal elites. More careful analysis, however, has now revealed the significant role of changing notions of subjectivity. Second-order emancipation has given rise to norms of subjectivity and self-realisation which, rather than demanding the implementation of a radical alternative, push for the accelerated development of the opportunities provided by the already-existing structures. The scope of environmental policy is correspondingly reduced to forcing new efficiency technologies, harnessing the capabilities of the market and improving the effectiveness of environmental management practices. Under the banners of sustainability, resilience and adaptation, its primary concern must be to fend off the pressures for structural change. Yet, with the limits to growth being more evident than ever and techno-managerial efficiency gains remaining well below the level required to compensate for the growing demand on finite resources, the resolve to sustain the established socio-economic structures inescapably implies that prevalent norms and patterns of self-determination and self-realisation can be sustained for only some sections of society and have to be accompanied by equivalent restrictions for others. Therefore, the politics of unsustainability is crucially about the management of – or societal resilience and adaptation to – increasing social injustice, marginalisation and exclusion. In the sense that it is guided and driven by radicalised claims to independence, self-determination and self-realisation, it continues the progressive and emancipatory project, yet, if measured against established norms of equality and social justice, it appears – as neo-Marxists suggest as well, albeit for different reasons – as 'inherently' or 'radically' reactionary (Swyngedouw 2007: 18; 2010: 228).

The primary challenge for this reactionary eco-politics is to practically organise and politically legitimate its agenda of social marginalisation and exclusion. In this respect, too, the analysis of the post-democratic turn and the new governmentality to which it gives rise provides important cues. Indeed, this practical dimension, i.e. the actual conduct of the politics of unsustainability, is a core element of post-ecologist governmentality. For political ecology and the emancipatory new social movements, democracy and ecology were inseparably connected to each other in that democracy was the political tool not only for the progressive and egalitarian struggle of the socially underprivileged but also for the liberation of nature which was accredited the same right to autonomy, integrity and dignity as the human subject. In the wake of the value shift outlined above, this relationship seems to change radically. Firstly, because with post-ecologist value orientations, more democracy is much more likely to further accelerate than to put an end to the unsustainable consumption of nature; and secondly, in a context of resource finiteness, the egalitarian principles of democracy run into conflict with the resolve to sustain patterns of self-realisation which cannot be generalised.

Yet, as outlined above, the post-ecologist turn goes along with an equally impactful post-democratic turn: second-order emancipation radicalises individualised demands for participation, representation and consumption-based self-realisation, and at the same time implies the emancipation from restrictive social imperatives and commitments. It devalues the democratic principle of egalitarianism vis-à-vis that of liberalism. Thus democracy metamorphoses from an emancipatory and egalitarian instrument of the oppressed and excluded into a tool of the (still) included for the defence of their established status. Following the post-democratic turn, democracy is no longer progressive in the traditional sense of fostering social solidarity, empowering the underprivileged and moving towards social equality, but in a revised contemporary sense of the individualised struggle to secure an optimal strategic position for succeeding in an inherently unsustainable – and therefore highly competitive – socio-economic environment. Whilst for the socially underprivileged democracy entails ever less of a promise, project or perspective, the still included are claiming it as a tool for the stabilisation and legitimisation of lifestyles which, more visibly than ever, can be sustained only at the cost of increasing social injustice and exclusion (national and international) and accelerated environmental exploitation.

Thus, the symbiotic relationship between democracy and ecology is actually maintained, albeit in a perverted manner: in its reconfigured form democracy – far from becoming undesirable or fading into insignificance – actually turns into the most important tool for the politics of unsustainability. Neo-Marxist demands for a 'return to the polis' (Swyngedouw 2008: 16) and eco-activist calls for 'reclaiming democracy for the citizenry' (Hamilton 2010: 223) not only fail to recognise that after the post-ecologist turn more democracy is most unlikely to result in more sustainability. More importantly, they also disregard to what extent, following the post-democratic turn, the populist claim to more authentically democratic decision-making is actually itself a means of sustaining the unsustainable: in a context of resource scarcity and austerity, in particular, the populist call for authentic democracy and the mobilisation of civil society against (alleged) threats of eco-dictatorship are a safe strategy for derailing any policy that might restrict the spending capacity and consumption power of parts of the population. Paradoxically, however, post-democratic democracy is also a powerful tool for the agenda of social inequality and exclusion: contrary to its explicit commitment to egalitarianism and giving a voice to the disempowered masses, democracy has, in fact, always had a tendency not to deliver 'the greatest good for the greatest number' but 'the greatest goodies for the best-organised few' (Putnam 2000: 340). By drawing on resources which are socially distributed very unequally, the new social movements, too, have reinforced this tendency and skewed the balance of political influence strongly in favour of the already privileged middle class. And beyond the post-ecologist and post-democratic turn, the new forms of decentralised, semi-participatory, flexible forms of stakeholder governance exploit and reinforce exactly this tendency of democracy to further privilege those who are already privileged. These new forms of governance engage a wide range of societal actors in the implemention of policies which are presented as systemic imperatives and without an alternative – and are designed to sustain the order of unsustainability. These inclusive forms of *stakeholder* governance are a powerful tool for reducing opposition and social conflict, and they generate a form of democratic legitimacy for policies which allow some sections of society to sustain their non-negotiable norms and forms of self-realisation but implement significant restrictions for others. Rather than being 'inherently contradictory' and the 'Trojan horse' of ideological neoliberals, these post-democratic forms of governance are, therefore, a highly efficient tool for the governance of unsustainability. They organise maximal social inclusion into the politics of exclusion. In a post-democratic sense, they *democratise* the politics of unsustainability.

So, whilst political ecology and the new social movements had conceptualised democracy as a means for the underprivileged to wrench power and material resources from the established elites, post-ecologist governmentality transforms democracy into a means for the privileged to wrench resources from social groups whose interests are less effectively organised and articulated. Interestingly, and worryingly, the execution of this agenda of social inequality and exclusion via the new forms of decentralised stakeholder governance no longer relies on the state as the central executive power. The new social movements had aimed to overcome the traditional dualism between the state and the private sphere and to replace both by something new, namely self-governing civil society which would empower citizens and give them autonomy and self-determination. The post-ecologist and post-democratic governance of unsustainability uses exactly this civil society and its self-organising networks to execute the marginalisation and control of some in order to sustain unsustainable lifestyles and norms of subjectivity for others. Its distinctive quality is that it is neither authoritarian nor egalitarian and that it continues the emancipatory project in a reactionary manner. Swyngedouw correctly notes that the 'new forms of governmentality' transform 'traditional disciplinary society' into a 'society of control through disembedded networks of governance' (Swyngedouw 2009: 608; 2007: 23, 26). Yet, contrary to the neo-Marxist account this is not really a matter of the Foucauldian 'conduct of conduct', i.e. of neoliberal elites strategically mobilising the commons for their anti-political and anti-egalitarian interests. Instead, this self-organised and self-managed governance of social exclusion is indicative of a new social contract (Blühdorn 2013a; 2013b) that engages a wide range of actors well beyond the neo-Marxists' neoliberal enemy.

Conclusion

This chapter has demonstrated that the paradigm of depoliticisation, post-democracy and post-politics can indeed be very productively employed for the analysis of eco-politics in advanced modern consumer societies. But in order to unlock its full explanatory potentials we need to move beyond the restricted perspective of post- and neo-Marxist thought. The analysis has given rise to an understanding of post-democracy, post-politics and the emancipatory project that is much richer – and much more disturbing – than the reassuringly simple narratives ritually rehearsed in activist discourses. Practices of depoliticisation, which have always been a strategy for increasing the authority and effectiveness of eco-politics, retain this function in the politics of unsustainability. Yet they take a form that is distinct from political ecology's categorical eco-imperatives as well as the science-based patterns of depoliticisation on which the techno-managerial politics of ecological modernisation rests. Just like the latter, the politics of unsustainability portrays its policies in terms of scientific and economic necessity, but beyond this, it ultimately draws its authority and legitimacy from presenting them as systemic imperatives. In doing so, it actually combines elements of both earlier patterns of depoliticisation. In advanced modern societies the kind of transcendental norms and pre-political fundamentalisms on which political ecology built its case are no longer plausible, while scientific truths and so-called economic necessities have also become highly contested. The politics of unsustainability transfigures the non-negotiable norms of subjectivity and self-realisation to which it is firmly committed into systemic imperatives. They thus acquire a status of objectivity (authority) which is on a par with the categorical imperatives emerging from political ecology's fundamentals. And the state, civil society and the private sector, supposedly all equally powerless vis-à-vis the almighty system, join forces in a new social contract to collectively execute the inevitable.

This exploration of depoliticisation, post-democracy and post-politics in contemporary eco-politics is very disturbing, not least because it leaves very little scope for effective policy suggestions and really promising political campaigns. Yet, beyond second-order emancipation, i.e. in the post-ecologist and post-democratic constellation, the role of critical sociology can neither be to present policy recommendations – which would invariably mean to join the new social contract for sustaining the unsustainable – nor to mobilise preconfigured notions of emancipation, authentic democracy or the truly political. If it wants to remain plausible, critical sociology needs to confine itself to approaching the politics of unsustainability from a descriptive-analytical perspective, fully focusing its efforts on revealing the mechanisms that make it work and exposing the post-ecologist governmentality that supports it. It may be hoped that this kind of description and analysis will release new political energies, but it is impossible to predict what kind of political campaign they might forge. This is an uncertain and potentially risky perspective. Yet, the hope and optimism which the neo-Marxist narrative conveys is most certainly false. It remains caught up in patterns of political analysis which do not fit the complexity of today's post-political constellation. It does not invest genuine trust in the emancipatory project but paternalistically channels any freshly emerging political energy into structures which are predictable and calculable. Ultimately, the neo-Marxist rhetoric may just be a discursive arena for the performance and experience of political norms which have become hopelessly outdated, but which still provide comfort and reassurance for the marginalised and excluded and for anybody struggling to come to terms with the irresolvable paradox that defines the politics of unsustainability.

References

Bauman, Z. (2000), *Liquid Modernity*, Cambridge: Polity.
Bauman, Z. (2007), *Consuming Life*, Cambridge: Polity.
Blühdorn, I. (2000), *Post-ecologist politics*. London: Routledge.
Blühdorn, I. (2002), 'Unsustainability as a frame of mind – and how we disguise it', *The Trumpeter*, 18: 1, pp. 59–69.
Blühdorn, I. (2004), 'Post-ecologism and the politics of simulation', in M. Wissenburg and Y. Levy (eds), *Liberal Democracy and Environmentalism*, London: Routledge, pp. 35–47.
Blühdorn, I. (2006), 'Self-experience in the theme park of radical action? Social movements and political articulation in the late-modern condition', *European Journal of Social Theory*, 9: 1, pp. 23–42.
Blühdorn, I. (2007a), 'Sustaining the unsustainable: Symbolic politics and the politics of simulation', *Environmental Politics*, 16: 2, pp. 251–75.
Blühdorn, I. (2007b), 'Self-description, self-deception, simulation: A

systems-theoretical perspective on contemporary discourses of radical change' *Social Movement Studies*, 6: 1, pp. 1–20.

Blühdorn, I. (2009a), 'Locked into the politics of unsustainability', in *Eurozine*, 30 October, available at: *http://www.eurozine.com/articles/2009-10-30-bluhdorn-en.html*.

Blühdorn, I. (2009b), 'Reinventing green politics: On the strategic repositioning of the German Green Party', in *German Politics*, 18: 1, pp. 36–54.

Blühdorn, I. (2010), 'Nachhaltigkeit und postdemokratische Wende. Zum Wechselspiel von Demokratiekrise und Umweltkrise', in *Vorgänge* 190: 2, pp. 44–54.

Blühdorn, I. (2011a), 'The politics of unsustainability: COP15, post-ecologism and the ecological paradox', *Organization & Environment*, 24: 1, pp. 34–53.

Blühdorn, I. (2011b), 'The sustainability of democracy: On limits to growth, the post-democratic turn and reactionary democrats', in *Eurozine*, 11 July, available at: *http://www.eurozine.com/articles/2011-07-11-bluhdorn-en.html*.

Blühdorn, I. (2013a), 'The governance of unsustainability: Ecology and democracy after the post-democratic turn', *Environmental Politics*, 22: 1, pp. 16–36.

Blühdorn, I. (2013b), *Simulative Demokratie*. Neue Politik *nach der post-demokratischen Wende*, Berlin: Suhrkamp.

Boggs, C. (2000), *The End of Politics: Corporate Power and the Decline of the Public Sphere*, New York: Guilford Press.

Crouch, C. (2004), *Post-democracy*, Cambridge: Polity.

Davies, J. (2012), 'Network governance theory: a Gramscian critique', *Environment and Planning A*, 44, pp. 2687–704

Die Grünen (1980), *Das Bundesprogramm*, Bonn: Die Grünen.

Dobson, A., and D. Bell (eds), (2006), *Environmental Citizenship*, Cambridge, MA: MIT Press.

Featherstone, M. (2007), *Consumer Culture and Postmodernism* (2nd edn), London: Sage.

Giddens, A. (2009), *The Politics of Climate Change*, Cambridge: Polity.

Goldsmith, E. (1972), *A Blueprint for Survival*, London: Penguin.

Guéhenno, J.-M. (1993), *La fin de la démocratie*, Paris: Champs Flammarion.

Hamilton, C. (2010), *Requiem for a Species. Why We Resist the Truth about Climate Change*, Washington, DC: Earthscan.

Inglehart, R. (1977), *The Silent Revolution: Changing Values and Political Styles among Western Publics*, Princeton, NJ: Princeton University Press.

Inglehart, R. (1997), *Modernization and Postmodernization: Cultural, Economic, and Political Change in 43 Societies*, Princeton, NJ: Princeton University Press.

Inglehart, R. (2007), 'Postmaterialist values and the shift from survival to self-expression values', in R. Dalton and H.-D. Klingemann (eds), *Oxford Handbook of Political Behaviour*, Oxford: Oxford University Press, pp. 223–9.

Inglehart, R., and C. Welzel (2005), *Modernization, Cultural Change and*

Democracy: The Human Development Sequence, Cambridge: Cambridge University Press.

Jacquesa, P. J., R. Dunlap, E. Riley and M. Freemanc (2008), 'The organisation of denial: Conservative think tanks and environmental scepticism', *Environmental Politics*, 17: 3, pp. 349–85.

Jordan, A., R. Wurzel and A. Zito (2013), 'Still the century of new environmental policy instruments? Exploring patterns of innovation and continuity', in *Environmental Politics*, 22: 1, pp. 155–73.

Kaase, M. (1984), 'The challenge of the *participatory revolution* in pluralist democracies', *International Political Science Review*, 5: 3, pp. 299–318.

Keane, J. (2009), *The Life and Death of Democracy*, London: Pocket Books.

Kellner, D. (1995), *Media Culture: Cultural Studies, Identity and Politics Between the Modern and the Postmodern*, London: Routledge.

Lodziak, C. (2002), *The Myth of Consumerism*, London: Pluto.

Micheletti, M. (2003), *Political Virtue and Shopping: Individuals, Consumerism, and Collective Action*, New York: Palgrave.

Mol, A., and D. Sonnenfeld (eds) (2000), *Ecological Modernisation Around the World*, London: Routledge.

Norgaard, J. (2011), *Living in Denial: Climate Change, Emotions and Everyday Life*, Cambridge, MA: MIT Press.

Porritt, J. (1984), *Seeing Green: The Politics of Ecology Explained*, Oxford: Basil Blackwell.

Putnam, R. (2000), *Bowling Alone: The Collapse and Revival of American Community*, New York: Simon and Schuster.

Rancière, J. (2006), *Hatred of Democracy*, London: Verso.

Seyfang, G. (2005), 'Shopping for sustainability: Can sustainable consumption promote ecological citizenship?', *Environmental Politics*, 14: 2, pp. 290–306.

Shearman, D. and J. W. Smith (2008), *The Climate Change Challenge and the Failure of Democracy*, Westport, CT: Praeger.

Soper, K. (2007), 'Re-thinking the good life. The citizenship dimension of consumer disaffection with consumerism', *Journal of Consumer Culture*, 7: 2, pp. 205–29.

Soper, K. (2008), 'Alternative hedonism, cultural theory and the role of aesthetic revisioning', *Cultural Studies*, 22: 5, pp. 567–87.

Swyngedouw, E. (2005), 'Governance innovation and the citizen: The Janus face of governance-beyond-the-state', *Urban Studies*, 42: 11. pp. 1991–2006.

Swyngedouw, E. (2007), 'Impossible/undesirable sustainability and the post-political condition', in D. Gibbs and R. Krueger (eds), *The Sustainable Development Paradox: Urban Political Economy in the United States and Europe*, New York: Guilford Press, pp. 13–40.

Swyngedouw, E. (2008), 'Where is the political?', unpublished manuscript, available at: *http://www.socialsciences.manchester.ac.uk/disciplines/politics/research/hmrg/activities/documents/Swyngedouw.pdf*.

Swyngedouw, E. (2009), 'The antinomies of the post-political city: In search of a democratic politics of environmental production', *International Journal of Urban and Regional Research*, 33: 3, pp. 601–20.

Swyngedouw, E. (2010a), 'Apocalypse forever? Post-political populism and the spectre of climate change', *Theory, Culture & Society*, 27: 2–3, pp. 213–32.

Swyngedouw, E. (2010b), 'The trouble with nature: Ecology as the new opium for the masses', in P. Healey and J. Hiller (eds), *Conceptual Challenges for Planning Theory*, Aldershot: Ashgate, pp. 299–318.

Swyngedouw, E. (2011a), 'Interrogating post-democratization: Reclaiming egalitarian political spaces', *Political Geography*, 30: 7, pp. 370–80.

Swyngedouw, E. (2011b), 'Depoliticized environments: The end of nature, climate change and the post-political condition', *Royal Institute of Philosophy Supplement*, 69, pp. 253–74.

Žižek, Slavoj (2009), *The Ticklish Subject: The Absent Centre of Political Ontology*, London: Verso.

Part II

Spectres of Radical Politics

8 Insurgent Architects, Radical Cities and the Promise of the Political

Erik Swyngedouw

It's useless to *wait* – for a breakthrough, for the revolution, the nuclear apocalypse or a social movement. To go on waiting is madness. The catastrophe is not coming, it is here. We are already situated *within* the collapse of a civilization. It is within this reality that we must choose sides.
(The Invisible Committee 2009: 138)

Insurgent architects: staging equality

The Taksim Square revolt in Istanbul and the Brazilian urban insurgencies are still in full swing at the time of writing, with uncertain and largely unpredictable outcomes. Romanian activists mobilise Occupy-type tactics sparked off by resistance to accumulation by dispossession and threatened socio-environmental destruction by Canadian company Gabriel Resources around planned gold mining in Rosia Montana. These urban rebellions are the latest in a long sequence of political insurgencies that unexpectedly erupted after Mohamed Bouazizi's self-immolation on 17 December 2010 ignited the Tunisian revolution. During the magical year 2011, a seemingly never-ending proliferation of urban rebellions sparked off by a variety of conditions and unfolding against the backdrop of very different historical and geographical contexts profoundly disturbed the apparently cosy neoliberal status quo and disquieted various economic and political elites. There is indeed an uncanny choreographic affinity between the eruptions of discontent in cities as diverse as Istanbul, Cairo, Tunis, Athens, Madrid, Lyon, Lisbon, Rome, New York, Tel Aviv, Chicago, London, Berlin, Thessaloniki, Santiago, Stockholm, Barcelona, Montreal, Oakland, Sao Paulo, Bucharest, and Paris, among many others. The *end of history* proved to be remarkably short-lived as incipient political movements staged – albeit in often inchoate, contradictory, and confusing manners – a profound discontent with the state of the situation and choreographed new urban modes of being-in-common.

A wave of deeply political protest is rolling through the world's cities, whereby those who do not count demand a new constituent process for producing space politically. The heterogeneous gatherers are outraged by and expose the variegated 'wrongs' and spiralling inequalities of autocratic neoliberalisation and actually-existing instituted democratic governance. The celebrated era of urban social movements as the horizon of progressive urban struggles (Castells 1993) seems to be over. A much more politicised if not radical mobilisation, animated by insurgent urban architects, is increasingly choreographing the contemporary theatre of urban politicised struggle and conflict (Swyngedouw 2013).

It is precisely the aftermath of such urban insurrections that provides the starting point for the arguments developed in this chapter. From a radical political perspective, the central question that has opened up, as the wave of insurgencies of the past few years has begun to peter out, revolves around what to do and what to think next. Is further thought and practice possible after the squares are cleared, the tents broken up, the energies dissipated, and everyday life has resumed its routine practices?

The spectral return of the political

For Jacques Rancière, democratising the polis is inaugurated when those who do not count stage the count, perform the process of being counted and thereby initiate a rupture in the order of things, in 'the distribution of the sensible', such that things cannot go on as before (Rancière 1998). From this perspective, democratisation is a performative act that both stages and defines equality, exposes a *wrong*, and aspires to a transformation of the senses and of the sensible, to render commonsense what was non-sensible before. Democratisation, he contends, is a disruptive affair whereby the *ochlos* (the rabble, the scum, the outcasts, 'the part of no part') stages to be part of the *demos* and, in doing so, inaugurates a new ordering of times and places, a process by which those who do not count, who do not exist as part of the polis become visible, sensible and audible, stage the count and assert their egalitarian existence. Egalitarian politics is about 'the symbolic institution of the political in the form of the power of those who are not entitled to exercise power – a rupture in the order of legitimacy and domination. It is the paradoxical power of those who do not count: the count of the "unaccounted for"' (Rancière 2000: 124). Egalitarian-democratic demands and practices, scandalous in the representational order of the police yet eminently realisable, are precisely those staged through mobilisations varying from the Paris and Shanghai communes to the Occupy, *Indignado*, and assorted other emerging political movements that express and nurture such processes of embryonic re-politicisation. Identitarian positions become, in the process, transfigured into a commonality, and a new common sense, and they can be thought and practised irrespective of any substantive social theorisation – it is the political itself at work through the process of political subjectivation, of acting in common by those who do not count, who are surplus to the police.

There are many uncounted today. Alain Badiou refers to them as the 'inexistent', the masses of the people who have no say, 'decide absolutely nothing, have only a fictional voice in the matter of the decisions that decide their fate' (Badiou 2012: 56). The inexistent are the motley assortment of apolitical consumers, frustrated democrats, precarious workers, undocumented migrants, and disenfranchised citizens. The scandal of actually existing instituted (post-)democracy in a world choreographed by oppression, exploitation and extraordinary inequalities resides precisely in rendering masses of people inexistent, politically mute, without a recognised voice.

For Badiou, 'a change of world is real when an inexistent of the world starts to exist in the same world with maximum intensity' (Badiou 2012: 56). In doing so, the order of the sensible is shaken and the kernel for a new common sense, a new mode of being in common becomes present in the world, makes its presence sensible and perceptible. It is the appearance of another world in the world. Was it not precisely the sprawling urban insurgencies that ignited a new sensibility about the polis as a democratic and potentially democratising space? This appearance of the inexistent, staging the count of the uncounted is, it seems to me, what the polis, the political city, is all about. Indeed, as Foucault reminds us, '[t]he people is those who, refusing to be the population, disrupt the system' (Foucault 2007: 43–4).

The notion of the democratising polis introduced above is one that foregrounds intervention and rupture, and destabilises the apparently cosy biopolitical order, sustained by an axiomatic assumption of equality. Democratisation, then, is the act of the few who become the material and metaphorical stand-in for the many; they stand for the dictatorship of the democratic – direct and egalitarian – against the despotism of the instituted 'democracy' of the elites – representative and inegalitarian (Badiou 2012: 59). Is it not precisely these insurgent architects that brought to the fore the irreducible distance between the democratic as the immanence of the presumption of equality and its performative spatialised staging on the one hand, and democracy as an instituted form of regimented oligarchic governing on the other? Do the urban revolts of the past few years not foreground the abyss between 'the democratic' and 'democracy', the surplus and excess that escapes the suturing and depoliticising practices of instituted governing? Is it not the re-emergence of the proto-political in the urban revolts that signals an urgent need to re-affirm the urban, the polis, as a political space, and not just as a space of biopolitically governed city life?

Of course, the social markers of the insurgencies are geographically highly differentiated: for example the resistance against the Morsi regime in Egypt; the attacks on Erdogan's combination of religious conservatism with a booming neoliberalisation of the urban process in Turkey;[1] or the spiralling discontent over the public bail-outs and austerity regimes mounted by assorted states and international organisations to save the global financial system from immanent collapse after the speculative bubble that had nurtured unprecedented inequalities and extraordinary concentration of wealth finally burst in 2008. The quilting points that sparked these rebellions were highly variegated too: a threatened park and a few trees in Istanbul; a religious-authoritarian but nonetheless democratically elected regime in Egypt; massive austerity in Greece, Portugal and Spain; social and financial mayhem in the UK and the US; a rise in the price of public transport tickets in Sao Paulo; the further commodification of higher education in Montreal; large-scale gold mining in Romania. Yet the urban insurgents quickly turned their particular, occasionally identitarian, grievances into a wholesale attack on the instituted order, on the unbridled commodification of urban life in the interests of the few, on the highly unequal socio-economic outcomes of actually-existing representational *democracy-cum-capitalism*. The particular demands transformed quickly and seamlessly into a universalising staging for something different, however diffuse and unarticulated this may presently be. The assembled groups ended up without particular demands addressed to the elites, to a Master. In their refusal to express specific grievances, they demanded everything, nothing less then the transformation of the instituted order. They staged in their socio-spatial acting new ways of practising equality and democracy, experimented with innovative and creative ways of being together in the city, and prefigured, both in practice and in theory, new ways of distributing goods, accessing services, producing healthy environments, organising debate, managing conflict, practicing ecologically saner life-styles, and negotiating urban space in an emancipatory manner.

These insurgencies are decidedly urban; they may be the embryonic manifestation of the immanence of a new urban commons (see García Lamarca 2013), one always potentially in the making, aspiring to produce a new urbanity through intense meetings and encounters of a multitude, one that aspires to spatialisation, that is to universalisation. Such universalisation can never be totalising as the demarcation line is clearly drawn, a line that separates the us (as multitude) from the them, i.e. those who mobilise all they can to make sure nothing really changes, captured neatly in the slogan of the 99 per cent versus the 1 per cent. The democratising minority stands here in strict opposition to the majoritarian rule of instituted democracy. As much as the proletarian, feminist or African-American democratising movements were (and often still are) also very much minoritarian in terms of politically acting subjects, they nonetheless stood and stand for the enactment of the democratic presumption of equality of each and all. The space of the political disturbs the socio-spatial ordering by re-arranging it with those who stand in for 'the people' or 'the community' (Rancière 2001). It is a particular that stands for the whole of the community and aspires towards universalisation. The rebels on Tahrir Square or Taksim Square are not the Egyptian or Turkish population; while being a minority, they stand materially and metaphorically for the Egyptian and Turkish people. The political emerges, Rancière attests, when the few claim the name of the many, to embody the community as a whole, and are recognised as such. The emergence of political space is always specific, concrete, particular and minoritarian, but stands as the metaphorical condensation of the generic, the many and the universal.

These attempts to produce a new commons offer perhaps a glimpse of the theoretical and practical agenda ahead. Do they not call for an urgent reconsideration of both urban theory and urban praxis? Does their acting not signal a clarion call to return the intellectual gaze, to consider again what the polis has always been, namely the site for political encounter and place for enacting the new, the improbable, things often considered impossible by those who do not wish to see any change, the site for experimentation with, the staging and production of new radical imaginaries for what urban democratic being-in-common might be all about? Re-centring the urban political therefore is for me one of the central intellectual demands adequate to today's urban life.

Spectres of the urban political re-scripted

For Alain Badiou, the political is not a reflection of something else, like the cultural, the social, or the economic. For him, the social sciences can at best be oppositional, operating within the standard contestation of 'democratic' rule (Badiou 1999: 94), and incapable of thinking of political transformation as the active affirmation of the egalitarian capacity of each and all to act politically. It is a site open for occupation by those who call it into being, claim its occupation and stage 'equality', irrespective of the place they occupy within the social edifice. It is manifested in the process of subjectivation, in the 'passage to the act'. It is precisely this process of political subjectivation that the social sciences rarely capture, if at all. In what follows, I shall further explore the understanding of the political that foregrounds the notion of equality as the axiomatic, yet contingent, foundation of democracy, that considers égaliberté (Balibar 2010) as an unconditional democratic demand, and that thinks the political as immanent process expressed in the rupture of any given socio-spatial order by exposing a wrong and staging equality. This wrong is a condition in which the axiomatic principle of equality is perverted through the institution of an order – what Rancière refers to as 'the police' – that is always necessarily oligarchic.

The political is not about expressing demands to the elites to rectify inequalities or unfreedoms, the daily choreographies of interest and conflict intermediation in public policy arrangements and rituals of governance, or a call on 'the state' to undertake action. It is the demand to be counted, named and recognised, theatrically and publicly staged by those 'who do not count', the inexistent. It is the articulation of voice that demands its place in the spaces of the police order. It appears, for example, when undocumented residents shout 'We are here, therefore we are from here!' and affirm their place within the socio-political edifice, or when the Spanish Indignados demand 'Democracia real ya!' and the Occupy movements claim to be the 99 per cent that have no voice. Their performative and localised inscriptions are the evental time-spaces from where a new democratising political sequence may unfold. Insurgent democratic politics, therefore, are radically anti-utopian; they are not about fighting for a utopian future, but are precisely about bringing into being, spatialising, what is already promised by the very principle upon which the political is constituted, i.e. equalitarian emancipation.

Such egalitarian staging of being-in-common, therefore, always operates at a certain minimal distance from the State/the police and invariably meets with the violence inscribed in the functioning of the police. Its spatial markers are not the parliament, meeting room or council chamber, but the square, the housing estate, the people's assembly, the university campus, the street, the park, the factory or office floor. Insurgent urbanity cannot do other than provoke the wrath of the state and has to confront, stare in the face, the violence that marks such a potential 'rebirth of history' as

Badiou provocatively calls it (Badiou 2012). Insurrectional interruption precisely incites the objective in-egalitarian violence of
the instituted order to become subjective, socially embodied, and
visible/perceptible, to render visible the irreducible gap between the
democratic as immanent process and the police as instituted and
taken-for-granted order (Žižek 2008). Confronting the violence of
the police and navigating a course that opens up trajectories of
change while preventing the confrontation descending into a spiralling abyss of violence is an urgent and difficult task, one that hinges
fundamentally on the process of organisation and the modalities of
its universalisation. Politics is indeed the moment of confrontation of
the axiomatic assumption of equality, the meeting ground between
police and the political, when the principle of equality confronts a
wrong instituted through the police order.

Politics understood in the above terms rejects a naturalisation of
the political, signals that a political *passage à l'acte* does not rely on
expert knowledge and administration (the partition of the sensible),
on re-arranging the choreographies of governance, or on organising
'good governance', but on a disruption of the field of vision and of the
distribution of functions and spaces on the basis of the principle of
equality. This perspective challenges a deep-seated belief that expert
knowledge and managerial capacity can be mobilised to enhance
the democratic governance of urban space, and that the horizon of
intervention is limited to the consensualising post-democratic management of the existing state of affairs (Swyngedouw 2009; 2011).
Of course, the above argument begs the question as to what to do.
How to reclaim the political from the debris of consensual autocratic
post-democracy?

The question of democracy: staging egalitarian dissensus

Rancière's notion of the political is characterised by division, conflict
and polemic (Valentine 2005). For him,

> democracy always works against the pacification of social disruption,
> against the management of consensus and 'stability' . . . The concern of
> democracy is not with the formulation of agreement or the preservation
> of order but with the invention of new and hitherto unauthorized modes
> of disaggregation, disagreement and disorder. (Hallward 2005: 34–5)

The politics of consensual urban design in its post-politicising guise,
therefore, colonises and contributes to a further hollowing-out of

what, for Rancière and others, constitutes the very horizon of the political as radically heterogeneous and conflicted. Disavowal of the political is pushed to its limits in such processes of foreclosure. Indeed and ironically, by inviting debate and discussion that eschews rupture, the political is de facto foreclosed. Consensus is precisely what suspends the democratic:

> Consensus is thus not another manner of exercising democracy ... [It] is the negation of the democratic basis for politics: it desires to have well-identifiable groups with specific interests, aspirations, values and 'culture' ... Consensualist centrism flourishes with the multiplication of differences and identities. It nourishes itself with the complexification of the elements that need to be accounted for in a community, with the permanent process of autorepresentation, with all the elements and all their differences: the larger the number of groups and identities that need to be taken into account in society, the greater the need for arbitration. The 'one' of consensus nourishes itself with the multiple. (Rancière 2000: 125)

Something similar is at work in the micro-politics of local urban struggles, dispersed resistances and alternative practices that customarily suture the field of urban social movements today. These are the spheres where urban activism dwells as some form of 'placebo'-politicalness (Marchart 2007: 47). This anti-political impulse works through colonisation of the political by the social through sublimation. Such urban social struggles identify ruptures, disagreements, contestations and fractures that inevitably erupt out of the incomplete saturation of the social world by the police order with a political act. The variegated, dispersed and occasionally effective (on their own terms) forms of urban activism that emerge within concrete socio-spatial interventions – concerning local pollution, road proposals, urban development schemes, airport noise or expansions, the felling of trees or forests, the construction of incinerators, industrial plants, mining ventures and so on – elevate the mobilisations of localised communities, particular groups, and non-governmental organisations to the level of the political. They become imbued with and are assigned political significance. The space of the political is thereby 'reduced to the seeming politicisation of these groups or entities ... Here the political is not truly political because of the restricted nature of the constituency' (Marchart 2007: 47). The identitarian elevation of matters of fact to matters of concern seems, in such a context, to constitute the horizon of the political, of what is possible, of what can be thought and done. In other words, particular urban conflicts are elevated to the status and the dignity of the

political. Rather than politicising, such particularistic social colonisation erodes and outflanks the political dimension of egalibertarian
universalisation. The latter cannot be substituted by a proliferation
of identitarian, multiple and ultimately fragmented communities.
Moreover, such expressions of protest that are framed fully within
the existing police order are, in the current post-politicising arrangement, already fully acknowledged and accounted for. In fact, these
protests, as well as their mode of expression, are called into being
through the practices of the existing order. They are positively invited
as expressions of the proper functioning of 'democracy', and become
instituted through public-private stakeholder participatory forms of
governance, succumbing to the 'tyranny of participation' (Cooke
and Kothari 2001). If they reject the post-democratic frame, they are
radically marginalised and symbolised as 'radicals' or 'fundamentalists', and are thereby relegated to a domain outside the consensual
post-democratic arrangement; they are rendered inexistent.

The more radical forms of urban activism become 'an unend-
ing process which can destabilize, displace, and so on, the power
structure, without ever being able to undermine it effectively' (Žižek
2002: 101), and as such are doomed to fail. The problem with these
tactics is that they not only leave the symbolic order intact and, at
best, 'tickle' the police order (see Critchley 2007), but also, as Žižek
puts it, 'these practices of performative reconfiguration/displacement
ultimately support what they intend to subvert, since the very fields
of such "transgressions" are already taken into account, even engen-
dered by the hegemonic form' (Žižek, 1999: 264). More problem-
atically, the ethical injunction, the humanitarian cause becomes the
ultimate horizon of the possible. In other words, such movements
point to a humanitarian ethics as the externally legitimising ground
for their interventions.

In contrast to these impotent passages of hysterical acting out, the
political as conceived in the context of this contribution is understood as an emergent property discernible in 'the moment in which
a particular demand is not simply part of the negotiation of interests
but aims at something more, and starts to function as the metaphoric
condensation of the global restructuring of the entire social space'
(Žižek 1999: 208). It is about the recognition of conflict as constitutive of the social condition, and the naming of the spatialities that
can become without being grounded in universalising notions of the
social (in the sense of an unfractured community or a sociological
definition of equality, unity or cohesion) or of a singular notion of
'the people'. The political becomes, for Žižek and Rancière, the space
of litigation (Žižek 1998), the space for those who are not-All, who
are uncounted and unnamed, not part of the police (symbolic or

state) order. A political space is a space of contestation inaugurated by those who have no name and no place.

The elementary gesture of politicisation is thus '[t]his identification of the non-part with the Whole, of the part of society with no properly defined place within it (or resisting the allocated place within it) with the Universal' (Žižek 2006a: 70). Such new symbolisations through which what is considered to be noise by the police is turned into speech signal an incipient re-politicisation of public civic space in the polis. Reclaiming democracy and the insurgent design of democratising public spaces (as spaces for the enunciation of agonistic dispute) becomes a foundation and condition of possibility for a reclaimed polis, one that is predicated upon the symbolisation of a positively embodied egalibertarian socio-ecological future that is immediately realisable. These symbolisations start from the premise that equality is being 'wronged' by the given urban police order, and are about claiming/producing/carving out a metaphorical and material space by those who are unaccounted for, unnamed, whose fictions are only registered as inarticulate utterances. Insurgency is, therefore, an integral part of the aesthetic register through which the re-framing of what is sensible is articulated and becomes symbolisable. This is a call for a de-sublimation and a decolonisation of the political or, rather, for a re-conquest of the political from the social, a reinvention of the political gesture from the plainly depoliticising affects of post-political and post-democratic policing.

Incipient urban politicisation

Alain Badiou has recently explored the significance of these insurrectional events (Badiou 2012). For him, the proliferation of these insurgencies is a sign of a return of the ideas of freedom, solidarity, equality and emancipation (which generically go under the political name of communism, the historically invariant 'name' for emancipatory struggle). The historical-geographical experimenting expressed through insurgent activities – that have not (yet) and may never acquire a political name or symbolisation (and surely a return to the name of 'communism' to designate these movements is unlikely) – nonetheless expresses for Badiou a certain fidelity to the generic communist hypothesis understood as a fidelity to the truth

> that a different collective organisation is practicable, one that will eliminate the inequality of wealth and even the division of labour. The private appropriation of massive fortunes and their transmission by inheritance will disappear. The existence of a coercive state, separate from civil

society, will no longer appear a necessity: a long process of reorganisa-
tion based on a free association of producers will see it withering away.
(Badiou 2008: 35)

A range of observers have systematically commented on and argued
for a more in-depth theoretical and practical engagement between
the insurrectional movements and the experimental practices that
articulate around new forms of egalitarian and solidarity-based management of the commons (see, for example, Badiou 2010; Bosteels
2011; Dean 2012; Douzinas and Žižek 2010; Swyngedouw 2010a;
Žižek 2013a).

Badiou thinks the recent urban insurgencies as 'historical riots'
that are marked by procedures of *intensification, contraction*, and
localisation (Badiou 2012: 90–1). First, intensification refers to the
enthusiasm marked by an intensification and implosion of time, a
radicalisation of statements, and an explosion of activities, condensed
in an emblematic space that is re-organised to express and mobilised
to relay this enthusiasm. All manner of people come together in an
intensive explosion, of an intensified process of being that energises
and incites others to share the enthusiasm inaugurated by the event.
A politics of encounter, of opening up, of joining-up animates such
intensification (Merrifield 2013). Radicalising statements, actions
and forms of taking sides coincide with an intensification of time in
place, creating 'an active process of correspondence . . . between the
universality of the Idea and the singular detail of the site and the circumstances' (Badiou 2012: 90–91). Such an intense state of collective
creation cannot be other that short-lived. Nonetheless, the Idea crystallised in the insurrectional event will last long after the return to the
'normality' of everyday life. What is at stake, then, is how to organise
the energy and to universalise the Idea inaugurated in the originary
event, how to engage in the slow, difficult and protracted process of
inaugurating a new sensibility, a new common sense, of nurturing
fidelity, after the initial enthusiasm that marks the historical moment
begins to dissipate.

Second, these enormous vital energies are mobilised for a sustained
period of time in a contracted manner. All manner of people come
together in an intensive explosion of acting, of an intensified process
of being-in-common. This intensity operates in and through the collective togetherness of heterogeneous individuals who in their mode
of being-in-common, in their multiplicity and process of political
subjectivation (that is, in becoming a political actant) and in their
encounter, stand for the metaphorical and material condensation of
the People (as political category). It is the emergence of a thinking
minority that takes the generic position of 'the people'. In doing so,

they 'replace an identitarian object, and the separating names bound up in it' (like Muslim, Christian, worker, intellectual, young, old, woman, man) with the common name of 'we, the People' (Badiou 2012: 92).

Finally, a political Idea/Imaginary cannot find ground and grounding without localisation. A political moment is always placed, localised, and invariably operative in public space. Squares and other (semi-)public spaces, like picket lines, workers' or women's houses, occupied factories, or the Italian *Centri Sociali*, have historically always been the sites, the geographical places, for performing and enacting emancipatory practices; these are the sites of existence, of exhibition, of becoming popular. Without a site, a place, a location, a political idea is impotent. The location produces intensity, unity and presence, and permits contraction. However, such intense and contracted localised practices can only ever be an event, originary, but ultimately pre-political. It does not (yet) constitute a political sequence.

In sum, the political emerges when the few claim the name of the many, the community as a whole, and are recognised as such. The emergence of political space is always specific, concrete, particular, minoritarian, but stands, in a sort of short-circuiting, as the condensation of the universal. This has to be fully endorsed and the consequences carefully considered. In particular, it pits a democratising process often against majoritarian, but ultimately passive and objectified, representative democracy. It is worth quoting Badiou at length here:

> It is then much more appropriate to speak of popular *dictatorship* than democracy. The word 'dictatorship' is widely execrated in our 'democratic' environment ... But just as movement democracy, which is egalitarian and direct, is absolutely opposed to the 'democracy' of the executives of Capital's power, which is inegalitarian and representative, so the dictatorship exercised by a popular movement is radically opposed to dictatorships *as forms of separated, oppressive state*. By 'popular dictatorship' we mean an authority that is legitimate precisely because its truth derives from the fact that it legitimizes itself. No one is the delegate to anybody else. (Badiou 2012: 59)

Such movement democracy, minoritarian yet presenting and recognised as the general will of the people, destabilises liberal notions of instituted democratic forms and forces us to consider 'the democratic' as process against democracy as constituted arrangement, or, in other words, to think, with Miguel Abensour, 'democracy against the state' (Abensour 2011). Indeed, the ultimate aim of politics is intervention, to change the given socio-environmental ordering in a certain manner. Like any intervention, this is a violent act. It at least partly erases what is there in order to erect something new and different. It is of central importance to recognise that politicising acts are singular interventions that (aspire to) produce particular socio-ecological arrangements and milieus and, in doing so, foreclose (at least temporarily) the possibility of others to emerge. Any intervention enables the formation of certain socio-ecological assemblages and closes down others. The subjective 'violence' inscribed in such choice has to be fully endorsed and its implications teased out. For example, one cannot simultaneously have a truly carbon-free city and permit unlimited car-based mobility, or socio-economic equality with the endurance of hereditary intergenerational wealth transfer. They are mutually exclusive. Even less can an egalitarian, democratic, solidarity-based and ecologically sensible future be produced without marginalising or excluding those who insist on a private appropriation of the commons of the earth and its mobilisation for accumulation, personal enrichment and hereditary transmission.

An egalitarian politics is radically inclusive; 'it is an inclusionary struggle' (Žižek 2013b: 126). Of course, the question then arises of how to confront those who remain on the outside, who will mobilise whatever dispositive to prevent the universalisation of the inclusionary struggle. Against their symbolic and objective violence, it is vital to think about ways to protect and defend the universalising process without descending into abyssal terror, about how to navigate the prospect of failure in the absence of effective defence as experienced by the Paris Commune or in the violence of political terror that marked so many past emancipatory transformations. Such violent encounters, of course, always constitute a political act, one that can be legitimised only in political terms. Neither philosophical musings nor substantive social theory can serve to legitimise such encounters.

Any political sequence is one that re-orders socio-ecological coordinates and patterns, reconfigures uneven socio-ecological relations (while foreclosing others), often with unforeseen or unforeseeable consequences. Consider, for example, how the historical struggle for political emancipation and equality was predicated upon sustained class and political struggle in the face of persistent and occasionally ruthless oppression and opposition. Such interventions that express a choice and take sides invariably signal an autocratic moment and the temporary suspension of the democratic understood as the agonistic encounter of heterogeneous views under the aegis of an axiomatically presumed equality of all. The gap between the democratic as a political given, predicated upon the presumption of the equality on the one hand and the autocratic moment of political intervention as the (temporary) suspension of the democratic on the other needs to be radically endorsed. While a pluralist democratic politics, founded on a presumption of equality, insists on difference, disagreement, radical openness and exploring multiple possible futures, concrete spatial-ecological intervention is necessarily about relative closure (for some), definitive choice, singular intervention and, thus, certain exclusion and occasionally even outright silencing. For example, tar sand exploitation and 'fracking' (hydraulic fracturing) cannot coincide with a climate policy worthy of the name. While 'traditional' democratic policies are based on majoritarian principles, the democratic-egalitarian perspectives insist on foregrounding equality and socio-ecological solidarity as the foundational gesture.

A political truth procedure or a political sequence, for Alain Badiou, unfolds when, in the name of equality, fidelity to an event is declared; a fidelity that, although always particular, aspires to become public, to universalise. It is a wager on the truth of the egalitarian political sequence (Badiou 2008). Such a sequence can retroactively be traced through its process of de-localisation from or spatialisation of the originary site, encapsulated when, for example, the *Indignados* claimed 'We are here, but anyway it's global, and we're everywhere'. While aspiring to universalise, such a spatialising movement can never be totalising; while everyone is invited in, not all will accept the invitation. The repetition of the repertoires of action, the continuing identification with the originary Idea, and the moving-back-and-forth between insurrectional sites, may begin to tentatively open up new spatialiaties of transformation while prefiguring experimental relations for new organisational forms. Such a process of spatialisation renders concrete, gives content, to the 'equality' expressed in the originary event. In the process, equality becomes substantively embodied and expressed; and perhaps a new political name that captures the new imaginary and its associated new common(s) sense may emerge alongside it.

While staging equality in public squares is a vital moment, the process of transformation requires the slow but unstoppable production of new forms of spatialisation quilted around materialising the claims of equality, freedom and solidarity. In other words, what is required now and what needs to be thought through is if and how these proto-political localised events can turn into a spatialised political 'truth' procedure; a process that has to consider carefully the persistent obstacles and often-violent strategies of resistance orchestrated by those who wish to hang on to the existing state of the situation. This procedure raises the question of political subjectivation and organisational configurations, and requires perhaps forging a political name that captures the imaginary of a new egalitarian commons appropriate for the twenty-first century's planetary form of urbanisation. During the nineteenth and twentieth centuries, these names were closely associated with 'communism' or 'socialism', and centred on the key tropes of the party as adequate organisational form, the proletarian as privileged political subject, and the state as the arena of struggle and site to occupy. The present situation requires a re-imagined socio-ecological configuration and a new set of strategies that nonetheless still revolve around the notions of equality. However, state, party and proletarian may not any longer be the key axes around which an emancipatory sequence becomes articulated. While the remarkable uprisings of 2011 signalled a desire for a different political configuration, there is a long way to go in terms of thinking through and acting upon the modalities that might unleash a transformative democratic political sequence. Considerable intellectual work needs to be done and experimentation is required in terms of thinking through and pre-figuring what organisational forms are appropriate and adequate to the task, what is the terrain of struggle, and what or who are the agents of its enactment?

The urgent tasks now to undertake for those who maintain fidelity to the proto-political events choreographed in the new insurrectional spaces that demand a new constituent politics (that is a new mode of organising everyday environments) revolve centrally around inventing new modes and practices of collective and sustained political mobilisation, organising the concrete modalities of spatialising and universalising the Idea provisionally materialised in these intense and contracted localised insurrectional events and the assembling of a wide range of new political subjects who are not afraid to stage an egalitarian being-in-common, imagine a different commons, demand the impossible, perform the new and confront the violence that will inevitably intensify as those who insist on maintaining the present order realise that their days might be numbered. Such post-capitalist politics is not and cannot be based solely on class positions. As Marx long ago asserted, class is a bourgeois concept and practice. The insurgencies are not waged by a class, but by the masses as an assemblage of heterogeneous political subjects. It is when the masses as a political category stage their presence that the elites recoil in horror.

In the aftermath of the insurgencies of the past few years, a veritable explosion of new socio-spatial practices are experimented with, from housing occupations and movements against dispossession in Spain to rapid proliferation of experimenting with new egalibertarian life-styles and forms of social and ecological organisation in Greece, Spain and many other places, alongside more traditional forms of political organising. Not all experimentations will succeed.

Many will fail. In the face of inevitable setbacks – like the current catastrophe in Egypt – the fidelity to the democratising process needs to be maintained and sharpened. An extraordinary experimentation with dispossessing the dispossessor, with reclaiming the commons and organising access, transformation and distribution in more egalibertarian ways already marks the return to 'ordinary' life in the aftermath of the insurgencies. The incipient ideas expressed in the event are materialised in a variety of places and ways, and in the midst of painstaking efforts to build alliances, bridge sites, repeat the insurgencies, establish connectivities and, in the process, produce organisation, symbolise its practices and generalise its desire. The repetition of heterogeneous situations may well be – as Nick Srnicek argues – what is adequate today to sustain fidelity to the events choreographed by the incipient politicisations of recent insurgencies (Srnicek 2008). Such procedures require painstaking organisation, sustained political action, and a committed fidelity to universalising the egalitarian trajectory for the management of the commons. While staging equality in public squares is a vital moment, the process of transformation requires the slow but unstoppable production of new forms of spatialisation quilted around materialising the claims of equality, freedom and solidarity. This is the promise of the return of the political embryonically manifested in insurgent practices.

By way of conclusion: from ground zero to enacting the polis

The Real of the political cannot be fully suppressed and is now returning in the form of the urban insurgencies with which I opened this contribution. Yet if the political remains foreclosed, and the polis remains moribund in the face of the post-politicising suspension of the properly democratic, then what is to be done? How can the polis be reclaimed as a political space? How and in what ways can the courage of the urban collective intellect(ual) be mobilised to think through a design of and for dissensual or polemical spaces? I would situate the tentative answers to these questions in three interrelated registers of thought.

The first revolves around transgressing the fantasy that sustains the post-political order. This would include not surrendering to the temptation to act out. The hysterical act of resistance ('I have to do something or the city, the world, will go to the dogs') just answers the call of power to do what you want, to live your dream, to be a 'responsible' citizen. Acting out is actually what is invited, an injunction to obey, to be able to answer to 'What have you done today?' The proper response to this injunction to undertake action, to design the new, to be different (which is already fully accounted for within the state of the situation) is to follow Bartleby's modest, yet radically transgressive, reply to his Master, 'I'd prefer not to . . .' (Žižek 2006b). The refusal to act, to stop asking what they want from me, to stop wanting to be liked is not only an affirmation that the Master does not exist or, at least, that the emperor is naked, but also an invitation to think, or rather, to think again. The courage of the urban intellect(ual) is a courage to be an organic intellectual of the city qua polis. This is an urgent task and requires the formation of new imaginaries and the resurrection of thought that has been censored, scripted out, suspended, and rendered obscene. In other words, is it still possible to *think*, for the twenty-first century, the design of a democratic, polemical, equitable, free common urbanity? Can we still think through today the censored metaphors of equality, communism, living-in-common, solidarity, egalibertarian political democracy? Are we condemned to rely on our humanitarian sentiments to manage socially to the best of our techno-managerial abilities the perversities of late capitalist urbanity, or can a different politics and process of being-in-common be thought and designed? I like to be on the side of the latter.

The second moment of reclaiming the polis revolves around re-centring/redesigning the urban as a democratic political field of disagreement. This is about enunciating dissent and rupture, and the ability to literally open up spaces that permit acts that claim and stage a place in the order of things. This centres on rethinking equality politically; i.e. thinking equality not as a sociologically verifiable concept or procedure that permits opening a policy arena that will remedy the observed inequalities (utopian/normative/moral) some time in a utopian future (i.e. the standard recipe of left-liberal urban policy prescriptions), but as the axiomatically given and presupposed, albeit contingent, condition of democracy. This must include of course the constitution and construction of common spaces as collectivised spaces for experimenting and living differentially, to counter 'the hyper-exploitation or the time that is imposed and that one tries to re-appropriate' (Kakogianni and Rancière 2013: 24). Political space thereby emerges as the collective or common space for the institutionalisation of the social (society) and equality as the foundational gesture of political democracy (as its presumed, axiomatic, yet contingent foundation).

This requires extraordinary designs (both theoretically and materially), ones that cut through the master signifiers of consensual urban governance (creativity, sustainability, growth, cosmopolitanism, participation, and so on) and their radical metonymic re-imagination

(see Gunder and Hillier 2009; Swyngedouw 2010b). Such metonymic re-registering demands thinking through the city as a space
for accommodating equalitarian difference and disorder. This hinges
critically on creating egalibertarian public spaces. Most importantly, the utopian framing that customarily informs urban visioning
requires reversal to a temporal sequence centred on imagining concrete spatio-temporal utopias as immediately necessary and realisable. This echoes Henri Lefebvre's clarion call for the 'right to the
city' understood as the 'right to the production of urbanisation', and
urges us to think of the city as a process of collective co-design and
co-production (Harvey 2012).

Thirdly, and most importantly, transmutating insurgency into a
political sequence poses the need to traverse the fantasy of the elites,
a fantasy that is sustained and nurtured by the perverse imaginary
of an autopoietic world, the hidden hand of market exchange that
self-regulates and self-organises, serving simultaneously the interests
of the Ones and the All, the private and the common. The socialism
for the elites that structures the contemporary city is Really one that
engages the common and the commons in the interests of the elite
Ones through the mobilisation and disciplinary registers of post-
democratic politics (Beverungen, Murtola and Schwarts 2013). It is
a fantasy that is further sustained by a double fantastic promise. On
the one hand, there is the promise of eventual enjoyment – 'Believe
us and our designs will guarantee your enjoyment'. It is an enjoyment that is forever postponed, that becomes a veritable utopia,
a no-place. On the other hand, there is the recurrent promise of
catastrophe and disintegration if the elite's fantasy is not realised,
if one does not surrender to the injunctions of the Master. This
dystopian fantasy is predicated upon the relentless cultivation of
fear (of ecological disintegration and ecocide, excessive migration,
terrorism, economic-financial collapse), fears that are both relayed
by and managed through technocratic-expert knowledge and elite
governance arrangements. This fantasy of catastrophe has a cas-
trating effect – it sustains the impotence for naming and designing
truly alternative cities, truly different emancipatory spatialities and
urbanities.

Traversing elite fantasies requires the intellectual and political courage to imagine egalitarian democracies; the production of
common values and the collective production of the greatest collective *oeuvre*, the city; the inauguration of new political trajectories
of living life in common; and, most importantly, the courage to
choose, to take sides. Most importantly, traversing the fantasy of
the elites means recognising that the social, economic and ecological catastrophe that is announced every day as tomorrow's threat is

not a promise, not something to come, but *is* already the Real of the present.

Note

1. This is stunningly captured in the documentary *Ecumenopolis: City Without Limits*; see *http://www.ekumenopolis.net/#/en_US* (accessed 22 July 2013).

References

Abensour, M. (2011), *Democracy against the State*, Cambridge: Polity Press.

Badiou, A. (1999), 'Poirier Nicholas – Entretien avec Alain Badiou, *Le Philosophoire*, 9, 11–25.

Badiou, A. (2008), 'The communist hypothesis', *New Left Review*, 49, 29–42.

Badiou, A. (2010), *The Communist Hypothesis*, London: Verso.

Badiou, A. (2012), *The Rebirth of History: Times of Riots and Uprisings*, London: Verso.

Balibar, É (2010) *La Proposition de l'Égaliberté*, Paris: Presses Universitaires de France.

Beverungen, A., A.-M. Murtola and G. Schwarts (2013). 'The communism of capital', *Ephemera*, 13(3).

Bosteels, B. (2011), *The Actuality of Communism*, London: Verso.

Castells, M. (1993), *The City and the Grassroots: A Cross-Cultural Theory of Urban Social Movements*, Berkeley: University of California Press.

Cooke, B., and U. Kothari (eds) (2001), *Participation: The New Tyranny?*, London: Zed Books.

Critchley, S. (2007), *Infinitely Demanding – Ethics of Commitment, Politics of Resistance*, London: Verso.

Dean, J. (2012), *The Communist Horizon*, London: Verso.

Douzinas, C., and S. Žižek (eds) (2010), *The Idea of Communism*, London: Verso.

Foucault, M. (2007), *Security, Territory, Population: Lectures at the Collège de France 1977–1978,* London: Palgrave Macmillan.

García Lamarca, M. (2013), 'Insurgent practices and housing in Spain: Making urban commons?', paper presented at Symposium on 'Urban Commons: Moving beyond State and Market', George Simmel Centre for Metropolitan Research, Humboldt University, Berlin, 27–8 September.

Gunder, M., and J. Hillier (2009) *Planning in Ten Words or Less – A Lacanian Entanglement with Spatial Planning*, Farnham: Ashgate.

Hallward, P. (2005), 'Jacques Rancière and the subversion of mastery', *Paragraph*, 28, 26–45.

Harvey, D. (2012), *Rebel Cities*, London: Verso.

Kakogianni M., and J. Rancière (2013), 'A precarious dialogue', *Radical Philosophy*, 178 (September/October), pp. 18–25.

Marchart, O. (2007), *Post-Foundational Political Thought: Political Difference in Nancy, Lefort, Badiou and Laclau*, Edinburgh: University Press.

Merrifield, A. (2013), *The Politics of the Encounter: Urban Theory and Protest under Planetary Urbanization*, Athens, GA: University of Georgia Press.

Rancière, J. (1998), *Disagreement*, Minneapolis: University of Minnesota Press.

Rancière, J. (2000), 'Dissenting words. A conversation with Jacques Rancière (with Davide Panagia)', *Diacritics,* 30, pp. 113–26.

Rancière, J. (2001), 'Ten theses on politics', *Theory & Event, 5.*

Srnicek, N. (2008), 'What is to be done? Alain Badiou and the pre-evental', *Symposium,* 12, pp. 110–26.

Swyngedouw, E. (2009), 'The antinomies of the post-political city. In search of a democratic politics of environmental production', *International Journal of Urban and Regional Research,* 33, pp. 601–20.

Swyngedouw, E. (2010a), 'The communist hypothesis and revolutionary capitalisms: Exploring the idea of communist geographies for the twenty-first century', *Antipode,* 41, pp. 1439–60.

Swyngedouw, E. (2010b), 'The trouble with nature: Ecology as the new opium for the masses', in P. Healey and J. Hillier (eds), *Conceptual Challenges for Planning Theory*, Aldershot: Ashgate, pp. 299–320.

Swyngedouw, E. (2011), 'Interrogating post-democracy: Reclaiming egalitarian political spaces', *Political Geography,* 30: 7, pp. 370–80.

Swyngedouw, E. (2013), 'Where is the political? Insurgent mobilizations and the incipient "return of the political"'. *Space and Polity,* (forthcoming).

The Invisible Committee (2009), *The Coming Insurrection*, Cambridge, MA: MIT Press.

Valentine, J. (2005), 'Rancière and contemporary political problems', *Paragraph,* 28, pp. 46–60.

Žižek, S. (1998). 'For a leftist appropriation of the European legacy', *Journal of Political Ideologies,* 3, pp. 63–78.

Žižek, S. (1999), *The Ticklish Subject: The Absent Centre of Political Ontology*, London: Verso.

Žižek, S. (2002), *Welcome to the Desert of the Real*, London: Verso.

Žižek, S. (2006a), 'The lesson of Rancière', in J. Rancière (ed.), *The Politics of Aesthetics*, London: Continuum, pp. 69–79.

Žižek, S. (2006b), *The Parallax View*, Cambridge, MA: MIT Press.

Žižek, S. (2008), *Violence*, London: Profile Books.

Žižek, S. (ed.) (2013a), *The Idea of Communism 2: The New York Conference*, London: Verso.

Žižek, S. (2013b), *Demanding the Impossible*, ed. Y.-J. Park, Cambridge: Polity.

9 The Limits of Post-Politics: Rethinking Radical Social Enterprise

Wendy Larner

Over the past three years I have been working with an urban community organisation called Coexist, based in Bristol, a small provincial city in the United Kingdom. Coexist is a registered Community Interest Company based in Hamilton House, a disused office building in the formerly rundown, but now rapidly changing, inner-city area of Stokes Croft. It was set up to manage spaces in which people can 'coexist' with themselves, with each other, and with the environment. Coexist has drawn together a diverse array of artists, crafts people, community groups, health practitioners and social enterprises in their effort to provide a base for innovative and ethical social organisations at below-market rents. Their broader vision includes building networks with a diverse range of local groups and institutions that can be leveraged to create new opportunities for themselves and others. Examples of this wider engagement include engagement with local food restaurants, participation in the establishment of a 'Creative Commons' as part of Bristol's economic development zone, and networking to support Bristol social enterprises and develop a new generation of 'social entrepreneurs'. The expressed aim of all this activity is to establish Coexist specifically, and the city of Bristol more generally, as a 'beacon of good practice' that will enable others nationally and internationally to emulate their grassroots model of environmentally sensitive urban regeneration and social innovation.

At first glance Coexist would appear to be exactly the kind of partnering, networked, post-political and post-democratic initiative that the wider literature on post-politics worries about. While Coexist may think they are working towards a more inclusive and egalitarian future, and are developing novel environmental, economic and social arrangements to underpin their urban experiments in living and working, most commentators on post-politics would argue that grassroots organisations such as these are caught up in depoliticised frameworks that draw together 'enlightened technocrats and liberal multiculturalists' (Žižek 1998) and are inadvertently reinforcing the neoliberal status quo. It could be argued that their efforts are embedded within the now familiar conceptions of community resilience, local economies, and social enterprise that increasingly shape mainstream economic development agendas. Rather than engaging in oppositional forms of resistance and social activism, they are actively building relationships with more mainstream organisations and institutions. While Hamilton House is a grassroots creative space that has arisen from a dynamic other than that of conventional forms of urban economic development and place-making, and Coexist have explicitly resisted the imposition of both corporate businesses and formal political structures, they are increasingly articulated into more classical arts- and culture-led regeneration efforts taking place across the city. Seen in this light, it is easy to understand how initiatives like Coexist might be seen as exemplifying the post-political ideal behind the neoliberal 'Third Way'.

The more applied urban geography and policy studies literatures also encourage us to be sceptical about such efforts. Building on longstanding claims about community organisations becoming 'little fingers of the state' (Wolch 1990), there is now an enormous literature about the ever-present perils of collaboration and partnership. Endless social science analyses in very diverse geographical and political settings have shown that while relational forms of governance purport to offer community organisations access to decision-making processes, too often they become rubber-stamping 'consultations' rather than a genuine example of the co-production of policy and service delivery, let alone the radical political alternatives they might aspire to be. Indeed, in discussions of neoliberalism, such 'discontents', and the arrangements they give rise to, are now often seen as part of the way in which the imaginaries and practices of neoliberalism have mutated over time (Leitner, Peck and Sheppard 2007). More generally, these discussions of the changing relationships between states and community organisations are echoed by commentators worried about the blurring of the boundaries between public- and private-sector organisations, largely as a result of the introduction of competitive contractualism, the associated move towards greater professionalism and an increasing reliance on mainstream business models (see Raco, Chapter 1 of this volume).

This chapter will challenge recent social scientific arguments about post-politics in which it is argued that technologies of government that privilege partnership, consensus and agreement have displaced debate, disagreement and dissensus. More generally, I have begun to worry about the relentless pessimism that characterises almost all

social science scholarship on neoliberalism, whether it be the nor-
matively oriented political theory of post-politics or the pragmatic
considerations of applied policy studies. This worry is not simply
personal inclination, and it is certainly not political proclivity; rather
it reflects my agreement with Collier (2012) that too much has been
taken for granted in discussions of what neoliberalism is, and too
little attention has been paid to examining the actual initiatives, ideas
and techniques involved. I will frame this argument through a review
of recent debates about the relationships between neoliberalism and
other political projects. I then use the example of Coexist to highlight
why looking closely at such initiatives encourages us to ask new questions about contemporary forms of governance. I will show that in
contrast to the 'enlightened experts and political elites' who receive
attention in accounts of post-politics, there are multiple and heterogeneous actors assembling around this initiative. Their strategies do
not involve the competitive comparisons and top-down partnerships
that feature in technocratic management; rather they involve the
fostering of relational forms of governance premised on alternative
conceptions of leadership, courage, willpower and fortitude. The
networked polyvalent political formations that emerge are not the
depoliticised post-democratic institutions highlighted in the existing
literature on post-politics. Instead, they fundamentally question the
status quo and actively seek political alternatives. In doing so, they
illustrate how social movements may welcome, enact and live radically different possibilities, thereby exemplifying a broader emphasis
on anticipating the future (Anderson 2010; Gibson-Graham and
Roelvink 2009). This approach, I would argue, is more useful in the
current conjuncture than one that makes invisible or even invalidates
the ongoing struggles of those who want political change in the here
and now.

Neoliberalism and post-politics

It is widely accepted that the processes associated with neoliberalism
have reshaped political projects, policy arrangements and governing
practices both nationally and internationally since the mid–1980s.
Commentators also agree that this political project has mutated over
time; from the 'more market' versions of neoliberalism that characterised the 1980s to the institutionally embedded versions of the
1990s and 2000s. In these more recent formations the globalising
knowledge economy based on new high-skill, high-tech industries
is actively fostered through capacity-building and economic incentives, and new approaches to social development are co-produced

through strategies of partnership, community involvement and public 'responsibilisation'. The rise of more process-oriented accounts of 'neoliberalisation' (Peck 2010) or 'after neoliberalism?' (Larner and Craig 2005) have shown that these mutations continue to privilege market mechanisms and calculative practices, while at the same time attempting to address the failures of the 'red in tooth and claw' versions of earlier forms of neoliberalism and the attendant problems of social polarisation.

This terrain is too often taken for granted by those interrogating post-politics. Swyngedouw (2010: 215), for example, states that 'I shall begin by accepting the transformation to a post-political and post-democratic configuration at face value'. Ironically, in the same article he argues that climate change 'matters of concern' (to use the Latourian framing) have been relegated to a terrain beyond dispute, to one that does not permit dissensus or disagreement. In this chapter I want to turn Swyngedouw against himself, to argue that the post-political and post-democratic configuration accepted at face value in the wider literature on post-politics must itself be re-politicised as a 'matter of concern', not presupposed as a 'matter of fact', if we are to understand and work with the political possibilities of the current moment.

Let me spend a little time rehearsing the debate about post-politics before moving to literatures that suggest that the shift towards the post-political and post-democratic condition may not be as monolithic, or as uncontested, as proposed above. As will be well known to readers of this book, the theoretical and political pessimism of the post-politics literatures is based on the 'parallel and intertwined' (Swyngedouw 2010) processes of neoliberalisation and the post-politisation of the public sphere. The claims that underpin this argument will also be familiar: capitalism and the market economy are now pre-supposed as the basic organisational structure of social and economic order. This organisational structure is associated with a mode of governmentality structured around 'dialogical forms of consensus formation, technocratic management and problem-focused governance', sustained by 'populist discursive regimes' and 'post-democratic institutional configurations' (Swyngedouw 2009). It is argued that dispute and disagreement have been evacuated from spaces of public encounter, and there is no longer an agreed subject of politics (for example, the proletariat) from whom an embodied vision of the future can be realised. The result is that while we still, perhaps more than ever, need radical political change, we are largely caught within the contours of the existing situation. Politics, it is argued, has become rare, evental and cannot be pre-determined ahead of time. More recently, the persuasiveness of this analysis has been underwritten by the visibility of insurrectional forms of political activism which are seen as more truly political than the micropolitics of 'dispersed resistances, alternative practices and affects' (Swyngedouw 2011).

It is the assumptions about the nature and content of neoliberal governmentalities that I wish to specifically contest, although I will also have something to say about the pre-supposition of capitalism and the market economy and the downplaying of 'micro-politics'. Again the position is boldly stated in the post-political literature and there is little room for nuance: there is now a managerial logic in all aspects of life; there has been a reduction of the political to the administrative; and decision-making is understood to be a feature of expert knowledge not of political position. This is associated with the diffusion of governance into a host of non-state and quasi-state institutional forms that foster consensual understandings of political action, and the particularisation of political demands. The result is a multi-scalar politics in which states act with experts, NGOs and other 'responsible' partners, and conflict is defused and managed through dialogical processes. It is also argued that there has been an extension of the regulatory and interventionist powers of authorities through the inclusion of 'unauthorized actors defined as experts, managers, participatory governance arrangements, consultants and the like' (Swyngedouw 2011). This is a governmentality that involves participatory governance and explicit forms of self-management, self-organisation and self-disciplining. Consensus thus becomes the 'end of politics' and the efforts of social movements, community practitioners and social justice activists are seemingly inevitably either co-opted or futile.

This is a strong story. But there are other accounts of neoliberal governmentalities that would suggest that this bleak picture may not accurately capture contemporary forms of governance. This is not simply to argue that there are empirical exceptions to the wider canvas painted above, and to substantiate such an argument by focusing on the particularity of my admittedly – and typically – idiosyncratic case (Larner, Le Heron and Lewis 2007). Rather I want to explicitly mark my theoretical departure from accounts that start from assumptions about the coherence of a monolithic neoliberalism, and to emphasise instead the flexible and chameleon-like nature and neoliberalism. My position is similar to that of Collier (2012) who recently identified what he describes as the distinction between neoliberalism as a 'big Leviathan' – a macrostructure or explanatory background against which other things are understood, and neoliberalism as if it were the 'same size' as other things and with which associations could be traced. Of course these are not new debates;

in various guises they have pervaded the geographical and anthropological accounts of neoliberalism and neoliberalisation over the last decade. But they are still too often overlooked. While this is not the place to fully rehearse these claims (see, amongst others, Larner 2000; Gibson-Graham 2008), what I want to underline is the point that the tendency to position neoliberalism as all-encompassing has made it difficult to see already existing alternatives, and has stifled exploration of the political implications of such approaches. In the context of the argument made herein, it also means that post-politics is positioned as a 'matter of fact', not a 'matter of concern'.

But neoliberalism has never been fully outside of its others, including its political opponents within radical social movements. It is worth remembering that in recent decades various commentators have grappled with the relationships between capitalism and its critiques; perhaps most notably those of Boltanski and Chiapello (2005) and Hardt and Negri (2000). Such accounts attempt to grasp how it is that the so-called 'spirit of capitalism' incorporates some of the values of those who criticise it. It is now increasingly recognised that both cultural and social critiques have extended from marginal positions and have been 'scaled up' to reshape mainstream institutions and practices. Yet even when these processes and relationships receive attention in the literature on neoliberalism, commentators most often tend to argue that neoliberalism has 'undone' the gains of radical social movements. For example that feminism, civil rights movements and environmentalism have become the unwitting 'co-conspirators' (Eisenstein 2006) of neoliberalism; that grassroots opponents have been 'co-opted' by market-oriented processes; and that the harnessing of countercultural aspirations has simply underpinned more successful and subtle forms of exploitation.

Correspondingly, if we use the analytical lens provided by the literature on post-politics to understand the relationship between neoliberalism and radical social movements, what we see is depoliticisation. Neoliberalism continues to be seen as a homogenous ideology imposed by political-economic elites. But if we accept that neoliberalism and social movements are more actively articulated than previously acknowledged, what does this mean for our analyses? For example, how is it that concepts such as self-reliance, self-help and empowerment have become part of the taken-for-granted vocabulary of neoliberalism? What does it mean if we look hard at such phenomena, rather than dismissing them as 'ironic', 'paradoxes', or 'co-option'? What are the implications of such awkward articulations theoretically and politically? What is made visible, and what remains invisible and so is not validated? In sum, what happens to the arguments about post-politics if we begin from the recognition that radical social movements have shaped neoliberalism itself (Bockman 2012)?

The political projects of neoliberalism

This analytical starting point is not as peculiar as it might initially seem. There is now a longstanding and relatively well-developed discussion as to how best to analyse the changing processes critical social scientists have named as neoliberalism. Whereas many accounts focus on deregulation, privatisation and marketisation as regulatory projects, others have focused on the forms of governance that encourage institutions and actors to behave in market-like ways. Over the past decade or so the debates and ongoing discussions between neo-regulationist and governmentality inspired accounts have helped us to understand that neoliberalism is a situated, hybrid political project that takes multiple forms in multiple places. Indeed, it might be argued that the more these theoretical assertions have been substantiated by more detailed empirical research in an ever greater range of geographical settings, the less value the insights of structural analyses of neoliberalism have had to offer (Collier 2012). Instead the focus of many commentators on neoliberalism has turned to asking how this particular political project has been able to articulate with other political projects, and what happens to these projects as a result of that articulation.

For some, this has led to attempts to think about the different kinds of political projects that are found under the umbrella of neoliberalism itself. For example, early contributions to this discussion emphasised the differences between apparently unambiguously neoliberal policies such as deregulation, privatisation, marketisation and commodification (Clarke 2004; Bakker 2007). In our accounts of political-economic restructuring in New Zealand, my colleagues and I delinked globalisation, the knowledge economy, sustainability, creative industries and social development, showing how these projects had discrete origins and were multiply reworked as they became part of a new political formation (Larner, Le Heron and Lewis 2007; Lewis 2009). More recently, the increasingly influential literature on policy mobilities has drawn attention to the ways in which policy discourses and models become part of neoliberal political projects. This literature maps how ideas and techniques 'travel' within and across different social networks and are embodied in diverse forms (Larner and Laurie 2010; Newman 2012; Peck and Theodore 2010). Seen collectively, these literatures have provided a major challenge to the black box models of 'policy transfer' that once implicitly dominated discussions of neoliberalism, and have provided powerful analytics for nuanced accounts of state restructuring and policy-making that emphasise hybridisation and heterogeneity.

For others the concern is with how political projects from well outside the usual spectrum of understandings and techniques usually named as neoliberal have become part of the 'neoliberal assemblage'. Of course the ideological hybridity of neoliberalism has long been recognised. For example, Stuart Hall's (1988) early analyses of neoliberalism argued that a plurality of discourses were stitched together to create Thatcherism. In Hall's work neoliberalism was a contingent ideology that both spoke to the economic crisis of 1970s Britain through its emphasis on market individualism *and* re-shaped national subjectivities through an emphasis on moral conservatism. Yet in the plethora of writing that has followed, his observations were often forgotten as people presupposed necessary connections between very different political ideologies. In particular, neoliberalism and neoconservatism are often conflated. Yet whereas in the United Kingdom and United States neoliberalism and neoconservatism appeared in tandem during the 1980s, this was not necessarily the case elsewhere. For example, in my work on New Zealand I have emphasised how the new emphasis on the market occurred at the same time as the mainstreaming of feminist, environmental and Maori political claims (Larner 2000). More recently, a range of studies have shown that neoliberalism has had a wide variety of 'others', including Chinese socialism (Hoffman 2010), social democracy (Clarke 2008), and Friere and Gandhi (Sharma 2008). Increasingly we have come to understand that neoliberalism always exists in a highly variegated landscape of institutional, economic and political forms (Peck 2010). As Catherine Kingfisher has argued, neoliberalism 'is neither unitary nor immutable, and it is always in interaction with other cultural formations or discourses' (2002: 165).

The hybridity of 'actually existing' neoliberalism (Brenner and Theodore 2002) is further underlined by the work of scholars who have begun to ask how it is that political experiments that were initially on the margins have gradually become part of governmental initiatives. There are numerous examples (amongst others, feminism, civil rights, micro-finance, participatory budgeting, restorative justice) of ideas initially seen as radical that have come to be adopted by the mainstream. Commentators are now not just asking how such different ideological projects can be reconciled, but rather how it is that particular kinds of techniques are engaged, the forms in which they travel, and the subjects who are produced. In this context it is important to remember that 'advanced liberal' (Rose 1999) techniques such as auditing, contractualism and benchmarking are polysemic; they are understood to be equally effective whether governing World Bank programmes or used by local community organisations. Nor are they politically aligned in particular ways. For example, Kantola and Squires (2008) claim we are now seeing a new form of 'market feminism' in which calculative practices such as gender mainstreaming initiatives and gender audits are being used to advance women's economic and political status. Of course, translations, negotiations, compromises and mutations are integral to these processes, and emerging institutions, governmental techniques and regulatory forms often bear little resemblance to the initial formulations.

Seen collectively, these discussions suggest the need for a greater focus on the antagonisms and heterogeneities that cut through neoliberal political projects, and underline my insistence that 'doing politics' has not been simply reduced to a form of institutionalised social management based on the mobilisation of governmental technologies. For example, James Ferguson has recently asked important questions about what he calls 'the uses of neoliberalism'. 'What if politics is really not about expressing indignation or denouncing the powerful? What if it is, instead, about getting what you want?' (Ferguson 2009: 167). He calls for 'an exploration of the contemporary possibilities for developing genuinely progressive arts of government' (Ferguson 2009: 167). Can we imagine new 'arts of government' that might take advantage of (instead of simply denouncing or resisting) recent transformations in the spatial organisation of government and social assistance? In a very different context McGuirk and Dowling (2009) have shown that multiple governance agendas are reshaping privately governed residential estates in Sydney. These are not simply the top-down discourses of privatisation, citizen responsibilisation, sustainability and community cohesion we might expect, but also involve diverse negotiations of everyday life. Their conclusion, contra the vast majority of analyses of neoliberal urbanism and the commentary on so-called 'gated communities', is that these residential estates cannot be understood as simply reflecting the primacy of private interests. Such studies demand that we avoid easy generalisations and pay closer attention to developments that might once have been dismissed as simply 'more neoliberalism'.

There is, of course, the risk that such a position reflects what Swyngedouw (2009) calls a 'sociological' analysis of urban political-ecological transformations. He claims that while critical social theory offers an entry point into strategies of resistance and emancipatory political tactics, the political is not constituted by the social, and that we need to focus on the 'properly political'. This echoes the arguments about 'roll with it' neoliberalism made by Roger Keil (2009), in which political and economic actors have mostly accepted the governmentality of the neoliberal formation as the basis for their actions. The argument here is that discussion and dispute is tolerated, but the general frame is not contested. My view, on the contrary, is that the accounts focused on the heterogeneity of neoliberal assemblages problematise the accepted narratives about neoliberalism that frame the post-politics literature. They ask us to think harder about the processes involved in 'neoliberalisation', and challenge the usual pessimism of the normative positions taken by theorists of post-politics.

The Coexist project

I want to return to Coexist and Hamilton House in the context of these debates. The example of an abandoned building that has become an 'incubator' for alternative forms of living and working, creative industries, and social enterprise development is increasingly common in post-industrial cities. In the aftermath of the global financial crisis, and with the failure of property-led models of urban regeneration, there is a new focus on these utopian political-economic experiments, including those associated with diverse economies (Gibson-Graham and Roelvink 2009) and autonomous social centres (Pickerell and Chatterton 2006). However, there are very different versions of these new spaces, ranging from top-down government-sponsored versions aimed at stimulating economic development, to bottom-up autonomous spaces that have grown out of former squats and social centres (Novy and Colomb 2012; Vanolo 2012). In this context I will begin my discussion by looking more closely at what the members of Coexist say about themselves and their space, and how they position themselves in contemporary political debates. In doing so, the analysis will highlight how the Coexist project asks us to think differently about contemporary ideological formations and political strategies. It will also show how such initiatives are explicitly aimed at constituting particular kinds of political subjects.

Coexist claim that they exemplify a new form of environmental, economic and community development. Certainly they do not appear to fit neatly into existing boxes in either academic literatures or grassroots politics (Sefyang and Smith 2007). Their understanding of themselves and their activities draws on at least four different strands of discourse and practice. First, there is an explicit engagement with conventional community development discourses and strategies with their emphasis on social inclusion, consensus-building, partnerships and networking. Second, they draw on contemporary understandings of sustainability and grassroots environmentalism through their explicit engagement with the categories and understandings privileged in the UK Egan Review for Sustainable Communities. These environmental discourses and practices inform the choice of activities selected for inclusion in Hamilton House, as well as their distribution within the building (transport in the basement, food on the ground floor, creativity on the first floor, and finally the 'head' in the top floor of the building). Third, the language of anarchism, itself becoming much more widespread in recent years, is present in their explicit claims about the importance of prefigurative practices and in calls for the development of the commons. But fourth, and perhaps most puzzling of all, this community-building, grassroots environmentalism and alternative political orientation is overlaid with an explicitly entrepreneurial approach that also shapes their activities.

Further contradictions appear on closer inspection of the history of this initiative. The building itself was made available to Coexist by a local property developer interested in fostering sustainability and alternative energy initiatives through innovative construction projects; their activities have been supported by architect George Ferguson who was recently elected as Bristol's first mayor; and I was first enrolled by Coexist through the University of Bristol's 'Entrepreneur-in-Residence', who they had approached to help them with their ambition to build an 'incubator for social enterprises'. While Coexist is based on 'grass-roots leadership ... built on a culture of self-responsibility and co-inspiration', they are also explicit about the need to be environmentally and financially sustainable. This is not an anti-capitalist or even an anti-market initiative; indeed there is an explicit emphasis on identifying new forms of economic development and job creation that can underpin local economic development and on fostering these activities. There are also increasing signs of professionalisation amongst some of those involved, and in the organisation of the building and its inhabitants more generally. However, the core purpose and approach have remained consistent and continue to shape the overall project:

> The Coexist vision is to create a centre of excellence for the local community that provides the resources and skills needed to help Stokes Croft and Bristol develop in a sustainable manner. It puts the needs of the community above the needs for profit, and supports putting social inclusion, economic sustainability, education and forward-thinking at the centre of urban renewal programmes. (Coexist n.d.)

In the three years since I have been working with them I have come to think of Coexist as a form of 'radical social enterprise' (McRobbie

2011); environmentally and socially committed to fostering political alternatives but clear about the need to generate economic benefits that can be used for the social reproduction of those involved, as well as the diverse communities in which they are situated.

It is no coincidence that Coexist emerged in the aftermath of the 2008 financial crisis, which gave rise to a more generalised lack of confidence in top-down economic development strategies. While Coexist have now become a central part of Bristol's vibrant counter-cultural scene, they explicitly reject gentrification and conventional versions of arts and culture-led urban regeneration in which developers follow artists, and a formal public strategy follows grassroots activity. Rather this is a 'do it yourself' version of city living that privileges autonomy and anti-authoritarianism, and aims to demonstrate that a less commercial and more sustainable inner city is possible (Clement 2012). In order to deliver on this alternative vision, the directors of Coexist (who are themselves young people from a variety of backgrounds including dance therapy, photography, social sciences and engineering) see themselves as 'facilitators', who use their diverse skills and contacts to help a variety of political alternatives thrive. None of the directors accepts any more than a minimum 'living wage', and Hamilton House has been transformed from a derelict office building to a busy cultural hub through massive amounts of voluntary and in-kind labour.

Members of the group of directors (who change frequently and sometimes unexpectedly) all occupy multiple roles and are building 'portfolio careers' across diverse activities and interests. Nor are these activities and interests necessarily associated with the traditional community sector and/or grassroots politics. In addition to being part of Coexist, they do things like run local music venues and restaurants, manage alternative technology networks, and engage in environmental politics. They are also increasingly linked into entrepreneurial networks locally and nationally.

The initiatives found in Hamilton House include a variety of forms of artistic expression (supported by offering affordable studio space to a wider variety of creative practitioners); transport and energy (by supporting green transport and alternative energy initiatives); small businesses (by hosting diverse social enterprises and charitable organisations); and local food initiatives including a community kitchen that delivers education programmes and can be hired out for local events and fund raising. These diverse actors and activities are encouraged to engage and learn from each other, a position promoted through the affordable local food restaurant on site and regular scheduled tenants' lunches, and through collaborative forms of leadership and management structures. More generally,

Hamilton House is full of people who are seeking alternatives to conventional careers; identifying possibilities that generate a living wage in a context where they either cannot or do not want to have steady jobs and at the same time allow them to 'live their dreams'. Being in Hamilton House not only gives them a space within which to work on their own projects, it explicitly fosters collaboration and skill-sharing. The tenants themselves describe an experience of 'serendipitous encounters' between 'crazy arty people all doing their own thing'. Certainly the initiative draws together a very diverse set of actors; 'bourgeois bohemians' (Florida 2002) rub shoulders with those who regularly use the nearby and long established homeless hostel; community organisations and NGOs operate alongside a wide range of creative practitioners and their embryonic firms; alternative health practitioners occupy the space during the day, whereas hedonistic young people socialise in the space at night; and long-standing Stokes Croft residents meet people from across the city and region who now regularly enter into and use this space.

Those who orbit around Coexist and Hamilton House understand themselves to be actively producing alternative futures. Their activities are explicitly framed through a critique of 'unsustainable capitalism' and are characterised as representing the pursuit of a 'strong alternative'. The concept of 'prefigurative politics' associated with autonomous and anarchist politics is what provides the ideological and practical basis for this alternative; it is presupposed that everyone is able to empower themselves and people are encouraged to create projects that bring about 'harmony in their own lives and the lives of others'. These ambitions also inform the cooperative ethos, flat management structure, and relational approach that characterise Coexist more generally. Coexist also privileges 'creativity' and actively links this to a redistributive anti-poverty politics. This is not the individualised creativity so often criticised in the wider literature on precarity (Gill and Pratt 2012). Rather, in this formulation, aesthetic and relational labour is explicitly reclaimed by the creative 'precariat' themselves:

> To be creative is the act of doing something original that has value. This is a key tool and strength of Coexist. We approach situations and people with creativity, open to our own and that of others. We have the freedom to respond and solve situations creatively to achieve our core purpose. (Wells, n.d.)

In this setting the explicit performance of creativity (which can be environmental, economic or cultural) and the patterns of labour associated with that performance are not understood as neo-liberal exploitation but rather as an expression of 'living differently'. As the broader debates about immaterial labour and 'self-precarization' (Lorey 2011) underline, in many of these new organisational and occupational strategies attributes like communication, affect, opinion, attention and taste are actively engaged.

Coexist's approach and the political subjects it constitutes are thus very different from those presupposed in discussions of neoliberalism and community development found in the existing literatures. Rather than the processes of individualisation, self-responsibilisation and calculation privileged in these accounts, Coexist's aim is to generate partnering subjects who privilege creativity, relationship-building, facilitative processes and collaboration. There is a great deal of self-consciousness and reflexivity about this amongst the members of Coexist. Indeed, they explicitly understand themselves to be involved in the process of 'making up' particular kinds of political subjects (Rutland 2012). They mobilise discourses of collective engagement and community empowerment alongside those of 'open heartedness', self-responsibility and co-inspiration in their ambitions for alternative community building:

> We believe this can be achieved by working together to harness the skills already present within communities. Coexist doesn't think this is a hard task. In fact we are seeing that it can be done. We are all already entirely capable of innovation, of clarity and to effortlessly coexist with ourselves and with each other. Each of us is a pioneer. Each of us has a unique contribution to the whole. And each moment is ours to make the most of. Here, coexisting naturally, we see that together we are capable of so much. (Pike 2011)

The building and its activities represent neither the oppositional politics of familiar forms of grassroots politics and community activism, nor the increasingly professionalised terrains of urban regeneration, social policy and social work. Instead Coexist and Hamilton House work on a reconfigured political and institutional terrain that is one of the largely unrecognised legacies of neoliberalism; the categories of state, market and civil society no longer hold in the ways in which most political actors and indeed many social scientists presuppose. This helps explain the proliferation of new categories such as social economy, social enterprise and social entrepreneurship in the attempts to try and understand this reconfigured terrain and the hybrid organisational forms now emerging (cf. Westall 2007). Indeed, during the time I have worked with Coexist the language of social enterprise has been increasingly mainstreamed within the organisation itself as new forms of expertise have been named and cultivated, active networking is encouraged, research is conducted, business cases are developed, and learning opportunities have begun to proliferate.

But simply dismissing such developments as either 'more neoliberalism' or indeed 'post-politics' may be to lose sight of their wider significance and potential. It is important to recognise that these developments are framed by neither naive optimism nor complete disaffection with the status quo. Coexist recognise the ongoing challenges of 'being the change you wish to see', but believe it is crucial to move past the moment of critique. They understand their organisation and the networks it is building to be constitutive, and believe that by 'coexisting' it is possible to bring into being a world other than the one that we have. Coexist thus actively position themselves as a node for experimentation that may give rise to new political possibilities. Seen through the lens of broader literatures on political alternatives, Coexist are indeed attempting to 'enact new worlds in the confines of the present' (Newman 2012; see also Gibson-Graham 2008). I would argue that we should draw attention to such alternative forms of living, working and expressing, and pause before dismissing them as always and inevitably coopted.

Conclusion

This paper did not begin from the debates in political theory or philosophy that tend to dominate the literature on post-politics. Rather than pursuing my interest in the debates about post-politics through programmatic statements that assume both the content and the effects of neoliberalism as 'matters of fact', my approach has been to explore these issues through theoretically informed empirical research. Consequently the chapter began in my usual starting place; namely an empirical case that has made me wonder about the tenor of existing academic debates about post-politics. These academic debates are strong arguments and rightly encourage us to be sceptical about the new emphasis on partnering governmentalities. But do they too quickly foreclose the politics and potential of these new formations? We should take heed of Jodi Dean's (2009: 12) warning that the debate about post-politicisation 'not only overlooks the reality of politics on the ground but it cedes in advance key terrains of activism and struggle'. I also find Povenelli's (2011) recent observation that neoliberalism emerges from a series of uneven social struggles within the liberal diaspora provocative.

Let me stress that mine is not a naive or utopian story; I am not denying the very real tensions associated with realising an initiative like Coexist. Coexist's 'urban experiment in working and living' is explicitly positioned both inside and outside capitalism and neo-liberalism. It is not state-funded, and the members are proud of the fact that they are now almost self-sustaining. But nor is this a fully private-sector initiative in which rents, events and classes cover the costs of running the organisation. Goodwill, interns and volunteers are what make the place run. Of course, there are always attendant dangers in initiatives such as Coexist, in particular in the ways in which they privilege participatory and deliberative processes that invite self-management and self-organisation. There is also a high degree of self-exploitation in the formation and maintenance of Coexist's flexible management model and the flat hierarchies it involves. Nor is this a story of heroic actors and unconstrained choices; in a context of rapidly rising youth unemployment and austerity politics these alternative spaces are emerging as much out of necessity as they are out of innovation.

However while I do not wish to romanticise Coexist, in reflecting on the debates about post-politics in relation to their activities I would argue that – ironically – the risk is a depoliticised political imaginary, in which choosing one trajectory over another and exploring their articulation with specific programmes and alternatives is not possible. More generally, I think we need to think harder about the kind of worlds we, as critical social scientists, want to make (Law and Urry 2004: 391). My conclusion is that the post-politics literature works effectively to mobilise political sympathies but should be treated with scepticism. The sub-text of this chapter is that by making the content and form of contemporary political struggles more visible, it might be possible to overcome our cynicism about the impossibility of politics in the current conjuncture. In the context of a wider emphasis on uncertain futures and anticipatory action (Anderson 2010), it is no longer only social movements and activists who are trying to imagine and enact radically different futures 'in the here and now'. Indeed, active and deliberate experimentation in a wide range of spheres has become integral to the processes of political re-invention after neo-liberalism. My more general point is that rather than representing the demise of politics, it is out of (inevitably incomplete, paradoxical and compromised) experiments such as Coexist that new political formations will emerge.

References

Anderson, B. (2010), 'Preemption, precaution, preparedness: Anticipatory action and future geographies', *Progress in Human Geography*, 34: 6, pp. 777–9.

Bakker, K. (2007), 'The "Commons" versus the "Commodity": Alter-globalization, anti-privatization and the human right to water in the Global South', *Antipode*, 39: 3, pp. 430–55.

Bockman, J. (2012), 'The political projects of neoliberalism', *Social Anthropology*, 20: 3, pp. 310–17.

Boltanski, E. and E. Chiapello (2005), *The New Spirit of Capitalism*, London: Verso.

Brenner, N., and N. Theodore (2002), 'Cities and the geographies of "actually existing" neoliberalism', *Antipode*, 34: 3, pp. 349–79.

Clarke, J. (2004), 'Dissolving the public realm? The logics and limits of neoliberalism'. *Social Policy*, 33: 1, pp. 27–48.

Clarke, J. (2008), 'Living with/in and without neoliberalism'. *Focaal – European Journal of Anthropology*, 51, pp. 135–47.

Clement, M. (2012), 'Rage against the market: Bristol's Tesco riot', *Race & Class* 53: 3, pp. 81–90.

Coexist (n.d.), *Vision Statement*, copy available from author on request.

Collier, S. (2012), 'Neoliberalism as big Leviathan, or . . . ? A response to Wacquant and Hilgers', *Social Anthropology*, 20: 2, pp. 186–95.

Dean, J. (2009), *Democracy and Other Neoliberal Fantasies: Communicative Capitalism and Left Politics*, Durham: Duke University Press.

Eisenstein, H. (2006), 'Scouting parties and bold detachments: Towards a postcapitalist feminism', *Women's Studies Quarterly* 34 (1/2), pp. 40–62.

Ferguson, J. (2009), 'The uses of neoliberalism', in N. Castree et al., *The Point is to Change It: Geographies of Hope and Survival in an Age of Crisis*, London: Wiley-Blackwell.

Florida, R. (2002), 'Bohemia and economic geography', *Journal of Economic Geography*, 2, pp. 55–71.

Gibson-Graham, J.-K. (2008), 'Diverse economies: Performative practices for "other worlds"', *Progress in Human Geography*, 32(5), pp. 613–32.

Gibson-Graham, J.-K., and G. Roelvink (2009), 'An economic ethics for the anthropocene', *Antipode*, 41: 1, pp. 320–46.

Gill, R., and A. Pratt (2010), 'In the social factory? Immaterial labour, precariousness and cultural work', *Theory Culture Society*, 25: 7–8, pp. 1–30.

Hall, S. (1988), 'The toad in the garden: Thatcher amongst the theorists', in C. Nelson and L. Grossberg (eds), *Marxism and the Interpretation of Culture*, London: Macmillan Press.

Hardt, M., and A. Negri (2000), *Empire*, Cambridge: Harvard University Press.

Hoffman, L. (2010), *Patriotic Professionalism in Urban China: Fostering Talent*, Philadelphia: Temple University Press.

Kantola, J., and J. Squires (2008), 'From state feminism to market feminism?', paper presented to the International Studies Association Annual Convention, 26–29 March.

Keil, R. (2009), 'The urban politics of "roll-with-it" neoliberalism', *City*, 13: 2–3, pp. 230–45.

Kingfisher, C. (2002), *Western Welfare in Decline: Globalization and Women's Poverty*, Philadelphia: University of Pennsylvania Press.

Larner, W. (2000), 'Neo-liberalism: Policy, ideology, governmentality', *Studies in Political Economy*, 63, pp. 5–26.

Larner, W., and D. Craig (2005), 'After neoliberalism? Community activism and local partnerships in Aotearoa New Zealand', *Antipode*, 37: 3. pp. 402–24.

Larner, W., and N. Laurie (2010), 'Travelling technocrats, embodied knowledges: Globalising privatisation in telecoms and water', *Geoforum* 41: 2, pp. 218–26.

Larner, W., R. Le Heron, and N. Lewis (2007), 'Co-constituting "After Neoliberalism?": Political projects and globalising governmentalities in Aotearoa New Zealand', in K. England and K. Ward (eds), *Neoliberalization: States, Networks, People*, Oxford: Blackwell Publishing.

Lewis, N. (2009), 'Progressive spaces of neoliberalism?', *Asia Pacific Viewpoint*, 50, pp. 113–19.

Law, J., and J. Urry (2004), 'Enacting the Social', *Economy and Society*, 33: 3, pp. 390–410.

Leitner, H., J. Peck, and E. Sheppard (2007) *Contesting Neoliberalism: Urban Frontiers*, New York: Guilford Press.

Lorey I. (2011), 'Virtuoso of freedom: On the implosion of political virtuosity', in G. Raunig, G. Ray and U. Wiggenig (eds), *Critique of Creativity: Precarity, Subjectivity and Resistance in the 'Creative Industries'*, London: MayFlyBooks.

McGuirk, P., and R. Dowling (2009), 'Neoliberal privatisation? Remapping the public and the private in Sydney's masterplanned residential estates', *Political Geography*, 28, pp. 174–85.

McRobbie, A. (2011), 'Rethinking creative economy as radical social enterprise'. *Variant*, 41, pp. 32–3.

Newman, J. (2012), *Working the Spaces of Power: Activism, Neoliberalism and Gendered Labour*, London: Bloomsbury Press.

Novy, J., and C. Colomb (2012), 'Struggling for the right to the (creative) city in Berlin and Hamburg: New social movements, new "spaces of hope"?', *International Journal of Urban and Regional Research*, available on Early View.

Peck, J. (2010), *Constructions of Neoliberal Reason*, Oxford: Oxford University Press.

Peck, J., and N. Theodore (2010), 'Mobilizing policy: Models, methods, and mutations', *Geoforum* 41: 2, pp. 169–74.

Pickerell, J., and P. Chatterton (2006), 'Notes towards autonomous geographies: Creation, resistance and self-management as survival tactics', *Progress in Human Geography* 30: 6, pp. 730–46.

Pike, J. (2011), interview with Jamie Pike, inaugural director, Coexist, conducted on 11 June 2011.

Povenelli, E. (2011), *Economies of Abandonment: Social Belonging and Endurance in Late Liberalism*, Durham: Duke University Press.

Rose, N. (1999), *Powers of Freedom*, Cambridge: Cambridge University Press.

Rutland, T. (2012), 'Activists in the making: Urban movements, political processes and the creation of political subjects', *International Journal of Urban and Regional Research*, available on Early View.

Seyfang, G., and A. Smith (2007), 'Grassroots innovations for sustainable development: Towards a new research and policy agenda', *Environment Politics*, 16: 4, pp. 584–603.

Sharma, A. (2008), *Logics of Empowerment: Development, Gender and Governance in Neoliberal India*, Minneapolis: University of Minnesota Press.

Swyngedouw, E. (2009), 'The antimonies of the postpolitical city: In search of a democratic politics of environmental production', *International Journal of Urban and Regional Research*, 33: 3, pp. 601–20.

Swyngedouw, E. (2010), 'Apocalypse forever? Post-political populism and the spectre of climate change', *Theory Culture Society*, 27: 2–3, pp. 213–32.

Swyngedouw, E. (2011), 'Interrogating post-democratization: reclaiming egalitarian political spaces', *Political Geography*, 30: 7, pp. 370–80.

Vanolo, A. (2012), 'Alternative capitalism and creative economy: The case of Christiania', *International Journal of Urban and Regional Research*, available on Online Early.

Wells, O. (n.d.), 'Coexist approach and objectives', internal document.

Westall, A. (2007), 'How can innovation in social enterprise be understood, encouraged and enabled?', Office of the Third Sector, internal document.

Wolch, J. (1990), *The Shadow State: Government and Voluntary Sector in Transition*. Washington, DC: Foundation Center.

Žižek, S. (1998), 'A leftist plea for "Eurocentrism"', *Critical Inquiry*, 24: 4, pp. 988–1009.

10 Neither Cosmopolitanism nor Multipolarity: The Political Beyond Global Governmentality

Hans-Martin Jaeger

Taking Chantal Mouffe's (2005) discussion of cosmopolitanism and multipolarity as a vantage point, this chapter examines contemporary dynamics of the political and post-political in international relations through an investigation of the global governance projects of the European Union (EU) and the recently constituted BRICS group (Brazil, Russia, India, China, South Africa). Emerging against the background of the unipolar or neo-imperial moment of the United States in early twenty-first-century world politics, EU and BRICS global governance programmes might be seen as important alternatives to recent American visions of world order, which seem to point in rather different directions. Prima facie, the EU's commitment to a post-sovereign world of multilateral cooperation underpinned by globalisation, human rights and the rule of law appears to contrast with BRICS' call for a multipolar world order based on equal sovereignty. This is reminiscent of the distinction that Mouffe draws between cosmopolitanism and multipolarity. Mouffe criticises cosmopolitan theorists for promoting a post-political vision that simultaneously denies hegemonic and pluralistic dimensions of (world) politics by presuming or promoting an international consensus around liberal democracy, postnational identity, cosmopolitan rights and technocratic global governance. Against this homogenising and depoliticising conception of world politics, Mouffe endorses the agonistic pluralism of a multipolar world order as a preferable alternative. My chapter complicates Mouffe's critique of cosmopolitanism and advocacy of multipolar order by mobilising Foucauldian governmentality analysis and Jacques Rancière's conception of the political ('politics').

In a first move, it deconstructs the opposition between the cosmopolitanism of the EU's approach to external relations and the multipolar global governance project of BRICS by unfolding the

EU's 'governmentality of ambiguity' (cf. Best 2005, 2008) and BRICS' 'bricolage' of governmentalities. The governmentality analytic confounds Mouffe's cosmopolitan-multipolar binary by highlighting that the EU's ostensibly cosmopolitan (egalitarian, civilian, constitutional, supranational) approach is shot through with hierarchical, military, extra-constitutional and intergovernmental countercurrents, while BRICS' ostensibly multipolar project also features biopolitical, liberal and neoliberal rationalities of governance. In a second move, the chapter suggests that Rancière's (1995, 1999, 2010) understanding of politics in terms of 'dissensus' and 'subjectivation' provides a more productive avenue than Mouffe's multipolar order to make sense of the political (and post-political) in the BRICS-EU dyad. Despite 'multipolar' ambiguities, the EU's approach to global governance ultimately embodies a 'police' project in Rancière's sense. BRICS, while not absconding from international police, also mobilise a political moment by 'putting . . . two worlds' – cosmopolitanism and multipolarity, the EU and BRICS, governmentality and politics – 'in one and the same world' (Rancière 2010: 69). This confrontation of two worlds in one challenges both the naturalness of liberal international order taken for granted by the EU, and Mouffe's more limited understanding of the political in international relations in terms of the conventional dynamics of balance-of-power or identity politics.

More broadly, my analysis shows that the emergence of a post-Western world is a more complicated matter than often assumed. On the one hand, the Western world of yore (as exemplified by the EU) has always been – and continues to be – more ambiguous and incongruous than liberal-cosmopolitan narratives suggest. On the other hand, the 'rise of the rest' (as exemplified by BRICS) is both less and more transformative than commonly believed. Far from primarily constituting a multipolarising 'power shift', it reassembles multiple powers of extant governmentalities, while simultaneously entailing a potentially more radical (egalitarian) reimagination of international politics. Rather than understanding international politics in terms of ever-present power, institutions or identities alone, Rancière's political theory challenges us to conceive of it in terms of more intermittent egalitarian enactments of simultaneous division and community.

Cosmopolitanism versus multipolarity

Since the end of the Cold War, cosmopolitanism has (re-)emerged as a prominent vision for global community and governance portending new forms of loyalty and identity, citizenship and community, and political processes and institutions beyond the sovereign state and commensurate with the globalisation of social and economic life. While generally liberal in orientation, cosmopolitanism has been cast in a variety of different forms. Habermas's discourse-ethical update of Kant's cosmopolitanism envisions inclusive discourses leading to consensus on the juridification of global human rights norms; Beck's more sociological interpretation of cosmopolitanism sees the latter as a consequence of the globalisation of ecological, economic and political risks that call for 'subpolitical' deliberations between experts and activists; and Held and Archibugi's political-institutional variant of cosmopolitanism is especially concerned with the increasing institutionalisation of democratic processes of global governance (Brown and Held 2010).

Mouffe faults all of these variants of cosmopolitanism for an 'anti-political vision', which promises a world beyond conflict, hegemony and sovereignty that displaces inevitable political antagonisms towards a moral register. Following Carl Schmitt, Mouffe sees the root of liberal cosmopolitanism's depoliticisation in its privileging of abstract individualism over collective identities, and its rational faith in the possibility of universal consensus. Moderating Schmitt's views, she advocates the transformation of (the) antagonism (of friends and enemies) into a pluralistic agonism, which provides political channels for (fundamentally) dissenting voices and conflictual representations of the world. Absent the possibility for legitimate agonistic political expression, both domestic and international politics are liable to degenerate into more violent forms of antagonism, such as xenophobic populism or terrorism (Mouffe 2005).

In contemporary international politics, Mouffe (2005: 81–2) sees a 'drastically reduced' space for agonistic expression, especially for challenging 'the hegemony of the neo-liberal model of globalisation', due to the US-led Western dominance in many international organisations. Despite their criticisms of US government policies in the 'war on terror', Mouffe (2005: 83, 90) charges the supporters of cosmopolitan visions with feeding this 'negation of "the political"' by perpetuating the idea that Western democracies, especially in Europe, embody 'the "best regime" and . . . have the "civilising" mission of universalising it'. To Mouffe, the post-political character of the cosmopolitan perspective is particularly apparent in its concept of global governance, which sees politics as the 'resolution of technical problems', thereby denying the constitutive role of power relations for international order (Mouffe 2005: 104–7).

Given the deficiencies of cosmopolitanism, Mouffe advocates 'multipolar world order' as an alternative. The latter would 'acknowledge the deeply pluralistic nature of the world' (Mouffe 2005: 91) and would require multiple 'centres of decision' with an 'equilib-rium' among various powers or regional blocs 'based on the idea of regional poles and cultural identities' (Mouffe 2005: 116–17). The philosophical stake of Mouffe's 'multipolar project' is the recogni-tion of forms of modernity and subjectivity beyond the European historical experience. However, Mouffe still sees a role for a 'politi-cal Europe' in a multipolar world. Beyond a mere power-political rivalry with the US (though conducive to equilibrium), 'Europe' should 'assert its identity' by promoting a 'civilisational model' dif-ferent from American neoliberalism but without any cosmopolitan pretense (Mouffe 2005: 127–9).

Some of Mouffe's claims about cosmopolitan theory bear closer scrutiny. For example, it is debatable whether Habermas sidelines the political and calls for a wholesale moralisation of international poli-tics, as asserted by Mouffe. Habermas (2011: 47) acknowledges that European unification is not a mere laboratory for cosmopolitanism but also allows Europe to regain room for political manoeuvre and self-assertion in counteracting its shrinking geopolitical and economic weight in the world. He also seeks to guard against excessive morali-sation of his cosmopolitan project by limiting its reliance on moral outrage to 'egregious human rights violations and manifest acts of [interstate] aggression' without any further presupposition of norma-tive consensus (Habermas 2006: 143; cf. 116–17, 189). While this does not fully insulate Habermas's cosmopolitanism against Mouffe's charges, it indicates a need to interrogate her cosmopolitan-multipolar binary. Indeed, as suggested by Puymbroeck and Oosterlynck (Chapter 4 of this volume), it might also be analytically fruitful to be more specific about different modalities of depoliticisation at play in the various streams of cosmopolitan theory.

As for Mouffe's 'multipolar world order' and Europe's role in it, we might note three problems in turn. First, Mouffe's advocacy of the well-worn balance of power (or 'equilibrium') as an alternative to cosmopolitanism overlooks the fact that, despite all differences and ruptures, both of these visions share a European history that has moved from a juridico-political logic of sovereignty towards more cal-culative and economic modes of governance (Foucault 2007, 2008). The equilibrium element of Mouffe's multipolar approach already contains traces of the very depoliticising tendencies (for example, technical, expert forms of governance) which Mouffe laments in cos-mopolitanism. Secondly, and related to the first point, Mouffe seems unaware of the – at least semantic – implication of her multipolar approach in more recent (neo-)realist theories of the balance of power in International Relations, which aim at explaining and pre-dicting war and peace based on the polarity of the international system (Waltz 1979; Mearsheimer 2010). This approach is rooted in an abstract individualism and instrumental rationality (transplanted to the level of the state) no less implicated in Western modernity than liberal cosmopolitanism (Ashley 1986). Thirdly, despite their disagreement, Mouffe (2005: 128) seems to share a certain Euro-nostalgia with cosmopolitan theorists, when she calls on 'Europe' to promote an alternative 'civilisational model' for globalisation. This idea remains beholden to the Eurocentric idea of Europe's exemplary role for the world.

Shifting from theoretical critique to a more situated mode of investigation, we will now destabilise the very opposition between cosmopolitanism and multipolarity by examining how they operate as governmentalities in two different contexts: the EU's external-relations programme and the emerging global governance agenda of BRICS. Just as many cosmopolitan theorists tend to associate the EU with their agenda, Mouffe would presumably see BRICS as a promising development towards a more multipolar world order. While these impressions are not fully mistaken, a governmentality perspective on the EU and BRICS can offer a more sociologically and politically fine-tuned account of cosmopolitanism and multipolar order than Mouffe.

Rather than taking claims about cosmopolitanism and multipolar-ity as alternative forms of world order at face value, a governmental-ity perspective draws attention to various rationalities and practices of ordering which make it possible to present these as coherent – post-political or political – programmes of governance in the first place. Although Žižek (2002: 100) overstates the case when arguing that 'the fundamental feature of post-politics is the reduction of poli-tics to "biopolitics"', a Foucauldian governmentality analysis can add (or fill in) a layer of epistemic, discursive and practical substruc-tures potentially blunting antagonism and conflict, and underwriting the structures of consensus and technocracy that mark post-pol-itics. However, this sociologically richer account of post-politics also complicates and confounds Mouffe's very distinction between (post-political) cosmopolitanism and (properly political) multipolar order by exposing pastoral hierarchy (if you will, hegemony) at the heart of the former and rationalities of biopolitical regulation and management of populations within the latter. While this may be seen to defuse the political promise of multipolar order and the post-political perils of cosmopolitanism, it anticipates Rancière's (2010: 207) claim (to which we will return) that the political ('politics') and the post-political ('police') can never be pure but always exist in a world of mixture.

Two limitations of the following analysis should be noted. First, while Foucauldian governmentality analysis (Foucault 2007, 2008; Dean 2010) is often concerned with 'smaller' techniques and tactics, only the 'larger' rationalities and mentalities of governing will be considered for illustrative purposes here. Secondly, the illustration will be limited to a rather selective though symptomatic set of materials, namely the EU's external governance agenda in the Lisbon Treaty and the BRICS Summit Declarations from 2009 to 2012.

AmbigEUities and BRIColageS of global governmentality

The opening article of the provisions on the Common Foreign and Security Policy (CFSP) in the EU's Lisbon Treaty appears to exemplify a cosmopolitan agenda:

> The Union's action on the international scene shall be guided by the principles which have inspired its own creation, development and enlargement, and which it seeks to advance in the wider world: democracy, the rule of law, the universality and indivisibility of human rights and fundamental freedoms, respect for human dignity, the principles of equality and solidarity, and respect for the principles of the United Nations and international law. (Article 21(1), Consolidated Version of the Treaty on European Union)

From a governmentality perspective, we may note two initial points. First, while the enumerated principles have certainly been important to modern European political thought and practice, it is less clear to what extent they have inspired the 'creation' and 'development' of the EU as such. The political rationalities effectively governing the constitution and evolution of European integration have varied considerably without consistently emphasising principles of democracy, the rule of law, human rights, and so on (see Walters and Haahr 2005). While these principles have been important criteria in the evaluation of candidate countries for EU enlargement, this may evoke imperial governance (Behr 2007). Secondly, aside from its ideological content we can consider the CFSP opening statement as a governmental programme. Foucault understands government as a 'conduct of conduct(s)', a conduct both of oneself and of others (Foucault 2000: 341). In the phrase about the principles said to have inspired the 'creation, development and enlargement' of the EU as well as the advancement of these principles 'in the wider world', we can see both of these senses of government (that of self and that of others) at play.

Mitchell Dean (2010: 19) indicates that government is 'an intensely moral activity' in the sense that it engages with 'how both the "governed" and "governors" regulate themselves', and that it stipulates 'what constitutes good, virtuous, appropriate, responsible conduct'. For the EU, such conduct is defined by, broadly speaking, liberal-cosmopolitan principles. However, the governmentality analytic highlights an ambiguity here. Notwithstanding the liberal content of these principles, Article 21 of the Lisbon Treaty suggests that those already exhibiting them in their own conduct are in a privileged position to 'advance' them in the conduct of others ('in the wider world') as well. This implies more pastoral or pedagogical, or as previously mentioned, imperial forms of regulation of conduct. The ambiguity is that egalitarian principles of governance (democracy, rule of law, and so on) coexist with hierarchical ones in the definition of the EU's role in the world.

So far, our analysis seems to support Mouffe's apprehensions about the post-political tendencies of a 'cosmopolitan Europe'. However, beyond any cosmopolitan 'civilising mission', further ambiguities mark the EU's external relations as mapped by the Lisbon Treaty, ambiguities which destabilise Mouffe's opposition between cosmopolitanism and multipolarity. In contrast to 'contradictions' within an otherwise homogeneous (say, 'cosmopolitan') governmentality, ambiguities may be constructive rather than disruptive elements of governmentality (Best 2005, 2008). Apart from the 'liberal-imperial' ambiguity, at least three further ambiguities make EU external relations governable: (1) an ambiguity between a self-understanding of the EU as a 'civilian' (or 'normative') and a military power; (2) an ambiguity between the 'constitutional' and 'extra-constitutional' character of EU external relations; and (3) a (continuing) ambiguity between the supranationalism and intergovernmentalism of the CFSP.

The upshot of these ambiguities is that a 'cosmopolitan' reading of the EU as a civilian, constitutional and supranational entity would be too one-sided because they contain elements (military power, 'extra-constitutional' procedures, and intergovernmentalism) that demonstrate that the EU is more prepared to participate in a multipolar world order than either cosmopolitan theorists or Mouffe recognise. Owing to the EU's assembly of ambiguities, a 'multipolar' orientation (towards hegemony, conflict and traditional sovereignty) lurks beneath its ostensible cosmopolitanism. However, turning to the multipolar trend presumably signalled by the emergence of BRICS, we will see that Mouffe's multipolar agenda also faces some intrinsic challenges.

The inauguration of a multipolar world order is perhaps the most widely cited rationale or consequence of the emergence of the BRICS group. Both journalistic coverage and academic treatments have highlighted this aspect of BRICS more than any other (for example Tisdall 2012; Yardley 2012; Roberts 2010a, 2010b; Glosny 2010; Sinha and Dorschner 2010). Of course, the fascination with multipolarity in relation to BRICS is not merely a journalistic or academic chimera. All four BRIC(S) summit declarations have explicitly stated support for a multipolar world order. However, the following analysis demonstrates that multipolar objectives are merely one piece in a more complex puzzle – or 'bricolage' – of global governmentalities at play in the emergence of BRICS.

My analysis highlights two more specific but equally central aspects of governmentality, namely the biopolitical concern with population and the oft-mentioned concern with economy. Both of these concerns reorient politics and sovereignty from their more agonistic dimensions (whether in the internal exercise of popular sovereignty or external competition among sovereignties) towards more regulatory, managerial and ultimately depoliticised forms of conduct. A survey of BRICS' summit declarations shows that traditional concerns of sovereignty (territory, law, and so forth) are indeed supplemented and recast in terms of biopolitical concerns with the wealth, welfare and health of the population (Foucault 2003: 243–4; 2007: 104–8), especially the population of BRICS and the 'developing' world. Foucault (2003: 249) notes that biopolitics is a 'technology of security' which aims at 'achieving an overall equilibrium that protects the security of the whole from internal dangers'. It is in this light that we can read BRICS' (2012: para 1) self-identification as a 'partnership for global stability, security and prosperity'. Specifically, BRICS seek to address 'challenges to global well-being and stability' with reference to 'global recovery', sustainable development (BRICS 2012: para 2), and food and energy security, seen as 'central to addressing economic development, eradicating poverty, and combating hunger and malnutrition in many developing countries' (BRICS 2012: paras 28, 41). One could of course also describe these areas of biopolitical concern in terms of cosmopolitan solidarity.

Two specific ways of inducing biopolitical equilibrium and security include the organisation of 'milieus' (both natural and artificial) and 'circulations' (of people, merchandise, and so on), thereby constituting them as fields of governmental intervention (Foucault 2007: 20–3, 29). Organising circulation involves 'a division between good and bad circulation, and maximising the good circulation by diminishing the bad' (Foucault 2007: 18). Organisational logics of milieus and circulations are clearly operative in BRICS' global governmentality. BRICS are concerned over the 'uncertain environment for global growth' and call for 'an improved international monetary and financial architecture' (BRICS 2012: paras 5–7). They also pledge their support for addressing the degradation of the natural environment, especially with respect to climate change (BRICS 2012: para 30). A concern with the balance between 'good' and 'bad' circulations is apparent in warnings against 'volatile cross-border capital flows' (BRICS 2012: para 6) and terrorist finance (BRIC 2010: para 23) on the one hand, and calls for 'enhancing the flow of development finance' (BRICS 2012: para 11) and 'trade and investment flows among our countries' (BRICS 2012: para 18) on the other.

Entwined with the problem of population, governmentality also involves the deployment of economic knowledges, especially statistics, and the constitution of 'the economy' as a 'field of intervention' (Foucault 2007: 95). The centrality of economy to BRICS' global governance approach is evident in their pervasive concern with economic growth (BRICS 2012: paras 5, 28, 35; 2011: paras 13, 23; 2010: paras 6–8). And, of course, Goldman Sachs economist Jim O'Neill's designation of 'the BRICs' as 'emerging economies' inspired the birth of BRIC(S) in the first place. 'Economy' then is not only a matter of practice, but even one of identity – indeed, the very *raison d'être* – for BRICS. A Joint Statistical Publication[1] presenting nationally disaggregated data on 'population', 'economically active population' and 'people's living standards', as well as chapters on 'milieus' ('resources and environment', and so on) and 'circulation' (imports and exports, tourism, and so on), is one of the most tangible results of BRICS cooperation to date.

Foucault (2007, 2008) marks a number of moments and passages in the genealogy of economic government from *raison d'Etat* to neoliberalism. For our purposes, two points are important. First, while once voicing doubt about the liberal belief in self-regulating markets (BRIC 2010: para 13), BRICS generally come strikingly close to invoking a version of the liberal utopia of permanent 'collective enrichment' and 'perpetual peace' which Foucault (2008: 44, 51–8, 61–2) associates with the 'globalisation' of the market in late eighteenth- and early nineteenth-century European liberalism. Secondly, BRICS' approach to governance also appears to reflect a particular, ordoliberal version of neoliberalism which requires a vigilant government acting on the legal and institutional 'framework' of the economy (rather than intervening in the economy itself) (Foucault 2008: 120–1, 138–40, 163–4). The assumption of such an enframing (or 'monetary and financial architecture') for the world economy is prominent in BRICS' pronouncements on global governance.

Given BRICS' novelty, much of this analysis remains preliminary. Accounts of BRICS' governmentalities are certainly not exhausted by the forms of biopolitics, liberalism and neoliberalism outlined by Foucault. Through their support of international initiatives for sustainable development, the Millennium Development Goals and counter-terrorism, BRICS are additionally connected to a 'rhizome' of existing environmentalities, developmentalities and anticipatory rationalities (Luke 1995; Ilcan and Phillips 2010; Aradau and van Munster 2007). Of course, BRICS may interpret, rationalise and implement these in ways that defy their original 'intentions'. Nevertheless, it should be clear that BRICS cannot be reduced to expressing 'multipolar world order', but manifest and are inserted into a much broader 'bricolage' of governmentalities, many of which could be equally at home within a cosmopolitan framework. More generally, the partial ideological convergence between the EU and the BRICS global governance agenda illuminated by a governmentality perspective highlights the significant redirection of the political-economic projects of at least some of the individual members of the BRICS group (especially Russia, India, and China) since the end of the Cold War. It can therefore be seen as symptomatic of the particular post-political condition (the end of political divisions and utopian projects) that Rancière (1995: ch. 1) and others have associated with this historical juncture.[2]

The (post-)political beyond governmentality and multipolarity

While highlighting ambiguity and complexity beyond cosmopolitanism and multipolarity, a governmentality analysis may not fully capture the political character of governance projects such as those of BRICS or the EU. Indeed, Mouffe might object that governmentality elides the political (conflict, hegemony, and so on) in a way similar to liberal cosmopolitanism (see Mouffe 2005: 107–15). In my view, this objection would miss the basic point of a Foucauldian analysis that power and politics may manifest themselves in more microphysical forms than pervasive hegemony or overt antagonism. Yet, governmentality is not co-extensive with politics. According to Rancière (2010: 93), Foucault's question of the biopolitical 'individualisation of bodies and . . . socialisation of populations . . . is not the same as that of politics'. We therefore now turn to Rancière's political theory with two overlapping purposes: first (vis-à-vis Mouffe), to think the political and post-political in international politics in terms other than multipolarity and cosmopolitanism, namely in terms of 'politics' and 'police' (without however positing these as a new binary); and second (vis-à-vis our Foucauldian analysis), to explore the political surplus or deficit of BRICS' and the EU's global governance projects beyond governmentality. Rancière provides a particularly suitable point of reference here because his analysis of 'ordinary' politics overlaps with Foucault's notion of police, and because he simultaneously shares Mouffe's concern with restoring an agonistic element to politics to (re-)open political space beyond technocratic management and consensus.

However, two differences in Rancière's approach should be noted at the outset. First, Rancière departs from both thinkers in denying power and identity central stage in his political theory (Rancière 1999: 32, 42; 2010: 27). Secondly, compared to the more historicising temper of governmentality analysis, Rancière's political theory engages in considerable abstraction. Despite these differences, it can provide a corrective for Mouffe's problematic conception of the political (multipolarity) and post-political (cosmopolitanism) in the international sphere, and for the partial oblivion of the political in governmentality analysis. Substantively, this section demonstrates that while both the EU and BRICS (in different ways) partake in the reproduction of a post-political international ('police') order, BRICS additionally (albeit intermittently) mobilise political moments with the potential of exceeding this order.

The latter claim necessitates a third caveat. Much as Foucault's concept of governmentality raises questions of scale (relationships between micro- and macro-processes), Rancière might resist the 'application' of his emancipatory conception of politics to states or international coalitions like BRICS, given the underlying post-foundational understanding of politics in his work (see Marchart 2010). However, the point here is not to ascribe some kind of transcendental political agency to BRICS. Rather it is to argue that the political ('politics') is always mobilised *in situ* including, perhaps unexpectedly, in practices overtly more geared to governance than resistance. While this way of engaging Rancière may not be 'leftist' in a traditional sense, it is at least not merely 'speculative' (see Loftus, Chapter 11 of this volume) but rather, as in our case, it is attuned to particular geopolitical practices.

Like Mouffe, Rancière distinguishes genuinely political practices and relationships from the often depoliticised 'official' institutions and practices (falsely) called politics (elections, bureaucratic decision-making, and so on). Rancière (1999: 28) borrows (and broadens) Foucault's notion of 'police' to refer to the latter set of activities, while reserving the term 'politics' for those actions that disrupt police. However, for Rancière, the role of police is both more general and more specific than for Foucault. At a general level, police defines the very 'configuration of the perceptible' or 'the allocation of ways of doing, ways of being, and ways of saying'; at a more specific level, it determines the 'shares' (places, roles, positions, identities) of different parties in the social order (Rancière 1999: 28–9). To Rancière (2010: 95) then, 'police designates not an institution of power but a distribution of the sensible[3] within which it becomes possible to define strategies and techniques of power'.

Both the EU and BRICS reproduce (international) police order in Rancière's sense. Constructivists in International Relations have highlighted that international organisations wield powers of classifying the world, defining categories of actors and action, fixing meanings, and articulating and diffusing norms (Barnett and Finnemore 2004: 29–34). While perhaps overly voluntaristic (as though such powers were original and exclusive to international organisations), this analysis captures important dimensions of how international organisations like the EU (re)produce a particular configuration of the sensible, which is central to Rancière's conception of police. It is revealing that Barnett and Finnemore (2004: 24–5) ascribe much of the 'police' capacity of international organisations to 'the appearance of depoliticisation' they project by relying on bureaucratic mechanisms and technical expertise. Leaving aside questions of the appearance or reality of depoliticisation, this perhaps makes it less plausible to ascribe police capacity to the as yet relatively weakly institutionalised BRICS group. Nevertheless, both the EU and BRICS participate in international police by configuring discursive space and allocating the shares of different parties.

Broadly speaking, the EU seeks to (re)produce a discursive space of international relations with states and organisations sharing its liberal principles and interest in international order, globalisation, multilateral cooperation and 'good global governance' (art. 21, CVTEU). As previously seen, the EU sees itself as a pastor, teacher, or exemplary civil(ising) power with a special mission to benefit the less 'advanced' within this (ambiguously) liberal universe. We also saw that BRICS' bricolage of governmentalities contains a dose of liberalism defining the visible, doable and sayable in ways not entirely dissimilar from the EU. This includes commitments to international law, multilateral cooperation, growth of the global economy, and so on. However, two differences should be noted. First, while both the EU and BRICS invoke the United Nations as a pillar of international (police) order, the EU does so in a largely backward-looking and 'conservative' manner, pointing to the UN Charter as the guideline for maintaining international order (art. 21(2c), CVTEU). Diverging from a mere conservation of the post(Cold-)war world, BRICS perceive a world of 'far-reaching, complex and profound changes' (BRICS 2011: para 7; see also 2012: para 2; 2010: para 1) in which the UN ought to (continue to) play a central role, while also requiring reform itself (BRICS 2012: para 26–7; 2011: para 8; 2010: para 4; 2009: para 14). Secondly, and related to the global changes, BRICS are also concerned with police in the more specific sense of the (re-) allocation of the shares of different parties; namely, in demanding quota and voting reform in the international financial institutions to 'enhance the voice and representation of emerging market and developing countries' (BRICS 2012: paras 8–9). BRICS then seek both preservation and transformation of international order. This is where Rancière's understanding of the political, or 'politics', becomes relevant.

Rancière understands politics as involving particular forms of conflict, which he calls *dissensus* or *disagreement,* as well as the emergence of new political subjects, which he calls *subjectivation.* He further defines politics in terms of three related elements, namely as a *staging* of *equality* that exposes a *wrong* (Rancière 1995: 96–7). Let us consider these three elements, their contextualisation within dissensus and subjectivation, and how they may relate to BRICS. First, contrary to thinkers such as Aristotle, Arendt or Habermas who ground politics in speech, Rancière argues that politics has less to do with speech as such than with what counts as speech. Before any communication of interests in the medium of speech, politics is 'conflict over the existence of a common stage and over the existence and status of those present on it' (Rancière 1999: 26–7; see also Hallward 2009). Rancière locates this theatrical element of politics within 'dissensus', that is, a dispute not simply over interests, opinions or values, but over the very 'partition of the sensible': what is (and what is not) sayable (or visible), who can (and who cannot) say it, and what counts (and what does not count) as a political statement or political space. Dissensus simultaneously creates division and community by 'placing ... two worlds in a single world' (Rancière 1999: 27).

BRICS' political theatricality emerges when we look beyond the 'speech' of BRICS' declarations to the very speech situation in which they are placed. A recent paper by Russian diplomat and BRICS coordinator Vadim Lukov can provide some inklings here. Vis-à-vis the Western 'inclination "not to notice"' the establishment of BRICS 'or to expect its quick demise', Lukov (2012) proclaims it 'one of the most significant geopolitical events of the new century'. The title of his paper, 'A global forum for the new generation: The role of the BRICS and the prospects for the future', evokes both a shared stage (a global forum) and different worlds (the new and, by implication, an older generation of 'informal global institutions' such as the G–7 or the G–77), which are thereby placed in a single world; a world in which BRICS may 'revive a "bloc approach"' (creating division), while simultaneously providing 'a new model for global relations . . . that overrides the old East-West and North-South barriers' (thereby creating community at the same time).

Secondly and perhaps most importantly, Rancière argues that politics involves a 'presupposition of equality' by those who are not supposed to 'have a part' in the community and yet identify themselves with it (Rancière 1999: 61–3). Rather than a mathematical proportion (as for the ancients) or a legal-political or economic construct (as for the moderns), the presupposition of equality refers to an assumption that 'the people' can 'verify' through action (Rancière 1995: 45–8, 85; cf. 1999: 33).[4] With regard to BRICS, the presupposition of equality is a complex issue. While BRICS claim to validate this presupposition on behalf of the 43 per cent of the world's 'people' they comprise (BRICS 2012: para 3), they simultaneously face daily challenges from (the) people acting under a presupposition of equality.[5] Moreover, internationally BRICS simultaneously appear as 'having a part' (as 'great powers') and not having a part (as erstwhile 'developing countries') in the 'international community'. Bearing in mind these qualifications, certain key points in the BRICS summit documents (perhaps along with the very staging of BRICS summits) do suggest a presupposition of equality. Specifically, BRICS call for 'greater democracy in international relations' based on 'equality' and 'mutual respect' and an enhanced 'voice of emerging and developing countries' (BRICS 2011: paras 5, 7; 2009: para 12; cf. 2010: para 2).

By contrast, the EU's pronouncements in support of democracy and equality (in art. 21(1), CVTEU) effectively make a 'presupposition of inequality' between the EU and 'the wider world'. When considering EU and BRICS democratic and egalitarian speech in juxtaposition, we are faced with what Rancière (1999: x–xi) calls 'disagreement', that is, a speech situation in which the parties 'both understand and do not understand the same thing by the same words'. Similarly to dissensus, disagreement is a function of breaching assumptions about who is entitled to speak a certain language rather than the content of speech. The Lisbon Treaty may see democracy and equality as attributes of certain institutional arrangements in EU member states, whereas BRICS emphasise democracy and equality among (rather than within) states. However, disagreement arises not from this difference of interpretation, but rather from the fact that BRICS appropriate the words of democracy and equality to 'verify' them in practice. Such a postulation of a world of shared meaning constitutes a 'transgressive', genuinely political action whose objective is

> not to found a counterpower susceptible of governing a future society, but simply to effect a demonstration of *capacity* which is also a demonstration

of *community* ... not secession, but self-affirmation as a joint-sharer in a common world, with the assumption, appearances to the contrary notwithstanding, that one can play the same game as the adversary. (Rancière 1995: 49)

'Politics occurs', says Rancière, when supposedly natural orders of inequality, (such as that implied by art. 21(1), CVTEU), are 'interrupted' by a presupposition of equality (Rancière 1999: 16–17). 'The essence of equality is ... to undo the supposed naturalness of orders and replace it with controversial figures of division' (Rancière 1995: 32–3).

Rancière's generic term for such figures of division, and the third element of politics, is 'wrong' or 'an injustice that needs to be addressed' (Rancière 1995: 97). From BRICS' perspective, 'wrong' could be signified by a largely Western narrative of world history (Zakaria 2009: 34–5), colonial and postcolonial grievances, China's 'century of humiliation' (Kaufman 2010), Russia's post-Cold War humiliation, or (legacies of) apartheid in South Africa. As previously mentioned, a more immediate wrong of concern to BRICS as a group is the inadequate representativeness of international financial institutions. However, while wrong may concern the distribution of positions (such as voting shares in the IMF), its significance derives from its 'constitutive function ... in transforming egalitarian logic into political logic' (Rancière 1999: 35). Rather than an identifiable tort that could be redressed juridically or by enfranchisement, wrong signifies a fundamental irreconcilability of different parties; a 'radical otherness' exemplified in Aristotle's figure of the stranger to a city (Rancière 1995: 97), or in our context, BRICS' (partial) alterity vis-à-vis a putative Eurocentric *cosmopolis*.

The alterity exposed by wrong is not a form of identity politics. Rather than presupposing given identities, wrong constitutes parties to a conflict as political subjects. Politics is a mechanism of subjectivation creating political subjects rather than being created by pre-existing ones. More precisely, subjectivation transforms 'identities defined in the natural order of ... functions and places into instances of experience of a dispute' (Rancière 1999: 36). Subjectivation is a particularly useful lens to understand the political in BRICS. BRICS are alternately identified as 'emerging markets/economies', criticised as 'irresponsible stakeholders' (Patrick 2010), or admonished to become 'responsible stakeholders' in the international system (see Roberts 2010a; Etzioni 2011; Thakur 2012). What these 'natural' and depoliticising identifications and admonitions overlook is that the emergence of BRICS, rather than relying on pre-existing regional, cultural-civilisational, or functional identities (as in Mouffe's multipolar order), marks an instance of political subjectivation and 'disidentification' (Rancière 1999: 36). BRICS' collaboration problematises 'natural' identities (for instance, by juxtaposing 'developing countries' to 'emerging economies') and corresponding responsibilities as 'stakeholders' in an order not or only partially of their own making. BRICS do not have to exist as a political subject (say, a regional 'pole' with a 'civilisational' identity) to engage in politics. Rather, the extent to which BRICS effectively engage in politics (which may be quite rare) shapes their political subjectivity.

BRICS' subjectivation, rather than an ex nihilo creation, reworks what it may mean for 'emerging economies' to be 'responsible stakeholders'. While Western calls to responsible stakeholdership sound like parental admonitions to a teenager, BRICS may politicise these notions. As David Scott illustrates in an analysis of official Chinese interpretations of responsibility, being a 'responsible stakeholder' can be mobilised in various ways: as a form of 'discourse power' accompanying a 'peaceful rise'; as being 'reasonable'; as implying stakeholder rights; as a contrast with US 'irresponsibility'; or most importantly here, 'to suggest a crucial equality of status with the US' (Scott 2010: 74–83). Conversely, BRICS may invoke 'common but differentiated responsibilities' of 'developed' and 'developing' countries in international environmental policy to (re)claim the latter status and its exemptions (BRICS 2012: paras 29, 31; 2011: para 22; 2010: para 22; 2009: para 9). BRICS thus mark a gap between the 'natural' identities assigned to them ('responsible stakeholders', 'emerging economies') and a more contentious experience (for example, as postcolonial or 'underdeveloped' countries) behind these identities. In contrast to identity politics in the name of multipolarity, this disidentification may be the hallmark of BRICS' political subjectivation.

A political understanding of BRICS has to be kept in perspective. BRICS' implication with multiple governmentalities and international police may more often attenuate rather than incite their dissensual potentials. However, while Rancière sharply distinguishes politics and police in principle, in practice they are entangled whenever egalitarian logic confronts police logic (Rancière 1999: 31–3; see also Chambers 2011). In our context, this entanglement is perhaps most apparent in BRICS' call for voting reform in international financial institutions. Given their mutual entanglement, 'police' and 'politics' cut across the binary of cosmopolitanism and multipolarity. 'Police' may be cosmopolitan or non-cosmopolitan, and the political is more contingent, incalculable and intermittent than images of multipolarity and equilibrium suggest.

Conclusion

Using the EU and BRICS global governance projects as an illustration, this chapter has attempted to build a bridge between discussions of the political and post-political in Mouffe's and Rancière's political theories and Foucauldian governmentality analysis. In one direction, the traffic across this bridge supplements accounts of post-politics with the governmental and biopolitical rationalities and infrastructures that make possible the domestication of hierarchy and antagonism in the first place. In the other direction, it restores to governmentality analysis agonistic 'themes of conflict, contestation, dissonance and struggle' which sometimes seem to elude it (Walters 2012: 148). However, rather than deriving this agonism from a Schmittian antagonism between friends and enemies (like Mouffe), my analysis has followed Rancière in locating it in certain forms of social practice (or, if you will, quasi-Foucauldian counter-conducts) at least partially disruptive of governmentality. Recognising the 'world of mixture' (Rancière's 2010: 207) of governmentality and politics in the EU-BRICS dyad allows for thinking the political and post-political in international relations beyond Mouffe's binary of cosmopolitanism and multipolarity. While cosmopolitanism is more ambiguous and insidiously political than Mouffe recognises, her focus on multipolar equilibrium as a somewhat 'left-Huntingtonian' clash of civilisational identities misses out on several at least equally important dimensions of the political not bound up with power and identity; specifically, the theatricality, presupposed equality, and concern with (in)justice foregrounded by Rancière.

However, rather than as a(n unlikely) new orthodoxy, Rancière's political theory should serve as a provocation to thinking about the meaning of global democracy. For Rancière '[d]emocracy is not a regime or a social way of life. It is the institution of politics itself' (Rancière 1999: 101; cf. 2010: 31–2). To the extent that BRICS at least partially and momentarily activate a political moment in global governance, they could be – no doubt counterintuitively for many – a symptom of a certain kind of global democracy; a form of global democracy that does not find expression in representative institutions or deliberative procedures but intermittently disrupts these in the name of equality or wrong as well as a claim to shared (international) community. Global democracy may be more sporadic than we usually imagine, cropping up in unexpected places such as BRICS, not necessarily 'representing' the disenfranchised, but simply registering that their voice should count as political speech. While BRICS themselves ought to be challenged democratically 'from below', their partial disruption of post-political consensus in international relations should in itself be considered as a democratic challenge to global (police) order.

Notes

1. Available at *http://www.bricsindia.in/publication.html* (accessed 20 April 2012).
2. Thanks to the editors for suggesting this point.
3. That is, the naturalised and acceptable (Swyngedouw 2011: 375), and perhaps the sensual (*jouissance*) (Wilson, Chapter 5 of this volume).
4. For Rancière the people, the demos, is a desubstantialised notion. What the demos means sociologically emerges in the practical validation of equality. See Rancière (1999: 83, 99–100; 2010: 33).
5. Witness indigenous peoples' resistance in Brazil, 'Pussy Riot(s)' in Russia, Dalit mobilisation in India, environmental dissent in China, or independent unions in South Africa, to name only some conspicuous examples.

References

Aradau, C., and R. van Munster (2007), 'Governing terrorism through risk: Taking precautions, (un)knowing the future', *European Journal of International Relations*, 13: 1, pp. 89–115.

Ashley, R. (1986), 'The poverty of neorealism', in R. O. Keohane (ed.), *Neorealism and Its Critics*, New York: Columbia University Press, pp. 255–300.

Barnett, M., and M. Finnemore (2004), *Rules for the World: International Organisations in Global Politics*, Ithaca, NY: Cornell University Press.

Behr, H. (2007), 'The European Union in the legacies of imperial rule? EU accession politics viewed from a historical comparative perspective', *European Journal of International Relations*, 13: 2, pp. 239–62.

Best, J. (2005), *The Limits of Transparency: Ambiguity and the History of International Finance*, Ithaca, NY: Cornell University Press.

Best, Jacqueline (2008), 'Ambiguity, uncertainty, and risk: Rethinking indeterminacy', *International Political Sociology*, 2: 4, pp. 355–74.

BRIC (2009), 'Joint Statement of the BRIC Countries' Leaders', Yekaterinburg, 16 June, available at *http://www.brics.utoronto.ca/docs/090616-leaders.html* (accessed 19 April 2012).

BRIC (2010), '2nd BRIC Summit of Heads of State and Government: Joint Statement', Brasilia, 15 April, available at *http://www.brics.utoronto.ca/docs/100415-leaders.html* (accessed 19 April 2012).

BRICS (2011), 'Sanya Declaration', BRICS leaders meeting, Sanya, Hainan, 14 April, available at *http://www.brics.utoronto.ca/docs/110414-leaders.html* (accessed 19 April 2012).

BRICS (2012), 'Fourth BRICS Summit: Delhi Declaration' and 'Delhi Action

Plan', New Delhi, 29 March, available at *http://www.brics.utoronto.ca/docs/120329-delhi-declaration.html* (accessed 19 April 2012).

Brown, G. W., and D. Held (eds) (2010), *The Cosmopolitanism Reader*, Cambridge: Polity.

Castañeda, J. (2010), 'Not ready for prime time', *Foreign Affairs*, 89: 5, pp. 109–22.

Chambers, S. A. (2011), 'Jacques Rancière and the problem of pure politics', *European Journal of Political Theory*, 10: 3, pp. 303–26.

Council of the European Union (2010), 'Consolidated Version of the Treaty on European Union', *Official Journal of the European Union*, Vol. 53, C 83/01, 30 March 2010. Available at *http://eur-lex.europa.eu/LexUriServ/LexUriServ.do?uri=OJ:C:2010:083:0013:0046:en:PDF* (accessed 7 January 2014).

Dean, M. (2010), *Governmentality: Power and Rule in Modern Society*, 2nd edn, London: Sage.

Etzioni, A. (2011), 'Is China a responsible stakeholder?', *International Affairs*, 87: 3, pp. 539–53.

Foucault, M. (2000), 'The subject and power', in J. D. Faubion (ed.), *Power: Essential Works of Foucault 1954–1984, Vol. 3*, New York: New Press, pp. 326–48.

Foucault, M. (2003), *'Society Must Be Defended:' Lectures at the Collège de France 1975–1976*, New York: Picador.

Foucault, M. (2007), *Security, Territory, Population: Lectures at the Collège de France 1977–1978*, New York: Palgrave Macmillan.

Foucault, M. (2008), *The Birth of Biopolitics: Lectures at the Collège de France 1978–1979*, New York: Palgrave Macmillan.

Glosny, M. A. (2010), 'China and the BRICs: A real (but limited) partnership in a unipolar world', *Polity* 42: 1, pp. 100–29.

Habermas, J. (2006), 'Does the constitutionalisation of international law still have a chance?', in J. Habermas, *The Divided West*, Cambridge: Polity, pp. 115–93.

Habermas, J. (2011), 'Die Krise der Europäischen Union im Lichte einer Konstitutionalisierung des Völkerrechts – Ein Essay sur Verfassung Europas', in J. Habermas, *Zur Verfassung Europas: Ein Essay*, Berlin: Suhrkamp, pp. 39–96.

Hallward, P. (2009), 'Staging equality: Rancière's theatocracy and the limits of anarchic equality', in G. Rockhill and P. Watts (eds), *Jacques Rancière: History, Politics, Aesthetics*, Durham: Duke University Press, pp. 140–57.

Ilcan, S. and L. Phillips (2010), 'Developmentalities and calculative practices: The Millennium Development Goals', *Antipode* 42: 4, pp. 844–74.

Kaufman, A. Adcock (2010), 'The 'century of humiliation', then and now: Chinese perceptions of the international order', *Pacific Focus*, 25: 1, pp. 1–33.

Luke, T. (1995), 'Sustainable development as a power/knowledge system: The problem of "governmentality"', in Frank Fischer and Michael Black (eds), *Greening Environmental Policy: The Politics of a Sustainable Future*, London: Paul Chapman, pp. 21–32.

Lukov, V. (2012), 'A global forum for the new generation: The role of the BRICS and the prospects for the future', available at *http://www. brics.utoronto.ca/analysis/Lukov-Global-Forum.html* (accessed 27 July 2012).

Marchart, O. (2010), *Die politische Differenz: Zum Denken des Politischen bei Nancy, Lefort, Badiou, Laclau und Agamben*, Berlin: Suhrkamp.

Mearsheimer, J. J. (2010), 'Structural realism', in T. Dunne, M. Kurki and S. Smith (eds), *International Relations Theories: Discipline and Diversity*, 2nd edn, Oxford: Oxford University Press, pp. 77–94.

Mouffe, C. (2005), *On the Political*, New York: Routledge.

Patrick, S. (2010), 'Irresponsible stakeholders? The difficulty of integrating rising powers', *Foreign Affairs*, 89: 6, pp. 44–53.

Rancière, J. (1995), *On the Shores of Politics*, London: Verso.

Rancière, J. (1999), *Disagreement: Politics and Philosophy*, Minneapolis: University of Minnesota Press.

Rancière, J. (2010), *Dissensus: On Politics and Aesthetics*, London: Continuum.

Roberts, C. (2010a), 'Polity forum: challengers or stakeholders? BRICS and the liberal world order – introduction', *Polity*, 42: 1, pp. 1–13.

Roberts, C. (2010b), 'Russia's BRICs diplomacy: Rising outsider with dreams of an insider', *Polity* 42: 1 pp. 38–73.

Scott, D. (2010), 'China and the "responsibilities" of a "responsible" power – The uncertainties about appropriate power rise language', *Asia-Pacific Review*, 17: 1, pp. 72–96.

Sinha, A., and J. P. Dorschner (2010), 'India: Rising power or a mere revolution of rising expectations', *Polity*, 42: 1, pp. 74–99.

Swyngedouw, E. (2011), 'Interrogating post-democratisation: Reclaiming egalitarian political spaces', *Political Geography*, 30: 7, pp. 370–80.

Thakur, R. (2012), 'Cementing BRICS as a coalition of the Global South', in BRICS Research Group (ed.), *BRICS New Delhi Summit 2012: Stability, Security and Prosperity*, London: Newsdesk Media, pp. 84–5, available at *http://www.brics.utoronto.ca/newsdesk/index.html* (accessed 1 August 2012).

Tisdall, S. (2012), 'Can the Brics create a new world order? Brazil, Russia, India, China and South Africa seek a multipolar world – but some argue they're bound by anti-Americanism', *The Guardian*, 29 March, available at *http://www.guardian.co.uk/commentisfree/2012/mar/29/brics-new-world-order* (accessed 19 April 2012).

Walters, W. (2012), *Governmentality: Critical Encounters*, London: Routledge.

Walters, W., and J. Henrik Haahr (2005), *Governing Europe: Discourse, Governmentality and European Integration*, London: Routledge.

Waltz, K. N. (1979), *Theory of International Politics*, Reading, MA: Addison-Wesley.

Yardley, J. (2012), 'For group of five nations, acronym is easy, but common ground is hard', *New York Times*, 29 March, A4.

Zakaria, F. (2009), *The Post-American World*, New York: W.W. Norton.

Žižek, S. (2002), *Welcome to the Desert of the Real*, London: Verso.

11   Against a Speculative Leftism

Alex Loftus

One may term 'Byzantinism' or 'scholasticism' the regressive tendency to treat so-called theoretical questions as if they had a value in themselves, independently of any specific practice . . . It can further be deduced that every truth, even if it is universal, and even if it can be expressed by an abstract formula of a mathematical kind (for the sake of the theoreticians), owes its effectiveness to its being expressed in the language appropriate to specific concrete situations. If it cannot be expressed in such specific terms, it is a byzantine and scholastic abstraction, good only for phrasemongers to toy with. (Gramsci Q 9, § 63; 1971: 200–1)

Periods of revolutionary insurrection prompt periods of reflection on the nature of politics. What may only be tentative signs of the abilities of subaltern groups to reshape social relations provoke treatises on the successes and the frustrations of such interventions, treatises which often turn on a reconceptualisation of the political. In the wake of Occupy's dramatic emergence and equally sudden disappearance, the attempt to delineate the bounds of the truly political event has yet again acquired a new urgency. In this chapter, I argue that how we engage with actually existing movements such as Occupy – and how we understand 'politics' in relation to them – matters enormously. It matters not only for the nature of our work as scholars but also for the power relations shaping knowledge production. The form of our engagement with social movements, moreover, will be shaped by where we see the conditions of possibility for future change. My focus in this chapter is largely confined to the political conceptions of Antonio Gramsci – which were developed in the wake of the Factory Councils and the reversal of a revolutionary moment as Italy descended into fascism – and their posthumous reception in post-Althusserian scholarship, which has influenced more recent readings of the political and post-political (Laclau and

Mouffe 1985; Butler, Laclau and Žižek 2000). Moving between post-Althusserian Marxist scholarship and Gramscian readings of the political, I argue for a conception of the political based on a philosophy of praxis, and criticise the privileging of conceptual abstraction over contextualised readings of historically and geographically specific practices.

The question of speculative leftism and the relation of philosophy to praxis frames Jacques Rancière's first book, *Althusser's Lesson*, published in 1974, in which he dissects the philosophy of his former mentor, Louis Althusser, and the directions Althusserianism had taken in the six years after May 1968. The text is crucial for mapping some of the lineages of post-Althusserian political thought. Rancière frames the split within Althusserianism as one between a 'speculative leftism' and a 'speculative Zhandovism' (Rancière 2011). Speculative leftism refers to the preoccupation with ideological state apparatuses; an understanding of ideology as 'illusion'; and a subsequent distancing from the hopes, fears and ideas that motivate individuals and classes. The book is developed around the simple idea that Althusser and his speculative leftist followers should listen more and cease their patronising, abstract sermonising. Taking its title from Althusser's particularly patronising 'lesson' in his 'Reply to John Lewis', a British communist philosopher, Rancière demonstrates how the position adopted by Althusser within the exchange reinstated a hierarchy of knowledge production as well as a theoreticist detachment from historically and geographically specific practices. In several respects, Rancière's critique of the pedagogical elitism assumed by Althusser prefigures *The Ignorant Schoolmaster* (Rancière 1991), in which he engages with Marx's *Theses on Feuerbach* and particularly the third thesis in which Marx claims, against the old materialism, that 'the educator too must be educated'. Rancière's critique therefore defines a Marxist praxis fundamentally at odds with speculative leftism. Against the detachment from historical and political events, Rancière restates the *historical* in historical materialism.

Resurrecting Rancière's critique of speculative leftism, Bruno Bosteels similarly detects a revival of metaphysics within contemporary writings on the 'idea of communism':

> What is speculative about this leftism is not the simple fact of being out of touch with reality in the style of plain old idealism but the way in which actual political events and historical filiations, while purportedly taken into account, in reality vanish and are replaced by theoretical operators that continue to be the sole purview of the Marxist philosopher as the master and proprietor of truth. (Bosteels 2011: 25)

Bosteels draws from Ranciere's critique but also situates this critique within a longer trend of rejecting certain forms of 'leftism'. Focusing at one point on 'a small French genealogy of this trend', he writes of how

> Louis Althusser and his disciples were accused of 'authoritarian' or 'speculative leftism' early on by the rebellious disciple Jacques Rancière; Rancière, in turn, is accused of radical 'apoliticism' by his older classmate Alain Badiou; and, closing the circle in the style of a winged Ouroboros, Slavoj Žižek goes on to accuse the ex-Althusserians Badiou, Rancière and Balibar of dreaming up, in typical leftist fashion, a form of 'pure politics'. (Bosteels 2010: 36)

In a more serious vein, Bosteels demonstrates how the allure of metaphysics is in dialectical tension with his own project to investigate the 'actuality of communism': he thus constructs an argument that can be read as an engaged and sympathetic critique of *some* aspects of post-foundational political debates (while remaining profoundly sympathetic to other aspects), at the same time as calling for an engaged praxis, building in particular on Bolivian social movements and the praxis-based perspectives of Álvaro García Linerá. He thus concludes one of his contributions with a call for the 'construction of a common horizon – beyond leftism yet also in dialogue with its invaluable lessons – in which it might be possible to take stock of and learn from the most radical political experiments of our present' (Bosteels 2010: 66).

In this chapter I make an argument that parallels the ambivalent relationship with leftism seen in the critiques of Rancière, Bosteels and Žižek. However, rather than building directly on this ambivalence, I seek to put some of the insights of Antonio Gramsci to work, while also showing how his reception has ultimately been shaped by the ambiguities of leftism. Gramsci's approach 'was defined by a singular and consistent concern: the attempt to elaborate a political theory which would be adequate to give expression to – and, just as importantly, to shape and guide – the popular and subaltern classes' attempts to awaken from the nightmares of their histories and to assume social and political leadership' (Thomas 2009a: 159). *The Prison Notebooks* outline a project that is antithetical to speculative forms of thought, and that seeks to wrestle with the fragmented conceptions of the world that define the subaltern's condition (Green and Ives 2009). However, demonstrating the relevance of Gramsci to a critique of the post-political condition requires, paradoxically, a defence of Gramsci against a certain reading imposed upon him by key interlocutors in the debates around the post-political. Thus,

I will seek to show how Laclau and Mouffe's Althusserian reading of Gramsci imposes a speculative leftist reading on the *Prison Notebooks*. Intriguingly, the curious ability to turn Gramsci's writings on their head is made possible through a particular reading of the latter's conception of the political. The result has been a cooptation of Gramsci within Byzantine debates that obscure his desire 'to speak in the language appropriate to specific concrete situations' (Gramsci Q 9, § 63; 1971: 201).

I begin with a brief introduction to Gramsci's philosophy of praxis before looking at the manner in which Gramsci's writings have been mediated within the Anglophone world through a speculative framework. Developing the claim that Laclau and Mouffe's highly influential reading of Gramsci rests on a misreading of Gramsci on the political, I seek to advance an alternative interpretation, rooted in the philosophy of praxis, in Gramsci's linguistic studies and in his distinctive reading of Machiavelli. I conclude by making the case for a living philology against the violence of theoretical abstraction.

Gramsci's philosophy of praxis

Gramsci is best known for his concept of hegemony, which bears some surface resemblance to certain understandings of the post-political condition. In his conceptualisation of hegemony, Gramsci analyses how moral and intellectual leadership comes to be asserted by social groups through a particular combination of consent and coercion. Diagnosing forms of bourgeois hegemony, Gramsci also considers the potentials for subaltern groups to constitute their own moral and intellectual leadership as a countervailing, and yet dialectically related, set of relations of force. Understanding Gramsci's distinctive contributions to a theorisation of hegemony is aided by situating it within his philosophy of praxis, the term he applies to his own reading of Marx.

Gramsci consistently relates the philosophy of praxis to three distinctive yet interrelated moments: absolute historicism; absolute immanence or the 'absolute secularisation and earthliness of thought'; and an absolute humanism of history (Gramsci Q 11, § 30; 1971: 465). Gramsci's absolute historicism refers to his situated analyses of conjunctural moments and to the inventories he compiles of the conceptions of the world that are fought over within such conjunctural moments. Absolute immanence refers to Gramsci's attention to Marx's (and his own) transformation of 'speculative' or idealist philosophies into a grounded form of critique that emerges from historically and geographically specific practices. And Gramsci's absolute humanism of history develops a relational understanding of the person and of the historically and geographically specific conditions of possibility for her becoming (see Thomas 2009a). Hegemony, therefore, cannot be divorced from historically and geographically specific practices and their articulation with already existing forms of intellectual and moral leadership. The possibilities for an immanent critique (and the transformation of hegemony) lie in both a reading of these practices and an understanding of the person who emerges from them, a person always viewed in relation to both others and her 'relations to nature'.

Profoundly influenced by both the *Theses on Feuerbach* and Marx's 1859 Preface to *A Contribution to Political Economy*, Gramsci was deeply sensitive to a form of dialectical pedagogy – in which the educator too must be educated – and to the conditions of possibility for particular conceptions of the world. As I go on to argue, such insights comprise a unique contribution to the debates about the possible return of the political. Crucially, Gramsci emphasises the importance of historically and geographically specific practices for the grounding of new political possibilities. However, as I will argue in the next section, these contributions to contemporary debates are complicated by the mediation of the philosophy of praxis through certain key gatekeepers.

Mouffe, Gramsci and the political

> If the history of marxist theory during the 1960s can be characterised by the reign of 'althusserianism', then we have now, without a doubt, entered a new phase: that of 'gramscism'. (Mouffe 1979a: 1)

Gramsci's writings have been noticeably absent from the flourishing body of work on post-foundational political thought (Marchart 2007); on the post-political and its discontents (see this collection); and on the idea of communism (Douzinas and Žižek 2010). This absence is particularly notable given that the Italian communist thinker had been so prominent in earlier debates around a (post-) Marxist politics. In these earlier debates, Chantal Mouffe discovered within Gramsci a non-reductionist theory of the autonomy of the political, something she viewed as a radical departure from the canon of Western Marxism. Gramsci's theory of hegemony, furthermore, shed light on a 'specifically political moment' (Mouffe 1979: 180), which Mouffe interpreted through a non-reductionist reading of ideology. Together with Ernesto Laclau (Laclau and Mouffe 1985), Mouffe was to take Gramsci's conception of the political further, only to find that vestiges of essentialism remained in the *Prison Notebooks*. In expunging this final essentialism, Laclau and Mouffe moved 'beyond' Gramsci, and discovered a radically democratic conception of the political within linguistic theory. It is surely no exaggeration to claim that the majority of scholars (and also, perhaps, activists) now encounter Gramsci's theory of hegemony through Mouffe's writings. And yet in claiming to move beyond Gramsci, Laclau and Mouffe (1985) effectively sutured the possibilities within the former's conception of politics. Tracing Mouffe's reading of Gramsci, and reading it alongside Rancière's critique of speculative leftism, enables a radically different interpretation of Gramsci that can more effectively take on the challenges of the post-political.

Despite referring to her turn to Gramsci as a turn away from Althusser, Mouffe's reading of Gramsci is deeply influenced by the French structuralist Marxist.[1] In an early essay, Mouffe attempts a 'symptomatic reading' of Gramsci, in which Althusser's definition of ideology as 'a practice producing subjects' is taken as the starting point, and according to which the 'basic tenet' of historical materialism is its conception of determination in the last instance by the economy (1979b: 200). Yet while Mouffe imposes an Althusserian reading of Gramsci, she also places some clear distance between her new position and the work of her former mentor. Thus, in a positive review of Gramsci's contributions to a theorisation of the 'autonomy of politics and ideology', Mouffe rejects Althusser's (1970) flawed but highly influential critique of Gramsci's 'historicism'. Instead Mouffe makes the bold claim that 'Gramsci's problematic anticipated Althusser in several respects' (1979b: 188). Beyond this anticipation, Mouffe emphasises the manner in which Gramsci's concept of hegemony surpasses reductionist conceptions in order to demonstrate that the subjects of political action are 'collective wills', in which different 'inter-class subjects' are created. The formation of such 'collective wills' is a result of the transformation of the previous ideological terrain and the 'rearticulation of existing ideological elements'. Thus, it is 'by their articulation to a hegemonic principle that the ideological elements acquire their class character which is not intrinsic to them' (1979b: 193). Overlooking Gramsci's grounding in linguistics, Mouffe already damns with faint praise, writing that

> I am not claiming that all the problems of the marxist theory of ideology are solved by Gramsci – even in the practical state. In any case the conceptual tools which he had to use have been completely superseded, and nowadays we are equipped to deal with the problem of ideology in a far more rigorous fashion thanks to the development of disciplines such as linguistics and psychoanalysis. (Mouffe 1979b: 199)

This comment foreshadows the problematic 'genealogy' of hegemony that was to form the prefatory basis for *Hegemony and Socialist Strategy,* a genealogy that can only be made on the basis of a deep chauvinism for the modern and an anachronistic account that sees linguistics emerging *after* Antonio Gramsci's own studies in the discipline under Mateo Bartoli. Notwithstanding such curious genealogies, Mouffe's reading of Gramsci is largely positive, due to the 'conception of politics' found within the latter's theorisation of hegemony, ideology and the 'integral state'. According to Mouffe, her Gramscian non-reductionist conception of the political provides the possibility for a new approach to power. She concludes her essay with the bold claim that

> It is in fact quite remarkable to see the extraordinary way in which some contemporary research – such as that of Foucault or Derrida which brings out a completely new conception of politics – converges with Gramsci's thought, and having recognised the anti-reductionist character of his thought I do not think it too hazardous to predict that the topicality of Gramsci's work and his influence will go on increasing in the future. (Mouffe 1979b: 201)

Whether such a prophecy would have been borne out or not, Laclau and Mouffe's 1985 work *Hegemony and Socialist Strategy* did much more to endorse and yet simultaneously reject the topicality and influence of what they claim to be a Gramscian conception of the political. The reason for Laclau and Mouffe's paradoxical endorsement and critique of Gramsci lies, in part, in their positioning of Gramsci within a linear trajectory that moves inexorably towards *their own* reading of the political, the latter then being equipped with the developments within linguistic theory alluded to in Mouffe's reading of Gramsci. In *Hegemony and Socialist Strategy,* Gramsci can be read as a progressive but ultimately flawed figure. Laclau and Mouffe script a history of the Second and Third Internationals as a futile quest to try and retain the principles of historical materialism (determination in the last instance by the economy, according to Mouffe (1979b)) while at the same time seeking to expunge historical materialism of essentialist hangovers. Only Gramsci emerges from these debates 'with a new arsenal of concepts'. Hegemony is thereby defined as 'new political logic' and a 'Gramscian watershed' is highlighted. However, just as this Gramscian watershed appears likely to be tapped for its political potential within a radically democratic project, Laclau and Mouffe discover that the 'articulatory role' of hegemony is 'assigned by the material base'. Indeed 'the naturalist prejudice, which sees the economy as a homogenous space unified by necessary laws, appears once again with all its force' (1985: 69). Gramsci is simultaneously vindicated and vilified. Both the 'Gramscian watershed' and Mouffe's earlier declaration of an era of 'Gramscism' are quickly superseded. For Laclau, the period following his engagement with Gramsci entails a much deeper engagement with the work of Jacques Lacan: for Mouffe, it entails an engagement with Carl Schmitt, amongst others, within whose work she finds the basis for an adversarial politics and the possibility for a radical critique of deliberative democracy.

On the autonomy of the political

Laclau and Mouffe's reading of Gramsci overlooks his attention to historical and geographical specificity, to the terrain of the conjunctural, and to the importance of developing a theoretical form or 'a language appropriate to specific concrete situations'. Against the claim that Gramsci's contribution to rethinking the political lies in an understanding of the *autonomy* of the political, I would argue that the philosophy of praxis moves in precisely the opposite direction. Indeed the notion of the political existing autonomously runs against Gramsci's dialectical approach. At the heart of this dialectical approach is an objection to speculative and metaphysical modes of theorising:

> It is affirmed that the philosophy of praxis was born on the terrain of the highest development of culture in the first half of the nineteenth century, this culture being represented by classical German philosophy, English classical economics and French political literature and practice . . . in the new synthesis, whichever 'moment' one is examining, the theoretical, the economic or the political, one will find each of the three movements present as a preparatory 'moment' . . . the unitary 'moment' of synthesis is to be identified in the new concept of immanence, which has been translated from the speculative form, as put forward by classical German philosophy, into a historicist form with the aid of French politics and English classical economics. (Gramsci Q 10II, § 9; 1971: 399–400)

The specificity of the philosophy of praxis, therefore, lies not in a claim for the autonomy of the political but rather in a dialectical framing of the relationship between the economic, the political and the philosophical. Neither in the first nor in the last instance is any individual moment the sole determinant. In a set of exchanges with Judith Butler and Ernesto Laclau, Slavoj Žižek rejects the implicit need to make such a choice, by stating 'Class struggle or postmodernism? Yes, please!' (Žižek 2000: 98). Here Žižek directs his ire at the false choice between a critique of political economy *or* 'postmodernism', arguing that the latter 'does *not* in fact repoliticize capitalism, because *the very notion and form of the "political" within which it operates is grounded in the "depoliticization" of the economy*' (italics in original). More recently, however, he has targeted his critique at those he refers to as 'post-Althusserian partisans of "pure politics"' (Žižek 2004: 75). Such partisans, 'from Balibar through Rancière and Badiou to Laclau and Mouffe' aim at 'the reduction of the sphere of economy to the "ontic" sphere deprived of ontological dignity' (Žižek 2004: 75), forcing one to make a choice between the political *or* the economy.

If such a choice is anathema for Žižek, it is equally anathema for Gramsci. Indeed the latter's conception of the political is defined in opposition to attempts to define a 'pure politics', a trend that Žižek suggests has plagued post-Althusserian scholarship. Delineating an abstract science of the political was the job of Benedetto Croce, the liberal Italian philosopher, and contemporary of Gramsci, against whom large parts of the *Prison Notebooks* are directed. Croce praised Machiavelli for developing an understanding of the political as a fixed set of laws, immutable, universal and transhistorical. Gramsci, by contrast, recognised the power relations unfolding within such a perspective. For behind Croce's conception of the autonomy of the political lies a thinly disguised bid to preserve the distinction between those who rule and those who are to be ruled:

> The purpose and function of the political is to render (or keep) the masses passive and malleable; the political encompasses the means and methods through which the people are brought to accept the rule of the 'aristo-democracy'. Thus politics is the activity that maintains the distinction between those who rule and those who are ruled. (Fontana 1993: 10)[2]

Gramsci negates this Crocean Machiavelli and reinterprets the author of *The Prince* as 'the democratic philosopher' or 'the Italian Luther' (Fontana 1993: 1). Thus, against Croce, Gramsci argues that Machiavelli's key contribution was to advocate for a new relationship with the masses. The prince's authority relies not on his ability to secure a distinction between the purity of politics and the messiness of 'common sense' but on his ability to nurture, develop and transform a new relationship between leader and led, educator and educated. As on numerous other occasions within the *Prison Notebooks*, Gramsci's analysis is based on an interpretation of the *Theses on Feuerbach*. In this instance (as for Rancière) it is the third thesis that is of crucial importance:

The materialist doctrine concerning the changing of circumstances and upbringing forgets that circumstances are changed by men and that it is essential to educate the educator himself. This doctrine must, therefore, divide society into two parts, one of which is superior to society. The coincidence of the changing of circumstances and of human activity or self-changing can be conceived and rationally understood only as revolutionary practice. (Marx 1975: 422)

Gramsci's theorisation of hegemony builds on Marx's conceptualisation of the education of educators (as embodied in revolutionary practice). However, the antecedent is to be found in Machiavelli. Thus, against a delineation of politics as an autonomous realm whose abstract laws can be decided *avant la lettre* and applied universally, Gramsci 'formulates a view of the political that is both the product and the carrier of a transformative and innovating praxis' (Fontana 1993: 72). Mouffe's claim that Gramsci's originality lies in his move against 'economism', owing to economism's 'misrecognition of the distinct autonomy of politics and ideology' (Mouffe 1979b: 168), should therefore be approached with a certain degree of scepticism. Gramsci's project can in fact be seen as the elaboration of a conception of politics that is dialectically related to philosophy, history and economics without being determined by any single one of these moments. Mouffe, by contrast, transforms Gramsci into a Crocean thinker. As a Crocean, Gramsci is better able to speak to 'post-marxism' and also to the 'post-Althusserian partisans of pure politics' identified by Žižek. Mouffe then goes on to develop a fundamentally Crocean insight that isolates the political as an autonomous sphere whose laws can be deduced by abstract philosophical thought, opening the way further for a reading of Gramsci as a speculative leftist. The ability to speak in a language appropriate to specific concrete situations is forgotten or obliterated. Taken forward within *Hegemony and Socialist Strategy* and within her later works, this becomes an extended attempt to better understand the concept of the political, which has little to do with the concerns of Gramsci. If Gramsci's *Prison Notebooks* are to speak to contemporary debates over the post-political and its discontents, it would seem that the starting point must be a fundamentally different one from Mouffe's misreading (and subsequent superseding) of the Sardinian. None of the dialectical tension between leftism and historically and geographically specific practices is to be found in such work. Instead, the contextual is absent from view.

'A political of a completely different type'

In a richly generative reading, Peter Thomas (2009b) has distinguished Gramsci's conception of the political from what he refers to as 'Platonizing' and 'transcendental' frameworks. Thomas positions Gramsci's political thought in relation to some of the debates considered within this collection, while distancing Gramsci's reading from metaphysical and abstract conceptualisations of 'pure politics':

> *The Prison Notebooks* attempt to rethink the concept of the political in both non-metaphysical and concrete terms by means of a theory of hegemony. According to this reading, Gramsci does not provide a theory of 'the political' as such, even less than he provides a 'general theory of politics'. Rather, he attempts to provide an analysis of the 'production' or, more exactly, 'the constitution of the political'. (Thomas 2009b: 28)

Instead of approaching the political with a preconceived notion of the workings of its abstract laws, Gramsci is interested in how a specific type of political comes to be constituted, in which the conditions of possibility for a political of a completely different type might lie. Thomas focuses on Gramsci's rejection of the claims of essentialism in Marxism, finding instead a fundamentally new understanding of 'structure as an ensemble of active social relations' (Thomas 2009b: 30). Such a reconceptualisation of praxis relies heavily on *The Theses on Feuerbach* as well as a thoroughgoing rejection of speculation as a form of metaphysics.

Foreshadowing recent work on the 'post-political suturing of the terrain of the public encounter' (Swyngedouw 2010: 215), Gramsci seeks to understand how 'the political' is constituted by the bourgeois 'integral state', finding its embodiment in the separation of political and civil society. As Thomas (2009b: 31) argues, 'The practice of bourgeois hegemony itself ... has been the means by which "the political" as a distinct realm of social experience has been concretely produced and institutionally formalized as the foundation of any possible "politics".' Thomas concludes that

> The main challenge for contemporary socialist political theorists and philosophers ... does not consist in the attempt to elaborate an 'alternative' leftist conception of the political, in order to gain, finally, its own mastery of politics ... Rather the task is to put politics 'in command' within philosophy itself: that is to practice philosophy as an organizational form of social relations that seeks to formulate adequate theoretical 'translations' of the concrete social and political relations and practices of

resistance that alone will be able to give rise to a 'political of a completely different type'. (Thomas 2009b: 35)

By putting politics in command within philosophy, Gramsci challenges the speculative currents of his own time and provides a fitting retort to forms of speculative leftism in other historical moments. Before concluding I will briefly put this conception to work in considering the possibilities for the emergence of "a political of a completely different type" within the city in which I live, London. How might we begin to understand the stuttering, staccato rhythms of political emergence and disappearance within this increasingly divided and revanchist city?

Major outbreaks of violence erupted in London and across the UK in August 2011, initially in response to the police shooting of Mark Duggan. Commentators rushed to explain these events as 'pure criminality' – the favoured expression of the political Right; as a challenge to the racist police policy of stop-and-search – certainly one of the initial causes of anger; or as unleashing a hidden underbelly of crude consumerism that had been tantalised and yet frustrated by growing poverty. Others questioned whether the violence had a genuinely political basis. Each of the 'explanations' that emerged tended to abstract from single events, reducing the violence to one singular vector, rather than seeking to understand the multiple forms of common sense that motivated differing social groups. As eloquent teenagers raged against the removal of their Educational Maintenance Allowance or challenged the entrenched institutional racism of the London Metropolitan Police, there were glimpses of conditions that may well open up new political possibilities. But virulent forms of xenophobia were mixed with these more fragmented conditions for democratic change. In the fragmented shards or in 'the crude, unsophisticated version of the populace' (Gramsci Q 11, § 12; 1971: 342), there are the possibilities for something different. Nevertheless, to unravel this crude, unsophisticated vision in all its contradictions necessitates a richly contextual and historicist approach that compiles the very inventories of sedimented knowledges needed to move from a flash of radicalism to a more sustained political movement. It is precisely such questions – always retaining a faith in the abilities of subaltern peoples to make such a move – to which Gramsci addressed his entire *Prison Notebooks*. To achieve such a project necessitates *listening* as much as developing new conceptual models to capture the inherent complexity.

By October of the same year, London was engulfed in a far more explicitly political movement, as protestors sought to occupy the London Stock Exchange (or failing that, Paternoster Square, or failing that, the steps of St Paul's Cathedral). Inspired by occupations in a range of locations, anger poured out at the global wave of austerity unleashed on the most vulnerable. Briefly, Occupy appeared to take back the streets; it exposed the cracks within authority; and it challenged corrupt, outdated forms of governance. Notably, Occupy appeared to come from nowhere, just as the violence in August and the student protests of the previous year had, apparently, come from nowhere. However, with a more detailed contextual reading of the events, we see the methods and tactics passed on from earlier environmental struggles from the Climate Camps to Reclaim the Streets. There is a forgotten (or unheard?) history of such struggles which articulates with a new set of conditions – an organic crisis, if you will. Recognising the possibility for exploiting such a conjunctural moment, Gramsci pushes us to understand the different possibilities such a movement might exploit, always viewing any practice in relation to the spatial and temporal rhythms of organisation, the contradictory and sedimented conceptions of the world and the classed, raced, gendered and sexed forms of identity that have emerged. Against both a Byzantinism and an abstract reading of the events, Gramsci pushes us to avoid eliding the differences between the different manifestations of Occupy or the political moments in Tahrir Square or Syntagma Square. Instead, there is a need to look for deeper historicised and spatialised understandings of the conditions of possibility within such movements. A philosophy of praxis seeks a dialectical pedagogy in which a politics of a completely different type is shaped in continual exchange with such movements in all their historical and geographical specificity.

Against the violence of abstraction. For a living philology.

Notwithstanding the brilliant manner in which scholars have been able to diagnose the current political malaise through work on the post-political, I worry that the antidote is too often divorced from the particularities of different historical geographies as well as the feelings, passions, hopes, fears and beliefs that emerge from situated practices. A form of abstraction is put to work that risks inflicting violence on the very political movements that scholars should be seeking to learn from. In the shibboleths that now abound, a language has developed that risks speaking neither to immediate particulars nor to the popular feelings within movements seeking to wrestle with those concrete particulars. My argument in this chapter, however, has not been to call for a retreat into empiricism. Nor has it been to advocate either an anti-theoretical or an anti-philosophical argument. Instead, I have sought to demonstrate the importance of a particular type of theory rooted in what might be termed, following Gramsci, a philosophy of praxis. There are intimations of similar approaches within recent writings and I have sought to emphasise Bosteels' (2010; 2011) creative reading of the political in particular; however there are also potential pitfalls that are worth rethinking through a critique of what Žižek refers to as a partisanship to the 'pure political'.

Most of my critique of speculative forms of leftism has been directed at Mouffe's peculiar reading of Gramsci's conception of the political in which she views the latter as an autonomous sphere. This repeats the trend that Žižek detects within other post-Althusserian traditions that force a false analytical choice between the political *or* the economy. Rejecting such non-dialectical, post-Marxist conceptualisations of Gramsci, and tracing how they emerged through a speculative leftism derived from Althusserian legacies, I have instead sought to build on an entirely different reading of the relationship between Gramsci and the political. How we understand the political clearly matters. Not simply within the confines of the seminar room, but within the movements from which we seek to learn and with whom we wish to work in challenging the one-dimensionality of austere capitalism. Indeed the stakes are higher than ever, in large part because of the very evacuation of the political that is so accurately detailed in this volume. But how we find a way out of this mess, and the extent to which we are willing to relinquish our own authority – indeed our own 'lessons' – within the definition of a political of a different type is still up for grabs.

Notes

1. The distinctions between Gramsci and Althusser can be overstated, and are far more complicated one than can be dealt with in this essay. What I find problematic is the reading of Gramsci that Althusser appears to enable in Mouffe. Such a reading fits precisely those tendencies criticised by Rancière (2011): a distance from practice and a preoccupation with the ideological state apparatuses as opposed to the hopes, fears and dreams of classed individuals.
2. It's important to note that Fontana's terminology here does not map easily onto the reading of politics as the ontic and the political as the ontological. In Gramsci, if this distinction is to be found, it is more present in his distinction between *piccola politica* and *grande politica*. The bourgeois state is able to reduce the latter to the former in the same way as the suturing of the political is said to occur in conditions of post-politics.

References

Althusser, L. (1970), 'Marxism is not a historicism', in L. Althusser and É. Balibar, *Reading Capital*, London: New Left Books.

Bosteels, B. (2010), 'The leftist hypothesis: communism in the Age of Terror', in C. Douzinas and S. Žižek (eds), *The Idea of Communism*, London: Verso.

Bosteels, B. (2011), *The Actuality of Communism*, London: Verso.

Butler, J., E. Laclau and S. Žižek (2000), *Contingency, Hegemony, Universality: Contemporary Dialogues on the Left*, London: Verso.

Douzinas, C., and S. Žižek (2010), *The Idea of Communism*, London: Verso.

Fontana, B. (1993), *Hegemony and Power: On the Relation between Gramsci and Machiavelli*, Minneapolis: University of Minnesota Press.

Gramsci, A. (1971), *Selections from the Prison Notebooks*, London: Lawrence and Wishart.

Gramsci, A. (1995), *Further Selections from the Prison Notebooks*, London: Lawrence and Wishart.

Green, M. E., and P. Ives (2009), 'Subalternity and language: Overcoming the fragmentation of common sense', *Historical Materialism*, 17: 1 pp. 3–30.

Laclau, E. (2005), *On Populist Reason*, London: Verso.

Laclau, E., and C. Mouffe (1985), *Hegemony and Socialist Strategy*, London: Verso.

Marchart, O. (2007), *Post-Foundational Political Thought: Political Difference in Nancy, Lefort, Badiou and Laclau*, New York: Columbia University Press.

Marx, K. (1975), *Early Writings*, London: Pelican.

Mouffe, C. (1979a), 'Introduction: Gramsci Today', in C. Mouffe (ed.), *Gramsci and Marxist Theory*, Abingdon: Routledge.

Mouffe, C. (1979b), 'Hegemony and ideology in Gramsci', in C. Mouffe (ed.), *Gramsci and Marxist Theory*, Abingdon: Routledge.

Mouffe, C. (1995), *On the Political*, Abingdon: Routledge.

Rancière, J. (1991), *The Ignorant Schoolmaster: Five Lessons in Intellectual Emancipation*, Stanford, St Redwood: Stanford University Press.

Rancière, J. (2011), *Althusser's Lesson*, London: Continuum.

Swyngedouw, E. (2010), 'Apocalypse forever? Post-political populism and the spectre of climate change', *Theory Culture Society*, 27: 2–3, pp. 213–32.

Thomas, P. (2009a), *The Gramscian Moment*, Leiden: Brill.

Thomas, P. (2009b), 'Gramsci and the political: From the state as "metaphysical event" to hegemony as "philosophical fact"', *Radical Philosophy*, 153, pp. 27–36.

Žižek, S. (2000), 'Class struggle or postmodernism? Yes, please!', in J. Butler, E. Laclau and S. Žižek (eds), *Contingency, Hegemony, Universality*, London: Verso.

Žižek, S. (2004), 'Afterword: The lesson of Rancière', in J. Rancière, *The Politics of Aesthetics*, London: Continuum.

12 Spatialising Politics: Antagonistic Imaginaries of Indignant Squares

Maria Kaika and Lazaros Karaliotas

Inspired by the so-called Arab Spring, the Spanish *Indignados*, Greek *Αγανακτισμένοι* (Indignants), and London and New York Occupy protests generated a broad range of spatial practices and hegemonic discourses that reasserted the importance of urban public spaces in expressing political dissent (Madden and Vradis 2012; Merrifield 2013; Smith 2013). The protests were met in academic and media analysis with a combination of excitement and cynicism. On the one hand, they kindled hopes for the emergence of a new political imagination and practice, and were therefore hailed as early signs of a nascent global political movement. On the other, they were condemned as a cacophony of disparate voices, with no clear political direction or claims.

This chapter[1] departs from accounts that either deify Indignant Squares as a model for twenty-first-century political praxis (Douzinas 2011, 2013; Rogkas 2011), or demonise them as apolitical/postpolitical crowd gatherings (Pantazopoulos 2011). By performing a closer ethnographic reading of the Indignant protests at Athens' Syntagma Square, we depict the Indignant Squares as a consensual and profoundly spatialised staging of dissent (Dikeç 2005; Swyngedouw 2011), which nevertheless harbours in its underbelly internally conflicting and often radically opposing political imaginaries (Castoriadis 1987; Kaika 2010, 2011). Grounding its analysis on the Greek *Αγανακτισμένοι* at Syntagma Square, the chapter charts the multiplicity of organisational practices, discourses and spatial configurations at the square, in order to depict the events that took place there neither as a cacophony of apolitical voices, nor as the beginnings of a coherent political movement. A closer look at the organisation, practice and discourses at Syntagma Square unearths the existence of not one, but two distinct Indignant Squares, both at Syntagma, each with its own topography (upper and lower square) and its own discursive and material practice.[2] Although both squares staged dissent, they nevertheless generated different (even opposing) political imaginaries. The upper square began as a gathering of people united by the desire to protest against corruption and political and economic instability, but concluded in xenophobic and racist discourses. The lower square equally began as a gathering of people united by the desire to protest, and evolved into more organised efforts to stage an open democratic politics of solidarity.

The chapter suggests that, rather than focusing on the homogenising term 'Indignants' movement' or 'Indignant Square', we should instead be trying to unpack the plurality of politics and internal contradictions within these events. A more nuanced theoretical understanding of different types of politics and the political, and a more finely grained empirical analysis of the discursive and spatial choreographies of these events would allow us, we argue, to go beyond either celebrating them as new political imaginaries, or condemning them as expressions of a post-political era. Talking of Indignant Squares in the plural helps us explore in more grounded ways both the limitations and the possibilities that these events offer for opening up (or closing down) democratic politics.

The chapter's first section engages with theoretical debates that unpack different understandings of politics and the political and explores how these underpin understandings of the relationship between politics and space. The following sections chart the discourses and practices that underpinned the material choreographies of the upper and lower Syntagma Squares, and assert the centrality of space in imagining and materialising alternative (democratic or non-democratic) politics. The final section explores the limitations between this specific spatialisation of political imaginaries and democratic politics. The empirical analysis in the chapter is based on participant observation and discourse analysis of the press, social media and Syntagma's Popular Assembly votes and minutes.

Space, politics and *the political*

The dialectic between space and politics has a long history in geography and political theory since 'spatialization ... becomes the very condition of politics precisely because it constitutes an integral element of the disruption of the natural order of domination' (Dikeç 2005: 181). Margaret Kohn (2003: 7) emphasises the link between the spatial and the political, by arguing that 'space is not just a tool for social control ... spatial practices can contribute to transformative politics. All political groups – government and opposition, Right and Left, fascist and democratic – use space, just as they employ language, symbols, ideas and incentives'. In this sense, 'there can be no politicisation in isolation from the field of spatial representation: antagonism can only surface within space – conflicts between socio-political forces can only be articulated in and through spaces' (Stavrakakis 2011a: 313). However, the debates on space and politics are often disembodied and abstract/theoretical. The Indignant Squares, we argue, offered a contemporary living laboratory for embodying and exploring these debates further in three distinct ways. First, by reasserting the centrality of space in the process of questioning the structuring principles of the established order (Žižek 1991), which Rancière defines as *the police*. Secondly, by becoming a potential material/spatial outlet where *the police* and *the political* could meet, a meeting that Rancière would define as *politics* (Swyngedouw 2011: 376). Finally, by highlighting the limitations of the spatialisation of *the political* in entering a praxis of *politics* even when it succeeds in becoming 'the place where community as such is brought into play' (Nancy 1991: xxxvii).

Before we explore further the ethnography of Syntagma Square and the insights this can bring to the debate on the dialectic between politics and space, it is necessary to clarify the ways in which we employ the terms *political*, *politics* and *police*. For a number of contemporary authors, *politics* is not what conventional political science understands as its object of enquiry, i.e. the ensemble of practices, processes, discourses and institutions of a specific constituted political order (parties, legislative bodies, and so on). Instead, politics necessarily moves beyond 'the locus of [existing] power relations' (Nancy 1991: xxxvii), and implies the questioning of instituted ensembles and practices. *The political* proper calls into question the very structuring principles of the established order (Žižek 1991), and entails the production of new social imaginaries and new institutions (Castoriadis 1987). The inherently antagonistic dimension of human relations is central in generating the political (Stavrakakis 1999; Mouffe 2005; Marchart 2007) as 'the place where community as such is brought into play' (Nancy 1991: xxxvii). Rancière attempts to explain what accounts for the contemporary closure of *the political* by introducing the notion of *the police*. For Rancière *the police* is the ensemble of practices associated with the institutionalisation of the social:

> an order of bodies that defines the allocation of ways of doing, ways of being, and ways of saying; it is an order of the visible and the sayable that sees that a particular activity is visible and another is not, that this speech is understood as discourse and another as noise. (1999: 29)

The police evolves around 'all the activities which create order by distributing places, names, functions' (Rancière 1994: 173) or what Rancière calls the 'partition of the sensible' (2001: 8).

Politics, then, becomes the point where the police and the political meet (Swyngedouw 2011: 376); the disruptive engagement with the police order, revolving around 'the properties of spaces and the possibilities of time' (Rancière 2006b: 13). Rancière defines political activity in profoundly spatial terms. It is 'whatever shifts a body from the place assigned to it or changes a place's destination. It makes visible what had no business being seen, and . . . makes understood as discourse what was once only heard as noise' (Rancière 1999: 30). In this sense, politics involves 'produc[ing] the spatiality that permits exercising [the] right [to speak]' (Swyngedouw 2011: 376). *Politics*, therefore, evolves around the production of 'dissensual spaces' (Swyngedouw 2011: 376) that can become hosts for 'voicing speech that claims a place in the order of things, demanding "the part for those who have no part"' (Swyngedouw 2011: 375). In staging dissent, such spaces become political in the sense that they 'modify the map of what can be thought, what can be named and perceived' (Rancière, quoted in Swyngedouw 2007: 72).

However, staging dissent alone does not constitute *politics*. Rancière reserves the term *politics* for practices that evolve around the democratic presupposition of equality. The Indignants of Syntagma Square have been depicted as a key moment of staging dissent in contemporary politics (Douzinas 2011, 2013; Kioupkiolis 2011; Korizi and Vradis 2012). But to what extent have these produced spaces of dissent become 'the meeting point of the police and the political' (Swyngedouw 2011: 376) that Rancière defines as politics? How far did the Indignant Squares go beyond staging dissent and into becoming properly political spaces, i.e. spaces that modified 'the map of what can be thought, . . . named and perceived' (Rancière, quoted in Swyngedouw 2007: 72)? To what extent did they produce a spatiality that offered the right to speak to those whose voice was only recognised as noise? Following Rancière's suggestion that politics arises through the 'disruption of [the] order of . . . the police' (1999: 99), in the following section we chart the spatial and discursive choreographies of Syntagma Square in order to analyse the extent to which events moved from indignation to a proper spatialisation of politics.

Indignant squares: the occupation that split the square

The occupation of Syntagma Square cracked the mirror of general consensus. This can only be understood against the background of the specific police ordering of the centre of Athens in the years that preceded the crisis. Since the mid–1990s the privatisation of public land had transformed what used to be public spaces into private niches catering for global tourism and international capital. The process of urban restructuring reached its climax in the years preceding the Athens Olympic Games (Gospodini 2009; Leontidou 2010). The predominance of the retail and service sectors, and the commission of new architectural 'icons' by banks, department stores and global chains in expensive neighbourhoods accounted for an intensive privatisation and commodification of Athenian urban space (Petropoulou 2008). The transformation of the Athenian landscape was accompanied by the establishment of practices of surveillance-induced social control, which in turn became absorbed into the citizens' stock of social values (Petropoulou 2010; Leontidou et al. 2008). The spaces that emerged out of this process and became the symbols of a new set of power relations (Stavrides 2008) are today the remnants of the utopian vision of glamour and enjoyment that followed Athens' successful Olympic bid in 2004 (Afouxenidis 2006). In the aftermath of the games, the Athenian urban fabric – and the city centre in particular – became an unprecedentedly polarised space, where islands of extreme wealth and power were interspersed with places of deprivation, exclusion and poverty (Noussia and Lyons 2009). At the same time, however, the Athenian city centre became the privileged site of 'the return of the repressed . . . in the form of urban violent insurgencies' (Swyngedouw 2011: 377). These peaked with the December 2008 riots that followed the killing of fifteen-year-old Alexis Grigoropoulos by a police officer in Athens city centre (Dalakoglou and Vradis 2011).

It is within this specific socio-spatial police ordering, and not simply within the context of an intense economic and political crisis, that the Indignant Squares movement emerged in Greece. The first large gathering at Syntagma Square took place on Wednesday, 25 May 2011, ten days after the occupation of Puerta del Sol in Madrid by the *Indignados*. This was in the aftermath of the proposal of a set of draconian austerity measures (Hadjimichalis 2011). The call for a gathering in Syntagma Square à la Tahrir Square and Puerta del Sol was launched through social media and gained increasing popular support, with the movement's Facebook group counting more than 1,000 new members per hour (*To Vima* 2011a). Similar initiatives proliferated in several Greek cities. The unknown social media administrators were calling for peaceful demonstrations, without party banners, without flags and without party-political slogans. Only national Greek flags would be welcome and everyone should participate as an individual and not as a member of a wider political group of any kind.[3] The people's gathering in Syntagma Square was baptised *Αγανακτισμένοι* (the Indignants) in homage to the Spanish initiative, and directly referring to the pamphlet *Indignez Vous!* penned by French Resistance elder Stéphane Hessel (2010). Reading through the early social media messages, there is no doubt that anger and indignation provided the spark for the protests. As Jean-Luc Nancy put it in the early 1990s:

> Anger is the political sentiment par excellence. It brings out the qualities of the inadmissible, the intolerable. It is a refusal and a resistance that with one step goes beyond all that can be accomplished reasonably, in order to open possible paths for a new negotiation of the reasonable but also paths of an uncompromising vigilance. (1992: 375)

In the days that followed, the Indignant protests in Athens evolved into a massive – though in no sense homogeneous – staging of popular dissatisfaction, anger and pressure against the so-called 'Greek Crisis' (Korizi and Vradis 2012; Douzinas 2013). During their best days, the gatherings attracted up to 200,000 people on the Square and the surrounding streets. Over several weeks – up until early July 2011 – thousands of people emerged out of the anonymity of everyday urban life, and staged their presence by re-appropriating public spaces in and around Syntagma Square, which up until then were occupied mainly by tourists and the clientele of nearby cafes and restaurants. The emerging crowds claimed the square as a stage to 'enunciate their dissent towards the hegemonic crisis politics which at the same time were effacing democracy' (Popular Assembly Vote (PAV) 2011c). The occupation of Syntagma Square continued despite brutal repression by police forces on several occasions, most notably on 15, 28 and 29 June 2011 (Korizi and Vradis 2012).

However, as more people gathered, a topographic differentiation started to occur within the square itself. Two distinct sets of practices and slogans emerged: the upper part of the square, directly facing the parliament, which started off as the quintessential space for expressing dissent, with direct curses and gesticulations against the parliament building, and evolved into harbouring right-wing slogans; and the lower square, where spontaneous efforts were made to articulate a voice beyond dissent with the institution of a popular assembly, with regular meetings, blog and Twitter accounts, collective food supplies and temporary tent accommodation. Each part of the square expressed opposing imaginaries for the future.

Upper square: reactionary indignation

During the first couple of days, the gathering in Syntagma Square was a *mélange* of people of different ages, social positions, occupational backgrounds and political beliefs, all united by the desire to express their discontent. In that sense, beyond personal anger and indignation, there was no clear political or other message emanating from the square. Characteristically, when the public electricity company workers (who were on strike) entered the square to demonstrate, they were spontaneously booed, and accused of hijacking the square for demonstrating as union members and not as individuals (Kyriakopoulos 2011). The prevailing attitude uniting all involved was that all politicians were corrupt thieves and since workers' unions were affiliated to political parties, they too had no place in the square, which should steer clear of party politics. In a nutshell, any ideological connotation beyond the unity of indignation was unwelcome in Syntagma Square. Interestingly, during these early days the hegemonic media and political elites were uncharacteristically sympathetic to the Syntagma Indignants. They provided wide coverage of the gatherings and congratulations for 'the most peaceful demonstrations in months!' (*To Vima* 2011b), but advised them to keep the gatherings apolitical, non-ideological and non-violent (see for example Skai 2011; *To Vima* 2011b). During the whole period, the area between the square and the parliament was heavily guarded by several rows of riot police in full gear.

Throughout May and June 2011, the square continued to be occupied by protesters, whose numbers and energy levels depended directly on the parliamentary activities of the day around the pending austerity measures. The upper part of the square, which is in direct visual contact with the parliament, became the key niche for launching direct protests against MPs. People from all socio-economic strata and cultural and political backgrounds, united by despair over the economic crisis which permeated Greek society (Gourgouris 2011), would visit the upper square to hurl abuse at their elected representatives on the opposite side of the road. With the most common cries being 'Thieves!' or 'Burn this brothel of a parliament', protests in the upper square often took the form of collective moans, cursing and gesticulating against the walls of the parliament.

But soon, apart from anger and indignation, two additional elements emerged as unifying the diverse crowd of the upper square.

First, there was a belief that the crisis was the outcome of recent corrupt political practices, which could be traced directly (and solely) to serving MPs. Secondly, there was a conviction that, despite it being the fault of a few corrupt politicians, the crisis was threatening the Greek nation as a whole, and could therefore become an element that would unite the nation like no other social or political ideology. Here, it was 'the people' against 'corrupt politicians' (Sotirakopoulos 2011). National unity and salvation could only be achieved through a 'properly Greek' anti-kleptocratic government that would imprison the traitors and restore national pride (Sevastakis 2011b, 2011d).

Yet the politics of this renunciation did not go beyond expressing collective indignation through cursing and shouting, and although it may have accurately expressed the breadth of indignation across the country, it is fair to say that it remained noise. It was a collective moan of desperation against the loss of the continuous enjoyment that was collectively promised at the publicly organised mass festivities at the very same Syntagma Square in 2004, when Greece won the European Football Cup, in expectation of the climax of glamour that the 2004 Olympic Games would bring.

The element that united the upper square – the imaginary of an innocent Greek public fooled by a bunch of corrupt politicians – also became the locus for nurturing reactionary politics. A number of right-wing and/or nationalist extremist groups carrying Greek flags made repeated attempts to re-appropriate Syntagma's occupation as a gathering for Greeks only (Sotirakopoulos 2011). A group that called itself the 'Greek Mothers' also featured prominently in the upper square and in the mass media, carrying banners demanding: 'Jobs for our children, not for foreigners'. According to the Greek Mothers, immigrants were mainly to blame both for the country's increasing unemployment rates, and for the increasing crime rates in the streets of Athens (Greek Mothers 2011). The following excerpts from their letter to Syntagma's popular assembly are indicative of the spirit that was prevailing in the upper square:

> The dire situation of our country dictates that only Greeks with pure national ideology can rescue her. Half-hearted statements will not do. Greece's problem is not economic. It is national . . . We were told that being a 'nationalist' is a bad thing . . . It is fanaticism, the wickedness of the Greeks against the 'poor illegal-immigrants'! I am Greek! I am a Nationalist! I am a Patriot! I do not belong to any party except to GREECE! I was not born and bred to hate, but I cannot ignore my enemies either! . . . All I care about is to be able to tell my children . . . that I did not quit; I did not sit back in comfort whilst useless individuals were

deciding the future of Greece's children; I was there, fighting for [my chil-
dren] to have the future they rightfully deserve!!! (Greek Mothers 2011)

The simplistic proposition that returning to an imaginary united
nation could pave the ground for solving the economic crisis had
severe political implications. This imaginary construction of an externalised other as the source of evil was not only confined to rhetoric.
Although only sporadic references to racist attacks within the square
itself were made, incidents of racist violence escalated during the
same period throughout Athens' city centre (*Eleftherotipia* 2011).
These practices intensified the tension amongst the protesters in the
square, and crystallised the separation of the square into two distinct
parts: the upper and the lower. As xenophobic incidents in the upper
square increased, tension between the protesters at the two squares
grew heavier (Popular Assembly Minutes (PAM) 2011).

Lower square: real democracy

At the area that became known as the lower square, and which occu-
pies Syntagma Square proper, the first chaotic days of protest gave
way to a series of efforts to articulate a more coherent political voice
and to better organise collective action. Specific action groups were
formed and took up places in different parts of the square. Amongst
these, the media group set up and provided daily content and updates
for the movement's website (*www.real-democracy.gr*), and issued
press releases for the mass media. A web radio was also set up,
streaming the proceedings of the square, whilst a translation centre
for non-Greek visitors, activists and foreign media correspondents
was also continuously populated (Popular Assembly Vote (PAV)
2011a, 2011e).

Despite its increasing organisational rigour, the formation of the
collectives at the lower square remained committed to being unaffili-
ated with political parties, despite objections by members of progressive political parties and groups, who were allowed to participate
only if they were not carrying party banners. For a country like
Greece, where the NGO sector is still nascent, and political parties
have traditionally been the key mechanism for articulating political
dissent, the banning of political parties from mass protests was an
extraordinary and unprecedented phenomenon.

An increasing number of people were spending significant amounts
of time in the square, with many of them coming from areas outside
the city centre. Collective practices of self-organisation thus became
imperative for sustaining the momentum of the gatherings: a

solidarity kitchen, clothes exchange, toilets, garbage collection, a first-aid station and informal hospital at the entrance of Syntagma metro station were set up by the protesters in the lower square. A neighbourhood organisation centre was coordinating actions that would reach beyond the squares into different parts of the city. A performing arts centre provided an outlet for expression and collective action. Most importantly, however, participants at the lower square set up an Open Popular Assembly Forum, where every evening people on the square took turns to develop their positions, with each allowed a minute and a half to speak – the measure serving as a guard against demagoguery (Douzinas 2011; Gourgouris 2011). This was a conscious attempt to institute proper democratic procedures and therefore it is not surprising that the demand for 'real and direct democracy' became the key slogan/signifier around which the discussions in the square's general assembly were articulated (PAV 2011c). The term 'direct democracy' deliberately encapsulates a double reference: the demand for democracy here and now and the demand for democracy in unmediated fashion (Kioupkiolis 2011).

The gathering of the anonymous majority, through direct participation and the use of communication technologies, created material and virtual public spaces with no unified or specified programme. These spaces were porous and spontaneous, free from entrenched power structures, leaders and exclusive identifications; they interacted in networked structures, where multiple and interchangeable actors participated in the genesis and development of joint actions (Kioupkiolis 2011). In that sense, we can argue that, although fragmented and contradictory, a self-cognizant process of political subjectivation was in the making in the lower square (Sevastakis 2011b). Although indignation against corruption and austerity measures emerged here as centrally as it did in the upper part of the square, the key focus went beyond a mere protest against the socio-economic strangulation of the country, and a demand for the radical change of Greek political institutions, practices and culture started to emerge as a (noisy) discourse – a proper demand for emancipation from the existing socio-spatial order. Indeed, the Popular Assembly repeatedly voted and made known via its website and social media that even if the Greek government were to stand up against the debilitating terms of the austerity measures, the Indignants would not vacate Syntagma Square until their goal for emancipation from current political institutions was achieved (PAV 2011b, 2011c, 2011d).

Operating within a context of increasing de-territorialisation of political and economic power to international financial markets and rating agencies, the lower square succeeded in conveying three important messages. First, it articulated a strong demand for reinstituting processes of direct democracy and universalising democratic politics. Second, it introduced new modes for re-(de)territorialising democratic politics: although spatially rooted in the square, the Indignants were associated with an international movement, and their actions were intertwined with events across the globe. These practices 'have preserved a nomadic de-territorialisation to the extent that they [were] opening virtual and material spaces' (Kioupkiolis 2011: 105). The 'passive space' of Syntagma Square 'that resign[ed] itself to passive encounters, where people meet each other in controlled environments, in spaces that are orderly, patrolled, secure' was turned into an 'active space . . . that encourage[d] active encounters of people' (Merrifield, Chapter 14 of this volume). Meanwhile, the mobilisation of social media and communication technologies for the internal organisation and external circulation of ideas (live-streaming popular assembly meetings, circulating information, furthering discussions that have been developed within the assembly, and so on), opened up the possibility for participation and for unexpected and anonymous interventions. Thus, the Indignant Squares attest to the centrality of 'meeting places between virtual and physical worlds, between online and offline conversations, between online and offline encounters' (Merrifield, Chapter 14 of this volume). Third, the noise that occasionally turned into proper debate amongst equals in the square forged 'a political ethos that promotes agonistic interconnection among equals' (Kioupkiolis 2011: 105). This was one of the most promising signals that the Indignant Squares sent across the world.

In this sense, the discourse emanating from the lower square's General Assembly can be read as a proper attempt to institute a form of democratic politics, albeit partial and fragmented; as an emancipatory struggle, wherein people took 'the right to their own time and their own place' (Swyngedouw 2011: 375), to collectively think and organise the spatialities of their political practices, to occupy and re-appropriate Syntagma Square from its allocation within the 'late capitalist post-political spatiality' (Swyngedouw 2011: 378). Syntagma Square could be seen as an arena where the originally populist and chaotic noise, or the fundamentalist discourses of the *ochlos* (Sevastakis 2011a, 2011b), entered a process of becoming a more articulate political voice (Rancière 1999, 2001). The lower square constituted a form of incipient politicisation, a public affair, unfolding both materially and symbolically in and through space, redefining the boundaries of the police ordering of space and re-imagining socio-spatial relations (see Swyngedouw, Chapter 8 of this volume). Whilst the efforts to articulate a more coherent political imaginary involved a certain element of closure, at the same time they opened up new possibilities for political action and practice. The performative and spatialised practices of the lower square constituted a public staging of equality 'where liberty and equality [were] no longer . . . represented in the institutions of law and state, but [were] embodied in the very forms of concrete life and sensible experience' (Rancière 2006a: 3).

However, the heterogeneity and open democratic procedures that became the lower square's biggest strength were also its key weakness. The engagement of large sections of the middle strata in the square's event increased its heterogeneity and made ideological identifications and political aims increasingly difficult to articulate (Sevastakis 2011b). Indeed, in earlier contemporary incarnations of the multitude of Greek politics (for example, the August 2007 protests against the devastating fires throughout Greece), the 'scepticism and frustration towards institutionalised polic(y)ing, allowed [a critical mass of post-democratic citizens] to coexist . . . with anarchist ideology . . . and [with] the socially marginalised' (Kioupkiolis 2011: 104). But at the lower Syntagma Square, whilst struggling to articulate a proper political imaginary and institute proper collective practices, this coexistence proved difficult to maintain (Kioupkiolis 2011).

Conclusion: the limits of Indignation in instituting democratic politics

Staged against the backdrop of the Parliamentary discussion and vote on the Greek austerity measures, the massive protests of 28 and 29 June 2011 constituted the last major event at both Syntagma Squares. Parliamentary approval of the austerity measures signalled the end of the gatherings in the upper and lower squares. The collective organisation infrastructure at the lower square was 'cleared' by municipal police on 30 July (Sevastakis 2011c; Korizi and Vradis 2012). Subsequent efforts – mainly on the part of political parties and NGOs – to reinvigorate the Indignant Squares never succeeded in mobilising the numbers involved during May and June 2011. Despite the initiation of a series of popular assemblies and neighbourhood movements in the aftermath of the Indignant Squares (Korizi and Vradis 2012), the movement withered away after the approval of the austerity measures. Retrospectively, one could say that the protests succeeded in expressing dissent, and in organising specific ways of being in common (see also Swyngedouw, Chapter 8 of this volume). However, they failed to institutionalise the spaces that could further facilitate democratic politics. The being-in-common produced as a discourse and practice in the lower square remained at the level of the carnavalesque, a big urban feast that did create, for a moment, the illusion of a community congealing around the need to oppose the loss of a promised enjoyment.

In this sense, in its failure to institute a proper democratic politics, Syntagma Square fuelled those who criticised it as 'post-political', or for adopting what Jodi Dean (Chapter 13 of this volume) calls 'a politics without politics'. However, its failure also asserted that 'events that punctuate the flow' (Rancière 2011: 80) cannot be expressed only through strikes or demonstrations. A new radical political imaginary (Castoriadis 1987) can only be produced through persistent and 'ongoing efforts to create forms of the common different from the ones on offer from the state, the democratic consensus, and so on' (Rancière 2011: 80). The gatherings at the lower square did assert 'the presupposition of equality' (Rancière 1999; 2006a) and attempted to imagine and materialise alternative ways of being, doing and saying in common. The performative staging of equality in the lower square, and in particular the daily meetings of the popular assembly and the collective self-organisation practices, constituted the spatialisation of the imaginary of *égaliberté* (Balibar 1993). Introducing and nurturing a nomadic re-territorialisation of democratic politics – mainly through the initiation of local popular assemblies and the use of social media – and an agonistic ethos of collective self-management, the lower square conveyed valuable new elements for democratic politics. However, the movement failed to move beyond the temporalities and spatialities of the police order in institutionalising democratic spaces that could last beyond the staging of the event. For Lefebvre, '[i]deas, representations or values' that fail in 'making their mark on space (. . .) lose all pith and become mere signs, resolve themselves into abstract descriptions, or mutate into fantasies; (1991: 416–17). Hence, the chapter insists that challenging the hegemony of neoliberalisation and the struggle for emancipation together with the 'ability to promote the idea of a continuous re-enacting of the [political] act' will also require efforts towards imagining and constructing conceptual, affective and material democratic spaces (Stavrakakis 2011b: 8). The institutionalisation, in other words, of a new radical democratic imaginary in the here and now.

Notes

1. This chapter draws on Kaika and Karaliotas 2014.
2. In describing the movement, the term 'Indignants' has been favoured by mainstream media and participants in the upper square, while the

lower square activists and popular assembly members favoured the term 'movement of the squares'. The rest of the chapter will refer to the movement as 'Indignant Squares' in an effort to capture both the element of anger and indignation that has been central for the mobilisation as well as its spatial articulations and connotations.
3. See *https://www.facebook.com/AganaktismenoiStoSyntagma.*

References

Afouxenidis, A. (2006), 'Urban social movements in Southern European cities: Reflections on Toni Negri's *The Mass and the Metropolis*', *City*, 10: 3, pp. 287–93.
Balibar, É. (1993), *Masses, Classes, Ideas: Studies on Politics and Philosophy Before and After Marx*, London: Routledge.
Castoriadis, C. (1987), *The Imaginary Institution of Society*, Cambridge, MA: MIT Press.
Dalakoglou, D., and A. Vradis (2011), 'Spatial legacies of December and the right to the city', in A. Vradis and D. Dalakoglou (eds), *Revolt and Crisis in Greece: Between a Present Yet to Pass and a Present Still to Come*, Oakland, CA: AK Press, pp. 77–90.
Dikeç, M. (2005), 'Space, politics and the political', *Environment and Planning D*, 23: 2, pp. 171–88.
Douzinas, C. (2011), 'In Greece we see democracy in action', *The Guardian* 15 June, available at: *http://www.theguardian.com/commentisfree/2011/jun/15/greece-europe-outraged-protests.*
Douzinas, C. (2013), 'Athens rising', *European Urban and Regional Studies*, 20: 1, pp. 134–8.
Eleftherotipia (2011), 'Racist groups attack immigrants in Monastiraki and Omonia', *Eleftherotipia*, 30 May, available at: *http://www.enet.gr/?i=news.el.article&id=279692* (in Greek).
Gospodini, A. (2009), 'Post-industrial trajectories of Mediterranean European cities: The case of post-Olympics Athens', *Urban Studies*, 46: 5–6, pp. 1157–86.
Gourgouris, S. (2011), 'Indignant politics in Athens – democracy out of rage', *Greek Left Review*, 17 July, available at: *http://greekleftreview.wordpress.com/2011/07/17/indignant-politics-in-athens-%E2%80%93-democracy-out-of-rage/.*
Greek Mothers (2011), 'Greek Mothers to the Popular Assembly of direct democracy in Syntagma Square', 19 July, available at: *http://spithathriasiou.blogspot.com/2011/07/blog-post_19.html* (in Greek).
Hadjimichalis, C. (2011), 'Uneven geographical development and socio-spatial justice and solidarity: European regions after the 2009 financial crisis', *European Urban and Regional Studies*, 18: 3, pp. 254–74.
Hessel, S. (2010), *Indignez Vous!*, Barcelona: Indigene Editions.
Kaika, M. (2010), 'Architecture and crisis: Re-inventing the icon, re-imag(in)

ing London and re-branding the City', *Transactions of the Institute of British Geographers*, 35: 4, pp. 453–74.

Kaika, M. (2011), 'Autistic architecture: The fall of the icon and the rise of the serial object of architecture', *Environment and Planning D: Society and Space*, 29: 6, pp. 968–92.

Kaika, M. and L. Karaliotas (2014), 'The spatialization of democratic politics: Insights from indignant squares', *European Urban and Regional Studies*, DOI: 10.1177/0969776414528928. Published online first on May 8, 2014.

Kioupkiolis, A. (2011), 'Indignant Squares: Beyond the common place of the multitude', *Sychrona Themata*, 113, pp. 103–6 (in Greek).

Kohn, M. (2003), *Radical Space*, Ithaca: Cornell University Press.

Korizi, S., and A. Vradis (2012), 'From innocence to realisation', *City*, 16: 1–2, pp. 237–42.

Kyriakopoulos, A. (2011), 'With no party, no syndicate, only wrath', *Eleftherotipia*, 26 May, available at: *http://www.enet.gr/?i=news. el.article&id=278646* (in Greek).

Lefebvre, H. (1991), *The Production of Space*, Oxford: Blackwell.

Leontidou, L. (2010), 'Urban social movements in "weak" civil societies: The right to the city and cosmopolitan activism in Southern Europe', *Urban Studies*, 47: 6, pp. 1179–203.

Leontidou, L., A. Afouxenidis, E. Kourliouros and E. Marmaras (2008), 'Infrastructure-related urban sprawl: Mega-events and hybrid peri-urban landscapes in Southern Europe', in C. Couch, L. Leontidou and G. Petschel-Held (eds), *Urban Sprawl in Europe: Landscapes, Land-use Change and Policy*, Oxford: Blackwell, pp. 69–101.

Madden, D. J., and A. Vradis (2012), 'From Athens to Occupy and back', *City*, 16: 1–2, pp. 235–6.

Marchart, O. (2007), *Post-Foundational Political Thought: Political Difference in Nancy, Lefort, Badiou and Laclau*, Edinburgh: Edinburgh University Press.

Merrifield, A. (2013), *The Politics of the Encounter: Urban Theory and Protest under Planetary Urbanization*, Athens, Georgia: University of Georgia Press.

Mouffe, C. (2005), *On the Political: Thinking in Action*, London: Routledge.

Nancy, J.-L. (1991), *The Inoperative Community*, Minneapolis: University of Minnesota Press.

Nancy, J.-L. (1992), 'La comparution/the compearance: From the existence of "communism" to the community of "existence"', *Political Theory*, 20: 3, pp. 371–98.

Noussia, A., and M. Lyons (2009), 'Inhabiting spaces of liminality: Migrants in Omonia, Athens', *Journal of Ethnic and Migration Studies*, 35: 4, pp. 601–24.

Pantazopoulos, A. (2011), 'The Indignant wants law and disorder', *To Vima*. Athens, 17 July 2011 (in Greek).

Petropoulou, C. (2008), 'Non/de/re/regulation and Athens' urban development', Athens: *INURA International Congress*, available at *http://inura08.files.wordpress.com/2008/10/introductiontoathens.pdf*.

Petropoulou, C. (2010), 'From the December youth uprising to the rebirth of urban social movements: a space–time approach', *International Journal of Urban and Regional Research*, 34: 1, pp. 217–24.

Popular Assembly Minutes (PAM) (2011), *Syntagma Popular Assembly Minutes 30th of May 2011*, available at: *http://real-democracy.gr/minutes/2011–05–30-praktika-laikis-syneleysis-syntagmatos* (in Greek).

Popular Assembly Vote (PAV) (2011a), *Syntagma Popular Assembly Vote 3rd of June 2011*, available at: *http://real-democracy.gr/votes/2011–06–03-apofaseis-laikis-syneleysis-plateias-syntagmatos* (in Greek).

Popular Assembly Vote (PAV) (2011b), *Syntagma Popular Assembly Vote 16th of June 2011*, available at: *http://real-democracy.gr/votes/2011–06–16-psifismata-laikis-syneleysis-plateias-syntagmatos–1606* (in Greek).

Popular Assembly Vote (PAV) (2011c), *Syntagma Popular Assembly Vote 29th of May 2011*, available at: *http://real-democracy.gr/content/votes/2011–05–29-%CF%88%CE%AE%CF%86%CE%B9%CF%83%CE%BC%CE%B1-%CE%BB%CE%B1%CF%8A%CE%BA%CE%AE%CF%82-%CF%83%CF%85%CE%BD%CE%AD%CE%BB%CE%B5%CF%85%CF%83%CE%B7%CF%82-%CF%83%CF%85%CE%BD%CF%84%CE%AC%CE%B3%CE%BC%CE%B1%CF%84%CE%BF%CF%82-%CF%84%CE%BF%CF%82-%CE%BE%CF%84%CE%BC%CE%B3%CE%B3%CE%B5%CF%82-%CE%BE%CE%BC%CE%B1%CE%B1-%CE%B3%CE%BC%CE%B5%CE%BF%CF%82-%CF%82%CE%BF%CE%BA%CF%82%CF%82-%CE%BC%CF%82%CE%BF%CE%BA%CE%AE%CF%82-%CE%BB%CE%B1%CF%8A%CE%BA%CF%82%CF%82-%CF%88%CE%BC%CF%82%CF%82-%CE%B8%CF%82%CE%BF%CF%82-%CE%B1%CE%B3%CE%BC%CF%82*

Popular Assembly Vote (PAV) (2011d), *Syntagma Popular Assembly Vote 30th of June 2011*, available at: *http://real-democracy.gr/votes/2011–06–30-psifismata-laikis-syneleysis-30062011* (in Greek).

Popular Assembly Vote (PAV) (2011e), *Syntagma Popular Assembly Vote 30th of May 2011*, available at: *http://real-democracy.gr/votes/2011–05–30-psifisma-laikis-syneleysis-syntagmatos* (in Greek).

Rancière, J. (1994), 'Post-democracy, politics and philosophy: An interview with Jacques Rancière', *Angelaki*, 1: 3, pp. 171–8.

Rancière, J. (1999), *Disagreement*, Minneapolis: University of Minnesota Press.

Rancière, J. (2001), 'Ten theses on politics', *Theory & Event*, 5: 3, available at *http://muse.jhu.edu/journals/theory_and_event/v005/5.3ranciere.html*.

Rancière, J. (2006a), *Hatred of Democracy*, London: Verso.

Rancière, J. (2006b), *The Politics of Aesthetics*, London: Continuum.

Rancière, J. (2011), 'Democracies against democracy', in G. Agamben (et al.), *Democracy in What State?*, New York: Columbia University Press, pp. 76–81.

Rogkas, V. (2011), 'June of agonistic democracy', *RedNotebook*, 22 June, available at *http://rednotebook.gr/details.php?id=2719* (in Greek).

Sevastakis, N. (2011a), 'The charm of the enlightened oligarchy', *Enthemata*, 5 June, available at: *http://enthemata.wordpress.com/2011/06/05/sevastakis–17/* (in Greek).

Sevastakis, N. (2011b), 'The holy purism and squares of "indignation"',

RedNotebook, 30 May, available at *http://www.rednotebook.gr/details. php?id=2588* (in Greek).

Sevastakis, N. (2011c), 'On the "aesthetic intervention" in Syntagma Square', *RedNotebook*, 31 July, available at *http://www.rednotebook.gr/ details.php?id=2979*.

Sevastakis, N. (2011d), 'Two summers: 2004/2011', *Enthemata*, 26 June, available at: *http://archive.avgi.gr/ArticleActionshow.action?articleID= 624831* (in Greek).

Skai (2011), 'Indignant Greeks protest', *Skai.gr*, 25 May, available at: *http://www.skai.gr/news/greece/article/170384/aganaktismenoi-ellines-organonoun-diadiloseis-meso-facebook/* (in Greek).

Smith, A. (2013), 'Europe and an inter-dependent world: Uneven geo-economic and geo-political developments', *European Urban and Regional Studies*, 20: 1, pp. 3–13.

Sotirakopoulos, N. (2011), 'The rise of the Greek Multitude (and why we need to move a step beyond)', *Journal of Critical Globalisation Studies*, 20 June, available at: *http://criticalglobalisation.com/blogs/nikoss_rise_ of_greek_multitude.html*.

Stavrakakis, Y. (1999), *Lacan and the Political*, London: Routledge.

Stavrakakis, Y. (2011a), 'The radical act: Towards a spatial critique', *Planning Theory*, 10: 4, pp. 301–24.

Stavrakakis, Y. (2011b), 'On acts, pure and impure', *International Journal of Žižek Studies*, 4: 2, pp. 1–35.

Stavrides, S. (2008), 'Urban identities: Beyond the regional and the global. The case of Athens', in J. Al-Qawasmi, A. Mahmoud and A. Djerbi (eds), *Second International Conference of CSAAR*, Tunis: CSAAR.

Swyngedouw, E. (2007), 'The post-political city', in BAVO (eds), *Urban Politics Now*, Rotterdam: Netherland Architecture Institute, pp. 58–76.

Swyngedouw, E. (2011), 'Interrogating post-democratization: Reclaiming egalitarian political spaces', *Political Geography*, 30: 7, pp. 370–80.

To Vima (2011a), 'Dozens of new members in the Indignants Group', 25 May, available at: *http://www.tovima.gr/society/article/?aid=402691 &wordsinarticle=%CE%B1%CE%B3%CE%B1%CE%BD%CE% B1%CE%BA%CF%84%CE%B9%CF%83%CE%BC%CE%B5% CE%BD%CE%BF%CE%B9* (in Greek).

To Vima (2011b), 'Indignants continue', 29 May, available at: *http://www. tovima.gr/society/article/?aid=403534&wordsinarticle=%CE%B1% CE%B3%CE%B1%CE%BD%CE%B1%CE%BA%CF%84%CE %B9%CF%83%CE%BC%CE%B5%CE%BD%CE%BF%CE%B9* (in Greek).

Žižek, S. (1991), *For They Know Not What They Do: Enjoyment as a Political Factor*, London: Verso.

13 After Post-Politics: Occupation and the Return of Communism

Jodi Dean

In 2011, Europe and the USA experienced the most significant political movement on the Left since 1968. Weirdly, a vocal portion of those participating claimed that the occupations, demonstrations and assemblies were not in fact political: theirs was a politics of no politics. Why would they say this?

On the one hand, people were signalling that they were not interested in the usual politics of cynical, compromised parties. They were alerting everyone – governments, neighbours, world – that they were not going to be contained, channelled and reduced to the corrupted terms of the dominant electoral systems. But the other, speculative, hand is more interesting: people were claiming that their movements were not political because they had absorbed the ideological message of democratic hegemony – ours is a post-political era. Democracy has won. Since it has defeated all competing political ideologies, the only remaining political task is extending it, enforcing it, tweaking the procedures, refining the process. In such an era, the primary concerns are inclusion, participation and discussion rather than the fundamental antagonism of class conflict.

Spain, Greece, Occupy, on the heels of and inspired by Tunisia and Egypt, allied with protests against cuts in the UK and Madison, Wisconsin, these movements of hundreds of thousands of people in protest against inequality, austerity and the expropriation of lives and futures reset the political course of the second decade of the twenty-first century. Construing them in post-political terms not only repeated a serious theoretical mistake, but also unnecessarily fettered their movement toward economic egalitarianism. Occupiers, the precarious and those resisting austerity too often spoke and thought in post-political terms of democracy even as their struggles pushed in directions historically associated with the name communism.

Two steps back

During the 1990s, a peculiar diagnosis of the political condition of Europe and the US became prominent. We were said to be 'post-political'. This was a curious diagnosis for various reasons. The countries formerly part of the Soviet bloc were actively writing new constitutions and developing new political practices. The US Right was engaged in rabid, focused, culture wars at multiple levels. Capitalists as a class were developing new modes for expropriating the work and futures of the people – ways that included cutting taxes, the privatisation of public utilities, deregulation (such that previous regulations were either eliminated or unenforced) and financialisation (where goods-producing industries started pursuing profit through financial services such as insurance and credit). In short, capital as a class was using the state to pursue the policies and practices generally flagged by the term 'neoliberalism'.

Rather than emphasising the political character of these attacks on what remained of the achievements of over a century of workers' struggle, an array of theorists used notions of depoliticisation, de-democratisation and post-politics to specify the situation of politics and its lack in the 1990s. Reversing the terms of the end of ideology thesis offered by neoconservative (Francis Fukuyama) and 'Third Way' (Anthony Giddens) thinkers, a wide array of Left and liberal thinkers writing in activist and academic contexts critically redescribed the orientation toward consensus, administration and technocracy lauded as benefits of the post-cold war age (Dean 2009).

Several aspects of this redescription stand out: the primacy of the economy, the individual and the police. Our condition is post-political, went the argument, because the spread and intensification of neoliberal economic policies subject states to the seemingly inevitable logic of the market. To the extent that state authority is less able to constrain corporate power, politics has become less significant. Over the course of the following decade this post-political argument would be repeated in the context of technocratic attempts to replace elected governments with managers focused on cutting services and paying debts (whether at the national level, as in Italy, or at more local levels, as in US municipalities). That it was another way of saying that the state serves as an instrument of capitalist control generally remained unsaid, a symptom of the actuality the term post-politics tries, but fails, to address the Left's turn away from communism.

The inability of democratic politics to produce viable solutions to social and economic problems resonates with a second component of what is described as post-political – the celebration of the individual in communicative capitalism. The individualisation of politics into commodifiable 'lifestyles' and opinions subsumes politics into consumption. That consumer choices may have a politics – fair trade, green, vegan, woman-owned – morphs into the sense that politics is nothing but consumer choices, that is, individuated responses to individuated needs. With politics seemingly reduced to consumer choice, government similarly contracts in some domains, concerning itself with traumatised victims, while it expands in others (especially to the extent that it can outsource its responsibilities to the private sector). Under neoliberalism, government's role is less to ensure public goods and solve collective problems than to address the personal issues of subjects. Accordingly, pollsters assess individual preference and satisfaction, as if the polled were the same as the politicised people, as if the aggregation of dispersed individuals through the unifying assumptions of the poll were capable of expressing a political, that is, divisive, truth. Not surprisingly, politics on the Left generally conformed to rather than confronted this individuation, joining in with the rejection of discipline, solidarity and collectivity urged by capitalism unrestrained.

Finally, insofar as the economy alone cannot fulfill all the functions of government even under neoliberalism, one element of the state rises to the fore – security (Passavant 2005). Thus, diminished governmental influence on economic and social policy is accompanied by the intensification and extension of the state as an agency of surveillance and control. Policing as necessary, whether for the maintenance of order or for protection from terrorists, emerges as that aspect of the state beyond question and reproach, giving another sense to Margaret Thatcher's notorious claim for economic competition, 'there is no alternative'. Here, at least, the Left has been active and alive, yet insofar as its opposition has been uncoupled from the critique of capitalism, it has become indistinguishable from libertarianism, leading to increasingly odd couplings like that of libertarian-communism.

The capitalist economy, the fragile, consuming individual, and the surveilling, controlling state are worth emphasising. Yet post-politics, depoliticisation and de-democratisation are conceptually inadequate to this theoretical task. The claim that states are decreasing in significance and impact because of the compulsions of the market ignores the millions of dollars regularly spent in political campaigns. Business and market interests as well as corporate and financial elites expend vast amounts of time and money on elections, candidates, lobbyists and law-makers in order to produce a political climate suitable to their interests. Capitalising on Left critiques of regulation and retreats from the state, neoliberals have moved right in, deploying state power to further their interests. Similarly, social conservatives in the US persistently fight across a broad spectrum of political fronts – including local school boards, state-wide ballot initiatives, judicial appointments and mobilisations to amend the Constitution. The left-wing lament regarding post-politics not only overlooks the reality of politics on the ground, but also cedes in advance key terrains of activism and struggle. Not recognising these politicised sites as politicised sites, the Left has failed to counter conservative initiatives with a coherent alternative.

It's even worse. The contemporary Left claims not to exist. Whereas the Right sees left-wing threats everywhere, those on the Left eschew any use of the term 'we', emphasising issue politics, identity politics and their own fragmentation into a multitude of singularities. The absence of a common programme or vision is generally lamented, even as this absence is disconnected from the setting in which it appears as an absence, namely, the loss of a Left that says 'we' and 'our' and 'us' in the first place. There are issues, events, projects, demonstrations, blogs, sometimes even affinity groups, but the Left claims not to exist – and this is the truth underlying the claim of post-politics.

One step forward

Theoretical accounts of post-politics tend to slip between two different positions: post-politics as an ideal of consensus, inclusion and administration that must be rejected and post-politics as a description of the contemporary exclusion or foreclosure of the political. Chantal Mouffe and Jacques Rancière hold versions of the former view, Slavoj Žižek takes the latter, and Wendy Brown specifies this latter point in terms of de-democraticisation.

Mouffe is the most compelling as she takes aim at Third Way politics, the liberalism of John Rawls, and the deliberative democracy of Jürgen Habermas. Arguing that these approaches 'negate the inherently conflictual nature of modern pluralism,' she concludes, 'they are unable to recognize that bringing a deliberation to a close always results from a *decision* which excludes other possibilities and for which one should never refuse to bear responsibility by invoking the commands of general rules or principles' (Mouffe 2000: 105). Consensus-based ideals fail to acknowledge that politics is necessarily divisive. A decision for one course rather than another excludes some possibilities and positions. Part of the challenge of politics is the ability to take responsibility for such exclusion.

Key to the strength of Mouffe's argument is her careful use of Carl Schmitt's critique of liberal parliamentarianism. Schmitt argues that liberalism seeks to evade the core political opposition between friend and enemy, attempting instead 'to tie the political to the ethical and subjugate it to economics' (1996: 61). Yet the political cannot be avoided, and attempts to submerge or efface it as intellectual deliberation or market competition result only in the displacement of the intensity characteristic of the political to another, potentially even more violent, realm. In Schmitt's words,

> the political can derive its energy from the most varied human endeavors, from the religious, economic, moral and other antitheses. It does not describe its own substance, but only *the intensity of an association or dissociation* of human beings whose motives can be religious, national (in the ethnic or cultural sense), economic, or of another kind and can effect at different times different coalitions and separations. (1996: 38; emphasis added)

The political marks the intensity of a relation, an intensity that characterises the antagonism constitutive of society (around which society forms).

Mouffe's accentuation of the unavoidability of antagonism and division points to a weakness in Rancière's discussion of post-politics (and post-democracy since for him democracy and politics are interchangeable). While attuned to the ways contemporary practices of counting opinions and managing preferences presume community and disavow political conflict and division, Rancière tends to write as if the disappearance of politics were possible, as if the evacuation of politics from the social were a characteristic of the current conjuncture (1999).[1] For example, he argues that today 'the identification between democracy and the legitimate state is used to produce a regime of the community's identity as itself, to make politics evaporate under a concept of law that identifies it with the spirit of the community' (Rancière 1999: 108). Rancière is right to emphasise the convergence between presumptions of democracy and of legitimacy. But he is wrong to imply the existence of a string of identifying moves that turn politics into law and law into unified community. In the US and the EU, law is the site of open and avowed political conflict that undermines even the fiction of community, a conflict that brings to the fore the relations of power and privilege already (and necessarily) inscribed in law. Rancière's claim that 'the state today legitimizes itself by declaring that politics is impossible' simply does not apply to the US or the EU, where battles rage around the economic fault-line denoted by terms like 'debt', 'foreclosures', 'cuts' and 'austerity' (1999: 110).

Žižek's account of post-politics grows out of his reading of Rancière

(1999: 198–205). He, too, oscillates between post-politics as the ideal behind the neoliberal Third Way, liberal multiculturalism and the therapeutic administrative state, and post-political as a description of today's 'liberal-democratic global capitalist regime' (1999: 209). Although Žižek's position is weakest when he uses the term 'post-political' descriptively, his explanation is nonetheless insightful: what makes the contemporary setting post-political is the exclusion of the possibility of politicisation. Žižek's point is that politicisation entails raising the particular to the level of the universal. A specific crime, issue or event comes to stand for something more than itself. Rather than a singular problem to be resolved, it indicates a series of problems confronting the system as a whole. It is the symptomal point of antagonism in a given constellation. For example, unemployment is not a matter of a particular person being laid off or unable to find a job. It is a necessary and constitutive feature of the capitalist mode of production. Working-class struggle politicises unemployment, demonstrating the necessity underlying what appears as contingent. 'What post-politics tends to prevent', Žižek explains, 'is precisely this metaphoric universalisation of particular demands: post-politics mobilizes the vast apparatus of experts, social workers, and so on, to reduce the overall demand (complaint) of a particular group to just this demand, with its particular content . . . ' (1999: 204). Of course, politicisation does occur today. The Right does it particularly well when they present liberals, feminists and gays as standing in for the larger crime of contemporary selfishness, prurience, decadence and weakness.

Žižek attributes contemporary post-politics to 'the depoliticization of economics, to the common acceptance of Capital and market mechanisms as neutral tools/procedures to be exploited' (1999: 353). Taken as a broad description of US politics, this argument is unconvincing: jobs, deficits, surpluses, taxes, inflation, interest rates, outsourcing, the strength of the dollar, trade imbalances, consumer spending, sub-prime mortgages, bubbles and budgets are key terms in the contemporary political lexicon. The economy appears as the site of politics, its most fundamental concern. Žižek's point, then, is better read as a critique of the Left – the real political problem today is that *the Left* accepts capitalism. The Left is caught in a post-political situation because it has conceded to the Right on the terrain of the economy: it has surrendered the state to neoliberal interests. Present leftists rarely view capitalism as the fundamental problem. Most blame the state as such (again, joining rather than combating libertarians). 'Depoliticised' thus well describes the contemporary Left's inability to raise particular claims to the level of the universal, to present issues or problems as standing for something beyond themselves. The Left prides itself on just this unwillingness, an unwillingness to say 'we' out of a reluctance to speak for another as well as an unwillingness to signify or name a problem, to take it out of its immediate context and re-present it as universal.

The US Left has not been completely without vision. It uniformly asserts the primacy of democracy. In a rich discussion of the convergence of neoliberalism and neoconservatism, Wendy Brown highlights de-democratisation as its central force and threat (2006). The details of Brown's analysis are evocative, but her overall account is unpersuasive because it both presumes a prior democracy, a previous acceptance and practice of democracy that is now unravelling, and neglects the hegemony of democratic rhetoric today. Democracy was long a contested category in US politics, subordinated to individual and states' rights, and valued less than elites' property and privilege. Anxieties over the tyranny of the majority, the great unwashed, immigrants, Catholics, workers, women, blacks and the young infused the American system from its inception. The combination of civil rights, students and new social movements in the 1960s with rapid expansion in communications media enabling people to register their opinions, contact representatives and organise gatherings and protests has, *contra* Brown, realised democratic aspirations to a previously unimaginable degree. Far from de-democratised, the contemporary ideological formation of communicative capitalism fetishises speech, opinion and participation. Communicative capitalism materialises and repurposes democratic ideals and aspirations in ways that strengthen and support globalised neoliberalism. In fact, the proliferation, distribution, acceleration and intensification of communicative access and opportunity produce a deadlocked democracy incapable of serving as a forum for progressive political and economic change.

The problem of the last decades is not de-democratisation. It has been the Left's failure to defend a vision of economic equality and solidarity, in other words, its betrayal of communism. When democracy appears as both the condition of politics and the solution to the political condition, capitalism cannot appear as the violence it is. Rather than assuming the underlying class conflict, one assumes a field generally fair and equal enough for deliberation and voting to make sense, the basic assumption of post-politics.

In some settings, an emphasis on democracy is radical, like the French Revolution, the Haitian Revolution, the initial fight for political freedom that led to the Russian February Revolution, as well as in struggles against colonialism and imperialism, and even in opposition to the authoritarianism of the party-state bureaucracies of the former East. To stand for democracy in these instances was to stand against an order constituted through the exclusion of democracy. In contemporary parliamentary democracies, however, for leftists to refer to their goals as a struggle for democracy is strange. It is a defence of the status quo, a call for more of the same. Democracy is our ambient milieu, the hegemonic form of contemporary politics.

Bowing to deliberation

That democracy is widely accepted did not stop the 2011 protest movements from presenting themselves in its name. In fact, democracy was the other side of the 'politics of no politics' urged in Greece, Spain and Occupy Wall Street. The 2011 Spanish protest camps and street occupations opted explicitly for a politics of no politics. Opposing high unemployment and steep spending cuts, thousands of people from throughout Spanish society took to the streets in a massive mobilisation. Multiple voices, participants as well as commentators, emphasised that no common line, platform or orientation united the protesters; they were not political. For many, the intense, festive atmosphere and break from the constraints of the usual politics incited a new confidence in social change. Discussion groups in the multiple assemblies approved a wide variety of motions that included raising taxes on the rich, eliminating the privileges of the political elite, controlling banks and providing for inexpensive and ecologically friendly public transportation. At the same time, the refusal of representation and reluctance to implement decision mechanisms hampered actual debate, enabling charismatic individual speakers to move the crowd and acquire quasi-leadership positions (no matter what position they took), and constraining possibilities of working through political divergences toward a collective plan (prominent voices insisted that the movement was not political). The mobilisation of thousands, the experience of occupation and resistance, was a vital political step, a clear indication of mass opposition to a state serving the interests of capital (Schneider 2011). For a while, it broke with 'the network of inert habits' previously inhibiting and displacing oppositional struggle (Badiou 2011: 35). Yet insofar as the assemblies were deliberative rather than executive bodies (in an unfortunate inverse of the Paris Commune), the action they set in motion was foreshortened, ineffective.

The occupation of Athens' Syntagma Square that began on 25 May 2011 similarly rejected representation, introducing a number of organisational innovations that prioritised the inclusion of individual voices over the inclusion of tendencies, groups and previously developed political positions. The innovations included the formation of a set of working groups, thematic assemblies and a general assembly with the Right to make decisions and before which speakers were chosen by lot.[2] These arrangements expanded opportunities for political expression. They installed a gap in the everyday, allowing a glimpse into the possibility of another world. According to some commentators, though, the large general assembly also re-induced passivity as people started to equate action with voting and to refrain from engaging in direction action.[3] The participation without representation approach hindered the development of a specific plan, strategy or vision of an alternative to the austerity programme the Greek government ultimately acquiesced to under IMF pressure. The movement of the squares risked becoming an end in itself rather than an element of a larger political strategy aiming towards ending capitalism and developing equitable and common relations of production.

These same patterns reappeared in Occupy Wall Street. On the one hand, the openness of the movement, its rejection of party identification, made it initially inviting to a wide array of those discontented with continued unemployment, increasing inequality and political stagnation in the US. On the other, when combined with the consensus-based process characteristic of the General Assemblies (adopted from the Spanish and Greek occupations), this inclusivity had detrimental effects, hindering the movement's ability to take a strong stand against capitalism and for collective control over common resources.

The 'politics of no-politics' meme seeking to trump class and economic struggle in the Spanish, Greece and US protests was not new. It was a reappropriation of the idea of post-politics. From post-politics' initial appearance as a description of a technocratic state intent on managing populations in the service of capital, to its subsequent deployment in critical analyses of governance under neoliberalism, it manifested itself again in activists' misunderstanding of their own oppositional movement. Avoiding the division and antagonism that comes with taking a political position, they displaced their energies onto procedural concerns with inclusion and participation, as if the content of the politics were either given – a matter of identity – or secondary to the fact of inclusion, which makes the outcome of political struggle less significant than the process of deliberation. As Manuel Castells described the Spanish *acampadas*: 'what is transformative is the process rather than the product' (2011). Many in Spain, Greece and Occupy named their goal democracy, envisioning their struggles specifically as a struggle for democracy (rather than for the abolition of private property, collective ownership of the means of production, and economic equality within an already democratic setting). Some

Occupy Wall Street activists, for example, tried to make money in politics the primary issue, as if inequality were primarily an effect of a broken political system rather than a constitutive attribute of capitalism.

If occupation is understood as a tactic, it becomes clear that these movements are not primarily democratic, and framing them as such is a symptom of the continued ideological suasion of post-politics. Occupation is not a democratic process; it is a militant, divisive tactic that expresses the fundamental division on which capitalism depends. Occupiers actively reject democratic institutions, break the law, disrupt public space, squander public resources, and attempt to assert the will of a minority of vocal protesters outside of and in contradiction to democratic procedures. This assertion is what made Occupy and the other movements so strong, so invigorating – they were divisive in a setting that attempted to reduce division to matters of personal opinion, taste or faith. Unfortunately, emphases on democracy led activists and commentators to underplay this component of the movement.

One of the clearest early statements of the democratic underpinnings of the 2011 movements came from Michael Hardt and Antonio Negri, who viewed them not only as calls for a 'real democracy' but also as experiments in a democracy liberated from the constraints of representation. Further developing their argument in the short book *Declaration* (2012), they emphasise direct and horizontal participation in political decision-making, again viewing the movements as nascent and local forms of what is needed on a larger scale.

The problem with Hardt and Negri's democratic depiction of the movements is not that it clashes with the self-understanding of participants, for many share their view. Nor is the problem their emphasis on participation and decision-making rather than execution, itself another instance of the way enthusiasm for horizontality results in a Left disregard for what Marx noted as a key achievement of the Paris Commune, namely, the fact that it acted as an executive rather than a parliamentary body. The problem is that the language of democracy is post-political. It avoids the fundamental antagonism of class conflict and proceeds as if the only thing really missing were participation. This avoidance of antagonism leads to a disavowal of division within the movements – and thus effectively to the post-political move that seeks to individualise, displace and manage political division.

Consider, for example, one of the early challenges facing Occupy Wall Street: with what was it concerned? To what wrong or crime was the movement responding? Early reluctance to name capitalism the crime and the wealthiest 1 per cent the enemy made it seem as if Ron Paul supporters, anti-Fed (the US Federal Reserve Bank) conspiracy theorists and anti-tax libertarians were as much a part of the movement as those demanding jobs for all, a guaranteed minimum income, campaign finance reform, and the restoration of the Glass-Steagall legislation separating commercial and investment banking. Because the movement was committed to a consensus-based approach to democratic decision-making, capitalism's supporters could install themselves as permanent obstacles to the articulation of any goals or demands deemed unacceptable by virtue of being too pro-union, socialist or communist.

Or consider the debate over demands (Deseriis and Dean 2012). In Occupy Wall Street, the debate over whether Occupy should issue demands obscured the fact that the people coming together in the name of the 99 per cent were an assemblage of politically and economically divergent subjectivities, not an actual social bloc. The refusal to be represented by demands was actually the refusal or inability to make an honest assessment of the social composition of the movement so as to develop a politics in which different forces and perspectives do not simply neutralise each other in the search for a position with which everyone could agree. Such inability was further obfuscated by emphases on democratic processes and participation. In order to avoid conflicts and pursue the myth of consensus, the movement produced within itself autonomously operating groups, committees and caucuses. These groups were brought together through structures of mediation such as the General Assembly and the Spokes Council, which struggled to find a common ground amidst the groups' members' divergent political and economic positions. Positions were so divergent and the likelihood of achieving even modified consensus so small that even before the eviction of Zuccotti Park, activists realised that getting anything done required working in smaller, separate or local groups rather than seeking the approval of the GA. In short, the democratic emphasis on consensus and refusal of demands that incited the movement became a serious blindspot with regard to real divergences, a blindspot that had high costs in terms of political efficacy as serious proposals got watered down in order to secure agreement from those who rejected their basic premises.

Critics of demands were right to argue that demands are divisive. Demands animate distinctions between 'for' and 'against' and 'us' and 'them'. This is the source of their mobilising strength insofar as the expression of a demand does not provide something that people can get behind if they choose to as individuals but something that they must get behind if they are part of a movement or on the same side in a struggle. The primary slogan associated with Occupy Wall Street politicised a division – as 'We are the 99 per cent' – yet preoccupations with direct democracy that resulted in countless, pointless meetings, endless deadlocked discussions and, ultimately, mistrust and fragmentation prevented the movement from acknowledging this politicisation of division as a strength. So despite being a movement named for its opposition to Wall Street, Occupy hesitated in presenting either the capitalist mode of production or the capitalist class as an enemy that must defeated. Dominant tendencies in the movement replaced ideology critique with the supposition that each individual opinion should be valued and respected as a legitimate perspective (as if dominant forces had no effect on subjectivity). For them, the movement was more about multiple opportunities to say 'I', to speak for oneself rather be spoken for, than it was about saying 'we'.

Scepticism toward invocations of 'we' and 'us' often arises from misinterpreting we-statements as sociological statements requiring a concrete, delineable, empirical referent. The misinterpretation is an effect of the erasure of the division necessary for politics as if interest and will were only and automatically attributes of a fixed social position. As a consequence, sceptics neglect the performative component of the first-person plural, overlooking the point where, as Žižek puts it, 'objective social analysis breaks down and a subjective political attitude directly inscribes itself' (2010: 203). The power of Occupy, a power expressed in the slogan, 'We are the 99 per cent,' arose out of such a direct inscription of a political attitude, the inscription of a political subject. No one thought that 99 per cent of the people in the US were actually saying 'we'. The slogan was not an empirical claim; it was a political representation.

For some in Occupy, often but not always adopting an anarchist position, 'we' is a problem because it posits an impossible unity. They assume that first-person plural statements imply uniformity across the entirety of the group (and here they sneak in some of their sceptical allies' reductive empiricism, as if groups or collectives designated via the first-person plural were necessary outgrowths of fixed social positions). This argument is weak because there is no reason to assume such a unity. Insofar as a 'we' can be constituted through the mutual recognition of 'you' and 'I', 'we' begins from, is premised on, constitutive difference (Dean 1996). That we differ and disagree doesn't mean we aren't us. It's not necessary to assume that 'we' are all the same or that 'we' always agree. Unfortunately, some individualist tendencies in the occupation movement failed to recognise that 'we' can and always does include difference and so needlessly fetishised an individualism belied by the collective power at the heart of Occupy Wall Street.

A basic tenet of psychoanalysis is that the individual subject is constitutively divided. On this point, the collective subject is no different.

It, too, is constituted out of diverging tendencies, affects, fantasies, thoughts, desires, practices and influences. It, too, struggles through change and changes through struggle. In politics a 'we' is uttered in opposition to a 'they' – it's us and them. 'We' excludes. But this opposition is not an argument against the first-person plural. It's a point in its favour. Rather than remaining confined by the inclusivist presumptions of post-politics, leftists should embrace the first-person plural and accept exclusion: some positions are wrong and should be rejected, opposed, defeated. These positions are the ones that directly or indirectly reinforce capitalist domination.

Claiming division

The true innovation of the 2011 movements is the rupture with post-politics manifest in the assertion of division. Occupy Wall Street refused the fantasy that 'what's good for Wall Street is good for Main Street', claimed the division between Wall Street and Main Street, and named this division as a fundamental wrong: the wrong of inequality, exploitation, and theft. 'We are the 99 per cent' asserts it as the 'we' of a divided people, the people divided between expropriators and expropriated. It does not unify this collectivity under a substantial identity – race, ethnicity, religion, nationality. Rather in the setting of an occupied Wall Street, this 'we' is a class, one of two opposed and hostile classes, those who have and control wealth, and those who do not. The assertion of a numerical difference as a political difference, that is to say, the politicisation of a statistic, expresses capitalism's reliance on fundamental inequality – as 'we' can never all be counted as the top 1 per cent.

'We are the 99 per cent' also erases the multiplicity of individuated, partial and divided interests that fragment and weaken the people as the rest of us. The count dis-individualises interest and desire, politicising the very statistics allegedly rendering us 'post'. Against capital's constant attempts to pulverise and decompose the collective people, the claim of the 99 per cent responds with the force of a belonging that not only cannot be erased, but that is produced by capital's own methods of accounting. Capital has to measure itself, count its profits, its rate of profit, its share of profit, its capacity to leverage its profit, its confidence or anxiety in its capacity for future profit. Capital counts and analyses who has what, representing to itself the measures of its success. These very numbers can be put to use, as in 'We are the 99 per cent'. They aren't re-signified – they are claimed as the subjectification of the gap separating the top 1 per cent from the rest of us. With this claim, the gap becomes a vehicle for the expression of communist desire, that is, for a politics that asserts the people as a divisive force in the interest of overturning present society and making a new one anchored in collectivity and the common.

As the occupation movement unfolded in the US during the autumn of 2011, it was clear that the occupiers were a self-selected vanguard, establishing and maintaining a continuity that enabled broader numbers of people to join in the work of the movement. Into a field more generally configured around convenience, ease of use and individual preference – a field noted more for 'clictivism' than any more strenuous or exacting kind of politics, occupation installs demanding processes through which protesters select and discipline themselves – not everyone can devote all their time to the revolution. Most activists affiliated with a specific occupation did not occupy all the time. Some would sleep at the site and then go to their day jobs or schools. Others would sleep elsewhere and occupy during the day and evening. Still others would come for the frequent, multiple hour-long General Assemblies. Nonetheless, occupation involved people completely, as Lukacs would say *'with the whole of their personality'*. As the occupations persisted over weeks and months, people joined in different capacities – facilitation, legal, technology, media, medical, food, community relations, education, direct action – participating in time-intensive working groups and support activities that involved them in the movement even as they weren't occupying a space directly.

The continuity of occupation was a potent remedy to the fragmentation, localism and transitoriness of contemporary Left politics. Occupation unites and disciplines via local, self-organised assemblies. This 'unity' does not accord with a 'party line' or set of shared demands or common principles. Rather, it is 'practical unity' as an effect of the conscious sharing of an organisational form. Unity, then, is an affiliation around and in terms of the practice of occupation. One of the most significant achievements of Occupy Wall Street in its first two months was the change in the shape of the Left. Providing a common form that no one could ignore, it drew a line: are you with or against occupation?

Given the collapse of the institutional space of Left politics in the wake of the decline of unions and the Left's post-political fragmentation into issues and identities, occupation asserts a much needed and heretofore absent common ground from which to join in struggle. In dramatic contrast to communicative capitalism's promise of easy action, of a politics of pointing and clicking and linking and forwarding, Occupy Wall Street says, *'No! It's not so easy. You can't change the world isolated behind your screen. You have to show up, work together, and collectively confront the capitalist class'*. Protest requires living bodies in the streets.

Occupation is a political form that asserts a gap by forcing a presence. This forcing is more than simply of people into places where they do not belong (even when they may ostensibly have a right). It is a forcing of collectivity over individualism, the combined power of a group that disrupts a space readily accommodating of individuals. Such a forcing thereby puts in stark relief the conceit of a political arrangement that claims to represent a people that cannot be present, a divided people who, when present, instill such fear and insecurity that they have to be met by armed police and miles of barricades. It asserts the class division prior to and unremedied by democracy under capitalism. The incompatibility is fundamental, constitutive.

The Occupy movement took many forms in cities around the world, none of which reached a consensus around communism (as if communism could even name a consensus). Most emphasised some kind of post-political plurality of views, resisting attempts to direct or determine the movement. In some of the groups working out of the New York General Assembly, for example, red-baiting was wielded as a weapon against proposals for a massive public-works programme for quality union-wage jobs. Some responded to the GA demand for 'Jobs for All' with virtual screams of 'but that's communist!' and attempts to block discussion at every point. In the wake of a century of anti-communism in the US, these dismissals are not surprising. It makes sense that some activists internalised anti-communist sentiments and that anxieties about communism would be more pronounced in the setting of a movement attacking inequality, unemployment, corporate power and the rapacious speculation of an unrestrained finance sector.

Nonetheless, the horizon of Occupy, in connection with the broader global movement against capitalism expressed in Greece and Spain, is communist. Communism is one name we have for an emancipatory egalitarianism that uncompromisingly rejects capitalism (Dean 2012). The break with assumptions that capitalism is the only game in town, that there is no alternative, and that politics is nothing but democracy resulted from the emphasis on division. None of the occupations are traditional movements of a working class organised in trade unions; none specifically target workplaces. This is still a movement of class struggle, though, especially when we recognise with Marx and Engels that the working class is not a fixed, empirical class but a fluid, changing class of those who have to sell their labour power in order to survive. For example, Occupy's use of strikes and occupations targets capitalism as a system. It worked to interrupt attempts to privatise public schools as well as working to shut down ports and stock exchanges. People are not mobilised as workers; they are mobilised as people, as everybody else, as the rest of us, as the majority – the 99 per cent – who are being thoroughly screwed by the top 1 per cent in education, health, food, the environment, housing and work. People are mobilised as those who are proletarianised and exploited in every aspect of our lives – at risk of foreclosure and unemployment, diminishing futures, increasing debts, shrunken space of freedom, accelerated dependence on a system that is rapidly failing.

To reiterate, Occupy returned capitalism to the centre of Left politics. It engaged in class warfare without naming the working class as one of two great hostile forces but by presenting capitalism as a wrong against the people. Instead of locating the crime of capitalism, its excesses and exploitation, primarily in the factory, it highlighted the pervasive, intensive and extensive range of capitalist expropriation of lives and futures. Occupy Wall Street got its bearings from the communist horizon as it expressed the intensity of collective desires to organise in struggle against the class power of the corporate and financial elite. No wonder, then, that it opened up a new sense of possibility for so many of us: it reignited political will by reactivating Marx's insight that class struggle is a political struggle.

For over thirty years, the Left accepted liberal notions that political goals are strictly individual lifestyle choices and social-democratic claims that history had already solved basic problems of distribution with the compromise of regulated markets and welfare states – a solution the Right rejected and capitalism destroyed. Critical of a post-politics that its own premises preventing it from combating, the Left failed to defend a vision of a better world, an egalitarian world of common production by and for the collective people. Instead, it accommodated capital, succumbing to the lures of individualism, consumerism, competition and privilege, and proceeding as if there really were no alternative to states that rule in the interests of markets. For this Left, politics was thought primarily in terms of resistance, playful and momentary aesthetic disruptions, the immediate specificity of local projects, and struggles for hegemony within a capitalist, parliamentary setting. The movements of 2011 ruptured this setting, impressing on us the necessity of the abolition of capitalism and the creation of new international practices and institutions of egalitarian cooperation. They ruptured it, moreover, not by appealing to democracy but by asserting division.

Notes

1. Rancière's argument is further complicated by his reading of disruption as the essence of politics and of Plato as a seminal step toward depoliticisation. If disruption is the essence of politics, then governance is necessarily depoliticising. This view of governance allows for a kind of permanent contestation without any responsibility for actual decisions and implementation. The resulting Left politics is reduced to a politics of resistance. Additionally, if the problems of depoliticisation start with Plato, then how does the term contribute to a diagnosis of the contemporary situation? How is it nothing but the inevitable failure of order?
2. 'Democracy is born in the Squares', *http://www.occupiedlondon.org/blog/2011/06/09/613-democracy-is-born-in-the-squares/*.
3. 'Preliminary notes towards an account of the 'Movement of the popular assemblies', *http://www.occupiedlondon.org/blog/2011/07/15/preliminary-notes-towards-an-account-of-the-%E2%80%9Cmovement-of-popular-assemblies%E2%80%9D/#more–4878*.

References

Badiou, A. (2011), *Theory of the Subject*, London: Continuum.

Brown, W. (2006), 'American nightmare: Neoliberalism, neoconservatism, and de-democraticization,' *Political Theory*, 34: 6, pp. 690–714.

Castells, M. (2011), 'The disgust becomes a network', *Adbusters*, 2 August, available at: *http://www.adbusters.org/magazine/97/manuel-castells.html*.

Dean, J. (1996), *Solidarity of Strangers*, Berkeley: University of California Press.

Dean, J. (2009), *Democracy and Other Neoliberal Fantasies*, Durham, NC: Duke University Press.

Dean, J. (2012), *The Communist Horizon*, London: Verso.

Deseriis, M., and J. Dean (2012), 'A movement without demands?', *Possible Futures*, 3 January, available at: *http://www.possible-futures.org/2012/01/03/a-movement-without-demands/*.

Hardt, M., and A. Negri (2011), 'The fight for real democracy at the heart of Occupy Wall Street', *Foreign Affairs*, 11 October, available at *http://www.foreignaffairs.com/articles/136399/michael-hardt-and-antonio-negri/the-fight-for-real-democracy-at-the-heart-of-occupy-wall-street*.

Hardt, M., and A. Negri (2012), *Declaration*, New York: Argo-Navis.

Mouffe, C. (2000), *The Democratic Paradox*, London: Verso.

Passavant, P. A. (2005), 'The strong neoliberal state', *Theory & Event*, 8: 3.

Rancière, J. (1999), *Disagreement*, Minneapolis: University of Minnesota Press.

Schmitt, C. (1996), *The Concept of the Political*, Chicago: University of Chicago Press.

Schneider, S. (2011), 'Taking the streets in Spain,' *Socialist Alternative*, 23 May, available at: *http://www.sa.org.au/index.php?option= com_k2&view=item&id=6903:taking-the-streets-in-spain&Itemid= 390&tmpl=component&print=1*.

Žižek, S. (1999), *The Ticklish Subject*, London: Verso.

Žižek, S. (2010), *Living in the End Times*, London: Verso.

14 The Enigma of Revolt: Militant Politics in a 'Post-Political' Age

Andy Merrifield

Schuwalkin and us

In a remarkable essay on Kafka, written in 1934 on the tenth anniversary of his death, Walter Benjamin introduces Potemkin, Catherine the Great's partner and chancellor. Potemkin is a drunk afflicted by severe and regular fits of depression. In one unusually long low, he retreats to his room, barring everybody entry. But nothing can be done without Potemkin's signature. So official business piles up, policies can't be enacted and grave irregularities result; Russian ministries come to a standstill. Catherine and top civil servants are at their wits' end. Then, one day, in struts a young, headstrong minor clerk called Schuwalkin. 'What's up?' Schuwalkin wonders. The ministers explain. Schuwalkin isn't impressed. Such inactivity and passivity. He's zealous and wants action, now. 'If that's all it is, gentlemen,' he replies, 'give me those files, I beg you' (Benjamin 2009: 193). The ministers have nothing to lose. So Schuwalkin grabs the bundles of papers and sets off through the galleries, along the corridors, to Potemkin's gloomy bedchamber. In he marches, without knocking, without even saying a word, foisting the documents under the nose of the bedridden chancellor. Dipping his plume in ink, he hands it to the startled Potemkin. Absent-mindedly, sleepily, the latter executes the first signature, then a second, then a third, and eventually all of them. Schuwalkin bolts back to the ministers who bend over the documents.

> Not one says a word; the group stands frozen. Once again, Schuwalkin approaches, once again he inquires zealously: what is the reason for the gentlemen's consternation? Then his glance too fell on the signature. Document after document is signed: Schuwalkin, Schuwalkin, Schuwalkin . . .' (Benjamin 2009: 194)

This vignette, says Benjamin, strikes us like a messenger, heralding Kafka's work two centuries in advance. The zealous and light-hearted Schuwalkin, like Kafka's K. in *The Castle*, has a brush with authority, is partly assuaged, yet ultimately comes away frustrated and empty-handed. Those authorities, mysterious and secluded in their bedchambers, in their dark attics within attics, along corridors off corridors, are there, sometimes glimpsed, sometimes even challenged, yet always – or seemingly always – elude us and deflect us: their full panoply of power remains intact come what may. Schuwalkin's story is our story, almost 100 years after Kafka's death: Benjamin propels Kafka and his world into our world. It's a world in which we progressives either come on like the youthful, confident Schuwalkin, swashbuckling our way in, in head-on confrontation, yet achieve little – apart from often getting hurt – or else we stand idle like those feckless politicians around Potemkin, inactive and idealess, waiting desperately for better times ahead.

Schuwalkin's story is a political parable of a post-political world, a world that is currently our own, a world which gives us – if it gives us anything – light and facile victories, even as it sometimes crushes us like a dog, subjecting us to trials for crimes we have never committed. Addressing this post-political conundrum requires, then, a pragmatic and programmatic confrontation of two questions. The first, an internal one, is the great Kafkaesque question: how do we escape the Castle within us? The other, an external one, is a pragmatic and programmatic confrontation of the great Sartrean question: is struggle intelligible?

The two questions, of course, are intimately related and can be played off one another; and they offer respective resolutions to one another's dilemma. As far as the latter goes, Sartre says that struggle is indeed intelligible – though only if it is subjected to dialectical intelligibility, to an intelligibility of contradictions, an intelligibility of indetermination and over-determination sought 'in the thick of the battle' (Sartre 2006: 114). As for the former, all political economy, Sartre likewise knew, is political-psychology, the convolution of meta-tactics and micro-tactics, of external and internal struggle, of a struggle with the world and a struggle with the self, a struggle to define a political subjectivity that avoids paranoiac simplification and paranoiac complication.

Ontological morphing

The advent of Occupy lets us glimpse a new political subjectivity taking shape, an epistemological rift in the ontological morphing of our social, political and economic life – that subtle, creeping shift of our being in the world. Something different has unleashed itself, revealed itself, gotten created, something different from the past, different from 1968. It may fizzle out; some people think it has already fizzled out, think it was all overstated and overrated from the off. To a certain extent, it has fizzled out. Yet it has created enough effervescence to home in on, to imbibe, to analyse and project into a land of post-post-political possibility.

A lot of people have drawn similarities between Occupy and 1968. But Occupy's radicalism differs: its tactics and tempo are different from 1968, its terrain of struggle is different. The world differs, too, has changed enormously since the 1960s, changed in significant political ways. These changes have had their own punctuating refrains: in 1967, on the cusp of student protest, The Doors sang, 'We want the world and we want it now'; exactly a decade on, in 1977, a decade vilified by fiscal crisis and economic slump, the Sex Pistols cried, 'NO FUTURE! NO FUTURE FOR YOU AND ME!' And then, not quite a decade on again, in 1984, during the back-end of Ronald Reagan's first term and in the thick of Thatcherism, Michael Jackson and USA For Africa harmonised 'We are the World'. A strange, almost inexplicable act of incorporation and cooptation, of universal reabsorption, had taken place; from wanting the world in 1967, there was no world worth having in 1977: it could all go to fuck; only then, as we hobbled into the 1980s, we were told that now, somehow, we were the world. That same no future had been thrown back in our faces: we were this no future, this TINA, and we've been living with it ever since.

That infamous Orwellian year of 1984 isn't a bad starting point to reflect upon this post-political rift. In 1984, in his famous essay, 'Postmodernism, or, the cultural logic of late capitalism', Fredric Jameson announced, amongst many other things, something significant: 'the abolition of critical distance', the Left's 'most cherished and time-honored formula' (Jameson 1984: 87). Henceforth critical distance finds itself, perhaps for the first time ever, thoroughly outmoded and impotent. There's no longer any without, only within, no repositioning of ourselves beyond what we progressives are critically analysing, critically struggling against; now there is no way for us to get critical leverage on the beast whose belly we are all collectively inside.

This lack of outside – or reframing of what inside and outside might now constitute – also preoccupied Salman Rushdie in 1984. In 'Outside the whale', Rushdie provided a thicker humane texturing to what Jameson awkwardly affirmed, taking on George Orwell at the same time. In 'Inside the whale', written in the 1940s, Orwell suggested there was an outside to this grubby profane world of ours, a safe haven somewhere, at least an outside for intellectuals who can find warm wombs, proverbial Jonah's whales, within their texts and art. Inside this outside, great art is incubated, Orwell said, great art and literature that says bundles about our corrupt and venal political and economic system. But Rushdie was having none of this:

> the truth is that there is no whale. We live in a world without hiding places; the missiles have made sure of that. So we are left with a fairly straightforward choice. Either we agree to delude ourselves, to lose our-selves in the fantasy of the great fish ... or we can do what all human beings do instinctively when they realize that the womb has been lost forever – that is, we can make the very devil of a racket. (Rushdie 1991: 99)

So maybe 1984 signalled the real end to the 1960s, sealed its fate. 1984 meant the end of the without, the end of critical distance, the end of 1968, the beginnings of the post-political. Maybe it meant the end of continuing the old tradition of radical politics, using the same mindset, the same workerist politics, the same frames of reference and militancy. Making a racket 1960s style, or even 1970s and 1980s style, seems no longer tenable today, no more the required politics to tackle a capitalist beast that has absorbed us within it, wholescale and wholesale, lock, stock and barrel. Something else is needed than the desperation of Zoyd Wheeler, Thomas Pynchon's hippy anti-hero from *Vineland* – which, remember, was also set in 1984 – leaping through plate glass windows, breaking on through to the other side, trying to cling on to his government stipend as a mental degenerate. There is an innocent charm to Zoyd's antics, as well as a touching fatherly concern about his teenage daughter Prairie, about how she's going to grow up in a world whose value system is all bad karma for Zoyd. Yet the problem is that there's something pathetic about old Zoyd, too, trapped in his dope-hazed past, paranoid about the Reaganite present, paralysed about thinking of a post-Reaganite future (Pynchon 1990). Beneath the cobblestones there is no longer any beach; and if there is, its waters are now too polluted to permit nude bathing.

Joseph K. and Karl M.

Our world is a different place from what it was in 1968 and Zoyd knew it but couldn't admit it. Our world today permits different hopes and dreams, poses different threats and possibilities. Paradoxically, today's neoliberal, post-political reality is more easily critiqued than ever before using basic Marxist tools. At the level of analysis, it has perhaps never been simpler to adopt a classical Marxist stance and be right. And yet, at the level of political practice, there's little in this analysis and critique that leaves us with any guide to practical struggle, to how we might act on this knowledge. One of the difficulties is that the world we think about, the world that functions through the current economic model, is classically Capital-ist in the sense of M.'s great text (let's call our Kafkaesque Marx 'M.'); yet the world we have to act in, the world progressives have to organise in, resist from the inside, is tellingly Kafkaesque.

The present post-political conjuncture is Kafkaesque to the degree that castles and ramparts reign over us everywhere. These castles and ramparts are usually in plain view, frequently palpable to our senses, inside us, yet at the same time distant and somehow cut off, somehow out of reach and inaccessible; and their occupants are ever more difficult to pin down when we come knocking at their doors, providing we can find the right door to knock on. ('Official decisions', says Kafka in *The Castle* (1997: 155), 'have the shyness of young girls'). Kafka is better than M. at recognising the thoroughly modern conflict now besieging us under capitalism. M. understood the general dynamics of the production of castles and the trials this system subjects us to. But he understood less about its corridors of power and how its organisational bureaucracies function. M. understood the difficulty of waging war against a process; however, he wasn't around long enough to imagine how this process would one day undergo administrative (mis)management, how it wouldn't only get chopped up by massively complex divisions of labour: it would also beget even more massive bureaucratic compartmentalisations, done by unaccountable and anonymous middle managers.

Kafka knew how modern conflict isn't just an us-against-other-people class affair, but us against a world transformed into an immense and invariably abstract total administration. The shift Kafka makes between his two great novels, *The Trial* and *The Castle*, makes for a suggestive shift in our own supranational administered world. In *The Trial*, Joseph K., like a dog, stands accused in a world that is an omnipotent tribunal, a sort of state monopoly capitalist system. In *The Castle*, the protagonist K. populates a world that has suddenly shrunk into a village whose dominating castle on the hill seems even more powerful and elusive than ever before. Perhaps in this village with its castle we can now glimpse our own 'global village', a world shrunk by globalisation, a world in which the psychological drama of one man confronting a castle is now really a political parable of us all today – us having to conceive a collective identity to resolve the dark gothic mystery we ourselves have scripted, a mystery in which we are simultaneously inmates and warders. 'Dealing directly with the authorities was not particularly difficult', K. muses,

> for well organised as they might be, all they did was guard the distant and invisible interests of distant and invisible masters, while K. fought for something vitally near to him, for himself, and moreover, at least at the very beginning, on his own initiative, for he was the attacker . . . But now by the fact that they had at once amply met his wishes in all unimportant matters – and hitherto only unimportant matters had come up – they had robbed him of the possibility of light and easy victories, and with that of the satisfaction which must accompany them and the well-grounded confidence for further and greater struggles which must result from them. Instead, they let K. go anywhere he liked – of course only within the village – and thus pampered and enervated him, ruled out all possibility of conflict, and transported him into an unofficial, totally unrecognized, troubled, and alien existence . . . So it came about that while a light and frivolous bearing, a certain deliberate carelessness was sufficient when one came in direct contact with the authorities, one needed in everything else the greatest caution, and had to look round on every side before one made a single step. (Kafka 1997: 52)

K. marvels at a world that sounds eerily like our own: 'nowhere had he seen officialdom and life as interwoven as they were here, *so interwoven that it sometimes even looked as if officialdom and life had changed places*' (Kafka 1997: 53, emphasis added). It follows now that progressives need the greatest caution in everything we do; we need to look around on every side before we can make a single step. The gravity of the situation isn't lost on any of us. But the gravity of this situation nonetheless 'pampers' and 'enervates' us, too, and tries to rule out all possibility of conflict by absorbing us into its 'light and frivolous bearing'. It has integrated us into its reality, a reality that satisfies all our unimportant wishes and desires; it has integrated itself into us as an apparently non-alien force. 'Are there control authorities?' K. wonders of the castle. 'There are nothing but controlling authorities', the mayor tells him (Kafka 1997: 58).

In our own times, the Kafkaesque castle has become the Debordian 'integrated spectacle', a phenomenon that permeates all reality. If the dynamics of *The Trial* exhibited the traits (and the leakiness) of the 'concentrated' and 'diffuse' spectacles that Debord outlined in *The Society of the Spectacle*, then *The Castle* is late-Debord, and tallies with the *Comments on the Society of the Spectacle* he would make twenty-one years later. 'When the spectacle was concentrated', Debord says, 'the greater part of the surrounding society escaped it;

when diffuse, a small part; today, no part' (Debord 1991: 9). The society of the castle and the integrated spectacle is like a vast whirl-pool: it sucks everything into a singular and unified spiralling force, into a seamless web that has effectively collapsed and amalgamated different layers and boundaries. Erstwhile distinctions between the political and the economic, between form and content, conflict and consent, politics and technocracy have lost their specific gravity, have lost their clarity of meaning: integration functions through a conflat-ing process of cooptation and corruption, of re-appropriation and re-absorption, of blocking off by breaking down. Each realm now simply elides into its other.

Where K. goes astray, and where his quest borders on the hopeless, is that he's intent on struggling to access the castle's occupants; he wants to penetrate the castle's bureaucratic formalities and the 'flaw-lessness' of its inner circle. K. struggles for a way in rather than a way out. Using all the Cartesian tools of a land surveyor, he confronts the castle on the castle's own terms, on its own ostensibly 'rational' frame of reference. K.'s demands, consequently, are too restrictive and unimportant, and too self-conscious. He wants to render the world of the castle intelligible as opposed to rendering it unac-ceptable. Instead of trying to enter the inner recesses of our castle, of unpacking its meaning, of demystifying its fetishism, instead of trying to find doors to knock on and people to make rational com-plaints to, we need to rethink this enigma of revolt, rethink it on our terms, not theirs, not on the castle's terms, and not on the terms of any 'logic of capital' either.

'Public' politics?

For, in truth, there is no enigma of capital: there can no longer be any fetishism within neoliberal capitalist society. M. exposed bour-geois sleights of hand and revealed for people the hidden world of capitalist alienation, demonstrating the 'root' cause of their subjuga-tion and domination. But today people around the world don't need M. to reveal the root of their misery, to correct the lacunas in their vision of everyday reality: they know it all too well themselves; they are bludgeoned by a system that is all too obvious to them, that is based on raw, naked and highly visible power, on brute force that doesn't need unmasking by anyone. This ruling class wallows in the obviousness of its shenanigans because it knows that its opposition is too weak and feeble to stand up to its power.

Thus there is no enigma of capital, at least not for us. It's their enigma. For us, their circulation, their production and accumulation by dispossession are not enigmatic: they are obvious, blunderingly obvious, bludgeoningly obvious, an obviousness based on pure power, on obvious power. If there is an enigma, it is how this power is administered, how it is controlled, how its controlling centre has become 'occult' (as Guy Debord said). The enigma before us is an administrative conundrum, of how to struggle within this total administration, under whose writ politics and economics, the public and the private, state and civil society have all become indistinguishable, indistinguishable in the traditional way we understood these categories; public spaces are now privatised, public services are privatised, the public is now private; entrepreneurs become politicians, politicians get entrepreneurial; billionaires head up agencies whose budgets dwarf even the biggest supranational organisations; what was once public is now private.

The public realm of 'collective consumption' – goods consumed collectively, like transport and utilities infrastructure, hospitals, schools, public spaces, and so on – hasn't so much been abandoned by the state as sold off at bargain prices to private capital. Not only has the state retracted from paying for items of collective consumption; these items have actively been dispossessed, re-valorised for profit. The plot thickens, too, as elsewhere public goods become publicised private billboards. In financially strapped urban areas of America, like Baltimore, efforts to raise the municipal coffers now mean fire trucks are emblazoned with glossy corporate ads; in Philadelphia, subway riders now bear travel cards with McDonald's ads; Kentucky Fried Chicken logos embellish manhole covers and fire hydrants in urban Indiana; pizza chains advertise on public school buses (*The New York Times* 2012). So it goes, on and on, the medium is the message . . .

The whole nature of the public realm in this age of privatisation and neoliberalisation needs to be rethought, a privatisation that M. saw coming way back. Bourgeois society, he reminds us in *The Communist Manifesto*, would 'leave no other nexus between man and man than naked self-interest, than callous cash payment . . . drowning the most heavenly ecstasies of chivalrous enthusiasm, of philistine sentimentalism, in the icy water of egotistical calculation'. Bourgeois society 'resolves personal [and public] worth into exchange value', rips away halos of every sort, converts all erstwhile hallowed and holy realms, including the public realm itself, into another money realm, into another means to accumulate capital. M. leaves us with the bleak task of picking up the pieces of what 'the public realm' might still mean.

There's a consequent need to redefine not a public realm that's collectively owned and managed by the state, but a public realm that is somehow expressive of the people, expressive of their common notions, common notions that Spinoza always insisted were not universal notions, not some form of universal rights. Spinoza was against an abstract conception of universality, which was an inadequate idea. Common notions are general rather than abstract, general in their practical and contextual applicability. From this standpoint, when something is public, its channels for common expression remain open, negotiable and debatable, political in the sense that they will witness people encountering other people, dialoguing with other people, arguing with other people. In the urban realm these public expressions will likely be more loudly heard and more intensely felt. When the whole world has been privatised, the public realm might be defined by this idea of common notion, of a common practice, of people acting and expressing rather than simply being there.

Twenty-first-century spaces will be public spaces not for reasons of pure concrete physicality or centrality, nor even because of land tenure, but because they are meeting places between virtual and physical worlds, between online and offline conversations, between online and offline encounters. Space won't so much be divided between public and private as between passive or active; between a space that encourages active encounters of people and a space that resigns itself to passive encounters, where people meet each other in controlled environments, in spaces that are orderly, patrolled, secure. Space here isn't so much public as the Sartrean 'practico-inert': it envelops people as passive backdrop, like dead labour functions in redundant fixed capital, as plain old bricks and mortar, as concrete and steel that imprisons. As Sartre says, the free group organises to combat 'the passive action of the practico-inert', of the city as alienating objectification. For urban spaces to come alive, to be public, which is to say to be active, they need to be occupied, taken over by dynamic social relations between people, by people there and elsewhere, elsewhere in other urban spaces, bringing those to life as well, creating a living, organic spatiality which isn't so much a 'constituent objectification' as a 'constituted subjectivation' (Sartre 2004).

Thus people in active space come together to create a function, to protest, to express themselves; they're not responding to a function like a crowd of shoppers. In coming together they express active rather than passive affects; plazas, parks, squares, streets and civic buildings thereby become what Jeffrey Hou calls 'insurgent public space': 'as we envision the future of public space in North America and beyond', Hou writes

> it is clear that the focus of our efforts should be equally, if not more, on the making of the public than on the making of space. While space

remains critical as a vehicle for actions and expressions, it is through the actions and the making of a socially and politically engaged public that the struggle for public space as a forum of political dialogues and expressions can be resuscitated and sustained. (Hou 2012: 94)

One of the many interesting things about the Occupy movement, about why it is potentially so radical as well as so potentially flawed, is that it has reframed the whole nature and language of revolt and invented a new kind of public expression. For a start, it doesn't make any demands and has no designated leaders. It has unnerved the enemy because it has tried, inadequately for the time being, to utter a different vocabulary of revolt. It does everything that Kafka's K. tried not to do. K., after all, was obsessed with demanding his rights – 'I want no favors from the castle, I want my rights'. K. was obsessed with cracking the secret interior of the castle, of gaining entry. He became so obsessed with the castle that he'd begun to internalise its logic, was suffused by its logic to the extent that he could only think via its logic. Above all, he wanted clarity, wanted to clear up that which was unclear. K. needed to embody the castle, to get into the castle, to penetrate its ramparts; he sought out its physical presence and the Count's representative: Klamm. K. had to humanise the castle somehow, wanted to deal with it on personal terms, on moral terms.

Fortunately, the Occupy movement does none of those things. In fact, it doesn't pose questions to anyone in particular, doesn't personalise its grievance; instead, it indicts the system and has tried to infiltrate its capillaries and arteries of power as an abstract entity. And if protagonists occupy space somewhere, these spaces of occupation are curiously new phenomena, too, neither rooted in place nor circulating in space, but rather an inseparable combination of the two; they're insurgent public spaces expressive of active Spinozian affects. The efficacy of these spaces for any global movement is defined by what is going on both inside and outside these spaces, by the here and the there. It's a dialogue between inside and outside that knows all the while that the dichotomy represents only different moments within a unity of process, à la M.'s Introduction to *The Grundrisse*. M.'s famous schema of how capitalist production begets distribution, how distribution begets exchange, exchange consumption, consumption more production, distribution more exchange, exchange more distribution, distribution more production, etc., etc., now has to be a vision of the circulation of revolt, of its production and virtual circulation, of its emotional and empathetic exchange, of its consummation, of how all this hangs together in some complex, enigmatic global flow of counter-power.

The presence of absence

In Judith Butler's (2011) essay 'Bodies in alliance and the politics of the street', written when bodies occupied Zuccotti Park, she invokes Hannah Arendt's notion (from *The Human Condition*) that all political acts require a 'space of appearance'; people appearing collectively defines politics and the public realm: 'it is the space of appearance in the widest sense of the word', wrote Arendt, 'namely, the space where I appear to others as others appear to me, where people exist not merely like other living or inanimate things but make their appearance explicitly' (Arendt 1999: 198). 'To rethink the space of appearance', Butler says, pushing Arendt further,

> in order to understand the power and effect of public demonstrations for our time, we will need to understand the bodily dimensions of action, what the body requires, and what the body can do, especially when we must think about bodies together, what holds them there, their conditions of persistence and of power. (Butler 2011)

Butler is surely correct to urge us to understand 'the bodily dimensions of action'; yet does Arendt's idea still stand for how bodies would politically function in a post-Kafkaesque political space? Somehow the 'space of appearance' doesn't seem quite right; nor does an archaic and simplistic notion of 'public'. To be sure, the politics of bodies in public space isn't defined by appearance so much as by opacity and anonymity, by clandestinity and dissimulation, by invisibility. One of the most radically challenging themes emerging from *The Coming Insurrection*, authored by the suggestively provocative 'Invisible Committee' (2009), is precisely this notion of clandestinity, of invisibility, of how apparent absence can unnerve the powers that be. The power of surprise, of secret organisation, of rebelling, of demonstrating and plotting covertly, of striking invisibly, and in multiple sites at once, is the key element that the Invisible Committee affirm for confronting a power whose firepower is vastly superior. To be explicitly visible, to appear explicitly – in a manoeuvre, in organising, in an occupation – 'is to be exposed, that is to say above all, vulnerable' (The Invisible Committee 2009: 112).

Here black ski masks, head scarves and Guy Fawkes masks become emblems of veritable nobodies, of invisible underground men and women, of people without qualities who want to disguise their inner qualities, who shun visibility in public, who have little desire to be the somebody the world wants them to be. These bodies are publicly expressive bodies, yet are bodies weary of revealing too much of themselves. That's why they wear disguises and masks:

they are bodies revealing their true identities by dissimulating their facial identity, by disguising themselves, by transgressing where these bodies are supposed to be and how they are supposed to look and act. This, after all, is the whole point of the so-called 'black blocs' that have inspired so much Occupy activism, a tactic whereby hoods, caps and masks of varying sorts create an anonymity symbolising tacit solidarity, a militant togetherness in the face of danger, a collective identity voiced without words, because sometimes words can say too much, or too little. What we have here is an expressive politics that 'appears' in a different guise, in its true guise of invisibility, as simultaneously presence and absence in the public realm.

In fact, the realm of opacity and dissimulation, of clandestinity and anonymity is part and parcel of an 'archetype' of contemporary militant politics, part of its tactic and identity, part of the armoury of what dissent is and should now be. Perhaps it's possible to draw up a list of 'archetypes of dissent', progressive not reactionary dissent, archetypes that symbolise, as Jung would have had it, some innate disposition to make trouble, to dissent and protest, to revolt against the structures of modern power, against modern economic, political, military and administrative power; to let power know that ordinary people are still alive and kicking, and staying alive necessitates every once in a while kicking out at that power, at its structures of law and order, yet in a manner very different from K.'s lame knee jerks.[1] It is these archetypes, as a loose collectivity, who are remaking and redefining what a twenty-first-century public realm might be.

'Archetypes' of Left dissent

There are five archetypes of Left dissent I want to flag up: Secret Agents; Double Agents; Maggots in the Apple; Great Escapers; and Great Refusers. Let me look, briefly, at each in turn.

Secret Agents are people who devote their very lives and being to the radical cause. They may be professional organisers and tacticians, plotting and dissenting, often clandestinely, writing and printing militant literature, existing to spread the word and fight the power. Nowadays, they may be black bloc anarchists, Marxists, socialists and autonomous communists of assorted stripes and persuasions, both young and veteran alike, who, with Occupy, now have found some focus, some medium through which they can channel their energies and dissatisfactions. Their militancy is thus at once open and concealed, known to some yet hidden from others.

The label 'secret agent' appeals because it conjures up some shady radical presence, a presence through a certain societal absence, a menacing figure who haunts, like the Verloc character about whom Joseph Conrad ironised in his 1906 eponymous novel. Indeed, Verloc, the said secret agent, planned to dynamite the Greenwich Meridian much as Occupiers would love to see the whole Wall Street scene blow; Verloc who intended to assault the organisation of capitalist time much as occupiers seek to assault the whole organisation of capitalist finance. Of course, Conrad created a grotesque character with Verloc, a social and sexual deviant, partly because of his foreignness (he was half-French), partly because he didn't fit the standard norms of respectability. Whatever his domestic failings and selfish conceitedness, Conrad said Verloc's mind 'lacked profundity' (Conrad 2007: 185), that Verloc's failing was a failing of feeling, a failing of feeling the complexity of the situation, a failing of feeling real compassion for the dispossessed. We might say that as a secret agent Verloc was a stereotype not an archetype.

These days, secret agents conspire with a great deal more sophistication and complexity, with a great deal more feeling and compassion; at least they should do. Maybe *The Man Who Was Thursday*, G. K. Chesterton's whimsical retelling of the revolutionary mind, published a year after Conrad's, is more informative and sustainable. This is the suitably dialectical tale of raffish Lucian Gregory, the 'walking blasphemy, a blend of angel and sage' (who turns out to be the mysterious anarchist president, 'Sunday'), and poet-cop Gabriel Syme, whose 'rebellion against rebellion' eventually led him to rebel against his rebellion against rebellion (Chesterton 2007);

If Secret Agents have a 'cover', have some gig concealing their clandestine politicking, *Double Agents* are out in the open, there, as they conceal their dual identities from each other. Their being is not 'either/or', but 'both/and'. In practice, this makes for a strange, schizoid practice, a deeper political idealism lurking behind a socially conventional pragmatism, a person in society who is rebelling against society. The stuff of the 99 per cent doubtless consists of many double agents: they earn a living to equip themselves to overthrow what earning a living really means.

In *The Communist Manifesto*, M. affirmed double agents; his well-heeled friend and benefactor Friedrich Engels, after all, was one, managing the textile mill his communist ideals wanted to tear apart. M. recognised how the developmental impulse of modern capitalism dowsed claims to holy purity in the damp waters of market profanity, that everybody needed to find work to live, and that finding work inevitably meant producing capital for somebody else. M. knew that the resourcefulness of the bourgeoisie always meant there was a market for radical ideas, that modern capitalism could create specific market niches, could plunder these ideas, commodify them, charge a fee to read them, exploit the brains that created these ideas, re-appropriate them in order to generate more profit and accumulate capital. But M. knew at the same time how markets could also help disseminate radical ideas, help them find broader audiences and more general readerships, while providing an income for the double agents who had these radical ideas, and who wrote and worked at trying to bite the hand that fed them.

Trade unions should conspire to incubate double agents, a rank-and-file membership concerned with immediate pay and conditions yet that also has its horizons open, that works to live beyond work, that labours to transform the labour relations underpinning work, knowing in the meanwhile that workers, and their families, somehow need to live. Any radical artist, too, who wants their revolutionary art and wares to find a broader public knows about the hazards and possibilities of double agency. They follow what Walter Benjamin once said of poet Charles Baudelaire: that he was the 'double agent of his class', 'an agent of secret discontent of his class within its rule' (Benjamin 2003: 92), a species who is the very product of modern life, with its complex role-playing and ambivalences, its tangled loyalties and multiple identities. Double agents revel in the tormented freedoms and contradictions these ambivalences engender, for living as well as for creating, and sometimes thrive off the double binds and double liberties within a singular body politic;

Maggots in the Apple is the evocative and somewhat unsavoury phrase that Henri Lefebvre, in *Introduction to Modernity*, took from French novelist Stendhal. In the first few decades of the nineteenth century, Stendhal described a 'new romanticism' in the air, a brazenly utopian response to the problems of an emergent technological and industrial civilisation, problems which remain ours today. In the early 1960s, when Lefebvre wrote *Introduction to Modernity*, he spotted a renewal of both classical and modern romanticism fighting back against the crushing irrational rationality of a bourgeois modernity run amok, updating the project Stendhal had announced in the 1820s: 'At last', Stendhal wrote in *Racine and Shakespeare* (1823), 'the great day will come when the youth will awake; this noble youth will be amazed to realize how long and how seriously it has been applauding such colossal inanities'. 'It requires courage to be a romantic', Stendhal said, 'because one must take a risk' (quoted in Lefebvre 1995: 239).

Lefebvre concluded *Introduction to Modernity* by saying there was a 'new attitude' drifting in the breeze: revolts, acts of insubordination, protests, abstentions, rebellions were there, seen and felt; Stendhal was a man of the late twentieth century. Stendhal's romanticism affirmed disparate elements of society: 'women, young people, political rebels, exiles, intellectuals, half-crazed debauchees, drunks, misfits, successive and abortive geniuses, arrivistes, Parisian dandies and provincial snobs' (Lefebvre 1995: 302). Perhaps, today, their historical counterparts are the downsised 'post-work' victims of a right-sizing capitalist corporate ethic, which 'sets workers free' as business cycles dip; and the maggots now constitute a huge mass of sub-, under- and un-employed workers, a relative surplus population, working, if they ever find work, insecurely, in McJobs, on temporary contracts, on workfare programmes and in internships, students and post-students who know that before them lies a dark, deep abyss about to engulf them, a black hole of the labour market and debt.

This ragged array of people now attempt to live out within everyday bourgeois society their ideal solutions to bourgeois society, challenging its 'moral' economic order, surviving in its core, 'like a maggot in an apple', trying to eat their way out from the inside. They seek to reinvent the world not because they have nothing to lose; more because they know there is nothing left to gain; they see nothing worth gaining from the lures and promises of current society. So, using all their powers of symbolism, imagination and fiction, a new subjectivity is being born, a new lived experience. They are maggots eating their way out of our rotten apple, eating themselves out of the Big Apple. Perhaps, then, Stendhal is a man of the early twenty-first century, too.

Great Escapers take to flight as a form of fight and express a spirit of critical positivity. They have absolutely no truck with existing society and go it alone, alone with others, to create alternative radical communities and communes, frequently self-sufficient, both in the city and the countryside. Their modus operandi is precisely the opposite's of K.'s: instead of trying to enter the inner recesses of the castle, of the citadel of contemporary capitalism, instead of trying to find doors to knock on and people to complain to, demanding their 'rights', Great Escapers burrow out under the castle's ramparts and ask for nothing. They dig tunnels and construct exit trails; they organise, with great caution, invisible committees (as they have at Tarnac, France), escape committees; and they hope their tunnels will be long enough, deep enough, to reach the woods, ubiquitous enough to converge with other tunnels. And if enough people dig, they believe the surface superstructure might one day give away entirely, after everyone has left. What remains will implode in one great heap of rubble – like the Berlin Wall.

'The Great Escape' was the Allied mass escape attempt from the German prisoner of war camp Stalag Luft III, immortalised by John Sturges's 1963 film starring Steve McQueen as Captain Hilts, the

Cooler King. In real life, like capitalist reality, Stalag Luft III, built in 1942 near the Polish town of Zagan, was considered escape-proof. The camp housed US and British airmen whose planes had been shot down in German territory. For these captives, the Germans soldiers said, the 'war was over'. Yet inmates had other ideas, had a sworn duty to continue to fight the enemy, by surviving, by communicating information about this enemy, and, above all, by escaping. The notion of duty was and still is a powerful ideal. But Great Escapers today know that escape must be more carefully planned than ever; and because there are more inmates than before, tunnels must also be longer and more numerous. Dummy tunnels will doubtless be required, too. Perhaps most vital of all is that everybody keeps digging their own tunnel, keeps organising their escape committees where they can, and that the trails are staked out by people who see subversion as a duty, as a permanent duty to themselves. The Great Escape suggests something subterranean, something organised and tactical, practical and concrete. It begins below and at ground level and doesn't float up in the air, abstractly, plonking itself down, undemocratically.

Rather than dig below ground, many liberals and radicals believe that the central object of any struggle isn't to orchestrate escape tunnels but to destroy the social structures and institutions that underwrite human captivity, that support privilege and authority, that define the castle on the hill. They say that one needs to abolish the conditions of mass subordination, destroy the logic of prison camps as well as the processes that give rise to camp mentality. One needs to negate the contradiction between inmate and warder, they say, before one can begin to create a passage to freedom. But negating and actually demolishing a social structure is a project destined to suffer the same trials and frustrations K. suffered when he tried to break into his castle, when he tried to find a well-grounded confidence for further and greater struggles that should have followed, yet which always seemed to elude him;

Great Refusers take to fight as a form of flight and express a spirit of negative defiance, immortalised by Herbert Marcuse's *One Dimensional Man*, his no-holds-barred outcry 'against that which *is*' (Marcuse 1968: 63, emphasis added). In refusing to play the game, in voicing NO, in individually and collectively downing tools, great refusers already begin to create another dimension to life, give renewed breadth and depth to it, re-sublimate what has been de-sublimated, what has been denied by a delusional 'happy consciousness'. Better to sport an unhappy, dissatisfied mien, Marcuse thought, with a frustrated libido that still functions, that still flows with the energy of the Life Instinct, than have your vital centre bought off, de-eroticised, sensually deprived by the instant gratification of society's techno-gismos.

According to Marcuse, by the mid–1960s a 'Total Administration' had permeated all reality, possessing the bodies and souls of everyday people. Even stronger claims can now be made for the omnipotence of this administrative machine, for its in-built calibration in defence laboratories, executive offices, governments, timekeepers, middle managers, efficiency experts, mass communications, publicity agencies, multinational corporations, supranational organisations, schools and universities. The Total Administration's consenting mechanisms liquidate opposition, absorb opposition, or else try to; the Reality Principle vanquishes the Pleasure Principle, convincing people that Reality is the only principle. Even so, there are others who 'prefer not to', who desist from wanting in, both quietly (like the passive negation of Melville's rebellious scrivener, Bartleby) and noisily; and they're now not only a substratum of society's outcasts and outsiders, as Marcuse insisted, but ordinary folk as well, a growing majority, who find themselves outside the 'democratic' process, redundant and disenfranchised in a system of increasing technological rationality and economic inequality. The 'I prefer not to' cannot be entirely suppressed, the 'non-coincidence' between the self we are and the self that society wants us to be. It's a non-coincidence, says Sartre, between an individual subject and his or her social being, a gap that bequeathes dissent, has to breed dissent. It's a non-coincidence that means some people won't be squeezed into any whole, won't be a supernumerary after all the spreadsheets have been done, after everything has seemingly been accounted for: the non-coincidence is an affirmation of residue, of remainders, of people who won't go away and who refuse to fit in.

Revolting memes

Doubtless dissenters here can fall into more than one category, and can even fall between categories; their respective constitution, their organising causes, be they romantically idealist or pragmatically realist, can likewise change over time, can shift and morph subject to personal and political circumstances. Indeed, the changing nature of their revolt suggests that this falling in and out of categories, and between categories, will make dissent both positively and negatively charged, a collective and constant to-ing and fro-ing that makes revolt more flexible and adaptive, less rigid and dictatorial. Meanwhile, all categories somehow need each other, will somehow reinforce one another, offer both offensive fronts and rearguard defences. And the efficacy of any dissent will likely be predicated on how these dissenters organise themselves internally yet coordinate themselves externally, reach out to one another, create a bigger kaleidoscope, a more inclusive constellation of dissent that coexists horizontally, democratically, in a shape and form that gives expression to dissenters' respective activism.

Taken together, these archetypes express a cultural contraflow of revolt, a different meme that circulates and gets exchanged collectively, that distributes and consummates itself spatially, that has to reproduce itself temporally on an ever-expanding scale of activity and activism – otherwise it will die off in a process of natural political selection. Memes are cultural transmitters, messenger particles carrying ideas, symbols and buzz concepts that catch on, that are communicable between people, that solidify group identity. Memes in this sense are cultural analogues of dissenting genes, mutating and replicating themselves as they respond to internal and external selective pressure, to external political pressure.

The term 'meme', shorthand for the Greek *mimeme* (something imitative), is generally attributed to biologist Richard Dawkins in his book *The Selfish Gene* (1976). With the meme, culture could now enter a genetic model of evolution. As Dawkins says, 'fashions in dress and diet, ceremonies and customs, art and architecture, engineering and technology, all evolve in historical time in a way that looks like highly speeded up genetic revolution, but has really nothing to do with genetic revolution' (Dawkins 1989: 190). 'When you plant a fertile meme in my mind', Dawkins continues, 'you literally parasitize my brain, turning it into a vehicle for the meme's propagation in just the way a virus may parasitize the genetic mechanism of the host cell' (Dawkins 1989: 192). We might say that neoliberalism, as a political-economic paradigm, is a meme that has parasitised our brains over the past twenty years or more, and has entered our culture in a way that looks like highly speeded up genetic revolution, 'but has really nothing to do with genetic revolution'. There is nothing natural here: its agents and commissars, its institutions and lobbyists have cajoled and bullied us into accepting this meme as a given, ensuring that this idea has evolved memically, imitatively, to the short-term selfish advantage of the 1 per cent. Still, as Dawkins notes, seemingly despite himself, 'we, alone on earth, can rebel against the tyranny of the selfish replicators' (Dawkins 1989: 202).

So, more recently, we've heard an appeal for a permanent 'meme war', for revolters to battle under the banner of a new meme, to propagate a different political-economic paradigm, one antagonistic to the dominance of the old order, one transforming and even erasing the institutions that spread this old meme that has parasitised our brains like a virus.[2] Those archetypes of dissent can help us unravel what this new, alternative meme might be, how it might be less enigmatic, how it circulates, how it gets disseminated through actual revolt, how it might stick around or get wiped out, how it exists conceptually in the minds of recipients, and how it might one day become a reality out in the world, a practicable alternative.

For the moment, with Occupy, and with the movement beyond Occupy, a new meme has been loosely expressed, a radical hypothesis, a daring hunch that, for dissenters who care about democracy and who know our economic system is kaput, there's a big idea out there waiting to come true, a revolutionary Higgs boson: that underneath it all, underneath everything we see, everything we know, even beyond what we can currently imagine, there lies another reality, one uniting all hitherto ununited aspects of reality, all hitherto ununited social movements. It's a realm attainable only through political, economic and cultural experimentation, through trial and error, through conceptualisation and activation, through thinking and acting, through dialogue and debate, through struggle; nothing is knowable, achievable in advance, a priori. Experimentation gives a deeper sense to M.'s 'Eleventh Thesis on Feuerbach'. The point, rather, should be to experiment with the world, to engage in a form of activism that constantly tests out and overcomes its own limits, that pushes beyond its own limits and experiments with itself and the world; positing something not parallel to what 'they' do but superimposed upon what they do, reinscribing for ourselves something else; swarming over what they do, creating a new life-world within and beyond what they do, beyond their present political-economic reality, in another dimension, with a yellow brick road rather than a castle on the hill.

Notes

1. I recognise that much of what I am going to say about progressive dissent has its reactionary counterpart; and the latter's form might even resemble the former's. It is the content of this dissent, of course, where we would hope that differences reside.
2. The call for a 'meme war' has been most creatively and persuasively articulated by Adbusters editor Kalle Lasn in *Meme Wars* (Lasn 2012). Dedicated to Guy Debord among others, *Meme Wars* is a 400-page reincarnation of Situationist agitprop, full of wonderfully inventive graphics, peppered with slogans and polemical essays that voice the visceral gut feeling that society as we know it sucks. What we might be witnessing here is what Debord himself called 'domination's falling rate of profit': that as neoliberalism spreads to the scale of the whole of social space

it consequently devours its own comparative advantage and somehow 'plots against itself' (Debord 1991: 84).

References

Arendt, H. (1999), *The Human Condition*, Chicago: University of Chicago Press.

Benjamin, W. (2003), *Selected Writings Volume 2: 1927–1934*, Cambridge, MA: Harvard University Press.

Benjamin, W. (2009), 'Franz Kafka, On the tenth anniversary of his death', in W. Benjamin, *One-Way Street and Other Writings*, London: Penguin.

Butler, J. (2011), 'Bodies in alliance and the politics of the street', *Transversal*, available at *http://eipcp.net/transversal/1011/butler/en/* (accessed 19 August 2013).

Chesterton, G. K. (2007), *The Man Who Was Thursday: A Nightmare*, London: Penguin.

Conrad, J. (2007), *The Secret Agent: A Simple Tale*, London: Penguin.

Dawkins, R. (1989), *The Selfish Gene*, Oxford: Oxford University Press.

Debord, G. (1991), *Comments on the Society of the Spectacle*, London: Verso.

Jameson, F. (1984), 'Postmodernism, or, the cultural logic of late capitalism', *New Left Review*, 146: July-August.

Hou, J. (2012), 'Making public, beyond public space', in Ron Shiffman et al. (eds), *Beyond Zuccotti Park*, Oakland: New Village Press.

Kafka, F. (1997) *The Castle*, New York: Penguin.

Lasn, K. (2012), *Meme Wars: The Creative Destruction of Neoclassical Economics*, New York: Seven Stories Press.

Lefebvre, H. (1995), *Introduction to Modernity*, London: Verso.

Marcuse, H. (1968) *One Dimensional Man: The Ideology of Industrial Society*, London: Sphere.

Pynchon, T. (1990), *Vineland*, London: Secker and Warburg.

Rushdie, S. (1991), 'Outside the whale', in Salmon Rushdie, *Imaginary Homelands: Essays and Criticism, 1981–1991*, London: Penguin.

Sartre, J.-P. (2004), *Critique of Dialectical Reason Volume One*, London: Verso.

Sartre, J.-P. (2006), *Critique of Dialectical Reason Volume Two*, London: Verso.

The Invisible Committee (2009), *The Coming Insurrection*, Los Angeles: Semiotext(e).

The New York Times (2012), 'Your ad here, on a fire truck? Broke cities sell naming rights', 24 June.

There Is No Alternative

Erik Swyngedouw and Japhy Wilson

> The realization of the world as global market, the undivided reign of great financial conglomerates, etc., all this is an indisputable reality and one that conforms, essentially, to Marx's analysis. The question is, 'where does politics fit in with all this? What kind of politics is really heterogeneous to what capital demands?' – that is today's question. (Alain Badiou, in Žižek 2000: 90)

Slavoj Žižek raised this question at the turn of the millennium, in the midst of a fierce debate with Ernesto Laclau over the nature and possibility of radical politics in the post-political age. Their confrontation embodied the political tensions that persist within the literature on post-politics, and which permeate this book. For his part, Laclau (2000a, 2000b) continues to espouse the radical democracy project that he set out with Chantal Mouffe in *Hegemony and Socialist Strategy* (1985). This project was explicitly post-Marxist and anti-communist, and was devoted to creating a political space for new social movements and new political identities not reducible to the industrial proletariat and its limited struggles. In his early work, Žižek was also committed to radical democracy, and he actively participated in the pro-democracy movements that contributed to the fall of communism in Eastern Europe. Yet these movements quickly disappeared after legitimating the transition from bureaucratic socialism to 'free market' capitalism via the brutal methods of economic shock therapy. The outcome was a new hegemony of transnational capital in alliance with IMF technocrats and members of the old nomenklatura, in which increasing poverty, inequality and unemployment were legitimated by appeal to economic necessity, combined with the mobilisation of right-wing nationalism, anti-immigrant xenophobia, and the rapid degeneration of democracy into a set of post-democratic rituals. This profoundly disillusioning sequence was reproduced in different forms in other parts of the world, and forced many of the so-called 'new Left' to reconsider their commitment to radical democracy. The abandonment of the critique of capitalism and its replacement with a pluralistic play of differences no longer seemed subversive or liberating, but now appeared as a crucial component in the ideological machinery of the post-political order. This crisis opened a new political space on the Left, occupied by Žižek, Badiou, Jodi Dean and others, who held themselves apart from both orthodox Marxism and radical democracy, and sought to reformulate an explicitly anti-capitalist project on the absent ground of post-foundational theory.

We broadly subscribe to this iteration of the post-foundational project. But we are also committed to an understanding of democracy as *dissensus*. As editors of this book, we have sought to challenge the post-political by exposing its operations, its vulnerabilities and its points of rupture, without pursuing an illusory consensus around the nature of post-politics itself, or around a particular vision of what politics is or should be. The disagreements within this book are constitutive of our rejection of what Rancière calls 'consensus democracy' (Rancière 1999: 95). Readers will make up their own minds concerning whose arguments are more persuasive, and whose visions are more compelling. Rather than attempting to reduce this vibrant cacophony to a set of agreed principles, we prefer to reflect on what the contributions tell *us* about the nature of the post-political, and about the possibility of radical politics today. In doing so, we make no claim to speak for anyone but ourselves.

The contributions to this volume reveal both the extent of post-politicisation, and the incompleteness and vulnerability of this process. Some of the chapters convey a claustrophobic sense of closure, even as they dissect the overtly political processes through which the post-political is constructed. This is the case, for example, in Raco's assessment of the intertwining of capital and governance in public-private partnerships, in which 'notions of democratic accountability through representation lose their salience', and in Kamat's analysis of participatory development, which is based on 'the premise that capitalism cannot be externally imposed but must grow in capillary form to become the dominant rationale of society'. This claustrophobia is also evident in Diken's identification of the post-political with 'a society that cannot imagine radical events'; in Blühdorn's assessment of the obsolescence of 'first-order emancipation'; and in Wilson's claim that post-politicisation extends beyond the symbolic register, to colonise the libidinal structures of enjoyment.

Yet in contrast to this impression of monolithic domination, many of the chapters in this volume emphasise the dysfunctionality of post-politics, and its repeated failure to achieve the closure it desires. Reynolds and Szerszynski show how each attempt to frame the issue of genetically modified organisms in the depoliticised terms of science, nature and technology has been subverted by the politicisation of these terms themselves. Van Puymbroeck and Oosterlynck reveal the tensions between multiculturalism and nationalist populism within broader structures of depoliticisation. Jaeger draws attention to the fractures and rifts that traverse the quintessentially post-political space of 'global governance'. And while conveying the one-dimensionality of post-politics, Diken and Wilson's respective chapters also emphasise the violence and anxiety that underlie this seemingly smooth surface.

Many other chapters focus on the continuity or re-emergence of the political within the post-political present. Yet just as the volume reveals the fragility of the post-political order, it also illustrates the limitations of the political forms that manifest within it. In our opinion, the examples of the reassertion of the political offered by Jaeger and Larner – of the BRICS and 'radical social enterprise' respectively – are better understood as instances of the post-political itself. Without wishing to dispute the capacity for such projects to achieve certain ameliorative improvements, they seem to us to exemplify precisely the kind of 'politics' that the post-political thrives upon – namely, a politics that is entirely consistent with, and even conducive to, the expanded reproduction of capital.

The Occupy protests and the 'politics of the squares' are seen by several of our contributors – and ourselves – as potentially heralding a return to a genuinely radical and transgressive form of political engagement. In his chapter, Merrifield celebrates the incandescence and innovation of these uprisings as a new form of militancy. Swyngedouw considers the modalities and configurations that may turn such proto-political events into a transformative political sequence, which revolve centrally around inventing new modes and practices of collective and sustained political mobilisation, and the assembling of a wide range of new political subjects who are not afraid to stage an egalitarian being-in-common, imagine a different commons, demand the impossible, perform the new and confront the violence that will inevitably intensify as those who insist on maintaining the present order realise that their days might be numbered. The chapters by Loftus and by Kaika and Karaliotas also fully endorse the uprisings, but raise serious concerns regarding their long-term transformative potential. This circumspection would seem to be justified by the rapid decline of these movements after their initial explosions, even as other uprisings continue to burst to the surface. For Dean, the cause of their inconstancy lies in the tendency of these movements to prioritise a post-political commitment to consensus democracy over an insistence that 'some positions are wrong and should be rejected, opposed, defeated. These positions are the ones that directly or indirectly reinforce capitalist domination'.

This brings us back to the question of democracy. The roots of the literature on post-politics are in the radical democracy project. But as we have seen, the commitment to pluralism and identity politics that characterises this project can be accused of contributing to the constitution of the post-political itself, to the extent that it naturalises capitalism as the unquestioned horizon of our political possibilities. Without attributing political positions to any of our contributors, it is clearly the case that some of them would be more sympathetic to radical democracy than to the resuscitation of the idea of communism proposed by Žižek, Badiou and others (Badiou 2010; Douzinas and Žižek 2010; Bosteels 2011; Dean 2012). After all, the original problem of depoliticisation addressed by post-foundational theory was not post-politics, but the economic determinism of orthodox Marxism that had stifled the intellectual freedom of the Left (Marchart 2007: 35–8; Stavrakakis 2010: 16–17).

A return to the horrors of what went by the name of communism in the twentieth century would certainly be anathema to democracy, however defined. Yet in the ongoing fallout from the global financial crisis, even the least radical of democrats would struggle to disagree with Badiou's assertion that democracy now means 'nothing more than an eager willingness to service the needs of the banks' (Badiou 2010: 98), or his claim that what passes for democracy would be more accurately named 'capitalo-parliamentarism' (Badiou 2010: 99). This is the political form that has congealed around global capitalism since the end of the cold war. Just as its artificiality was concealed by the vicarious thrill of the democratic revolutions of Eastern Europe at that time (Žižek 1993: 200), so it is reaffirmed today in the spectacle of the so-called 'Arab Spring', in which the West is once again invited to enjoy a narcissistic representation of its own imagined 'democracy' (even as its governments ensure that these revolutions are reduced to vanishing mediators between twin forms of militarised oligarchy – a gesture now repeated in the unconditional support for the 'new' oligarchic regime in Ukraine). Meanwhile the anti-austerity protests subside, a new round of fictitious growth begins, and the post-political order is reconfigured around a new set of signifiers – 'big society', 'philanthrocapitalism', 'gross domestic happiness', and so on. The master of these new signifiers is surely now 'Mandela', whose life embodied the post-political transition from the violent confrontation of opposed world-views to the consensual endorsement of global capitalism, and whose death was marked by world leaders gathering in South Africa to invoke the sanctity of 'democracy'. The ceremony was strangely reminiscent of Saramago's fable with which this book began. Like the election that Saramago describes, this spectacular celebration of the triumph of democracy was met with popular indifference. The stadium was half-empty, many of the leaders were booed, and in a wonderfully Brechtian twist, Obama's soaring oratory was translated into gibberish by the interpreter for the deaf, who solemnly performed meaningless sign language beside him. The interpreter later claimed to have had a schizophrenic episode, but as Žižek has pointed out, 'his performance translated an underlying truth' by interpreting the words of the world leaders as 'what they effectively were: nonsense' (Žižek 2013). As in Saramago's story, the failure of the event was attributed to bad weather, but outside the stadium the economic inequalities were deeper than they had been under apartheid, and around the world the pomp and ceremony on our television screens could only briefly paper over what the global crisis has once again revealed: 'that capitalism is nothing but banditry, and is irrational in its essence and devastating in its becoming' (Badiou 2010: 96).

In this context, any commitment to democracy that precludes the urgent transformation of the capitalist mode of production can only be regarded as part of the problem. This is not an endorsement of Blühdorn's dismissal of the emancipatory potential of democracy in his chapter, in which he suggests that 'many of the priority tasks for personal fulfilment and social well-being ... can, it seems, be addressed much more effectively in non-democratic ways'. Rather, it is an assertion of fidelity to Rancière's principle of equality as the negative ground of democracy itself (Rancière 2004), and as the basis for a reimagining of utopia, the loss of which is perhaps the most insidious and crippling dimension of the post-political condition:

> We have to overturn the old verdict that would have us believe we are now living in the age of the 'end of ideologies'. We can now see quite clearly that the only reality behind their so-called 'end' is 'Save the banks.' Nothing could be more important than rediscovering the passion for ideas, or than contrasting the world as it is with a general hypothesis, with the certainty that we can create a very different order of things. (Badiou 2010: 99–100)

The communist hypothesis

The communist hypothesis is that a different collective organization is practicable, one that will eliminate the inequality of wealth and even the division of labour. The private appropriation of massive fortunes and their transmission by inheritance will disappear. The existence of a coercive state, separate from civil society, will no longer appear a necessity: a long process of reorganization based on a free association of producers will see it withering away. (Badiou 2008: 35)

For Alain Badiou, the scandalous name for the 'general hypothesis' that combines with 'the certainty that we can create a very different order of things' is communism. The use of the signifier 'communism' will undoubtedly raise a few eyebrows here and there. The persistent criminalisation of the name and its erasure from much of the intellectual debate over the past two decades or so has been so effective that even its utterance meets with suspicion, distrust and perhaps, a slight sense of curiosity. In an age in which anything and everything can be discussed, the very idea of communism as a positive injunction seems to have been tabooed, censored and scripted out of both everyday and intellectual vocabularies. It is only tolerated in anodyne accounts of the obscure disaster of the twentieth-century institutionalised version of communism, or in romanticised Hollywood renditions of the life and work of communist heroes such as Che Guevara. The idea of communism has either been criminalised beyond rescue or, at best, relegated to the dustbin of failed utopias.

Nonetheless, as Badiou noted in 2009 in the foreword to a landmark conference on 'the idea of communism',

[t]he communist hypothesis remains the good one, I do not see any other. If we have to abandon this hypothesis, then it is no longer worth doing anything at all in the field of collective action. Without the horizon of communism, without this idea, there is nothing in the historical and political becoming of any interest to a philosopher. Let everyone bother about his own affairs, and let us stop talking about it . . . What is imposed on us as a task, even as a philosophical obligation, is to help a new mode of existence of the hypothesis to deploy itself. (Badiou 2009)

The central metaphors that sustain the idea of communism are, of course, equality, solidarity and democracy, held together by a fidelity to the conviction that these can be realised geographically through continuous and sustained political struggle. The realisation of the practices of these principles involves the self-organisation and self-management of the people, and will eliminate the state as the principle organiser of political life. The communist hypothesis, therefore, combines the negativity of 'resistance' (to any relation or practice that perverts the presumption of political equality) with the positivity that declares a fidelity to the immanent practicability of free and equal self-organising forms of socio-spatial organisation. 'Communism' names 'the complete process by which freedom is freed from its non-egalitarian submission to property' (Badiou 2013: 46).

The idea of communism retains indeed a subversive edge, and this in spite of the disastrous experiments that went under its name in the twentieth century, precisely because the name still instils a sense that a really different world cannot only be imagined but is practically possible. Being-in-common in egalitarian and free ways that permit the self-development of each and all retains a genuine mobilising potential. An urgent and demanding intellectual task is ahead to rethink the social practices, political forms of organisation and theoretical reflections that will again give the idea of communism a positive content.

The notion of communism is, of course, no more than an idea, and a scandalous and illegitimate one, in the present sequence of things. The question is whether new and different significations can be inscribed in its name, rather than endlessly repeating the refrain, correct as it may be, of the ethico-moral bankruptcy of the former socialist states. Neither a repetition of the standard critiques of the disasters of the past nor a simple invocation of utopian possibilities suggested by its name will do. Nothing less than a radical invention of the new is required, on the basis of a sustained critical engagement with what is already embryonically there.

For us, communism is intimately connected to the contingent presumption of equality of each and everyone as political beings. Moreover, the presumption of equality is predicated upon the recognition of difference, differentiation, agonism and dissensus, while refusing to inscribe one particular antagonism as the One that prevents the realisation of the presumption of equality. The presumption of equality is radically open and inclusive: everyone is invited in. A communist practice, therefore, is one that fights for the positive realisation of equality (with its historically-geographically contingent content that is always contested and contestable), and that strives for the universalisation of egalitarian practices from the basis of always historically and geographically situated inequalities.

The demand for political equality is a necessary, but insufficient, condition for thinking through the communist hypothesis. Political equality prefigures and permits the agonistic expression of differential claims, particularly with respect to the forms of social organisation and the distribution of collective wealth (or surplus). Political equality assumes the capacity of all and everyone to govern, and affirms the capability of self-organisation and collective decision-making. This opens up a second terrain, after equality, that sustains the communist hypothesis: namely the belief in the capacity of each and everyone (and not just of the state, its technocratic managers, or propertied and moneyed elites) to govern and to decide the principles of appropriation and distribution of wealth and revenue. The communist hypothesis, therefore, prefigures the end of the coercive state and its replacement by forms of self-organisation and management. Thinking through the relations between emancipatory struggles and the transformation of governing the commons is indeed an urgent task. In particular, the articulation between different interlocking geographical scales of regulation, self-management and organisation on the one hand and their relation to changing state forms on the other remains a thorny issue.

The historical-geographical terrain of the communist hypothesis is of course the commons. The very name of communism not only invokes an egalitarian 'being-in-common' of all qua multiple and multitude, but also refers to the commons that is the earth, the world and, therefore, life itself. This latter sense of the commons refers fundamentally to the collectively transformed socio-ecological conditions and their associated socio-physical relations, such as water, air, carbon dioxide, knowledge and intellect, information, affective labours, the integrity of the body, biodiversity regimes, resources, urban space, and the like. The commons of socio-ecological arrangements and their conditions of rights of use, transformation, access and distribution, the modalities of their spatial organisation, and the configuration, access, ownership and distribution of collective knowledge/information are now the key domains around which the communist hypothesis has to be thought and developed. In particular, it raises the question of property and property relations with respect to common resources like those listed above. Framing the political argument around the commons as one between public versus private ownership, we would argue, misses the point if the public sphere is defined as or restricted to the domain of the state. As demonstrated throughout this collection, the state has become (and arguably has always been) just another instance of the private alongside private capital and private individuals, in relation to the commons, understood as the bio-political conditions of existence. The private reason embodied in both state and capital needs to be replaced by public reason articulated around the commons and the modalities of egalitarian being-in-common. The communist hypothesis is indeed structured around the commons as the 'property' of each and everyone under common stewardship. Communism is therefore a struggle against both the privatism of the state and that of capital – ultimately structured around property relations that fragment, privatise and monopolise the commons – and for the production of collective and public institutions for the democratic management of the commons, thereby turning the commons into a new use value. The communist idea concerns the transformation of the commons from private to collective and the re-affirmation of the capacity of all qua collective – the collective or communist intelligence – to govern the city, the commons in-common.

In sum, the communist hypothesis is articulated around several elements. First, it affirms the presupposition of equality and the political capacity of each and everyone. Second, the communist hypothesis contains a historical invariant – it stands for the eternal return of the heroic-tragic historical-geographies of emancipatory struggles on the one hand and the eternally returning desire/struggle for emancipation, freedom and equality on the other. Third, the communist hypothesis entails an utterly voluntaristic (subjective) moment that is the will of the individual to join up in common with others to realise politically the idea of communism (Hallward 2009). The communist idea is nothing without the will do something new, without the will to become political subject. Fourth, the communist hypothesis insists on the continuous transformation of this singularity of the egalitarian will and movement to the universality of being-in-common as part of a commons. Fifth, the realisation of the communist hypothesis demands the collective control over the commons qua common use values (rather than common property) and the gradual disappearance of the state as we know it today.

What is left to think?

The idea of communism may appear as little more than a mirage on the political horizon of the contemporary Left. Yet even as it has been pushed to the boundaries of our fantasy space, it continues to haunt the nightmares of global capital. As we write this, the second anniversary of Occupy Wall Street has recently passed. In the absence of any meaningful resurgence of the movement, Wall Street has been able to feign a smug indifference. When asked about the anniversary on CNN, for example, the CEO of Goldman Sachs replied, 'I must have missed it. I didn't know this was such a big anniversary. I must send flowers' (Lloyd Blankfein, in Zakaria 2013). Both interviewer and audience responded with sycophantic laughter. Yet when Occupy first exploded, the financial oligarchy had been far less self-assured. Indeed, despite the failure of the Occupy movement to frame its position in terms of communism or even anti-capitalism, the business press was suddenly filled with paranoid defences of capitalism and anxious discussions of the dangers of Marx and socialism. In January 2012, for example, the *Financial Times* launched a series entitled 'Capitalism in crisis', in which the representatives of global capital closed ranks to protect the system. They loudly insisted that 'Capitalism works far better than any other system' (Lawson 2012), and hurried to remind us of 'how profoundly communism was discredited by the collapse of the Soviet system' (Rachman 2012). Yet they could not help noting that 'opinion polls show public support for ... capitalism plumbing new depths' (*Financial Times* 2012), and could not conceal their concern that the ongoing economic crisis 'might yet produce the conditions for the revival of an anti-capitalist movement' (Rachman 2012). As we saw in the Introduction to this volume, Occupy Wall Street and Tahrir Square were enough to afflict the World Economic Forum with a paralysing fear that these 'seeds of dystopia' might let a thousand flowers bloom. Their choice of metaphor is significant here. In contrast to cold war representations of communism as a foreign evil empire, or as a shadowy ideology being insidiously promulgated by malevolent external forces, 'seeds of dystopia' suggests the immanent presence of a repressed antagonism that threatens to explode from within the structures of actually existing capitalism itself. The spectre of communism that torments today's global elites is therefore the same one that haunted Europe in 1848: the real possibility of communism now.

But the communism that haunts the contemporary Left is not a real possibility. It is a ghost – the spectre of a socialism that once really existed, of a communism that is dead. The idea of communism has been poisoned by the failure of its twentieth-century manifestation, a condition that, towards the end of the previous century, left the Left in a state of utter paralysis, both politically and intellectually. This is not to say that the obscure disaster of twentieth-century communism does not require urgent and critical attention. On the contrary, this is one of the tasks ahead, one that has to be undertaken in light of the communist hypothesis. In this context, we should resist the neurotic compulsion to act. The Left flees from the ghosts of communism past, and hurls itself into its obsessive commitments to 'do something', to 'act' in the names of humanity, cosmopolitanism, anti-globalisation, the environment, sustainability, climate change, social justice or any of the other empty signifiers that have become the stand-ins to cover up for the absence of emancipatory egalibertarian political fantasies. The failure of such obsessive activism is now clearly visible. Humanitarianism is hailed to legitimise military intervention and imperial war; the environment becomes a new terrain of capitalist accumulation and serves ideologically as a 'new opium for the masses' (Swyngedouw 2010); cosmopolitanism is cherished as the cultural condition of a globalised capitalism; and many of the proliferating manifestations of resistance and revolt have become predictable, albeit spectacular, short-lived Bakhtinian carnivals whose geographical staging is carefully choreographed by the state.

The relationship between our critical theories and the political as egalitarian-emancipatory process has to be thought again. It is undoubtedly the case that the three key markers of twentieth-century communist politics – state, party and proletariat – require radical reworking. We would insist that neither the state nor the party are any longer of use to think the communist hypothesis. This should not be read as an invitation to ditch forms of institutional and political organisation. On the contrary, it calls for a new beginning in terms of thinking through what institutional forms are required at what scale and what forms of political organisation are adequate to achieve this. The notion of the proletariat as a political subject equally needs a radical overhaul. In a context of mass dispossession and privatisation of the commons, the political fault lines become drawn around this axis, around which all manner of new political (proletarian) subjectivities arise. The name of the 'proletarian' stands, of course, for the political subject who, through egalibertarian struggle, aims to take control again of life and its conditions of possibility.

Communism as a hypothesis and political practice is much older than the twentieth century and will, in one guise or the other, continue in the future, albeit in different forms and perhaps with a different name. Excavating the historical-geographical variations and imaginations of the communist invariant requires re-examining and re-evaluation. Communism as an idea manifests itself each time people come together in common, not only to demand equality, to demand their place within the edifice of state and society, but also to stage their capacity for self-organisation and self-management, thereby revolutionising the very parameters of state and government. There are plenty of communist political sequences that have punctuated history. Consider, for example, the rebellion of the 'ochlos' (the rabble), demanding their rightful place as part of the 'demos' in the governing of the polis in ancient Athens; or the French revolutionaries who declared equality and freedom for all in the new revolutionary constitution of 1789. The most emblematic example is undoubtedly the 1870 Paris Commune – the first moment the proletariat showed, to the horror of the bourgeoisie, its capacity to self-organise and self-govern. This was later followed by the early Soviets, and the Shanghai commune of 1966, which was brutally smashed by the forces of the Chinese state.

The key task, therefore, is to stop and think, to think communism again, to think through the communist hypothesis and its meaning for a twenty-first-century emancipatory, free and egalitarian politics.

While the pessimism of the intellect over the past few decades usurped the will for radical change, the realisation of the communist hypothesis requires a new courage of the intellect to break down barriers and taboos, to dare to think universalising emancipatory and democratic politics again, to trust the demands formulated by those who have no voice, who have no part, to trust the will for change and to embrace the task of testing radically the truth of the communist hypothesis; a truth that can only be established through a new emancipatory political sequence.

The communist hypothesis forces itself onto the terrain of the political through the process of subjectivation, a coming into being through voluntarist actions, procedures and performances, of collective embodiments of fidelity to the presumption of equality and freedom. It is a fidelity to the practical possibility of communism, but without ultimate guarantee in history, geography, the party or the state. Communism is an idea without ultimate ground, but with extraordinary emancipatory potential. The proletarian (or revolutionary) subjects are those who assemble together, not only to demand freedom and equality but to take it, to carve out, occupy, organise the spaces for the enactment of this politics, already experimented with in localised practices of a wide range of militant groups. The historical-geographical invariant of the communist hypothesis requires serious intellectual engagement in order to tease out what an equal, free and self-organising being-in-common for the twenty-first century might be all about. This is a formidable task to be asked of the communist (common) intellect. It will require serious theoretical reconceptualisation, a restoration of trust in our theories, a courageous engagement with painful histories and, above all, abandoning the fear of failing again. The fear of failing has become so overwhelming that fear of real change is all that is left; resistance is as far as our horizons reach – transformation, it seems, can no longer be thought, let alone practised. The injunction scripted by the communist hypothesis is one that urges communist intellectuals to muster the courage to confront the risk of failing again. The choice we face is a simple one. In fact, it is no choice at all. We either indulge the fantasy that what exists can be perpetuated, and seek to improve it to the best of our humanitarian abilities, or we begin to seriously think through the possibilities of re-imagining and realising the communist hypothesis for the twenty-first century. Ironically, it is the first of these options that must be dismissed as dangerously 'utopian', in the sense that our catastrophe cannot be meaningfully addressed within the parameters of global capitalism. This conclusion can be posed as a question to our enemies: why do you keep saying there is no alternative, when there really is no alternative?

References

Badiou, A. (2008), 'The communist hypothesis', *New Left Review*, 49, pp. 29–42.

Badiou, A. (2009), 'Foreword', conference 'On the idea of communism', Birkbeck College, University of London, 13–15 March.

Badiou, A. (2010), *The Communist Hypothesis*, London: Verso.

Badiou, A. (2013), 'Our contemporary impotence', *Radical Philosophy*, 181: pp. 43–7.

Bosteels, B. (2011), *The Actuality of Communism*, London: Verso.

Dean, J. (2012), *The Communist Horizon*, London: Verso.

Douzinas, C., and S. Žižek (2010), *The Idea of Communism*, London: Verso.

Financial Times (2012), '*Financial Times* launches Capitalism in Crisis series', editorial, 9 January.

Hallward, P. (2009), 'The will of the people – notes towards a dialectical voluntarism', *Radical Philosophy*, 155, pp. 17–29.

Laclau, E. (2000a), 'Structure, history and the political', in J. Butler, E. Laclau and S. Žižek (eds), *Contingency, Hegemony, Universality: Contemporary Dialogues on the Left*, London: Verso, pp. 182–212.

Laclau, E. (2000b), 'Constructing universality', in J. Butler, E. Laclau and S. Žižek (eds), *Contingency, Hegemony, Universality: Contemporary Dialogues on the Left*, London: Verso, pp. 281–307.

Laclau, E., and C. Mouffe (1985), *Hegemony and Socialist Strategy: Towards a Radical Democratic Politics*, London: Verso.

Lawson, N. (2012), 'Forget Fred and focus on the real banking scandal', *Financial Times*, 6 February.

Marchart, O. (2007), *Post-Foundational Political Thought: Political Difference in Nancy, Lefort, Badiou and Laclau*, Edinburgh: Edinburgh University Press.

Rachman, G. (2012), 'Why I'm feeling strangely Austrian', *Financial Times*, 10 January.

Rancière, J. (1999), *Disagreement: Politics and Philosophy*, Minneapolis: University of Minnesota Press.

Rancière, J. (2004), 'Introducing disagreement', *Angelaki, Journal of Theoretical Humanities*, 9: 3, pp. 3–9.

Stavrakakis, Y. (2010), 'On acts, pure and impure', *International Journal of Žižek Studies*, 4: 2, pp. 1–35.

Swyngedouw, E. (2010), 'The trouble with nature: Ecology as the new opium for the masses', in P. Healey and J. Hillier (eds), *Conceptual Challenges for Planning Theory*, Aldershot: Ashgate, pp. 299–320.

Zakaria, F. (2013) 'GPS: Polarization nation; understanding China's foreign policy; interview with Lloyd Blankfein', available at *http://tran scripts.cnn.com/TRANSCRIPTS/1310/13/fzgps.01.html* (accessed 24 October 2013).

Žižek, S. (1993), *Tarrying with the Negative: Kant, Hegel, and the Critique of Ideology*, Durham: Duke University Press.

Žižek, S. (2000), 'Class struggle or postmodernism? Yes, please!', in J. Butler, E. Laclau and S. Žižek (eds), *Contingency, Hegemony, Universality: Contemporary Dialogues on the Left*, London: Verso, pp. 90–135.

Žižek, S. (2013), 'The "fake" Mandela memorial interpreter said it all', *The Guardian*, 16 December.

Index

Abensour, Michael, 180
activists/activism 58, 63, 193; *see also*
    Friends of the Earth; Greenpeace;
    social movements
Afghanistan, 135
Africa
    development, 120
    Millennium Villages, 115–16, 120
    philanthrocapitalism, 116, 119
    philanthropy, 111
    poverty, 118
    'sexual networking', 117–18
Agamben, G., 126, 132, 134, 138, 139,
    142, 143
agonism, 50, 52, 58, 91, 92
agriculture
    European Union, 60
    GMO, 53, 54, 55–60
    India, 79–80
Ahmed, S., 102
AIDS *see* HIV/AIDS
Albertsen, N., 140
alienation, 131, 141, 155
Althusser, Louis, 230, 231, 234
anarchism, 199
Anderson, Perry, 81
anger, 249; *see also* violence
antagonism
    and agonism, 91, 92
    and class, 112
    and cultural diversity, 101, 102–3
    to democracy, 3, 79, 81, 270
    and market choice, 48
    Mouffe and, 12, 14, 15, 91, 92, 210
    post-political, 130–8
    replacement of, 70, 90
    and space, 246
    and violence, 92

Žižek and, 14, 16, 266
    see also dissensus
Apocalypse Now (film), 135
apocalypticism, 130–3
Arab Spring, 4, 10, 136, 302, 308
archi-politics, 96, 97–8, 99, 102, 120
Archibugi, Daniele, 210
Arendt, Hannah, 50; *The Human*
    Condition, 289
Aristotle
    Politics, 139–40
    and power, 136
Athens
    ancient, 309
    Olympic Games (2004), 248
    Syntagma Squares, 268–9; mass
        protests, 247–50, 252–6; Open
        Popular Assembly Forum, 253
austerity
    and class, 4
    and discontent, 172, 241
    and elites, 9
    in Greece, 248, 255
    International Monetary Fund and,
        8–9
    and privatisation, 27
Australia: residential estates (Sydney),
    197

Badiou, Alain
    Bosteels on, 231
    on capitalism, 303
    and communist hypothesis, 90–1,
        303–4
    on democracy, 128–9, 302
    on dictatorship, 180
    and 'Idea', 128, 303
    on inequalities, 178–9

Badiou, Alain (*cont.*)
  on the inexistent, 171
  and insurrectional movements,
    178–80
  on love, 122
  and politics, 91, 93, 126, 173–4, 299,
    300
  and society, 94
  and truth, 182
  on violence, 174–5
Balibar, Étienne, 231, 237
Bangladesh, 75
banks
  bail-outs, 8
  legislation (United States), 271
  and self-help groups, 75, 78
  World Bank, 30, 34, 68, 71, 72, 74
bans, 128
Barnett, Michael, 219
Baudelaire, Charles, 292
Baudrillard, J., 135
Bauman, Zygmunt, 128, 154
Beck, Ulrich, 86, 210
Benjamin, Walter, 140–1, 142–3,
    279–80, 292
Berlin Wall, 7
Big Society, 97–8, 302
billionaires, 115; see also 'the rich'
biodiversity, 58
biopolitics, 215
biotechnology, agricultural see GMO
Bishop, Matthew and Green, Michael:
    *Philanthrocapitalism: How the
    Rich Can Save the World and Why
    We Should Let Them*, 109–10, 111,
    112, 114, 115, 121
'black blocs', 290
Blair, Tony, 29, 30, 136
Blankfein, Lloyd, 307
bodies: and languages, 128, 129
Boedeltje, M., 36
Bond, S., 102
Bono, 111, 117, 120
Bosteels, Bruno
    The Actuality of Communism, 5–6
    on leftism, 230–1
    on Rancière, 96
Bouazizi, Mohamed, 169
Boucher, G., 92–3
Braithwaite, J., 31
Brazil, 169; see also BRICS
BRICS (Brazil, Russia, India, China,
    South Africa), 208, 212
  aims of, 215–16
  circulations within, 215, 216
  and democracy, 221, 224–5

  and disagreement, 221
  and economy, 216
  and equality, 221
  and financial institutions, 223
  and governance, 216, 217
  and identity, 215, 223
  and international order, 220
  and multipolarity, 213–17
  and neoliberalism, 216
  and police, 219–20
  and politics, 220–1, 223
  and responsibility, 223
  and subjectivation, 222, 223
Brown, Wendy, 67, 68, 82, 264, 267
Buffet, Warren, 115
Butler, Judith, 236
  'Bodies in alliance and the politics of
    the street', 289

Cairo: Tahrir Square, 308
Cameron, David, 42
capitalism
  and anti-capitalism, 82
  Badiou on, 303
  and Christianity, 140
  communicative, 262–3, 267
  and communism, 16
  and cosmopolitanism, 308
  defence of, 308
  and environment, 308
  'free market', 299
  future of, 141
  and GM food, 48
  global, 8, 28, 89, 90
  and guilt, 140–1
  Kafka and, 283
  and the Left, 266–7, 276
  Marx and, 141–2, 285, 288, 291–2
  and microcredit, 75–6, 77
  and neoliberalism, 149, 262
  New Institutional Economics and, 73
  Occupy and, 275–6
  and philanthrocapitalism, 113
  and philanthropy, 122
  and power, 285–6
  and public sphere, 192
  and radical social movements, 194
  and 'the state', 28
  and sustainability, 25
  Third World, 73
  and value, 141
  Weber on, 140
  see also philanthrocapitalism
capitalo-parliamentarism, 302
caste: India, 78
Castells, Manuel, 269

Chambers, Ray, 111
Chambers, Samuel, 91
charity, 114, 122; *see also*
    philanthrocapitalism; philanthropy
Chesterton, G. K.: *The Man Who Was*
    Thursday, 291
children
    Africa: sick, 116
    India: effect of suicide on, 80
    mirror-stage of development, 119
China
    and responsibility, 223
    Shanghai commune (1966), 309
    see also BRICS
Christianity, 133, 140; *see also*
    protestant ethic
cities
    alternative, 186
    insurgencies in, 169–70
citizens
    as consumers, 6, 29, 48–9
    and democracy, 1, 2, 3, 40–1, 42,
        43–4, 76–7, 93, 161
    and sustainability planning, 27, 37
civic republicanism, 102
civil unrest, 4; *see also* protest
    movements; revolts; revolutions
Clarke, David B., 121
class
    and antagonism, 112
    and austerity, 4
    and hegemony, 234
    Marx on, 183
    and multiculturalism, 102–3
    Occupy Wall Street and, 12, 275
    and philanthrocapitalism, 112
    and post-politics, 112
    and protest, 248
    and self-help groups, 78
    subaltern groups, 231, 232
    and sustainability, 41
    working, 275, 276; *see also*
      proletariat
Žižek and, 14
climate change, 149
Clinton, Bill, 110, 114, 115
closure, 8, 11, 151, 182, 246, 254, 300,
    301
Collier, S., 193–4
commons, 90, 306
    creative, 189
    management of, 172–3, 179, 184,
      306–7
communism
    Badiou on, 122–3
    Bosteels on, 5–6

and capitalism, 16
and commons, 306–7
defeat of, 7, 8, 51, 299
and egalitarianism, 275
future of, 309
hypothesis of, 90–1, 303–7, 307–10
the Left and, 267, 308
libertarian, 263
Occupy movements as, 275
Žižek on, 15–16
see also Marx, Karl: *Communist*
    Manifesto; Marxism
communities, 104n3, 190, 202
competition, 38, 40
Conrad, Joseph: *The Secret Agent*, 291
consensus, 86
    and climate change, 149
    and democracy, 13, 79, 175–6, 271–3
    and development, 69
    and exclusion, 264
    and GM, 49
    normative, 79
    and participatory governance, 193
    and post-politics, 50–1, 127
    and self-help groups, 77, 79
    and sustainability, 36
    Washington Consensus, 74
    see also dissensus
consumers
    and choice, 263
    and GM, 48, 60, 61
continuous assessment, 129
contractualism, 33, 190
Corliss, Richard, 135
Cornips, J., 36
corporations, 30–1, 33
corruption: Greece, 251
cosmopolitanism
    and capitalism, 308
    European Union and, 214
    and governmentality, 217
    Mouffe and, 208, 210–12
    versus multipolarity, 209–13
counter-revolutions, 128, 131; *see also*
    revolutions
Cowley, J., 41
Crick, Francis, 54
critical distance, 281
Croce, Benedetto, 237
Crouch, C., 26, 30
cultural diversity, 100–3

DNA, 54, 55
Davies, J., 151
Dawkins, Richard: *The Selfish Gene*,
    296

Dean, Jodi, 121, 122, 203, 300
Dean, Mitchell, 214
Debord, Guy, 286, 297n2
  *Comments on the Society of the
    Spectacle*, 284–5
debt, 27, 146, 262, 265, 276
  and employment, 293
  and guilt, 140–1
  and PFI, 33, 36
  rural, 79–80
Deleuze, G., 141
Deloitte, 34
democracy
  ancient Athens, 309
  antagonism to, 3, 79, 81, 270
  Badiou on, 128–9, 302
  BRICS and, 221, 224–5
  citizens and, 1, 2, 3, 40–1, 42, 43–4,
    161; India, 76–7, 79
  and consensus, 13, 79, 176, 271–3
  and decision-making, 43–4
  democratic deficits, 88–9
  democratic hegemony, 261
  and development, 68
  direct, 253, 254
  as dissensus, 300
  and economy, 8–9, 37
  and emancipation, 156, 157, 160,
    163, 181
  and equality, 173
  erosion of, 4, 5, 28–9
  and experts, 31, 175
  Farm Scale Evaluations and, 58
  global, 2–3
  the Left and, 300
  liberal, 137
  and localism, 37
  and Marxism, 158
  Mouffe and, 11–12
  and neoliberalism, 67–8, 157–8
  and occupation, 269
  and the political, 174
  and political ecology, 159–60
  'radicalization of', 91–2
  Rancière on, 12, 170–1, 224, 300
  representative, 32
  and revolutions, 267–8
  Saramago on, 1–2, 303
  and science, 50
  Swyngedouw and, 92, 158
  United States, 267
  and unsustainability, 159–60
  Žižek and, 299
  see also post-democracy
democratisation, 171–2, 183–4
dependency, 27, 30, 39–40, 43, 76, 276

depoliticisation
  of conflicts, 130
  and cultural diversity, 100–3
  dynamics of, 5
  and identity, 155
  and Marxism, 302
  matrix of, 97–100; archi-politics, 96,
    97–8, 99, 102, 120; meta-politics,
    98, 99, 100, 102–3; para-politics,
    98, 99, 102; ultra-politics, 98, 99
  Rancière on, 95, 96–7
  and unsustainability, 162
Deranty, J. P., 94
Derrida, J., 132, 133–4, 235
despotism, 136–7
development
  Africa, 120
  and consensus, 69
  definition of, 38
  depoliticisation of, 71
  India, 68, 69, 70, 77
  and neoliberalism, 71
  New Institutional Economics and,
    73–4
  and philanthrocapitalism, 119
  social organisations *see* United
    Kingdom: Coexist project
  sustainable, 25, 30, 39, 68
devolution: United Kingdom, 37, 42
dictatorship, 180
Dikeç, M., 245
Diken, Bülent, 89, 98–9
Dillon, M., 132
disadvantage, 75–7, 102
disagreement, 5, 89, 91, 149, 176, 182,
    185, 192, 272
  Rancière on, 94, 96, 97, 127, 175,
    220, 221
  see also dissent
disavowal, 13, 14, 95, 96–7, 99–103,
    113, 118, 121, 130, 137, 176, 270
disease, 109, 114, 115, 117, 118
dissensus, 15, 50, 220, 300; *see also*
    antagonism; consensus
dissent
  archetypes of, 290–5, 296, 297;
    double agents, 291; Great Escapers,
    293–4; Great Refusers, 294–5;
    Maggots in the Apple, 292–3;
    secret agents, 290–1
  Greece, 249
  and revolts, 295–6
  spaces of, 247
  see also protest movements
division
  figures of, 222

ideological, 14, 148
international development, 69
organisational, 215
political difference, 12, 15, 89, 175, 209, 217, 220, 265, 269, 270, 271–2, 273–6
scientific, 61, 62
social, 99
The Doors, 281
Dowling, R., 197
Doyle, S., 135
dystopias, 4–5; *see also* utopias

EFSA *see* European Food Safety Authority
Eagleton, Terry, 122
eco-politics, 147
neo-liberal, 151
neo-Marxists and, 152–3, 159
Swyngedouw and, 149–51, 152
eco-villages, 96
ecology *see* political ecology
economics
New Institutional Economics, 72–4, 81–2
United States, 266
economies
Aristotle on, 139
BRICS, 216
and competition, 40
and democratic accountability, 8–9, 37, 41
and governmentality, 215
The Economist, 8
Edkins, A., 33
education: Indian self-help groups, 78, 79
égaliberté, 81, 174, 177, 178, 183, 184, 186, 256, 309
Egypt, 172, 308; *see also* Arab Spring
elections, 1, 2, 6, 9, 32, 263
elites
and austerity, 9
and democracy, 2
fear of communism, 308
private sector, 32
and socialism, 185
and sustainability, 26
see also experts
emancipation
and democracy, 156, 157, 160, 163, 181
and identity, 155
Engels, F., 291
English Nature, 58
enjoyment *see jouissance*

entrepreneurialism, 120, 199
environment
and capitalism, 308
GMO and, 51, 53, 55, 56, 58
policies, 147
equality
BRICS and, 221
concept of, 129
and democracy, 173
presumption of, 305
Rancière and, 12, 13, 221, 222
spatial, 40, 182, 255, 256
and unsustainability, 159, 160–1
eschatology, 131
ethnic minorities *see* cultural diversity; foreigners; multiculturalism
EuroCommerce, 57
Europe: identity of, 211
European Food Safety Authority (EFSA), 61
European Union
and austerity, 27
and disagreement, 221
global governance programme, 208
and GMO, 48, 49, 55–6; Conference on GM-Free Regions (2005), 62, 63; Deliberate Release Directive (1990), 55, 57–8, 59, 61
and international relations, 219
the Left's challenge to, 261
Lisbon Treaty, Common Foreign and Security Policy (CFSP), 213, 214
and police, 219
political condition of, 262
Private Finance Initiative, 34
experts, 14, 193
and austerity, 4
and democracy, 31, 175
dependence on, 30, 43
and global economy, 8
and growth planning, 39
and modernisation, 26
and policy, 30
and political contradictions, 6
and Private Finance Initiative, 34
and regulatory capture, 30
and sustainable development, 30

Facebook, 248
Farm Scale Evaluations (FSEs), 58
fascism, 121
feminism, 194, 196, 197
Ferguson, George, 199
Ferguson, James, 197
Feuerbach, L., 141
financial crisis (2008), 200

Financial Times, 9, 307–8
Finnemore, Martha, 219
Fontana, B., 237
food, genetically modified *see* GMO
foreclosure
  and consensus, 176
  and opposition, 43, 50, 79, 87, 89,
    100, 102, 181, 264, 276
  philanthrocapitalism and, 112
  Žižek and, 14–15, 113, 122, 130
foreigners, 99, 251; *see also*
    multiculturalism
Foucault, Michel
  on circulation, 215
  and governmentality, 129, 212, 213,
    216
  on the people, 171
  and politics, 217, 235
  and power, 88
  Rancière and, 89, 93–4
France
  banks, 8
  communes, 270, 309
fraternity, 74, 128, 129
free will, 138
freedom, 129, 132
Friends of the Earth, 58
Fukuyama, Francis, 7, 51, 133, 134, 262
fundamentalism, Islamic, 130

Gabriel Resources (mining company),
    169
García Linerá, Álvaro, 231
Gates, Bill, 109, 110, 114, 116, 117, 121
Gates Foundation, 71, 115
gender *see* women
genetically modified organisms/GMO,
    48, 49, 62–3
  controversy of, 51, 54–5, 56
  crops, 53, 54, 55–60; markets, 59;
    opposition to, 56–7, 58
  and health, 53, 55, 56, 57–8
  labelling of, 57, 59, 60, 61
  as a metonym, 53–5
  as regulatory objects, 56, 57, 59
  and risk, 61
Giddens, Anthony, 28, 29, 30, 262
globalisation
  BRICS and, 216
  GM crops and, 53
  Mouffe and, 14
  neoliberal model of, 12
glory, 139, 142
God
  Agamben on, 143
  in Christian theology, 138

  and post-politics, 142–3
  Taubes's concept of, 131
Goodchild, P., 141
governance
  BRICS and, 216, 217
  'democratic', 2, 30, 32
  diffusion of, 193
  good, 5, 25, 30–1, 34, 37, 70
  and government, 33
  New Institutional Economics view
    of, 73
  participatory, 72–3
  and power, 39–40
  'soft spaces' of, 77
  stakeholder model of, 73
  and sustainability, 151
  Third Way, 28
government
  'arts of', 197
  Dean on, 214
  and democracy, 1–2
  economic, 216
  in the 'Global South', 69
  and governance, 33
governmentality, 137
  and cosmopolitanism, 217
  European Union and, 213, 214
  Foucault on, 129, 212, 213, 216
  theological roots of, 138
Gramsci, Antonio
  and linguistics, 234, 235
  on Machiavelli, 237
  Marx's influence on, 233
  Mouffe on, 233–6, 238
  philosophy of praxis, 232–3, 236,
    239, 241
  and the political, 237, 238, 239–40
  The Prison Notebooks, 229, 231–2,
    234, 237, 238, 239, 240
  theory of hegemony, 232, 234, 238
grant coalitions, 32
Gray, John, 43
'The Great Escape' (film), 293–4
Greece
  austerity, 248, 255
  collectives, 252–3
  effects of global economic crisis, 9
  'Greek Mothers', 251–2
  Indignant Squares, 244, 246, 247,
    248–55
  Indignants, 244, 247, 249, 250, 252,
    253, 254
  politics of no politics, 264, 269
  racism, 251–2
  socio-spatial practices, 183
  see also Athens

Green, Michael *see* Bishop, Matthew and Green, Michael
Greenpeace, 56–7, 58
Grosrichard, A., 137
growth
  'growth machines', 32
  and localism, 40–1
and markets, 74
  of public sector, 41
  and sustainable development, 38–9, 68, 119–20, 159, 215–16, 302
Guattari. F., 141

HIV/AIDS, 117
Habermas, Jürgen, 50, 210, 264
Hall, J. R., 130–1
Hall, Stuart, 196
Hallward, Peter, 94, 175
happiness, 3, 302; *see also jouissance*
Hardt, Michael and Negri, Antonio
  Declaration, 270
  Empire, 194
health: GMO and, 53, 55, 56, 57–8; *see also* disease
hegemony
  bourgeois, 239
  democratic, 261
  Gramsci's theory of, 232, 234, 238
  Hegemony and Socialist Strategy (Laclau and Mouffe), 235–6, 238
Heidegger, Martin, 10
Held, David, 210
herbicides, 58
history
  absolute humanism of, 232, 233
  BRICS perspective of, 222
  'end of', 7–8, 48, 51, 54, 62, 133, 134, 169–70
  historical materialism, 235
  and violence, 174–5
Hobsbawm, Eric, 48, 50
Hou, Jeffrey, 287–8
humanitarianism, 308
The Hurt Locker (film), 134–5

IMF *see* International Monetary Fund
'Idea', 128, 180, 183
identities
  bourgeois-modernist tradition of, 154
  BRICS and, 223
  and depoliticisation, 155
  and emancipation, 155
  Gramsci and, 241
  and markets, 154
  and political ecology, 155–6

and self-help groups, 81
  and subjectivity, 156–7, 159
ideologies, 109, 113, 234
the Imaginary, 7
immigrants: Greece, 251
Inderst, G., 34
India
  agriculture, 79–80
  NGOs, 70
  neoliberalism, 67, 68
  self-help groups, 75, 76, 77–81; caste, 78; common interest, 77; rural, 76, 77–8, 80
  suicide, 79–80
  see also BRICS
Indignados, 10, 147, 171, 174, 182
inequalities
  Badiou on, 178–9
  and globalisation, 112
  and meta-politics, 98, 99, 100
  and political difference, 93
  and the post-political, 87
  and sustainability planning, 42
infrastructures, 33, 34
Inglehart, R., 155
insurrectional movements, 3, 4, 9–10, 174, 178–81; *see also* activists/ activism
International Monetary Fund (IMF), 8–9, 53, 71, 72, 74
invisibility, 289–90
The Invisible Committee, 169; *The Coming Insurrection*, 289
Islamic fundamentalism, 130
Istanbul: Taksim Square revolt, 169, 172
Italy: global economic crisis, 9, 229, 262

Jackson, Michael, 281
Jackson, T., 25
Jameson, Fredric
  'Future City', 8
  'Postmodernism, or, the cultural logic of late capitalism', 281
Jolie, Angelina, 111, 115–16
Jones, M., 40
jouissance (enjoyment)
  and philanthrocapitalism, 114–17, 118–19, 122
  Žižek and, 111, 113, 116–17, 121

KPMG, 39
Kafka, Franz, 116, 279–80
  The Castle, 283–4, 285, 288
  The Trial, 283, 284
Kakogianni, M., 185

Kantola, J., 197
Keil, Roger, 198
Kenya: Millennium Village, 115–16
Keynesianism, 40
Kingfisher, Catherine, 196
Kioupkiolis, A., 254, 255
knowledge economy, 191–2
Kohn, Margaret, 245–6
Krugman, Paul, 74

Lacan, Jacques
    childhood development, 119
    and *jouissance*, 116
    and reality, 7, 10
    and society, 94
Laclau, Ernesto
    and economy, 237
    and Gramsci, 233–4
    Hegemony and Socialist Strategy,
        235–6, 238, 299
    and post-politics, 14
    and 'radicalization of' society, 91–2
    Žižek and, 236–7
Lacoue-Labarthe, Philippe, 5
land ownership: United Kingdom, 41
languages: and bodies, 128, 129
Lasn, Kalle: *Meme Wars*, 297n2
Latour, Bruno, 48, 50, 51, 54, 55, 62
law: and conflict, 265
Lawson, Nigel, 308
Leal, Pablo Alejandro, 72
Lefebvre, Henri, 186, 256; *Introduction
    to Modernity*, 292–3
the Left
    archetypes of dissent, 290–5
    and capitalism, 266–7, 276
    challenges by, 263–4
    and communism, 267, 308
    and democracy, 300
    identity of, 264
    speculative leftism, 230–1
    see also Occupy protest movements
Levi-Faur, D., 32
Lewis, John, 230
liberalism, 264–5; *see also* neoliberalism
linguistics: Gramsci and, 234, 235
Lowcock, Mark, 70
Lukov, Vadim, 220

McChrystal, General Stanley A., 135
McGuirk, P., 197
McKinsey's, 39
Machiavelli, Niccolò, 237
mainstreaming, 196–7
malaria, 117, 118
Mandela, Nelson, 302–3

Marchart, Oliver, 10, 11, 86–7, 89, 176,
    246
Marcuse, Herbert: *One Dimensional
    Man*, 294–5
markets
    and competition, 38
    and depoliticisation matrix, 98
    'free', 8
    and GM, 48, 59
    and governance, 39–40
    and identity, 154
    local, 40
    mass, 63
    and neoliberalism, 67
    New Institutional Economics and, 73
    and states, 30
Marx, Karl
    and absolute immanence, 232
    and capitalism, 141–2, 283, 285, 288,
        291–2
    on class, 183, 276
    on commodities, 139
    The Communist Manifesto, 71–2,
        286, 291–2
    on criticism of religion, 126
    on money, 140, 141
    on Paris commune, 270
    Theses on Feuerbach, 230, 237–8
Marxism
    'actually existing', 302
    and democracy, 158
    end of, 7
    and the Left, 301
    and meta-politics, 98
    and neoliberalism, 9
    and post-politics, 10
    Rancière and, 16
    and unsustainability, 158
    Žižek and, 112
    see also communism; neo-Marxists
materialism, historical, 235
Mbembe, Achille, 116
media: and Indignants, 250, 252; *see
    also* social media
memes, 296–7
Merkel, Angela, 102
messianism, 130, 132–3
Millennium Development Goals, 119
Millennium Promise, 111
Millennium Villages Project, 111,
    115–16, 119–20, 121
Mitterand, François, 8
model villages, 119
modernity
    and apocalypticism, 130
    'liquid', 154, 155

and revolutions, 128
and secularisation, 127
money, 140, 141
Monsanto, 56
mosquitoes, 117
Mouffe, Chantal
  and antagonism, 12, 14, 15, 91, 92,
    210
  and cosmopolitanism, 208, 210–12
  and democracy, 11–12
  and dissensus, 50
  and economy, 237
  on Gramsci, 233–6, 238
  Hegemony and Socialist Strategy,
    235–6, 238, 299
  and neoliberalism, 12
  and the police, 15
  on the political, 246
  on politics, 11; post-politics, 14, 15,
    111–12, 264–5
  and Schmitt, 236
  and society, 91–2, 94
  and the Third Way, 12
multiculturalism, 101–2, 190, 266; *see
  also* cultural diversity
multipolarity
  BRICS and, 213–17
  and cosmopolitanism, 211, 212, 214
Murphy, Richard, 26

NGOs, 70, 193
  and development, 71
  environmental, 57, 58
  and self-help groups, 75, 76, 78
Nancy, Jean-Luc, 5, 246, 249
'the natural', 49, 52–3, 62
Negri, Antonio, 126; *see also* Hardt,
  Michael and Negri, Antonio
neoconservatism, 196
neoliberalism, 3, 5
  BRICS and, 216
  and capitalism, 28, 262, 263
  and democracy, 67–8, 157–8
  and ecological crisis, 148–52
  and GMO, 53
  hybridity of, 196
  India, 67, 68
  the Left's challenge to, 8
  and markets, 67
  and Marxism, 9
  and meta-politics, 98
  Mouffe and, 12
  and neoconservatism, 196
  and political economy, 28, 296
  political projects of, 195–8
  and post-politics, 191–5

revolts against, 169, 170
'roll with it', 197–8
'Third Way', 12, 28, 37, 69, 190
and Third World development, 71–2
uses of, 197
'zombie', 4
neo-Marxists
  and eco-politics, 152–3
  and stakeholder governance, 151–2
  and unsustainability, 159, 163
neutrality, 52, 58–9, 62
New Institutional Economics (NIE),
  72–4, 81–2
'new progressivism', 28
The New Yorker, 114, 116, 117
New Zealand, 195, 196
Nietzsche, F., 132, 138; *Thus Spoke
  Zarathustra*, 143

OECD *see* Organisation for Economic
  Co-operation and Development
Obama, Barack, 303
Occupy protest movements, 4, 9–10,
  147, 171, 174, 241, 268–9, 275–6,
  280–1, 288, 290, 297, 301; Occupy
  Wall Street, 264, 269, 270–1,
  273–5, 276, 280–1, 307, 308
Offe, C., 29, 43
O'Neill, Jim, 216
ontology, 10, 11, 112, 138, 141
Oosterlynck, S., 92
Organisation for Economic Co-
  operation and Development
  (OECD), 55
Orientalism, 136, 137
Orwell, George: 'Inside the whale',
  281–2

PFI *see* United Kingdom: Private
  Finance Initiative
partnerships
  BRICS as, 215
  citizens and, 29
  and collaboration, 190
  Local Enterprise, 40–1
  public private, 30, 32, 33, 34, 39
  and social development, 189, 191,
    192, 193, 198, 202
philanthrocapitalism, 302
  in Africa, 116, 119
  and capitalism, 113
  and class, 112
  critiques of, 110–11
  and development, 119
  and entrepreneurialism, 120
  as an ideological formation, 111–14

philanthrocapitalism (*cont.*)
  and *jouissance*, 114–17, 118–19, 122
  'the rich' and, 109, 110, 112, 115
philanthropy, 110, 112, 114, 122
Pickles, Eric, 41
Pike, J., 202
planning, sustainability *see* United
  Kingdom: sustainability planning
police
  Athens, 248, 250
  definition of, 246
  Mouffe and, 93
  and polis, 178
  Rancière and, 12, 15, 93, 94–5, 97,
    174, 218–19, 223, 246–7
  and security, 263
  and space, 246
  and ultra-politics, 99
  and violence, 175, 248, 249
polis
  democratising, 171, 173
  and police, 178
  reclamation of, 184–7
the political, 184–5
  Badiou and, 173–4
  and democracy, 174
  economic subordination of, 8–9
  Fontana on, 237
  and GMO, 59
  Gramsci and, 237, 238
  Mouffe on, 11, 246
  and politics, 10, 90–2
  Rancière on, 12, 88, 173, 175, 177–8,
    246, 247
  retreat of, 5
  Schmitt on, 265
  and space, 246
  Žižek and, 15, 177–8, 246
political difference
  purification approach, 90–1, 92–3
  relational approach, 93–5
  three-term approach, 91–2, 92–3
political ecology
  and democracy, 159–60
  and identity, 155–6
  reactionary, 157–62
  and subjectivity, 153, 154
political parties
  Andhra Pradesh (India), 76
  apathy towards, 3, 261
  and communism, 183, 309, 310
  Conservatives (UK), 36
  and democracy, 1, 81, 267
  Greece, 250, 252, 255
political space, 173, 179, 180, 185–6
political systems: legitimacy of, 29

politicians, corrupt: Greece, 251
politicisation, 266
politics
  archi-politics, 96, 97–8, 99, 102,
    120
  Badiou and, 91, 126, 299, 300
  banalisation of, 127–8
  biopolitics, 215
  BRICS and, 220–1, 223
  definitions of, 86, 246
  egalitarian, 170–1, 181
  Foucault and, 217
  and intervention, 180–2
  Laclau and, 299
  and London riots (2011), 240
  meta-politics, 98, 99, 100, 102–3,
    104n2
  Mouffe on, 11
  of no politics, 261, 268
  para-politics, 98, 99, 102
  and the political, 10, 90–2
  and post-politics, 126
  'prefigurative', 201
  Rancière on, 12, 15, 88, 94, 126, 217,
    220, 221–2, 247
  'scientisation of', 50
  self-help groups: India, 78
  and space, 247
  subjectivation of, 94
  Swyngedouw and, 91, 247
  ultra-politics, 98, 99
  Žižek and, 126, 299, 300
Pollock, Allyson, 26
pollution, 54, 58
Ponte, Stefano, 117
post-democracy
  and consensus, 50–1
  and emancipation, 157
  neoliberals and, 149
  post-political society as, 68–9
  Rancière and, 13, 14, 95
  Žižek and, 14
  see also democracy
post-political
  Agamben on, 134
  and consensus, 50–1
  and inequality, 87
  Swyngedouw and, 95, 96, 149, 192
  see also the political
post-politics
  Brown and, 264
  Dean on, 203
  and depoliticisation, 99
  as economic theology, 138–42
  and God, 142–3
  as an ideological fiction, 127

meaning of, 5–11; as a Borromean
    knot, 7; ontological (Real)
    dimension, 10; political
    contradictions, 6
Mouffe and, 14, 111–12, 264–5
and neoliberalism, 149, 191–5
and political difference, 95
as political theology, 130–8
and politics, 126
postpoliticisation process, 5
Rancière and, 264, 265
as revision, 127–30
and self-help groups, 81–2
Žižek and, 89, 212, 264, 265–7
Povenelli, E., 203
poverty
    Africa, 118
    and capitalism, 142
    and credit, 75–6
    and development: Third World, 71
    and disease, 117
    and entrepreneurialism, 120
    'poverty porn', 118
    and wealth, 115–16, 126
power
    and capitalism, 286
    and despotism, 136
    and dissent, 290
    and glory, 139
    God and, 138
    post-political, 138–9
praxis: Gramsci's philosophy of, 232–3,
    236, 239, 241
PriceWaterhouseCoopers, 32, 39
the private: and the public, 50
private sector
    elites, 32
    social movements see United
        Kingdom: Coexist project
privatisation
    and austerity, 27
    and experts, 31–2
    and 'risk', 31
    and sustainability, 26–7, 38; see also
        United Kingdom: Private Finance
        Initiative
    and welfare state, 27
Product RED organisation, 117
progress, 52
proletariat, 309
property, 306
protest movements, 244; see also Arab
    Spring; Indignados; Indignant
    Squares; Occupy
protestant ethic, 130, 140
public participation: and GMO, 60–1

public-private partnerships, 32–4
public sector
    and economic growth, 41
    and sustainability, 39
public sphere, 5, 50, 286–7, 306
Pynchon, Thomas: Vineland, 282

RSPB see Royal Society for the
    Protection of Birds
Rachman, Gideon, 308
racism, 102, 240, 251–2
Rancière, Jacques
    Althusser's Lesson, 230
    Bosteels on, 96, 231
    Chronicles of Consensual Times, 15
    on consumers, 6
    on consensus, 176
    on democracy, 12, 170–1, 224, 300;
        post-democracy, 13, 14, 96
    The Difficult Legacy of Michel
        Foucault, 93–4
    Disagreement: Politics and
        Philosophy, 96–7
    and dissensus, 15, 50, 220
    and economy, 9, 237
    and equality, 12, 222, 255
    and Gramsci, 242n1
    on history, 7
    The Ignorant Schoolmaster, 230
    The Philosopher and his Poor, 96–7
    and police, 12, 15, 93, 94–5, 97,
        218–19, 223, 246–7
    on polis, 185
    on the political, 12, 88, 173, 175,
        177–8, 212, 246, 247; political
        difference, 15, 93, 94–5; political
        space, 79
    on politics, 12, 15, 88, 94, 126, 217,
        220, 221–2, 247; depoliticisation,
        95, 96–7; post-politics, 264, 265;
        ultra-politics, 98
    on society, 10
    on subjectivation, 222, 223
    on utopias, 43
    on the visible, 80
    on 'wrong', 222
Rawls, John, 264
the Real, 7, 10, 184, 186–7
    Lacan and, 11
    Žižek on, 14, 113
Reality Principle, 295
Reformation, 133
religion
    Christianity, 133, 140
    Marx on, 126
    and modern civilisation, 127

religion (*cont.*)
  and post-politics, 142–3
  and terror, 131
republicanism, 120
revolts
  Arab Spring, 136
  and dissent, 295–6
  state control of, 308–9
  urban, 169–70, 172–3
  see also riots
revolutions, 128, 131, 153, 238, 267–8;
    see also counter-revolutions
'the rich'
  and philanthrocapitalism, 109, 110,
    112, 115
  and poverty, 115–16
  see also wealth
Richey, Lisa Ann, 117
the Right, 98, 99, 266
riots
  Athens, 248
  London, 240
  see also insurrectional movements;
    revolts
risk
  Farm Scale Evaluations and, 58
  and GMO, 61
  and Private Finance Initiative, 34, 42
  and privatisation, 31
Romania: revolts, 169
romanticism, 292–3
Royal Society for the Protection of
  Birds, 58
Rushdie, Salman: 'Outside the whale',
  281, 282
Russia *see* BRICS group; Soviet Union
Rwanda: Millennium Villages Project,
  120

Sachs, Jeffrey, 111, 115, 116, 120
  The End of Poverty, 117, 118, 119
Saramago, José: *Seeing*, 1–2, 303
Sarkozy, Nicolas, 102
Sartre, Jean-Paul, 280, 287, 295
Scharpf, F., 29
Schmitt, Carl, 49, 57, 131, 132–3
  'Age of neutralizations and
    depoliticizations', 51–2
  Mouffe and, 236
Scott, David, 223
security, 263
'Seed List Hearings', 58
self-help groups (SHGs), 75–82
  Andhra Pradesh (India), 75, 76,
    77–81
  and identities, 81

  and banks, 75, 78
  and class, 78
  and consensus, 77
  and NGOs, 75, 76
  and women, 75, 76
the Sex Pistols, 281
Shakira, 114, 115
Shaxson, N., 39
slaves, 136–7
Smith, Adam, 142
Smyth, H., 33
'the social', 50
social control: Athens, 248
social media: and Indignants (Athens),
  248, 250, 252, 253, 254; *see also*
  Facebook
social movements
  and capitalism, 194
  emancipatory, 153–4, 161, 170
  urban, 176–7, 178
  see also Friends of the Earth;
    Greenpeace
social order: disruption of, 86–7
social organisations, 189–90; *see also*
  United Kingdom: Coexist project
society
  bourgeois, 293
  foundationist account of, 89
  modernisation of, 153, 154; *see also*
    modernity
  survival of, 10
Soros, George, 109, 110, 111
South Africa *see* BRICS group
sovereignty, 130, 137
Soviet bloc, former, 262
Soviet Union, 309
soybeans, 56–7
space
  alternative *see* United Kingdom:
    Coexist project
  of appearance, 289
  democratic, 256
  police and, 246
  political, 79, 173, 185–6, 245–7
  public, 180, 287–8; *see also* Athens:
    Syntagma Squares
'spatial selectivity', 40
spatialisation, 182, 184
Spain
  politics of no politics, 264, 269
  socio-spatial practices, 183, 184
Spinoza, Baruch, 287
Squires, J., 197
Srnicek, Nick, 184
Stavrakakis, Y., 246, 256
Stendhal, 292

Stiglitz, Joseph, 74
'structured coherences', 32
subaltern groups, 231, 232
subjectivation, 222, 223
subjectivity
    and identity, 154–5, 156–7, 159
    and political ecology, 153, 154
suicide: Andhra Pradesh (India), 79–80
supermarkets, 55, 57, 59, 62, 63
sustainability
    anti-utopian utopian project, 26
    and capitalism, 25
    communities *see* United Kingdom:
        Coexist project
    and consensus, 36
    definition of, 39
    and elites, 26
    governance of, 151
    local, 41
    and 'modernisation', 26, 28
    planning *see* United Kingdom:
        sustainability planning
    Private Finance Initiative, 34–6
    and privatisation, 26–7, 30
    and 'the state', 26
    Swyngedouw on, 150
    and unsustainability, 158–9
sustainable: definition of, 38
sustainable development, 25, 30, 39, 68
Swyngedouw, E.
    and communist hypothesis, 90, 91
    on critical social theory, 197
    on decision-making, 44
    on democracy, 92, 158
    and environmental policy, 147
    on governmentality, 161
    on the particular, 80–1
    and the political, 88–9; political
        difference, 92; post-political, 51,
        87, 89, 95, 96, 149, 192, 193
    and politics, 91, 247; eco-politics,
        149–51, 152
    on sustainability, 150; sustainable
        development, 25
Sydney: residential estates, 197
the Symbolic, 7, 14, 113

Taubes, J., 131–2, 132–3
tax avoidance, 32
technology, 51–2, 62–3; biotechnology
    see GMO
terrorism, 14, 98, 130–1, 210
Thatcher, Margaret, 263
theology
    economic, 138–42
    political, 130–8

'Third Way', 12, 28, 37, 69, 190, 264
Third World, 67, 70
Thomas, Peter, 231, 239–40
time, 130, 132
The Times, 120
trade unions, 292
Tressell, Robert: *The Ragged Trousered
    Philanthropists*, 122
Tunisia: revolution (2010), 169
Turkey, 169, 172

ultra-politics, 14, 96
United Kingdom
    coalition government, 36–9, 40–1; *see
        also* Cameron, David
    Coexist project (Bristol), 189, 190,
        198–203, 203–4
    Department for International
        Development (DFiD), 70
    Department of Business, Innovation,
        and Skills (BIS), 38
    devolution, 37, 42
    Egan Review for Sustainable
        Communities, 199
    'GM Nation?' consultation, 49, 60
    land ownership, 41
    law, 265
    localism, 37–40; *Local Development
        Plans*, 37; Local Enterprise
        Partnerships, 40–1; Localism Act
        (LA) (2012), 37
    London protests (2011), 240–1
    London riots (2011), 240
    National Planning Policy Framework
        (NPPF), 25, 37–9
    political condition of, 196, 262
    Private Finance Initiative (PFI), 27,
        33–6, 42
    Regional Development Agencies
        (England), 38
    sustainability planning, 27, 33,
        36–44; 'delivery' model of, 41; and
        inequality, 42; local, 37
United Nations, 30, 219
United States
    banks, 271
    collective consumption, 286
    democracy, 267
    economy, 266
    GMO, 55–7
    law, 265
    Left wing challenges, 261, 263–4
    neoliberalism/neoconservatism, 196
    Occupy Wall Street, 264, 269, 270–1,
        273–5, 276, 280–1, 307, 308
    political condition, 262

United States (*cont.*)
  responsibility, 223
  and world order, 208
universalisation, 173
universality, 287
unsustainability
  and democracy, 159–60
  and depoliticisation, 162
  and equality, 159, 160–1
  and sustainability, 158–9
urban regeneration: Bristol (UK), 189,
  198, 200, 202
utopias
  and anti-utopias, 42–3
  and democratic engagement, 30
  end of, 7, 303
  Millennium Villages as, 121
  model villages as, 119
  as political-economic experiments,
  198
  spatio-temporal, 185, 186
  see also communism: hypothesis of;
  dystopias

value, 141
Vanity Fair (magazine), 117
violence
  Athens, 248
  and choice, 181
  ecstatic, 135–6
  insurgents and, 174
  London, 240
  and non-violence, 134
  police and, 175, 248, 249
  and political antagonism, 92
  sovereign, 130
  as ultra-politics, 96
  Žižek on, 14

WTO *see* World Trade Organization
'War on Terror', 14, 210
Washington Consensus, 74
Watson, James, 54
wealth: Aristotle on, 140; *see also* the
  rich
Weber, M., 140
welfare state
  and bureaucracy, 29
  and citizen choice, 29–30
  and dependency, 40
  and global capitalism, 28
  as a political necessity, 112–13
  privatisation of, 27, 37; Private
  Finance Initiative, 35
  sustainability of, 33

Wells, O., 201
Welzel, C., 155
women
  gender mainstreaming of, 197
  and self-help groups, 75; India, 76, 77
  effect of suicide on: India, 80
  see also feminism
World Bank, 30, 34, 68, 71, 72, 74
World Economic Forum, 308
World Risk Report (2012), 4
World Trade Organization (WTO), 9,
  53, 55, 56
'wrong', 222

Yeatman, Allison, 28

Žižek, Slavoj
  and antagonism, 14, 16, 266
  on anti-capitalism, 82
  Bosteels on, 231
  on capitalism, 109
  and class, 14–15
  on consensus, 272
  and democracy, 15, 299
  and depoliticisation, 98
  and economy, 236–7
  on fake Mandela memorial
  interpreter, 303
  on fantasy, 123n2
  on ideological 'closure', 8
  on insurrection, 175
  and 'interpassivity'/'substitution',
  114–15
  and *jouissance*, 111, 113, 116–17,
  121
  Living in the End Times, 90–1
  and Marxism, 112
  on multiculturalism, 101, 102
  and philanthropy, 110
  and the political, 15, 177–8, 185,
  246
  and political difference, 13, 93
  and politics, 126, 130, 299, 300;
  archi-, 120; post-, 81, 89, 111, 112,
  130, 212, 264, 265–7; ultra-, 15,
  98
  on Rancière, 15
  on self-help groups, 80
  and society, 94
  The Sublime Object of Ideology,
  116–17
  on Third World representations, 118,
  120
  on urban activism, 176
  on utopias, 43